2001

Of Pharohs
and Phreudians,

Happy Birthday
Edgar!

Love
Bruce Marija
+ Katja

Monographs of the
Hebrew Union College
Number 25

———

A Letter That Has
Not Been Read:
Dreams in the Hebrew Bible

Monographs of the Hebrew Union College

A LETTER THAT HAS NOT BEEN READ

Dreams in the Hebrew Bible

Shaul Bar

Translated by Lenn J. Schramm

HEBREW UNION COLLEGE PRESS
CINCINNATI

© 2001 by the Hebrew Union College Press
Hebrew Union College–Jewish Institute of Religion

Library of Congress Cataloging-in-Publication Data
Bar, Shaul
  A letter that has not been read: dreams in the Hebrew Bible / Shaul Bar;
  translated by Lenn J. Schramm.
  p.cm. – (Monographs of the Hebrew Union College; no. 25)
  Includes bibliographical references and index.
  ISBN 0–87820–424–5 (alk. Paper)
  1. Dreams in the Bible. 2. Bible. O.T.–Criticism, interpretation, etc. I. Title.
  II. Series.

BF1099.B.5 B27 2001
221.8'15463–dc21   201016542

Printed on acid-free paper in the United States of America
Typeset by Posner and Sons Ltd., Jerusalem, Israel
Distributed by Wayne State University Press
4809 Woodward Avenue, Detroit, MI 48201

Dedicated with love
to my mother, Bella Bobrow,
and to the memory of my father,
Jacob Bobrow ז״ל

מוקדש באהבה
לאמי, בלה בוברוב, עד מאה ועשרים,
ולזכר אבי, יעקב בוברוב

The I. Edward Kiev Library Foundation

In September 1976 the family and friends of Dr. I. Edward Kiev, distinguished Rabbi, Chaplain, and Librarian of the Hebrew Union College–Jewish Institute of Religion in New York, established a Library Foundation in his memory to support and encourage the knowledge, understanding, and appreciation of scholarship in Judaica and Hebraica. In cooperation with the Hebrew Union College Press, the Foundation offers this work by Shaul Bar as an I. Edward Kiev Library Foundation Book.

Contents

Acknowledgments

To start with, I would like to thank my teacher, Professor Baruch Levine, for providing guidance, support, and stimulating conversation, all of which inspired me to take on this challenging project. I am grateful as well to my colleagues who read early drafts of the manuscript and offered many perceptive comments and insights: Stephen Benin at the University of Memphis; Steve McKenzie at Rhodes College; Ed Bleiberg, Egyptologist at the Brooklyn Museum; Daniel Fleming, Assyriologist at NYU; and the late Egyptologist Bill Murnane, who is sorely missed at the University of Memphis. The support and encouragement of these fine scholars through the years have been invaluable to me.

I thank my computer-expert friend Paresh Sanghani, who helped me knock a plague of "bugs" out of my files. I am grateful as well for the resources and staff of the Harding Graduate School of Religion in Memphis, where Librarian Don Meredith graciously led me to materials, Carisse Beryhill patiently helped me to master footnote style, and Evelyn Meredith and Pat Hughes supported my research with great cheerfulness.

I am thankful as well for the generosity and support of Bert and David Bornblum, who established the Bornblum Judaic Studies Program at the University of Memphis. Philip Miller at the Hebrew Union College Library in New York has provided wondrous wisdom and friendship since our NYU days. The foundation honoring the memory of his predecessor I. Edward Kiev has generously provided funding for the publication of this volume. And Lenn J. Schramm translated my Hebrew with accuracy and style.

Anna S. Chernak read my manuscript and offered valuable advice and endless encouragment. And I cannot forget Henry Resnick, whose enthusiasm for sports and great knowledge of Judaica have inspired me through the years. I am grateful as well to Dr. Raphael Posner in Jerusalem, to Professor Shmuel Aḥituv of Ben-Gurion University in Beer Sheva, and to Jeffrey Cooley and Professor David Weisberg of Hebrew Union College in Cincinnati for their helpful suggestions. Finally, a special thank you to managing editor Barbara Selya of the Hebrew Union College Press for her dedication and expertise in transforming my manuscript into this book.

Memphis, Tennessee
March 2001

Abbreviations

AASOR	*Annual of the American Schools of Oriental Research*
AB	*Anchor Bible*
ABR	*Australian Biblical Review*
AfO	*Archiv für Orientforschung*
AHw	*Akkadisches Handwörterbuch.* W. von Soden. 3. vols. Wiesbaden, 1965-1981
AJSL	*American Journal of Semitic Languages and Literature*
AnBib	*Analecta Biblica*
ANET	*Ancient Near Eastern Texts Relating to the Old Testament.* Edited by J.B. Pritchard. 3rd ed. Princeton. 1969.
AnOr	*Analecta Orientalia*
AnSt	*Anatolian Studies*
AOAT	*Alter Orient und Altes Testament*
ARM	*Archives royales de Mari*
ARMT	*Archives royales de Mari, transcrite et traduite*
AS	*Assyriological Studies*
BA	*Biblical Archaeologist*
BASOR	*Bulletin of the American Schools of Oriental Research*
BDB	Brown, F., S. R. Driver and C. A. Briggs, *A Hebrew and English Lexicon of the Old Testament.* Oxford, 1907
BHK	*Biblia Hebraica.* Edited by R. Kittel. Stuttgart. 1973
Bib	*Biblica*
BibOr	*Biblica et Orientalia*
BN	*Biblische Notizen*
BZ	*Biblische Zeitschrift*
BZAW	*Beihefte zur Zeitschrift für die älttestamentliche Wissenschaft*
CAD	*The Assyrian Dictionary of the Oriental Institute of the University of Chicago.* Chicago, 1956-
CBQ	*Catholic Biblical Quarterly*
CP	*Classical Philology*
EncJud	*Encyclopedia Judaica.* 16 vols. Jerusalem, 1972
EMiqr	*Entsiqlopedia Miqrait–Encyclopaedia Biblica*
ErIs	*Eretz-Israel*
ExpTim	*The Expository Times*

GesB	W. Gesenius, *Hebräisches und aramäisches Handwörterbuch,* rev. F. Buhl, Berlin, 1921
HALOT	*The Hebrew and Aramaic Lexicon of the Old Testament.* L. Koehler, W. Baumgartner, and J.J. Stamm. Translated and edited under the supervision of M. E. J. Richardson. 4 vols. Leiden. 1994-1999
HAT	*Handbuch zum Alten Testament*
HKAT	*Handkommentar zum Alten Testament*
HSM	*Harvard Semitic Monographs*
HTR	*Harvard Theological Review*
HUCA	*Hebrew Union College Annual*
IB	*Interpreter's Bible.* Edited by G. A. Buttrick et al. 12 vols. New York, 1951-1957
ICC	*International Critical Commentary*
IDB	*The Interpreter's Dictionary of the Bible.* Edited by G. A. Buttrick. 4 Vols. Nashville, 1962.
IEJ	*Israel Exploration Journal*
IOS	*Israel Oriental Studies*
ITQ	*Irish Theological Quarterly*
JANESCU	*Journal of the Ancient Near Eastern Society of Columbia University*
JAOS	*Journal of the American Oriental Society*
JBL	*Journal of Biblical Literature*
JBR	*Journal of Bible and Religion*
JCS	*Journal of Cuneiform Studies*
JEA	*Journal of Egyptian Archaeology*
JEOL	*Jaarbericht van het Vooraziatisch-Egyptisch Gezelschap(Genootschap) ex oriente lux*
JJS	*Journal of Jewish Studies*
JNES	*Journal of Near Eastern Studies*
JPOS	*Journal of the Palestine Oriental Society*
JQR	*Jewish Quarterly Review*
JSOT	*Journal for the Study of the Old Testament*
JSS	*Journal of Semitic Studies*
JTS	*Journal of Theological Studies*
KHC(AT)	*Kurzer Hand-Commentar (zum Alten Testament)*
LexÄg	W. Heleck and E. Otto, *Lexikon der Ägyptologie,* Wiesbaden, 1972
LXX	Septuagint
MT	Masoretic Text
NBD	*New Bible Dictionary.* Edited by J. D. Douglas and N. Hillyer. 2d ed. Downers Grove,1982
NEB	*New English Bible,* Oxford, 1961–1970

NCBC	*New Century Bible Commentary*
NICOT	*New International Commentary on the Old Testament*
Or	*Orientalia* (NS)
OT	Old Testament
OTL	*Old Testament Library*
OTS	*Old Testament Studies*
PEQ	*Palestine Exploration Quarterly*
PRU	*Le Palais royal d'Ugarit*
RA	*Revue d'assyriologie et d'archeologie orientale*
RB	*Revue biblique*
RevQ	*Revue de Qumran*
SAK	*Studien zur altägyptischen Kultur*
SBLDS	Society of Biblical Literature Dissertation Series
SJLA	*Studies in Judaism in Late Antiquity*
SVT	Supplements to *Vetus Testamentum*
TDOT	*Theological Dictionary of the Old Testament.* Edited by G. J. Botterweck and H. Ringgren. Translated by J. T. Willis, G. W. Bromiley, and D. E. Green. 8 vols. Grand Rapids, 1974-
THZ	*Theologische Zeitschrift*
Tigr	*Tigrinya (Tigrina)*
UF	*Ugarit-Forschungen*
VAB	*Vorderasiatische Bibliothek*
VT	*Vetus Testamentum*
VTSup	*Vetus Testamentum, Supplements*
Vulg	Vulgate
WbÄS	*Wörterbuch der ägyptischen Sprache.* A. Erman and H. Grapow. 5 vols. Berlin, 1926–1931. Reprint, 1963
WBC	*World Biblical Commentary*
WTJ	*Westminster Theological Journal*
YOS	*Yale Oriental Studies*
ZÄS	*Zeitschrift für ägyptische Sprache und Altertumskunde*
ZAW	*Zeitschrift für die alttestamentliche Wissenschaft*

Introduction

Since Freud, the rational modern approach to human dreams has typically involved inquiry into past or current emotional states. Dreams are seen as manifestations of the subconscious. What we have not resolved, what we are unwilling to admit, and even what we dare not recognize while awake—all find expression while we are sleeping: wishes, anxiety, fear, lust, hatred, ambition, jealousy, longing.[1]

In contrast, the ancients, unfamiliar with the intricate byways of the human soul revealed by modern psychology, saw dreams as channels of communication between human beings and external sources. In sleep, they believed, messages were conveyed to the unconscious mind, messages often relating to the future and sometimes including clear and unambiguous announcements, advice, injunctions, or warnings. Several Akkadian sources referred to a "god of dreams," whose chief task was to send dreams to slumbering human beings.[2] Some have conjectured that this god was merely an emissary of various

---

1. Sigmund Freud, *On Dreams* (New York: Norton, 1952); *The Interpretation of Dreams,* in *Standard Edition of the Complete Psychological Works of Sigmund Freud,* vol. 4 (London: Hogarth Press, 1953); "A Metapsychological Supplement of the Theory of Dreams," in *Standard Edition,* vol. 14 (London: Hogarth Press, 1958). A summary of Freud's views can be found in the following works: C. S. Hall and G. Lindzey, *Theories of Personality* (London: John Wiley and Sons, 1957); H. Nagera, *Basic Psychoanalytic Concepts on the Theory of Dreams* (London: George Allan and Unwin, 1969); Isaac Lewin, *The Psychology of Dreams* (Tel Aviv: Dekel, 1980), pp. 47–56.

2. Several Mesopotamian documents refer to "the god of dreams" as bringing dreams to mortals. These sources include three different names for this deity: ᵈMamu is Sumerian, and means '(the god) dream'. Anzaqar, whose Akkadian equivalent is *zaqīqu,* 'zephyr', means 'tower'. Both of these terms are referred to as "the god of dreams." The Sumerian anzaqar appears very infrequently in both Akkadian and Sumerian literature (twice only): once in Hymn D in honor of Šulgi, king of Ur, in a context that is not clear; and once in the epic *Lugalbanda and ḫurumkurra,* in which the god appears to Lugalbanda in a dream and orders him to slaughter a wild ox and a kid and to spill their blood on the ground. According to Oppenheim (*EMiqr* 3:146), this reflects a very ancient belief in invisible dream spirits and their king, who are in many ways like the spirits known from Greek epic. The Akkadian

1

other deities. Others hypothesized that spirits and ghosts were also responsible for bad dreams. In some Mesopotamian sources, bad dreams and evil signs came from sorcerers who sought to harm a person, but charms and spells could be used to avert them.[3] It was also thought that the soul or part of it left the body of the sleeper and embarked on adventures and journeys. The content of the dream consisted of the incidents and experiences of the soul during its wanderings.

The Greeks, too, believed in the external and passive origin of dreams. They thought that gods and spirits who brought dreams entered through the keyhole, stood alongside the bed of the sleeper, conveyed a message to him or her, and then departed the same way they came. Sometimes the gods stood in front of the dreamer and acted out the content of the dream. Classical mythology refers to the "people of dreams" or "tribe of dreams"[4] who lived in the approaches to the underworld, in caves or under trees, from whence they dispersed dreams throughout the world at night.[5] The Greeks also seem to have believed, though, that the content of prophetic dreams depended not only on the gods and spirits, but also on the dreamer's psychological and physical condition: the hour, diet, age, and so forth. Wine was deleterious to dreams, but water beneficial. Onions, garlic, and beans had a bad effect. Hence the dream experience was dependent upon internal as well as external forces.

Although people in antiquity found it hard to digest the idea that a person's body could be lying in bed while he or she was touring other worlds, in the context of the polytheism of the ancient world, it seemed plausible that some god whispered in the dreamer's ear to convey a warning against other deities. In the Bible, however, with its monotheistic message of One God who rules the universe, there is no clear explanation as to why the Almighty should communicate with a sleeping person, rather than clearly and openly when the recipient was awake. Hence it is possible that nocturnal dream theophanies are meant to express the distance between human beings and

sources speak of "dreams that were brought" to the sleeper, or describe the god Anzaqar as sending dreams to human beings. Oppenheim adds, however, that we must not assume that this deity was an accepted member of the Mesopotamian pantheon or a "dream master" who lives in a tower, from which he dispatches dream spirits to visit slumbering people. The dream god is involved in the case of bad dreams, but has nothing to do with forecasts of the future or communication with a god.

3. A. Leo Oppenheim, "Mantic Dreams in the Ancient Near East," in G. E. Von Grunebaum and Roger Caillois, *The Dream and Human Societies* (Berkeley: University of California Press, 1966), p. 346.

4. Hesiod, *Theogony* 211ff.

5. *Odyssey* 24:11ff; see also "gate of dreams from which at night the dreams swarm out and visit mankind" (*Odyssey* 19:562ff.).

God. God appears in dreams in order to moderate the shock or danger of a direct waking revelation.[6] The dream represents a more refined and sophisticated state in the development of religion than that reflected in a direct encounter with the deity.

Such conjecture is the basis of the present work, and the subjective nature of the topic is part of its fascination. Oneirocritics interpret dreams according to the symbols and descriptions provided by the dreamers, but these descriptions are rendered even more imperfect by the transfer of the experiences into different media. The dreams in question are thousands of years old and almost certainly not written down by the dreamers themselves, yet there are those who would apply to them the tools of psychoanalysis.[7] Most scholars, however, regard dream stories as legends. Ernst Ludwig Ehrlich, explaining why he kept psychology out of his study of biblical dreams, wrote:

> The biblical authors who tell us about dreams did not have these dreams themselves. We are dealing with a stylistic device that they employed or only with the elements of a dream image that they wove into their descriptions. One should not treat such a literary product as if it were a genuine dream. Dreams in the Bible, rather than a psychological phenomenon, are first and foremost a phenomenon of the history of tradition and faith.[8]

Indeed, a survey of biblical dreams reveals that they have a standard format composed of several fixed elements. This suggests that biblical authors used dreams for their own purposes, fitting the details into the familiar paradigm. If this is the case, we must relate to biblical dreams as literature only, and not as manifestations of the heroes' personal experiences.

Be that as it may, a study of the dream stories of the Bible and ancient Near East indicates that two main types of dreams were collected in literature: prophetic dreams and symbolic dreams.[9] In the prophetic dream, the word of

---

6. Zeev Weisman, *From Jacob to Israel* (Jerusalem: Magnes Press, 1986), p. 105, n. 30.

7. On the topic of dreams, see: A. Leo Oppenheim, *The Interpretation of Dreams in the Ancient Near East: With a Translation of an Assyrian Dream Book,* Transactions of the American Philosophical Society (1956); Ernst Ludwig Ehrlich, *Der Traum im Alten Testament,* GZAW 73 (Berlin: de Gruyter, 1953); Robert Karl Gnuse, *The Dream Theophany of Samuel* (Lanham, Md.: University Press of America, 1984); Wolfgang Richter, "Traum und Traumdeutung im Alten Testament," *BZ* 7 (1963), 202-220; Serge Sauneron et al., *Les Songes et leur interpretation,* Sources orientales 2 (Paris: Le Seuil, 1959); Jean-Marie Husser, *Le Songe et la parole: Etude sur le rêve et sa fonction dans l'ancien Israël, BZAW* 210 (Berlin: Walter de Gruyter, 1994).

8. Ehrlich, *Der Traum im Alten Testament,* p. v.

9. The term "prophetic dream" is borrowed from Kaufmann, because we see the dream as a sort of prophecy and prediction of the future; see Yehezkel Kaufmann, *Toledot*

God is an announcement, injunction, or warning delivered to the dreamer in an unambiguous form that is instantly and fully understood. Its centerpiece is the appearance of the deity. God or an angel comes to a person in a nocturnal dream, stands nearby, and speaks to him or her. The message presented is chiefly verbal; the visual element is quite limited.

In a symbolic dream, however, the visual is crucial. While God himself does not appear, the dreamer has visions (tableaux or actions) that function as symbols with hidden meanings.[10] The fact that God does appear *in propria persona* in prophetic dreams led scholars to conclude that this kind of dream was, in Yehezkel Kaufmann's words, "appropriate to the spirit of the quest for the Israelite God." Kaufmann's view of these dreams as a peculiarly Israelite phenomenon was seconded by A. Leo Oppenheim, who noted that the Bible reserves prophetic dreams ("theological dreams" in his parlance) "for members of the chosen people and symbolic dreams for members of other peoples as well."[11]

In the first chapter, then, we shall discuss the prophetic dream. In this category we have included the dreams of Jacob (Gen. 28:10–22 and 31:10–13), Solomon (1 Kings 3:4–15), and Abimelech (Gen. 20:3–8). Oppenheim noted that dream narratives in the ancient Near East were constructed according to a fixed paradigm with three main stages: (1) the setting—who, when, where, and the conditions in which the dream took place; (2) the content of the dream—the message from the deity or angel to the dreamer; and (3) the response to the dream—the dreamer wakes up and reacts to the dream—followed by the fulfillment of the dream.[12] We shall attempt to determine whether Oppenheim's model is valid for biblical dreams as well. To this end, we shall consider the various parts of the dreams as well as their verbal texture, which is the rhetorical means used by the narrators to describe the dreams. The latter is extremely important, because it is through style and format design that the author creates emphases that attract the reader's attention.[13]

We will consider the word חלום itself, since the Bible employs various other

---

ha-'emunah ha-yisra'elit (Jerusalem: Bialik Institute, 1955), pp. 507–509. On the other hand, Oppenheim, *Interpretation,* 186, calls this kind of a dream a "message dream." In his article in the Biblical Encyclopedia, he refers to it as a "theological dream." See A. Leo Oppenheim, "Dream," *EMiqr* 3:143–144. Gnuse speaks of an "auditory message dream"; see Robert Karl Gnuse, *The Dream Theophany of Samuel,* p. 19. French scholars, by contrast, refer to these dreams as "théorématiques"; see André Caquot, "Selon Canaan et Israel," in *Les Songes et leur interprétation,* p. 106.

  10. Kaufmann, *Toledot,* pp. 507–508.
  11. Oppenheim, *Interpretation,* p. 209.
  12. Ibid., pp. 186ff.
  13. Frank Polak, *Biblical Narrative* (Jerusalem: Mossad Bialik, 1994), p. 11.

terms that seem to be synonymous. As for the message conveyed by the dream, we will consider how it is described and functions. On this basis we will assign the dreams to categories: dreams of promise and encouragement (Gen. 28:12ff.) and admonitory dreams (Gen. 20:6, 31:24). What role do the messages play? Why are they reported in the Bible? We will also note extrabiblical motifs borrowed by the biblical authors and how they were influenced by them. Finally, we will consider the dreamers' reactions to their experiences. Is there continuity between the dreams and waking reality? Nowhere does the Bible tell us how dreamers knew they had experienced prophetic dreams. An examination of their reactions, however, indicates whether they viewed their dreams as prophetic or merely ordinary.

In the second chapter we shall turn our attention to symbolic dreams, which, like prophetic dreams, are prefigurations of future events. Here dreamers see symbols but hear nothing, neither announcements nor injunctions. This category includes Joseph's dreams (Gen. 37:5-7, 9), the dreams of the butler and baker (Gen. 39:9-13 and 16-19), Pharaoh's dreams (Gen. 41:1-7), the dream of the Midianite soldier (Judg. 7:13-14), and Nebuchadnezzar's dreams (Dan. 2 and 4). Because God makes no appearance in these dreams, the question arises as to whether the messages conveyed originate outside the dreamers–from God–or whether the symbols express the dreamers' own unfulfilled yearnings or fears, set in their normal environments. Consequently his brothers refer to Joseph as "that dreamer" (lit. "that master of dreams") (Gen. 37:19), and see his dreams as reflections of his ambition to dominate them–"Do you mean to reign over us? Do you mean to rule over us?" (Gen. 37:8). His father, too, rebukes him: "What is this dream you have dreamed? Are we to come, I and your mother and your brothers, and bow low to you to the ground?" (Gen. 37:10). We may infer from these reactions that Jacob and his other sons believed that Joseph's dreams were not prophetic, but merely the expression of his aspirations and desires.

Similarly, in the Book of Judges we read how Gideon and his lad infiltrated the Midianite camp and overheard one soldier relating his dream to his comrade, who interpreted it for him:

> Gideon came there just as one man was narrating a dream to another. "Listen," he was saying, "I had this dream: There was a commotion–a loaf of barley bread was whirling through the Midianite camp. It came to a tent and struck it, and it fell; it turned it upside down, and the tent collapsed." To this the other responded, "That can only mean the sword of the Israelite Gideon son of Joash. God is delivering Midian and the entire camp into his hands" (Judg. 7:13-14).

Here the meaning of the dream is immediately clear to the second soldier. The apprehensions of the Midianite troopers occasioned by the preparations under way in the Israelite camp found an outlet in the dream. The dream was not prophetic, but reflected the mood among the Midianites. Gideon hears this evidence of the poor morale among his enemies because the Lord instructed him to "go down to the camp with your attendant Purah and listen to what they say; after that you will have the courage to attack the camp" (Judg. 7:10–11). In chapter two, then, we shall consider whether symbolic biblical dreams are the products of the dreamers' own imaginations, needs, and desires, or whether external forces plant them in the dreamers' minds.

Whether or not the message comes from God, it is conveyed through strange phenomena that sometimes contradict physical law. The message is expressed in symbols that must sometimes be deciphered and interpreted. According to the *amora* Rabbi Ḥisda, "A dream that has not been interpreted is like a letter that has not been read" (BT Berakhot 55b). Some symbolic dreams yield readily to interpretation (Joseph's in Gen. 37:5–9); others are arcane, so that only experts can determine whether or not they have a meaning, and if there is one, what it is.

Hence it is not surprising to find that there were professional dream interpreters in antiquity, and that books that provide clues and keys for the interpretation of dreams have been found in Egypt and Mesopotamia. In the third chapter we shall discuss those interpreters and examine some of their dream books. Specifically, we will consider some of the themes presented in them and consider how the dream symbols and allusions were deciphered. In that context we shall refer to the Talmud, which incorporates a sort of rabbinic dream book. Here too we shall consider the themes that appear in dreams, how they are interpreted, and how the Talmud relates to dreams and their sources.

As we shall see, most of the dreams in the Bible are found in Genesis. Beyond those, there are dreams in Judges 7:13–15, 1 Kings 3:5–15, and Daniel 2 and 4. Curiously, although in Genesis God reveals his word and wishes to the dreamer—words and wishes that lie at the very foundation of the Israelite faith—a look at the prophetic books of the Bible indicates that there is not even a single description of a dream experienced by a prophet. Instead we find descriptions of visions and spectacles. The prophets do use the word *dream*, but only to reject and ridicule dreamers. Zechariah says, "For the teraphim spoke delusion, the augurs predicted falsely; and dreamers speak lies and console with illusions" (Zech. 10:2). Jeremiah had already followed a similar path: "How long will there be in the minds of the prophets who prophesy falsehood—the prophets of their own deceitful minds—the plan to make My people forget My name, by means of the dreams which they tell each other, just as their fathers forgot My name because of Baal?" (Jer. 23:26–27).

How, then, did the prophets and wisdom literature relate to the phenomenon of dreams? Did they reject it because they believed dreams have an external source and do not contain any message from God?[14] Why would the prophets oppose a legitimate way for human beings to communicate with the divine? According to several traditions the revelatory value of dreams is self-evident (Num. 12:6).[15] Does the Bible purposely convey different attitudes toward their origins and value? If so, why?

In short, the line of demarcation between dreams and visions, or between God's appearance in a dream and a true waking theophany, is not always clear and distinct. Evidently persons who had those experiences were not careful to distinguish between them. It should be remembered that by the nature of things, God's appearance to a person who is awake and his appearance in a prophetic dream may be similar in both form and content. In the Bible we find "dream by night (חלום לילה)" (Gen. 20:3 and 31:24; 1 Kings 3:5), but also "vision by night (מראת הלילה)" (Gen. 46:2), "visions of the night (חזיון לילה)" (Job 4:13, 20:8, 33:15), "vision of the night (חזון לילה)" (Isa. 29:7), and "a night vision (Aramaic: חזוא דיליליא)" (Dan. 2:19). Sometimes these terms are used in parallel—"in a vision (מַרְאָה),... in a dream" (Num. 12:6); sometimes they appear in a construct, with "dream (חלום)" depending on "vision (חזון)" (Isa. 29:7 and Job 33:16); and sometimes "dreams (חלומות)" and "visions (חזיונות)" are parallel (Joel 3:1 and Job 7:14). Some believe, too, that the visions revealed to prophets, which serve as the introductions to their prophecies, are in fact dream visions, even though this is not stated explicitly (see Isa. 6:1, Jer. 1:11, 13; Ezek. 1:1–3 and 8:1–3; Joel 3:1; etc.).[16] Ehrlich believes that the difference between visions and dreams is that in the former the theophany is more mysterious and spiritual. Because a prophet may be vouchsafed both visions and dreams, however, it is often difficult to distinguish between them.[17]

In the fifth chapter we shall trace the terms מַרְאָה and מַחֲזֶה in an attempt to discover whether they have any connection with dreams and whether they

---

14. Lichtenstein believes that the prophets rejected only a particular type of dream—ambiguous dreams, which are not far removed from divining, but are not direct dream theophanies. See Murray Lichtenstein, "Dream Theophany and the E Document," *JANESCU* 1/2 (1968–1969), p. 49.

15. Ehrlich, *Traum,* p. 156, n. 1.

16. S.v. "dream," *EMiqr* 3:151.

17. Ehrlich, *Traum,* pp. 6 and 47.

describe the same phenomenon.[18] First we shall investigate their etymologies and meaning in the biblical text. Then we will look into the contexts in which they are found. Do they describe divine revelations? Do the recipients of the theophanies see, hear, or sleep? Are the idioms found in the various stages of dreams also found in visions? We will also consider the phenomenological aspect of visions; that is, whether they include the different stages found in dreams: (1) the appearance of the deity; (2) the message from the deity; (3) the end of the revelation and the dreamer's awakening and reaction. Can these stages be found in biblical visions?

In the last chapter, we shall consider the purposes served by the dream stories of the Bible. The narratives as we know them are the culminations of a protracted process. They have passed through many variants–first orally, then in the initial transcription, and finally in successive redactions. We shall compare the motifs of biblical dreams with ancient extrabiblical material and look for the underlying idea of all the dream stories. Are they intended to present information, depict a particular situation, or influence the thoughts and behavior of readers? For example, the story of Jacob at Bethel may be meant to explain the source of the sanctity of the shrine in Bethel and of its associated rites, such as why the Israelites anoint stones with oil and give tithes. Another possibility is that the narrative is an etiological story to explain the name *Bethel.* Similarly, what function is filled by the dreams in the Joseph cycle? The fact that the stories incorporate a number of motifs common in folk legends and myths has led some scholars to the conclusion that the story is fictional. Others note its authentic Egyptian backdrop–details that the author of a later legend could not have known–and believe it has an historical underpinning. And is Solomon's dream at Gibeon recounted in order to provide legitimacy for Solomon's rule over Israel, or was it originally a message of approval for Solomon's construction of the Temple? And why are Nebuchadnezzar's dreams presented? Is it to provide readers with information about his kingdom? Do these dreams have a theological message? These and other questions will be considered in the last chapter.

---

18. Readers will note that Hebrew words are vocalized throughout the book only when an unpointed reading would cause ambiguity.

1

The Prophetic Dream

A. Leo Oppenheim believed that the *message dream,* which I shall call the *prophetic dream,* is derived from the *incubation dream*–a dream visited upon one while sleeping in a sanctuary or holy place after ritual preparations, which he held was the archetype of the message dream of Scripture.[1] Working from this model, Oppenheim attempted to explain motifs found in various cultures, in which the description of the deity as a mighty figure standing by the head of the dreamer is only a distortion, typical of dreams, of the image of the deity before whom the suppliant is asking for a revelation.

The fact that one cannot find allusions to incubation in all of the dreams in Scripture seems to have led Oppenheim to the additional hypothesis that dreams of this sort describe theophanies that, for religious or literary reasons, were cast as dreams. Because it was believed that human beings tend to be left in shock and terror after a deity appears directly to them, the god's appearance in the dream softens the trauma of the experience. In a state of passive submission, the dreamer hears the words of the deity. Awe-struck, he cannot respond. The dream theophany thus expresses the distance between divine and human spheres. It is considered to be more refined and represents a later stratum in the development of religion.[2]

A scrutiny of the prophetic dreams in the Bible shows that they were set down according to a standard paradigm, which can be traced and reconstructed on the basis of sources that run from Sumeria of the third millennium BCE through the poems of Homer and on to Ptolemaic Egypt. As discussed in our introduction, Oppenheim noted the three main components of the message dream: the setting, the message, and the dreamer's reaction. In this chapter, after some preliminary etymological considerations, we shall examine whether Oppenheim's paradigm, as illustrated in Mesopotamian literature, fits the prophetic dreams described by the Bible as well. In so doing, we shall

---

1. Oppenheim, *Interpretation,* p. 190.
2. Weisman, *Jacob,* p. 105.

attempt to understand how biblical authors viewed dreams. Did they believe they were a legitimate phenomenon in which God actually appeared? If so, what language was used to describe such divine revelations? What topics or themes served to transmit the ritual annunciations, commands, or warnings contained therein? Finally, are there patterns in the dreamers' reactions to their dreams, from which we may draw broader conclusions about the function of these phenomena?

THE ETYMOLOGY OF חֲלוֹם

The biblical Hebrew word for dream is חֲלוֹם, derived from the root ח.ל.מ. The root appears in the Bible some 86 times, 60 of them as a noun: e.g., "And God said to him in the dream ..." (Gen. 20:6). There are also 26 occurrences of some verbal form–e.g., "He dreamt; a stairway ..." (Gen. 28:12). Of these, 24 are of the root ח.ל.מ in the *qal,* and two in the *hiph'il* (Jer. 29:8 and Isa. 38:16). There are 20 instances of the noun used as the internal accusative of the same verb–e.g., "Once Joseph dreamt a dream ..." (Gen. 37:5).

The etymology of the root ח.ל.מ still awaits a satisfactory explanation. It is found in other Semitic languages, including the various dialects of Aramaic (Jewish, Christian-Palmyrene, Samaritan, Mandaic), Ugaritic, Arabic, and Ethiopic.[3] In Arabic the root *ḥalama* means "dream," but also "to attain puberty, become mature." The cognate Tigre root has the meaning "come of age."[4] BDB explains the root ח.ל.מ as meaning "dream experience, an emission of the seminal fluid, attain to puberty."[5] A similar gloss is offered by the editors of *HALOT,* who see a semantic development from "come of age" through "have sexual dreams" to "dream" in general. Evidently they believe that the link between dreaming and sexual maturity is inherent in the fact that sexual dreams begin in adolescence–a hypothesis that seems to me to be extremely far-fetched.

The root ח.ל.מ also appears in the Bible in the sense of "strong, healthy": "My Lord, for all that and despite it my life-breath is revived; You have *restored*

---

3. M. Ottosson, "chālam," in *Theological Dictionary of the Old Testament,* ed. G. Johannes Botterweck and Helmer Ringgren, trans. David E. Green (Grand Rapids, Michigan: Eerdmans, 1980), 4:427.

4. *TDOT* 4:427; E. Littmann and M. Hofner. *Wörterbuch der Tigre-Sprache* (Wiesbaden: F. Steiner, 1962), p. 53b.

5. Francis Brown, Samuel Rolles Driver, and Charles Augustus Briggs, *A Hebrew and English Lexicon of the Old Testament* (Oxford: Clarendon Press, 1966), p. 321.

me to health and revived me" (Isa. 38:16);[6] "their young are healthy " יַחְלְמוּ (Job 39:4). The root ח.ל.מ has the same signification in Syriac, where we find the form *ḥelim* "powerful"; in Syriac the root means "well, healthy, whole, sound," and also "dream." Dahood pointed to the first king of the Ebla dynasty, king Igris-Halam. According to him, Halam was the God of Health. In Ugarit, the name *bn hlm,* "son of Halam," was borne by one of the citizens.[7] Both *BDB* and *GesB* suggest two different roots. Another possibility is that because sleep serves a healing function, the root ח.ל.מ is associated both with sleeping and with regaining one's health.

In Jer. 27:9–10, the root ח.ל.מ is used to designate the master of a particular art: "As for you, give no heed to your prophets, augurs, *dreamers,* diviners, and sorcerers, who say to you, 'Do not serve the king of Babylon.' For they prophesy falsely to you...." This verse designates four categories of practitioners: prophets, augurs, diviners, and sorcerers, but in Hebrew all are referred to by their products, with the noun חֲלֹמֹתֵיכֶם in the middle. It seems plausible that this word refers to the masters of a related craft, that is, professional dreamers, and that the expressions "who say to you" and "prophesy to you" apply to the dreamers along with the prophets and sorcerers and their colleagues.[8] In his commentary on the verse, David Kimḥi writes that "the meaning is 'the dreamers of your dreams'"–a precise rendering of Targum Jonathan's Aramaic. The Septuagint, Vulgate, and Peshitta follow a similar approach and have "your dreamers," rendering the word as an agent noun parallel to the others in the verse. These "dreamers" are obviously those who foretell the future by seeking dreams. The assumption that the reference is to professional dreamers is strengthened by Deut. 13:2–"If there appears among you a prophet or a dream-diviner and he gives you a sign or a portent"–and by the phrase "that dreamer" בַּעַל הַחֲלֹמוֹת הַלָּזֶה applied to Joseph (Gen. 37:19).

In Job, we find the word חַלָּמוּת "Does חַלָּמוּת have any flavor?" (Job 6:6). The Septuagint renders it as "in empty words," thus the translators of the Septuagint understood חַלָּמוּת as if it were "dreams." Tur-Sinai went in a similar direction and explained the entire section (6:3–7) as describing the nightmares with which God terrifies Job. In these dreams, God makes Job drink a liquid that he cannot abide swallowing. In verse 6, this liquid is described as "tasteless" and called the juice of חַלָּמוּת, the spittle of the divine figures who make

---

6. Ibid.; cf. BT Rosh Hashana 28a, "A man who is sometimes healthy (חלים) and sometimes crazy–when he is healthy he is sane in all respects."

7. M.J. Dahood, "Ebla, Ugarit, and the Bible," in G. Pettinato, *The Archives of Ebla* (Garden City, New York: Doublday, 1981), p. 307

8. M. Z. Segal, "Problems of words," *Leshonenu* 9–10 (1938–1940), p. 154 (Hebrew).

Job drink in his dream.[9] Other commentators have suggested that חֶלְמוּת is the name of a plant whose juice is insipid (perhaps the mallow), as in the Aramaic חלמיתא, or that it refers to the white of eggs (חלמון).[10] This was also the path followed by Abraham Ibn Ezra (1089-1164): "According to our Sages, חלמון inside; and some say that it is the sap of a plant that in their language is *ḥalama*."

The roots that describe חֲלוֹם designate sleep. In Sumerian, m a. m u means "dream" or "sleep."[11] The most common Akkadian word for dream is *šuttu*[12] (from the same root as *šittu*, "sleep"[ישׁי yšn]). Another Akkadian term for dream may be *munattu* (which ultimately has the same root as is found in Arabic *nāma*–meaning "sleep," in Hebrew נ.ו.מ as "be drowsy, slumber" and in Ethiopic, "dream.") In most Akkadian texts *munattu* signifies "the early morning hours."[13] Nevertheless, there are some texts in which it is necessary to gloss the word as "sleep" with the metonymous sense of "dream."[14] It is likely that *munattu* designates the sleep of the early morning hours. Another Akkadian expression that refers to dreams is *tabrīt mūši* "a nocturnal revelation"; this is literary and rare. In Akkadian a dream "is seen"; hence we find verbs like *amāru*,[15] *naṭālu*,[16] and rarely *naplāsu*, which refer to vision. Because a deity *causes* a dream to be seen, we also have the verb *šubrû* "to make see."[17] In Hittite, the word for dream is *tešḫaš*. The verb *tēšḫanna* means "to appear in a dream" and always refers to a dream theophany. The Egyptian word for dream is *rśw.t*,[18] which appears in expressions like "to see a dream," or "to see something in a dream." The word, which also means "awaken" (in both the

---

9. N. H. Tur-Sinai, *The Book of Job* (Jerusalem: Kiryat Sefer, 1967), p. 115.

10. Samuel Rolles Driver and George Buchanan Gray, *The Book of Job, ICC* (Edinburgh: T. & T. Clark, 1950), p. 60. A. S. Yahuda identified the slime or saliva (ריר) of חלמות with the insipid liquid exuding from a soft kind of cheese referred to in Arabic as *ḥalūm* or *ḥallūm*. See A. S. Yahuda, "Hapax Legomena im Alten Testament," *JQR* 15 (1903): 702–703.

11. See Oppenheim, *Interpretation,* p. 225.

12. *CAD* Š III:405–407.

13. *CAD* M II:200, "waking, waking times."

14. In the text of *Ludlul bēl nēmeqi*, the word *munattu* appears in a context where it may mean "sleep" as well as "dream": "[In] my sleep/dream ([*i-na*] *mu-na-at-ti*) they sent me a message." See Oppenheim, *Interpretation,* p. 225; W. von Soden, AHw II: 672, renders *munattu* as "Morgenschlummer" morning slumber. W. G. Lambert wrote that *munattu* was: "the early-morning period of light sleep and waking … but in all the passages where the meaning is plain 'waking time' is clearly correct." See: W. G. Lambert, *Babylonian Wisdom Literature* (Oxford : Clarendon Press, 1960), p. 295.

15. *CAD* A II:8, n. 6; TDOT 4:423.

16. *CAD* N II:124–125 G; TDOT 4:423.

17. Oppenheim, *Interpretation,* p. 226.

18. *WbÄS,* II, 452.

transitive and intransitive senses), has an open eye as its determinative, apparently representing dreaming as a special state of consciousness, something like watching during sleep.[19] According to Gunn,[20] *wp.t mȝ'.t* "message of truth" also refers to a dream revelation.

There are, however, languages in which the word for "dream" is associated with that for "sleep," while in other languages it is derived from roots associated with vision. Gordon notes that in Ugaritic the root *ḥlm* means "to see."[21] In Arabic, *ru'yā* "dream" is derived from the root *ra'ā* "to see." In Coptic, we have *nau*, "look behold" from the earlier f.s. *nw* (older *nwȝ)* "look, see," all the way through Demotic.[22]

THE THEOPHANY

The first stage in a prophetic dream is the theophany, which seems to follow a standard formula involving who the dreamer is, and when, where, and under what conditions the dream takes place. Oppenheim's formula seems to apply to the revelations in the Bible as well. Indeed, it is possible that the standard formula is used because many of the dream theophanies in the Bible occur to non-Hebrews.

Let us first consider *when* and *where* the dreams take place. "But God came to Abimelech in a dream by night" (Gen. 20:3); "but God came to Laban the Aramean in a dream by night" (Gen. 31:24); "that night God came to Balaam" (Num. 22:20).[23] Although these examples fail to specify the location of the theophanies, we can deduce from their contexts that God appeared to Abimelech in Gerar, to Laban at Mt. Gilead (Gen. 31:23), and to Balaam in his home.[24] In all three verses, however, God appears at night. As the Talmudic

---

19. Oppenheim, *Interpretation,* p. 226.

20. B. Gunn, "Notes on Ammenemes I," *JEA* 27 (1941): 2–6.

21. C. H. Gordon, *Ugaritic Handbook* (Rome: Pontifical Biblical Institute, 1947), p. 228, n. 674.

22. Jaroslav Černý, *Coptic Etymological Dictionary* (Cambridge University Press, 1976), p. 113.

23. It should be emphasized that the word חלום 'dream' does not appear in the last-cited verse; from a reading of the episode, however, it is obvious that we are dealing with a dream and perhaps with an incubation; see further below.

24. Gnuse noted that the scene of the theophany is missing in the dreams attributed to E and concluded that the message-dream paradigm did not exist independently in the individual stories but was the creation of the narrator who incorporated these descriptions in his narrative cycle. Nevertheless, we can infer from the story itself where the theophany took place, and the author simply saw no reason to specify this detail (Gnuse, *Dream,* pp. 74–75).

rabbis expounded: "It is like a king who had a wife and a concubine. When he went to his wife, he went in public, but when he went to the concubine, he did so secretly. So too the Holy One, blessed be He, does not appear to Gentile prophets except at night: God came to Balaam at night, to Laban at night, and to Abimelech at night" (Genesis Rabba 52, 20).[25]

But even when the dreamers are Hebrews, the Bible consistently reports that the dreams are nocturnal: בַּחֲלוֹם הַלַּיְלָה "a dream by night": "at Gibeon the Lord appeared to Solomon in a dream by night" (1 Kings 3:5). Of Jacob's dream in Bethel, we read that "he came upon a certain place and stopped there for the night, for the sun had set" (Gen.28:11). In contrast, when the angel appears to Jacob in the house of Laban, it is the time of year that is specified: "at the mating time of the flocks" (Gen. 31:10). This reference to the season has a direct link to the content of the dream, which deals with the natural increase of the herds tended by Jacob.

Unlike the Bible, however, the ancient Near East seems to have attached no great importance to when a dream took place, and this detail is omitted from most dream narratives. There are some exceptions, of course. The Akkadian literary work of *Ludlul bêl-nêmeqi* includes a dream said to take place in the morning hours.[26] The dream of Thutmoses IV, by contrast, occurs at noon.[27] From Mari we have a dream sent to King Zimri-Lim, warning him to stay home. The author is one Addu-duri, a woman of some influence at the royal court. She writes, "This dream of mine was in the evening-watch."[28] Some believe that the reference to the hour at which the dream occurs is meant to buttress its authenticity; in this instance, however, at the end of the account we are told that Addu-duri sent a lock of hair, and this seems to be intended as a warrant of the veracity of the dream.[29]

Not only do biblical dreams take place at night, but while experiencing the

---

25. In the dream of Amenhotep II, recounted on the Memphis stele, we read: "The majesty of his august god, Amon ... came before His Majesty [i.e., the pharaoh] in a dream" (Oppenheim, *Interpretation*, p. 188; *ANET* 246; Serge Sauneron et al., "Dans l'Égypte ancienne," in *Les Songes et leur interprétation*, p. 22.).

26. Ibid., p. 187, d. 17. Lambert, however, renders the text differently: "in dream and waking moments I am equally wretched." Two other dreams that occur in this opus are said to take place at night; see W. G. Lambert, *Babylonian Wisdom Literature* (Oxford: Clarendon Press, 1960), p. 49, l. 8; 22, 30.

27. Oppenheim, *Interpretation*, p. 187; "Egyptian Oracles and Prophecies," trans. John A. Wilson, *ANET*, 449.

28. *ARM* X:50, in "Akkadian Letters," trans. William L. Moran, *ANET* 631(p); W. L. Moran, "New Evidence from Mari on the History of Prophecy," *Biblica* 50 (1969): 38.

29. Joel Sweek, "Dreams of Power from Sumer to Judah," Ph.D. dissertation, University of Chicago, 1996, p. 112.

dream, the dreamer is always asleep: "He came upon a certain place and stopped there for the night, for the sun had set. Taking one of the stones of that place, he put it under his head and lay down in that place" (Gen. 28:11). To this we should compare: "For God speaks time and again–though man does not perceive it–in a dream, a night vision, when deep sleep falls on men, while they slumber on their beds. Then He opens men's understanding, and by disciplining them leaves His signature" (Job 33:14–16). Similarly, the idioms that signify the dreamer's awakening from the dream reflect the fact that he was sleeping: "Jacob awoke from his sleep" (Gen. 28:16); "Jacob got up early in the morning" (Gen. 28:18); "Abimelech got up early in the morning" (Gen. 20:8); "When You are aroused You despise their image, as one does a dream after waking, O Lord" (Ps. 73:20). The indication that the dreamer is sleeping while dreaming is very important, because it is one of the touchstones for distinguishing dreams from visions.[30]

In extrabiblical sources, too, there is a tendency to emphasize that the dreamer had gone to bed or was already asleep. In an Assyrian text about the dream of a priest of Ishtar, we find the verb *utullu* "being in bed."[31] In the *Annals of Ashurbanipal* there is a description of the dream of a young man that depicts the outcome of the war between Ashurbanipal and his brothers. He dreams about an inscription that relates the downfall of the rebels. The dream begins with the following words: "In these days, a man went to bed in the middle of the night and had a dream as follows."[32]

And during the theophany itself, the dreamer is passive; he waits to hear what God has to say to him.[33] God, by contrast, is the active party: "God came" (Gen. 20:3 and 31:10); "The Lord appeared" (1 Kings 3:5; 2 Chronicles 1:7); "I make Myself known" (Num. 12:6); "The Lord was standing beside him" (Gen. 28:13); "He said" (Gen. 20:3 and 31:11). Sometimes God calls the dreamer by name: "And in the dream an angel of God said to me, 'Jacob!' 'Here,' I answered." (Gen. 31:11).[34] In other dreams the Lord identi-

---

30. André Caquot, "Selon Canaan et Israel," in *Les Songes et leur interprétation,* p. 111.

31. Oppenheim, *Interpretation,* pp. 187, 249, section 8, no. 10.

32. Ibid., loc. cit., no. 11.

33. In contrast to the passivity of the dreamer, the Bible includes two exceptional cases in which the dreamer conducts a dialogue with God: the dreams of Abimelech (Gen. 20:3–5) and Solomon (1 Kings 3:5–14).

34. There is another double vocative addressed by the Lord to Jacob in Genesis 46:2: "God called to Israel in a vision by night: 'Jacob! Jacob!' He answered, 'Here.'" David Kimḥi explains that the Lord called his name twice because several years had passed during which Jacob had not had any revelation, and "He called twice so he would know that it was the [holy] spirit calling him." A similar double vocative occurs in Samuel 3:10: "The Lord came, and stood there, and He called as before: 'Samuel! Samuel!' And Samuel answered,

fies himself: "He said, 'I am the Lord, the God of your father Abraham and the God of Isaac'" (Gen. 28:13); "I am the God of Bethel" (Gen. 31:13). Evidently the inclusion of the Lord's name is meant to suggest that there is a close relationship between the deity and the dreamer–that is, the deity is the dreamer's patron and protector. In extrabiblical sources, too, there are dreams in which the deity identifies himself. For example, in the dream of Thutmoses IV, we read: "I am your father, Harmakhis-Khepri-Re-Atum."[35] And in another Egyptian dream, that of Djoser, we read: "I am Khnum, your creator."[36]

Although biblical literature emphasizes the fact that God is the active party in the dream, the Bible includes no detailed attempt to describe the image of the deity, as is found in extrabiblical sources. As Barr noted: "Thus we see that in many cases the description of the theophanic appearance is less important than registering the words spoken; or perhaps more probably, that the recording of the appearance in detail was felt by writers often to be too serious and difficult to attempt except in special cases."[37] Another possibility is that this is an echo of the idea that "a man cannot see Me and live" (Ex. 33:20)

Unusually, the dream at Bethel indicates that the Lord "was standing beside him" (Gen. 28:13)–perhaps to emphasize the extent to which the appearance of God was real and substantial. The verb "standing" also occurs in the account of Samuel's theophany: "The Lord came, and stood there" (1 Sam. 3:10). In Sumerian and Akkadian, we have a similar expression indicating that the deity "stands" next to the dreamer's head. For example, in the dream of Eannatum, we read: "For him who lies (there) ... he (the appearing deity) took his stand at his head."[38] In the poem of *Ludlul bêl-nêmeqi* we read: "He (the deity) entered and took his stand."[39] We can also compare the Egyptian literature of the Hunger Stele: "standing over against me."[40] In the literature of the ancient East, the author even describes the deity. In the dream of Gudea, Ensi

---

'Speak, for Your servant is listening.'" The repetition of the name is an expression of affection and encouragement, just as we find with regard to Moses (Exod. 3:4) and Abraham (Gen. 22:11).

35. Oppenheim, *Interpretation,* p. 251, section 8, no. 15.

36. Ibid.

37. J. Barr, "Theophany and Anthropomorphism in the OT," *SVT* 7 (1960), p. 32.

38. Oppenheim, *Interpretation,* p. 189.

39. Ibid.

40. Ibid., p. 189; "Egyptian Myths, Tales, and Mortuary," trans. John A. Wilson, *ANET* 31–32. See also the extensive bibliography in M. Lichtheim, *Ancient Egyptian Literature* (Berkeley: University of California Press, 1980), vol. 3: 95. The inscription is apparently an ancient forgery; see further in the next chapter.

of the Sumerian city of Lagash, he describes the image of the deity that appears from earth up to the sky.[41] The dream of the pharaoh Merneptah incorporates the description of a titanic figure "as if a statue of Ptah were standing before Pharaoh. He was like the height of [x cubits]."[42]

In sum, the prophetic dream of the Bible, like its counterpart in the ancient Near East, takes place at night, comes to a sleeping dreamer, and includes both audible and visual elements. The dreamer is passive, whereas the deity is active and comes to convey a message through the dream.

THE CONTENT OF THE DREAM

The nucleus of the prophetic dream is the message from the god, which is conveyed in plain language, without symbols. The core of the message is verbal, although it is sometimes accompanied by a dream vision. The dream anticipates and emphasizes certain events of concern to the protagonist; sometimes it warns the dreamer about the future or admonishes him against performing certain acts. The themes of such dreams are directly related to the dreamer's life, but the strange phenomena and fantasies we usually associate with the world of dreams are absent.

Because the themes of biblical prophetic dreams are fixed and recurrent, it is possible to divide them into two groups: dreams of encouragement and dreams of admonition. In Jacob's dreams (Gen. 28:12–19, 30:10–13, and 46:1–5)[43] and Solomon's dream (1 Kings 3), God's appearance serves to encourage the sleepers. In the admonitory dream, God cautions the dreamer not to harm His chosen one: Abimelech is warned about Sarah (Gen. 20), and Laban about Jacob (Gen. 31:24). Below we shall analyze the themes and objectives of these specific dreams.

DREAMS OF ENCOURAGEMENT AND PROMISE

The Dream at Bethel
God appears to Jacob in three dreams, each of which occurs at an important crossroads in the patriarch's life, just before he sets out on a journey. The

---

41. Thorkild Jacobsen, *The Harps that Once–: Sumerian Poetry in Translation* (New Haven: Yale University Press, 1987), Cyl. A IV:15, p. 392; Oppenheim, *Interpretation,* p. 189.

42. Ibid., p. 189; Max Müller, *Egyptological Researches: Results of a Journey in 1904* (Washington, DC: Carnegie Institution of Washington, June 1906), Plates 22:28–29.

43. According to Genesis 46:1 (MT 46:2), God calls to Jacob "in a vision by night" (Gen. 46:2). In the next chapter we shall consider whether such a nocturnal vision is in fact a dream.

dream at Bethel follows close upon Jacob's departure from his father's house en route to Haran (Gen. 28:10). This departure marks the end of his youth and introduces the period of his sojourn in the house of Laban, where he becomes the father of a family. His dream in Laban's house takes place on the eve of his hasty decamping to return to Canaan (Gen. 31:11) and marks his assumption of the role of independent agent. Lastly, Jacob's dream in Beersheba is mentioned before he descends to Egypt (Gen. 46:2) and raises the curtain on the last chapter in his life. It is plausible that at each juncture he receives instructions from God, aimed, as we shall see below, at strengthening and encouraging him for the future, both personally and nationally. These messages manifest his closeness to God, who identifies Himself in each of the three dreams and, in Gen. 31 and 46, even calls Jacob by name.

Citing the alternation in the names of the deity—Elohim and YHWH—and the different forms taken by the theophany—in one case direct, in the other a dream—advocates of the documentary theory have identified two literary strands in the biblical passage, one attributed to E (vv. 11b–12, 17–18, 20–22), the other to J (vv. 11a, 13–16, 19a). However, there is substantial disagreement among scholars concerning the details of this division.[44] De Pury, for example, divides the story between E and J; the promises and naming of Bethel (vv. 13–16 and 19a) are assigned to J, but vv. 11–12, 17–18, 20–21a, and 22–the dream, the erection of the pillar, and Jacob's vow—to E. There is no critical consensus about v. 10 (J or E), v. 19b (J or redactor), and v. 21b (E or redactor).

In contrast, R. Rendtorff[45] expresses doubts as to the division of the dream into separate sources, arguing that the story went through a number of revisions during which additional material was added. Accordingly he suggests that the earliest material is found in vv. 11–12 and 16–19 and that the divine promises in vv. 13–15 were added to link this story to the patriarchal narratives. Verses 20–22 constitute an independent account of a vow with expansions in v. 22b and later in 21b. Moreover, Fokkelman's literary examination uncovers a correspondence between Jacob's preparations for sleep, his dream in which God promises to protect him on his journey (vv. 11–15), and his

---

44. See Ehrlich and the division he proposes (Ehrlich, *Traum,* pp. 27–28). See also Victor P. Hamilton, *The Book of Genesis* (Grand Rapids, Eerdmans, 1994), p. 245; Gnuse, *Dream,* p.67; Gerhard von Rad, *Genesis, A Commentary,* trans. John H. Marks (Philadelphia: Westminister Press, 1972), p.283; A. de Pury, *Promesse divine et légende cultuelle dans le cycle de Jacob: Gen. 28 et les traditions patriarcales,* Études bibliques (Paris: Gabalda, 1975).

45. R. Rendtorff, "Jacob in Bethel, Beobachtungen zum Aufbau und zur Quellenfrage in Gen. 28:10–22, *ZAW* 94 (1982), pp. 511–523.

reaction when he wakes up and proceeds to consecrate the pillar to the Lord and make his vow (vv. 16–22).[46]

The dream at Bethel is unique because its verbal message is complemented by a vision (v. 12), to which the dreamer himself provides an interpretation (v. 17).[47] It should, however, be emphasized that the link between the meaning of the vision (v. 17) and the verbal message (vv. 13b–15) is indirect.[48] The narrator describes a ladder in the dream whose top reaches to heaven and on which angels of God are ascending and descending.[49] There is a strong argument that the biblical author was influenced by multiple extrabiblical sources. The ladder reminds us of the Mesopotamian ziggurats or sacred towers,[50] which soared dozens of meters skyward and which were often described as having their tops in the heavens. Gudea of Lagash says of the Eninnu temple that "it lies in heaven." And a text from Manipur refers to a tower "whose peak reaches the sky."[51] There was a lower sanctuary at the base of that tower. At its summit was an upper sanctuary where the godhead was believed to have its permanent abode. The tower itself was the link between the two sanctuaries. Sometimes there were stairs in the tower, which the deity could descend in order to appear to mortals.

Similarly, the angels' ascent and descent of the ladder in Jacob's dream parallel those of the Assyrian version of the myth of Nergal and Ereshkigal, where we read that the gods came down "the long stairway *(simmiltu)* of

---

46. On the literary structure of the tale of Jacob's dream in Bethel, see: J. P. Fokkelman, *Narrative Art in Genesis* (Assen / Amsterdam: Van Gorcum, 1975), pp.71–81; Frank Polak, *Biblical Narrative* (Jerusalem, Bialik, 1994), pp. 223–225.

47. Some scholars, however, believe that the vision is left uninterpreted. See: Ehrlich, *Traum*, p. 29; Wolfgang Richter, "Traum und Traumdeutung im Alten Testament," *BZ* 7 (1963), p. 210; Gnuse, *Dream*, p. 69.

48. De Pury, *Promesse divine*, p. 337.

49. The word סלם 'ladder' in v. 12 is a hapax whose etymology is quite difficult. It may be derived from the root ס.ל.ל. 'heap up' and designates a "stairlike pavement or ramp." See: Von Rad, *Genesis*, p. 284; E. A. Speiser, *Genesis, AB* (Garden City, NY: Doubleday, 1964), p. 218. Another possibility is that the root is related to the Akkadian *simmiltu* 'stairway'; see: A. R. Millard, "The Celestial Ladder and the Gate of Heaven" (Genesis xxviii.12,17), *ExpTim* 78 (1966/67), pp. 86–87; H. Hoffner, Jr., "Second Millennium Antecedents to the Hebrew 'ÔB," *JBL* 86 (1967), p. 397, n. 30; H. R. Cohen, *Biblical Hapax Legomena in the Light of Akkadian and Ugaritic* (Missoula, MT: Scholars Press, 1978), pp. 34 and 108. See also Westerman, *Genesis*, 2:454, who connects *sullām* with both *sālāl* and Akkadian *simmiltu*.

50. Speiser, *Genesis*, pp. 219–220; Nahum M. Sarna, *Understanding Genesis* (New York: Schocken Books, 1966), p. 193. On the connection between סולם and *ziqquratu*, see M. Jastrow, *Religious Belief in Babylonia and Assyria*, p. 290, n. 1.

51. Nahum M. Sarna, *Genesis: The JPS Torah Commentary* (Philadelphia: Jewish Publication Society, 1989), p. 83.

heaven."[52] Furthermore, in the myth we read that after Nergal and Ereshkigal ascended the long ladder of the sky, they reached the "gate" of the heavens. The tradition that the name of the city Babylon is derived from *bab-ilim* "gate of the god" is also reminiscent of our passage.[53] In another source, the Pyramid Texts, the dead king climbs a ladder to rejoin his mother, Nut; the expression "gate of heaven" also appears in these texts."[54] Thus the many extant examples of the ladder motif, referring to the transmission of a divine embassy, suggest that the biblical author borrowed it, discarded its mythological elements, and adapted it to this story of Jacob, allowing it to serve as a framework for the transmission of the divine promise to the patriarch.

From an account of the angels ascending and descending the ladder[55] (v. 12), the biblical author proceeds to report the appearance of the Lord who "was standing beside him" (v. 13).[56] The ladder and angels are only stage props, whose main function is to lead up to the climax—the appearance by the Lord, and His promise, which is the nucleus of the dream. Perhaps the

---

52. Millard, "The Celestial Ladder and the Gate of Heaven," pp. 86–87; O. R. Gurney, "The Myth of Nergal and Ereshkigal," *AnSt* 10 (1960), pp. 105ff.

53. In rabbinic aggada the gate of heaven is conceived of as a Temple on high that corresponds to the Temple on earth; see the comment on our verse by R. Simeon bar Yoḥai in Genesis Rabba 69. Because the Temple was located in Jerusalem rather than in Bethel, the Sages had to resort to an exegesis whereby "the ladder stands in the Temple and its slope reaches to Beth El." The view that the Temple in Heaven is opposite Beth El has an echo in the Temple Scroll from Qumran (29:9–10).

54. J. G. Griffiths, "The Celestial Ladder and the Gate of Heaven (Gen. 28:12 and 17)," *ExpTim* 76 (1964/65), pp. 229–30; 78 (1966/67), pp. 54–55.

55. The famous question is how angels could climb up before climbing down, since it is well known that angels must first descend from heaven and then go back up. Rashi explains: "Ascending first and then descending. The angels that escorted him in the Land of Israel do not leave the land and ascended to the heavens and the angels of outside the land came down to escort him."

56. It is not clear whether the preposition and its object refer to Jacob (as trans. here) or to the ladder ("was standing *on it*"). The Septuagint, Vulgate, and Peshitta all believe that the Lord is standing on the ladder. It is difficult to accept this interpretation, however, because, if the Lord was standing on the ladder, it is hard to fathom how the angels could ascend and descend it. More plausible is the view that the Lord was standing beside Jacob, as in NEB and NAB. The idiom נצב על with the sense of "stand over" or "stand beside" is found in a number of places (Exod. 7:15, Num. 23:6 and 17; 1 Sam. 19:20 and 22:9). Compare Gen. 18:2, where the angels stand by (*or* over) Abraham (נִצָּבִים עָלָיו). Similarly, Abraham's servant stands near (נצב על) the well. On the other hand, נצב על, in the *nif'al*, also occurs in the sense of "stand atop something" (see Exod. 17:9, 33:21, and 34:2); in the *hif'il* it means "put something on top of something" (2 Sam. 18:17). See Hamilton, *The Book of Genesis*, p. 241; C. Houtman, "What did Jacob See in his Dream at Bethel? Some Remarks on Gen. 28:10–22," *VT* 27 (1977), p. 348.

angels are scouting out the land and then returning to heaven to report to God. Or perhaps they represent Jacob's hopes and fears and his prayer that the Lord will protect him. All of these ascend to heaven, where they are answered.[57]

The promises to Jacob that constitute the heart of the dream (vv. 13–15) include a personal promise (v. 15) as well as others that have more national dimensions–possession of the land and the promise of offspring (vv. 13b–14).[58] These pledges are quite astonishing; we might more likely have expected this theophany to include a rebuke of Jacob for having misled and defrauded his brother and father. But that reproof comes later, in the form of various punishments.[59] From the thematic perspective, God's promises are quite similar to those He made to Abraham in Genesis 13:14–16. The land will be given to Jacob and his children, who will be like the dust of the earth.[60]

When God promises the land to Jacob, the text emphasizes that the reference is to "the ground on which you are lying"–wording appropriate to Jacob's present situation. Jacob is concerned that he may not see his homeland again; the Lord promises that not only will he do so, but it will become the permanent possession of himself and his children in the distant future. On the other hand, the personal promise at the end of the dream has more immediate implications: "Remember, I am with you: I will protect you wherever you go and will bring you back to this land. I will not leave you until I have done what I have promised you" (Gen. 28:15). This pledge is meant to encourage Jacob, who, totally indigent, is now fleeing Esau's rage and journeying to an unknown land, believing that God has abandoned him.

It is obvious that the Lord's promise to Jacob is appropriate to his personal situation and will be realized in his own lifetime.[61] It should be emphasized that the promise of returning "to this land" is also a recurrent motif in Jacob's

---

57. Sarna, *Genesis,* p. 198.

58. The motif of inheriting the land and having many descendants is very frequent in Scripture. See: Gen. 12:2; 17:20; 18;18; 21:13 and 18; 46:3; Exod. 32:10; Num. 14:12.

59. Jacob was punished measure for measure for his deceitful actions. He deceived his blind father Isaac; on his wedding night, when Jacob could not see anything, Laban substituted Leah for Rachel. Jacob deceived his father with the skin of a kid; his sons deceived him when they drenched the coat of many colors in the blood of a kid. He was also punished by the death of Rachel, the rape of Dinah, and Joseph's sale into slavery by his brothers. When Jacob appears before Pharaoh, he tells him that "few and hard have been the years of my life" (Gen. 47:9).

60. In v. 14, there is a promise of progeny and becoming a blessing for all the families of the earth, a blessing that will be realized through Jacob and his descendants. On this see Genesis 12:3, 18:18, 22:18, and 26:4.

61. Westermann, *Genesis,* pp. 455–456.

other two dreams (31:13 and 46:4) and highlights Jacob's bond to his birth-place. And just as the promise of a son is a recurrent motif in the Abraham cycle, the motif of divine assistance and protection is prominent in the stories of Jacob and Esau (Gen. 26:3; 24; 28:15 (20); 31:3; 32:10; 46:3; 48:15, 21; 50:24).[62] This motif appears in chapters 26–50 but never in the first half of Genesis. The expression "I am with you" is usually accompanied by other promises (Gen. 26:2–5), but God's promise is meant only for the person ad-dressed by Him, and is vouchsafed to someone leaving his homeland or start-ing on a journey. The divine promise to accompany, protect, and guide the patriarch is appropriate to the life of nomads,[63] but similar expressions are relatively rare in extrabiblical sources.[64]

Whereas the Bible assigns Jacob's dream a narrow meaning that relates exclusively to him, the midrash Tanḥuma goes beyond the confines of the story to give the dream a much broader significance, one that relates not merely to Jacob, who is leaving his country, but to the people of Israel wan-dering in exile from its homeland. As the midrash states:

> "And behold the angels of God descending and ascending": These are the princes of the heathen nations that God showed Jacob our father. The Prince of Babylon ascended seventy steps and descended; Media fifty-two and descended; Greece one hundred steps and descended; Edom ascended and no one knows how many! In that hour, Jacob was afraid and said: "Peradventure this one has no descent?" Said the Holy One blessed be He to him: "Therefore fear thou not, O my servant Jacob … neither be dismayed, O Israel [Jer. 30:10]. Even if thou seest him, so to speak, ascend and sit by Me, thence will I bring him down! As it is stated (Obad. 1:4): 'Though thou exalt thyself as the eagle and set thy nest among the stars, thence will I bring thee down, saith the Lord.'"[65]

The medieval exegete Obadiah ben Jacob Sforno (c. 1470–c. 1550) explained the dream in accordance with this midrash:

> "Ascending and descending"—indeed ultimately, having gained

---

62. Westermann believes that the promise of protection has no connection with the genre of stories that describe the discovery of a holy place. He accordingly believes that J interpolated this promise of divine protection at the start of Jacob's flight from Esau. Pledges of protection and assistance are generally given at the start of a journey and are appropriate to the nomadic way of life.

63. C. Westermann, *The Promises to the Fathers,* trans. David E. Green (Philadelphia: Fortress Press, 1980), pp. 140–143.

64. Ibid.

65. Midrash Tanḥuma, *Vayetze* 2.

ascendancy, the Gentile princes will go down, and the Almighty who forever stands above will not forsake His people as He promised (Jer. 30:11): "For I will make a full end of all the nations whither I scattered you, but I will not make a full end of you."

Thus the Tanhuma views the ladder as symbolizing history and the angels as empires that rise and fall.[66]

The inspiration for this interpretation is probably the vision of the four kingdoms in the Book of Daniel. The homilist saw before his eyes three empires that had ruled over the Jews and disappeared—namely Babylonia, Media/Persia, and Greece. The fourth empire is Edom/Rome, which was still dominant in the time of the homilist. Jacob leaving Canaan represents the people of Israel, who are going into exile. Jacob's fright parallels the Jews' fear that the ascendancy of Rome may have no end. The author of the midrash, who lived under Roman rule, could not predict when Rome and its offspring, referred to in the rabbinic literature of the Middle Ages as "Edom," would lose their dominion. But he quotes a verse from Obadiah (v. 4) that confidently predicts the downfall of Edom. Every ascent of the ladder depends on the descent of someone else. Nor is it a ladder that has no end, for God stands at the top of it. It is the Lord who directs history. He raises up and lowers down and will bring low the Roman Empire too.

In another midrash (Genesis Rabbah 68:12), the early third-century sage Bar Kappara holds that every dream contains its own solution and cites the ladder seen by Jacob. The sage interprets the dream using a method that replaces the symbols with future events and refers them not to Jacob but to the distant future.[67]

Bar Kappara taught: No dream is without its interpretation (אין חלום שאין לו פתרון).

"And behold a ladder" (Gen. 28:12) refers to (זה) a stairway;

"Set up on the earth" (ibid.) refers to (זה) the altar, as it says: "An altar of earth you shall make for Me" (Exod. 20:24);

"And the top of it reached the heaven" (Gen. 28:12) refers to (אלו) the sacrifices, the odors of which ascended to heaven;

"And behold the angels of God" (ibid.) refers to (אלו) the High Priests;

66. Nehama Leibowitz, *Studies in Bereshit (Genesis)*, trans. Aryeh Newman, 4th rev. ed. (Jerusalem: World Zionist Organization, 1981), p. 299.

67. Maren Niehoff, "A Dream Which is Not Interpreted is Like a Letter Which is Not Read," *JJS* 43 (1992), pp. 72–73.

"Ascending and descending on it" (ibid.): ascending and descending on
the stairway;
"And behold the Lord stood beside him" (Gen. 28:13): "I saw the Lord
standing beside the altar" (Amos 9:1);
The rabbis solved it by reference to Sinai (פתרין ליה בסיני).
"And he dreamt, and behold the ladder" (Gen. 28:12) refers to (זה) Sinai;
"Set up on the earth" (ibid.), as it says: "And they stood at the nether
part of the mount" (Exod. 19:17);
"And the top of it reached the heaven" (Gen. 28:12), as it says, "And the
mountain burned with fire unto the heart of heaven" (Deut. 4:11);
"And behold the angels of God" (Gen. 28:12) refers to (זה) Moses and
Aaron;
"Ascending" (ibid.), as it says, "And Moses went up" (Exod. 19:3);
"Descending" (ibid.), as it says, "And Moses went down from the moun-
tain" (Exod. 19:14).
"And behold the Lord stood beside him" (Gen. 28:13), as it says, "And
the Lord came down upon Mount Sinai" (Exod. 19:20).[68]

In the midrash, Bar Kappara identifies the ladder in Jacob's dream with the
ramp leading up to the altar in the Temple, based on its shape and orientation
toward Heaven. In his interpretation, Bar Kappara uses the same standard
idioms, such as זה and אלו, that are used in the interpretation of symbolic
dreams in the Joseph cycle (Gen. 40:12, 18). His interpretation proceeds by
analogy: "And the top of it reached the heaven" parallels "these are the
sacrifices whose aroma reaches the heavens"; "And behold the angels of
God" is paralleled by "these are the high priests ascending and descending
it." He compares the angels' ascent and descent with the priests' ascent and
descent of the ramp leading to the altar. The appearance of the Lord in the
dream, "the Lord stood beside him," is juxtaposed with a similar verse from
the book of Amos, in which the Lord is described as standing by the altar.

A different interpretation of Jacob's dream is found in the midrash, presented in the name of the Sages, that begins with the expression פתרין ליה. Here
the ladder is identified with Mount Sinai. The midrash goes on to point out
that the words סלם "ladder" and Sinai have the same numerical value. Here
too the interpretation is by way of analogy and the angels on Jacob's ladder
are said to be like Moses and Aaron. The angels' ascent and descent prefigure
Moses' ascent and descent of Mount Sinai. Here too the midrash finds allusions in the dream to events in the future of the people Israel rather than in
the life of Jacob.

---

68. Genesis Rabba *Vayetze* 68, 12.

Jacob's Dream in the House of Laban

Another dream theophany visited on Jacob is described in Gen. 31:10–13. The text as we have it is corrupt, but it is apparent that we are dealing with two separate experiences that have been merged.[69] One involves the stratagem by which Jacob made his flocks proliferate. This theophany took place in the narrative past and featured an angel of God[70] with a visual element, supplemented by the angel's words (v. 12). In the second theophany, however, the God of the Bethel dream appears to Jacob and commands him to rise and leave Laban's house and return to the land of Canaan—a revelation that refers to the present and immediate future.[71] The message in the second theophany is verbal only. According to our text, the angel who told Jacob the secret of breeding the ewes now addresses him and tells him to go back to his homeland. But some time must have passed between the genetic counseling and the injunction to go back to his homeland. Further, verse 12 is an almost literal reprise of verse 10. The angel tells Jacob to lift up his eyes and see what he has already seen. For this reason, some have proposed inverting the order of the verses.[72]

Commentators disagree about whether this is a single or a double dream. Nachmanides (Moses b. Naḥman, known as Ramban, 1194–1270) evidently sensed that there were two separate revelations here. In his commentary on v. 13, he writes: "This is not a single dream: Note well that 'lift up your eyes and see all the he-goats' was when the sheep were in heat during one of the earlier years, but 'I am the God of Bethel' was spoken later, at the time of the journey, because after He told him to rise and leave this land he did not tarry any longer in Haran." S. D. Luzzatto (1800–1865), by contrast, in his commen-

---

69. On the corruption of the text, see Sarna, *Genesis,* p. 214, Westermann, *Genesis 12–36,* p. 491. Some, however, point out that the structure of the dream sequence in our text is identical to that of other dreams in Genesis:

v. 10	"saw in a dream and behold" (הִנֵּה)	cf. 28:12a	15:12a
	vision (he-goats mounting)	28:12b–13a	15:12b, 17
vv. 11–12	explanation of the vision	28:13b–15	15:13, 15, 18–21
v. 13	consequent command	28:20–22	15:13, 15, 818–21

See Wenham, *Genesis 16–50,* vol. 2, p. 272.

70. Some consider the verses that describe the proliferation of the sheep to be an expansion and supplement to Gen. 30:28–43, where Jacob's method is explained. See Westermann, *Genesis 12–36,* p. 491.

71. Verses 11 and 13 are really an expansion of v. 3: "Then the Lord said to Jacob, 'Return to the land of your fathers where you were born, and I will be with you'" (Gen. 31:3). Westermann argues that this verse stood in place of vv. 11 and 13 in the original text. See Westermann, *Genesis 12–36,* p. 492.

72. Westermann, *Genesis 12–36,* p. 491.

tary on verse 13, sees it all as a single dream, in which the description of the he-goats is a flashback:

> "I am the God who has been with you until now and saw to it that the sheep bore speckled young. I am the one who now tells you to rise and leave this land and I will help you." For it is all one dream that comes to him now, when the sheep were in heat that year.

Whether part of a single or a double theophany, verse 13 is phrased in the imperative: "Arise and leave this land"—and is evidently meant to encourage and reinforce Jacob, who is afraid of Laban. Laban has already deceived him several times—especially on his wedding night, when he substituted Leah for Rachel. Jacob, though furious, could do nothing. When Laban overtakes the fugitive Jacob, he rebukes Jacob for what he has done. Jacob retorts: "I was afraid because I thought you would take your daughters from me by force" (Gen. 31:31). Jacob has long been nursing his sense of being defrauded. His anger and frustration erupt in the serious charges with which he castigates Laban. The biblical author employs a flashback technique and quotes Jacob's complaints about past wrongs: Laban has repeatedly changed his terms of employment and has demanded that Jacob make good for animals eaten by predators. Jacob paid up even though he was not legally required to do so.[73] Jacob's wives share this sense of frustration; they tell him that they feel like alien women in their father's house because he has sold them and consumed their money.[74]

In the light of Laban's deceit, we can understand why the text recalls the revelation in Bethel, where God promised to protect Jacob and return him safe and sound to Canaan.[75] The verse depends on the story of the dream at Bethel—whether by recalling God's promise to "bring you back to this land" (Gen. 28:15) or as the fulfillment of Jacob's request in his vow that God return him in peace to his father's house. The instruction to Jacob to leave Laban's

---

73. According to the Code of Hammurabi, as well as Exod. 22:12, a hired shepherd was liable only for strayed or stolen lambs. See at length: S. E. Loewenstamm, "אנכי אחטנה," *Leshonenu* 29 (1965), pp. 69–70; J. N. Postgate, "Some Old Babylonian Shepherds and Their Flocks," *JSS* 20 (1975), pp. 1–21; C. Mabee, "Jacob and Laban: The Structure of Judicial Proceedings (Genesis XXXI 25-42)," *VT* 30 (1980), pp. 192–207.

74. They are referring to the dowry received by the father of the bride, part of which he was supposed to set aside for her benefit; Laban evidently did not do so. See Westermann, *Genesis 12–36*, p. 491.

75. The word אֲשֶׁר 'where' appears twice in v. 13, to make it clear that Bethel is the name of a place and not of the deity. The language "I am the God Bethel" (Gen. 31:13) is somewhat crabbed; both the Septuagint and Onkelos render it as "I am the God *who appeared to you in* Bethel."

house has already appeared at the beginning of the chapter: "Then the Lord said to Jacob, 'Return to the land of your fathers where you were born'" (Gen. 31:3). Because this verse does not refer to a dream, proponents of the documentary theory consider it to be a Yahwist version of the divine injunction to Jacob to return to his homeland. It seems at least as plausible that the verse is a précis of sorts, with the later ones merely filling in the details of the theophany.

Jacob's dream in the house of Laban incorporates motifs from daily life into its description of sheep mating. In it, the angel alludes to three different ram styles: the rams that are mounting the ewes are streaked, then speckled, and finally mottled (Gen. 31:12).[76] In verse 8, however, Jacob mentions only two violations of the agreement by Laban, omitting the case of the spotted rams. That Laban did in fact breach their contract three times is indicated by the fact that Jacob mentions three instances of intervention by God: "But the God of my father has been with me" (v. 5); "God, however, would not let him do me harm" (v. 7); and "God has taken away your father's livestock and given it to me" (v. 9). Why did the angel reveal to Jacob the secret of sheep-breeding? According to the text, it is because God has "noted all that Laban has been doing to you" (v. 12). God is helping Jacob so as to redress the wrongs done him by Laban. The dream makes no reference to the peeled rods of chapter 30; Jacob's prosperity is ascribed solely to God. For this reason, some believe that the tale of the rods (30:25ff.) is a Yahwist version of the story, whereas the description in our chapter stems from the Elohist tradition (31:2, 4–16). Against this theory, however, there is the view that the stratagem Jacob employs to increase the number of his sheep is not the result of a divine blessing and that the dream never in fact took place. Because Jacob does not want to humiliate Laban and tell his wives how their father had tricked him, he tells them that the multiplication of his own flock was the result of a divine revelation in which he was told what to do.[77]

Solomon's Dream

Solomon's dream at Gibeon also belongs to the category of dreams of promise and encouragement. Only recently enthroned, the new king needs divine rec-

---

76. Ehrlich, *Traum*, p. 133, n. 2. Ehrlich pointed out the use of בְּרֻדִּים 'spotted' in Zechariah (6:3 and 6). Evidently our verse adds בְּרֻדִּים because it rhymes with נְקֻדִּים, עֲקֻדִּים, and הָעֲתֻדִים. The play on words is a frequent characteristic of symbolic dreams. The interpretation of symbolic dreams seems to involve a phonetic association between the words that appear in the dream and those in its interpretation, as we shall see in chapter 3. In the present instance, though, "spotted" has nothing to do with the interpretation of the dream, which is in any case prophetic and does not require interpretation.

77. Sarna, *Genesis*, p. 214.

ognition and legitimacy. The dream, a direct continuation of his waking life, deals with the king's qualifications and role, as well as the charismatic traits that a king must possess, such as "a wise and discerning mind" (1 Kings 3:12). In form, the dream is similar to other royal dreams in the Bible—those of Abimelech and Nebuchadnezzar, especially the dialogue format in Abimelech's. In content, however, Solomon's dream is very different, in that the other two have nothing to do with how the monarch deals with his subjects.

God's first words to Solomon in the dream are "Ask, what shall I give you?" (1 Kings 3:5). This opening is appropriate for a theophany that comes in response to the dreamer's request: God duly responds, appears to the suppliant, and lets him state his petition. God's question recalls Abram's query of God in the Covenant between the Pieces: "What will You give me?" (Gen. 15:2), in response to the Lord's promise that "I am a shield to you; your reward shall be very great" (Gen. 15:1). The Lord promises Abram that his descendants will take great wealth with them when they leave Egypt, and that "As for you, you shall go to your fathers in peace; you shall be buried at a ripe old age" (Gen. 15:15). Similarly, the Lord promises Solomon surpassing wealth and longevity. Solomon's description of his subjects as "a people too numerous to be numbered or counted" (1 Kings 3:8) combines two blessings allotted to Abraham: "I will make your offspring as the dust of the earth, so that if one can count the dust of the earth, then your offspring too can be counted" (Gen. 13:16); and "Look toward heaven and count the stars, if you are able to count them" (Gen. 15:5). The motif of a petition addressed to the Lord is evidence of the antiquity of the story of the theophany at Gibeon, for this motif was widespread in biblical literature and the literature of the ancient Near East.[78]

In his dream, Solomon requests wisdom and prefaces his petition with the disclaimer that he is "a young lad, with no experience in leadership" (1 Kings 3:7). Some read these words as self-effacement, of the sort displayed by kings and high officials in texts that describe their anointing or consecration (e.g., Judg. 6:15; 1 Sam. 9:21; Jer. 1:6). Solomon's reference to himself as "a young

---

78. One of the most common petitions addressed to the Lord is for victory over one's enemy in an impending battle. Before the war against Aram, Ahab and Jehoshaphat inquire of the Lord through the band of prophets and also through Micaiah son of Imlah (1 Kings 22): Should they go out and fight a battle at Ramot-Gilead? In other words, will the Lord assist them in combat? In some cases, of course, the Lord does not respond: "And Saul inquired of the Lord, but the Lord did not answer him, either by dreams or by Urim or by prophets" (1 Sam. 28:6; see also 1 Sam. 14:37–38). In Psalm 20, the king who requested the Lord's assistance is promised that the enemy will be routed and the Lord will grant his petition. On the motif of petitions addressed to the Lord, see Saul Zalevsky, "The Revelation of God to Solomon in Gibeon," *Tarbiz* 42 (1973), pp. 215–218.

lad" has a parallel in the description of the statue of Rameses II sucking his finger under the protection of Horus in the guise of a giant hawk.[79] Another text speaks about the coronation of the infant Thutmoses III: "[The god Amon] is my father, and I am his son. He commanded me that I should be upon his throne while I was [still] a nestling...."[80]

In yet another Egyptian text, Sesostris III states that while he was still a small boy he was designated to rule the kingdom; even before his birth it was determined that he would reside in a palace.[81] These statements are commonly viewed as part of the propaganda of the pharaohs, who alleged that they received their kingships at a young age. Our text may serve a similar purpose, proclaiming that Solomon was legitimately enthroned while still a youth. This idea is supported by the expression "with no experience in leadership" (literally, "I do not know how to go out and come in"), which refers to the daily conduct of affairs of state (cf. 1 Sam. 18:16 and Deut. 31:2). Another signification of the idiom involves leading the nation out in battle and returning at its head after the war (Josh. 14:11 and 1 Sam. 29:6).[82] Thus Solomon seeks God's gift of wisdom to help him overcome his inexperience in running the state and performing his royal duties successfully.

Solomon also seeks wisdom because of the size of the population over which he rules, which makes it difficult for him to judge them.[83] Moses, too, was hard pressed to judge the people because there were so many of them.

---

79. John Gray, *I and II Kings* (Philadelphia: Westminster Press, 1963), p. 122.

80. "Egyptian Oracles and Prophecies," trans. John A. Wilson, *ANET*, 446a, I.

81. S. Herrmann, "Die Königsnovelle in Ägypten und in Israel: ein Beitrag zur Gattungsgeschichte in den Geschichtsbüchern des Alten Testament," in *Wissenschaftliche Zeitschrift der Karl-Marx Universität Leipzig* 3 (1953–1954), p. 54.

82. E. A. Speiser, "Coming and Going 'at the city gate,'" *BASOR* 144 (1956), pp. 20–23; G. Evans, "'Coming' and 'Going' at the City Gate: A Discussion of Professor Speiser's Paper," *BASOR* 150 (1958), pp. 28–33.

83. Scholars do not agree about the signification of the word שפט. Was Solomon asking to judge the people in the limited sense of the word–that is, the judicial function only? Or should we understand the root ש.פ.ט in the broader sense of government? See Z. W. Falk: "Ruler and Judge," *Leshonenu* (30) (1965-1966), pp. 243–247 (Hebrew). Falk maintains that, according to 1 Sam. 8:8 and 2 Kings 15:5, the root ש.פ.ט has the latter and more comprehensive sense. Speiser, too, relying on 1 Sam. 8, believes that it has the sense of "rule": see E. Speiser, "The Royal Rule," in *The Patriarch and the Judges* (Tel Aviv: Masada, 1967), pp. 297–300 (Hebrew). S. E. Loewenstamm, "Ruler and Judge," *Leshonenu* 32 (1968), pp. 272–274, shows that in Ugaritic the verb *tpt* has two senses, law and rule. S. Zalevsky, "The Lord's Appearance in Gibeon," pp. 242–244 (Hebrew), believes that *tpt* refers only to law. Similar views are expressed by J. A. Montgomery, *The Books of Kings* ICC (New York: Scribners, 1951), p. 107; J. Gray, *1 and 2 Kings*, p. 122. M. Weinfeld, *Deuteronomy and the Deuteronomic School* (Oxford: Clarendon, 1971), p. 245.

He was forced to institute a new judicial arrangement (Exod. 18; and the second version of the story in Deut. 1). The request for wisdom is also related to one of the chief functions of the king—namely, to impose justice on society and judge with equity. The king must redress social wrongs, protect the virtuous, and act against the wicked. Isaiah cites these as the distinguishing traits of the ideal monarch, one whose kingdom is established "in justice and in equity, now and evermore" (Isa. 9:5–7). On such a king will descend "a spirit of wisdom and insight, ... a spirit of devotion and reverence for the Lord" (Isa. 11:2). He "shall judge the poor with equity ... [and] justice shall be the girdle of his loins" (Isa. 11:4–5).

The newly enthroned Solomon turns to the Lord and asks for His help in instituting justice and leading the people. The granting of his petition, supplemented by promises of wealth, honor, and longevity, indicates the Lord's full support of the young monarch. The divine promise,"I grant you a wise and discerning mind," is the culmination of a series of reasons for God's gift:

> Because you asked for this thing—
> You did not ask for long life,
> You did not ask for riches,
> You did not ask for the life of your enemies,
> But you asked for discernment in dispensing justice—
> I now do as you have spoken" (1 Kings 3:11–12).

The passage rises to a number of climaxes.[84] It begins with "this thing," followed by an enumeration of the favors that Solomon did not request, in order of increasing importance. The first two, longevity and riches, relate only to Solomon. But victory over his foes involves his subjects as well. The specific request, for discernment, is not material but spiritual.

Herrmann, drawing on Egyptian parallels, assigns the story of Solomon's dream to the literary genre known as *royal novella*. In his view, the dream is meant to glorify the king and legitimize his rule. Kings outside of Egypt, too, cited prophetic dreams to justify their dominion. The Hittite king Hattushili asserted that the goddess Ishtar appeared to him and his wife in their dreams, foretold his ascension to the lofty position, and declared her support for him.[85] We must not forget that Solomon ascended the throne after being nominated by his father David (1 Kings 1:30–48). His rule had not yet received popular approval in the form of a covenant between the people and the monarch (of

---

84. Polak, *Biblical Narrative,* p. 51.
85. Oppenheim, *Interpretation,* p. 197.

the sort recounted in 2 Kings 16:1–13). Both prophet and people had been deprived of their natural and primary initiative of election.

In addition, Solomon's ascension to the throne was accompanied by bitter struggles. His brother Adonijah had the support of broad and influential circles, including Joab son of Zeruiah, Ebiathar the priest, his brother princes, and leading figures of the tribe of Judah. After the executions of Adonijah and Joab, Solomon needed the ceremony at Gibeon to confirm and underscore his unchallenged rule over all Israel and unite the people behind him. The ceremony in Gibeon was paralleled by one held in Jerusalem. The reason for conducting two ceremonies may have been the need to expand his support. One was held in the northern part of his realm, with the intention of binding the northern tribes to him; while the second took place in the capital and was meant to win the loyalty of David's loyal supporters.

Hence the story of the dream provides legitimacy to Solomon's assumption of power. Enthroned by the Lord–"And now, O Lord my God, You have made Your servant king in place of my father David" (v. 7)–he has also received the charismatic qualities that a king must have. All of these are given to Solomon in his dream by the Lord.[86]

THE ADMONITORY DREAM

Abimelech's Dream
Abimelech's dream (Genesis 20:3–7) falls into the category of the admonitory dream.[87] In it, God appears to Abimelech and warns him, "You are about to

---

86. Weisman sees Solomon's dream as one of vocation. According to him, the ritual aspect of the dream has been deflected towards the commission aspect typical of prophetic revelation. In the dream the Lord designates Solomon as king. In the Bible we find the commission model has several elements, such as (1) distress, (2) the commission, (3) refusal to undertake the commission, (4) a promise of divine assistance, and (5) the provision of a sign. Although not all of these stages are found here, this model helps us understand "I am a young lad, with no experience in leadership" as Solomon's attempt to decline the commission. Weisman's conjecture may be answered by noting that Solomon is king; hence the commission paradigm does not seem to apply. See Z. Weisman, "The Charismatic Personality in the Bible," doctoral dissertation, Hebrew University of Jerusalem, 1972, pp. 233–235 (Hebrew).

87. Proponents of the documentary theory assign this story to E, except for v. 18, which they see as a gloss because of its use of the Tetragrammaton instead of Elohim. There are four reasons for ascribing chapter 20 to E: the use of the divine name Elohim, the use of אמה for "slave-girl" (v. 17), the use of a dream for a divine revelation (vv. 3 and 6), and the parallel story in 12:10–20, which is ascribed to J. Recently scholars such as Westermann, Alexander, and Rooning have followed the lead of Van Seters and argued that chapter 20 is not a freestanding unit parallel to 12:10–20 but in fact assumes the existence of chapter 12. What is more, our chapter is meant to answer several questions raised by 12:10–20, such as why

die."[88] The reason: "Because of the woman you have taken; moreover she is a married woman."[89] Abraham is not mentioned by name, but only as the husband of the woman who was taken by Abimelech. He is also referred to as "the man," "he," and "a prophet"–perhaps to indicate the distance between Abraham and Abimelech.

God's warning is concise and unambiguous. It is phrased in the present tense, as was noted by Sforno, who paraphrased it as "You are going to succumb to a disease that will begin with you because the Lord has closed fast...." Indeed, the chapter concludes with the report that the Lord healed Abimelech and his wife and his slave-girls (v.17). On the surface the text seems to be speaking of infertility, but S. D. Luzzatto believed that the reference was instead to some sort of venereal disease that prevented the king from having sexual relations with his wife and concubines. After Abraham prayed on their behalf, the king and his wives were cured and the latter could give birth.

The need for Abraham to intercede is somewhat strange, because Abimelech himself conducts a dialogue with the Lord. Why, then, did Abraham have to pray for the king? We can only note that tradition ascribed to various prophets–Moses (Num. 12:13), Elijah (1 Kings 17:20–22), and Elisha (2 Kings 4:33–35)–the ability to make supplications and heal others.

God's appearance to Abimelech resembles a judicial proceeding. There are several stages in the process: the indictment (v. 3), the accused's presentation of his defense (vv. 4–5), and the acceptance of his argument and reversal of the original verdict (vv. 6–7). Although the sin for which Abimelech was to

---

the Lord punished Pharaoh, who did not know that he had taken a married woman, and why Abraham lied and said that Sarah was not his wife. Van Seters believes that these problems are answered in chapter 20, which is an expansion of the more ancient stratum of Genesis found in 12:10–20 but antedates the main J redaction of Genesis. See the survey in Gordon J. Wenham, *Genesis 16–50,* vol. 2 (Dallas, Texas: Word Books, 1994), pp. 68–69; T. D. Alexander, "Are the Wife / Sister Incidents of Genesis Literary Compositional Variants?" *VT* 42 (1992), pp. 145–153; J. Rooning, "The Naming of Isaac: The Role of the Wife / Sister Episodes in the Redaction of Genesis," *WTJ* 53 (1991), pp. 1–27; Westermann, *Genesis 12–36,* pp. 318–319; J. Van Seters, *Abraham in History and Tradition* (New Haven: Yale University Press, 1975), pp. 171–175. On the literary aspect and the link between the two stories, see: R. Polzin, "'The Ancestress of Israel in Danger' in Danger," *Semeia* 3 (1975), pp. 81–98; P. D. Miscall, "Literary Unity in the Old Testament Narrative," *Semeia* 15 (1979), pp. 27–44. G. Coats, "A Threat to the Host," in *Saga, Legend, Tale, Novella, Fable,* ed. G. Coats, *JSOT* Sup 35 (Sheffield, England: *JSOT* Press, 1985), pp. 71–81.

88. Cf. Deut. 18:20 and Isa. 38:1. See also W. F. Stinespring, "The Participle of the Immediate Future and Other Matters Pertaining to Correct Translation of the Old Testament," in *Translating and Understanding the Old Testament: Essays in honor of H. G. May,* ed. H. T. Frank and W. L. Reed (Nashville: Abingdon, 1970), p. 66.

89. בעלת בעל has the same meaning in Deut. 22:22.

be punished is adultery,[90] even before he answers God, the text emphasizes–using the euphemism קָרַב 'approached'–that Abimelech has not had sexual relations with Sarah.[91] Answering God as if he is conversing with his own deity, he asks: "O Lord, will You slay people even though innocent?"(Gen. 20:4). Interestingly, this question about the nature of divine justice echoes Abraham's with regard to the impending doom of the Sodomites (Gen. 18:23). Then shifting the blame to Abraham, who misled him–"She is my sister"–and Sarah, who corroborated this statement–"He is my brother"–Abimelech goes on to argue that he had not known that Sarah was a married woman. The Lord, however, accepts Abimelech's defense and tells him that He had in fact been aware of his innocence.

Such a dream, dealing with past events, is rare, since dreams are usually future-oriented. But the Lord's warning to Abimelech is in fact meant to keep him from sinning. Hence He instructs Abimelech as to what he must do to clear his name–return Sarah to Abraham. Then God repeats His earlier warning ("You are about to die"–v. 3); here, however, the Lord says to him: "You will surely die."[92] The duplication מוֹת תָּמוּת emphasizes the gravity of God's warning. It applies not only to Abimelech, but to everything that belongs to him–"Know that you shall die, you and all that are yours" (Gen. 20:7).[93] Thus the dream is based upon two admonitions, supplemented by instructions as to how the admonished one can purge himself of guilt.

---

90. Abimelech's rebuke of Abraham uses the expression חֲטָאָה גְדֹלָה 'a great guilt', which recurs in Joseph's protest to Potiphar's wife"How then could I do this most wicked thing (הָרָעָה הַגְּדֹלָה הַזֹּאת), and sin (וְחָטָאתִי) before God?" (Gen. 39:9) again in the context of adultery.

91. The root ק.ר.ב. frequently has a sexual connotation in the Bible. See Lev. 18:6, 14:19; Deut. 22:14; and Isa. 8:3.

92. Abimelech must return Sarah because Abraham is a *prophet.* This is the first occurrence of the word in the Bible. Its original meaning is not as clear as we might like. Some associate it with the Akkadian *nabû* 'to call'. The king of Assyria was known as "the one called," that is, someone who had been called by the gods. In Hebrew the word נביא has two different significations: a prophet who is the recipient of a divine call or summons, and a person who transmits a message from God. The second sense is appropriate to texts such as Exodus 4:15 and 7:11. In the Bible the נביא is the spokesman of God and man alike, delivering the former's promises and warnings but also intervening with the Lord to forgive mortals their transgressions. The use of the epithet נביא here to refer to Abraham is intended to highlight another aspect of his personality. The same Abraham who tried to intercede for the Sodomites will now do so for Abimelech. See Sarna, *Genesis*, p. 142. See also the cognate word from Ebla, *na-ba-um*. M. J. Dahood, "Ebla, Ugarit, and the Bible," in G. Pettinato, *The Archives of Ebla* (Garden City, New York: Doubleday, 1981), p. 278.

93. In a similar vein, the entire people are punished for David's sin (2 Sam. 24:15).

Laban's Dream

Another warning is found in Laban's dream (Gen. 31:24). As noted previously, dreams play a decisive role in Jacob's life. When he is a fugitive leaving his father's house desperate and alone, he hears God's encouraging promises in a dream (Gen. 28:15). Many years later, when Jacob is under the thumb of his father-in-law, who has deceived and tricked him, a dream reveals how he can receive his due (Gen. 31:10–13). Now, when Laban wants to harm Jacob, the Lord warns *Laban* off in a dream and deters him from acting.

The dream is described in a single verse: "But God appeared to Laban the Aramean in a dream by night and said to him, 'Watch yourself lest you say anything to Jacob, good or bad.'" (Gen. 31:24). Unlike Abimelech's dream, here the name of the patriarch is mentioned–perhaps because Jacob had spent two decades in Laban's household and they were intimately acquainted. Rashi (Solomon ben Isaac, 1040–1105), citing the Talmud (BT Yevamot 63), explains "good or bad" as meaning "the bounty of the wicked is bad for the righteous." Nachmanides goes further and glosses the message as meaning: "Watch yourself, lest you say to him that you will treat him well if he returns with you from his way, and lest you frighten him that you will harm him if he does not come with you, because I have commanded him to return to his land." The phrase "good or bad" is also found in the response of Laban and Bethuel to Abraham's servant: "The matter was decreed by the Lord; we cannot speak to you bad or good" (Gen. 24:50)."[94] This expression is an example of a *merism*, the expression of a whole by means of contraries (see Num. 24:13; 2 Sam. 13:22; Zeph. 1:12; Jer. 10:5). Some accordingly maintain that here it means that Laban should not speak to Jacob at all.[95] Benno Jacob, by contrast, says that the phrase does not mean that Laban must refrain totally from interaction with Jacob, but only that he must not harm him and must not take anything from him or compel him to return to Haran.[96] In fact, according to verse 29, Laban does speak with Jacob and rebukes him for his conduct, while mentioning the warning he has received from God.

---

94. "Good" is missing from GK and the Vulgate, so that the phrase is the same as in verse 29.

95. A. M. Honeyman, "Merismus in Biblical Hebrew," *JBL* 71 (1952), p. 12, would render the phrase as "not any word at all."

96. B. Jacob, *The First Book of the Bible: Genesis,* abridged, edited, and trans. by Ernest I. Jacob and Walter Jacob (New York: Ktav, 1974), p. 211.

REACTION TO THE PROPHETIC DREAM

If the nucleus of the prophetic dream is the message from the deity, equally significant is the formula indicating the end of the dream–to which we can add the dreamer's reaction. This stage is frequently a part of prophetic dreams in the Bible: "Abimelech got up early in the morning" (Gen. 20:8); "Jacob got up early in the morning" (Gen. 28:18); "Jacob awoke from his sleep" (Gen. 28:16); "When You are aroused You despise their image, as one does a dream after waking, O Lord." (Ps. 73:20); "Then Solomon awoke: it was a dream" (1 Kings 3:15).[97] In Akkadian we find the word *nagaltû* "to wake up"–that is, the dream has suddenly ended.[98] To this we should compare: "a seer reclined and saw a dream: when he awoke Ishtar showed him a night vision."[99] And in the Epic of Gilgamesh: "[As at night] he lay, he awoke from a dream."[100] In the Egyptian dream of Djoser, we read: "Then I awoke refreshed (?), my heart determined and at rest."[101] The dream of Thutmoses IV concludes: "When he had finished these words, then this king's son awoke, because he had heard these [words]."[102] This awakening from a dream is also found in the second dream of Gudea: "He woke up with a start; it was (but) a dream"[103] Oppenheim believes that the explicit reference to the dreamer's waking up serves to convey the suddenness of the transition between dreaming and waking and to describe the astonishment that a person feels upon discovering that he or she has been dreaming.[104] Specifying that the sleeper wakes up is an attempt to add an objective dimension to the dream and thereby underscore its authenticity. Perhaps the ultimate awakening is attributed to Jacob, who awoke from his sleep and said, "Surely the Lord is present in this place, and I did not know it!" (Gen. 28:16).

The dreamer's reaction to his experience is extremely important because it provides us with a basis for distinguishing a prophetic dream from a delusive one. We should not forget that the Bible acknowledges the possibility of false dreams. Deuteronomy 13:2–6 deals with the case of a prophet or dreamer

---

97. Here the wake-up formula is identical to that found in the legend of Keret: "Keret awakes and it was a dream" (Cyrus H. Gordon, *Ugaritic Literature* [Rome: Pontifical Biblical Institute, 1949], p. 71, line 154).

98. Oppenheim, *Interpretation,* p. 191; *CAD* N I:106., W. von Soden, Ahw II:709.

99. "Akkadian Oracles and Prophecies," trans. Robert H. Pfeiffer, *ANET,* 451.

100. "Akkadian Myths and Epics," trans. E.A. Speiser, *ANET,* IX 1, 13, p. 88.

101. Oppenheim, *Interpretation,* pp. 191, 251, section 8, no. 19.

102. "Egyptian Oracles and Prophecies," trans. John A. Wilson, *ANET,* p. 449.

103. Oppenheim, *Interpretation,* p. 212; Jacobsen, *The Harps that Once,* XII:12–13, p. 403..

104. Ibid., p. 191.

who seeks to mislead the people with vain dreams. The prophet or dreamer must provide a *sign,* a natural phenomenon that reinforces his words, or a *portent,* a supernatural phenomenon.[105] Even if these come to pass, it does not prove that the dream was prophetic. And even from its content, one cannot infer whether the dream is prophetic, or simply a normal dream.[106]

It is interesting to note that in several letters from Mari, descriptions of dreams are followed by statements that the authors are enclosing some personal signs associated with the prophet-dreamer—the hem of their robe or a lock of hair: "I m[yself] hereby seal my hair and fringe and send (them) to my lord."[107] In another letter, already referred to above, we read: "By the *ḥurru*-bird I have examined this matter and she could see *(naṭlat)* (the dream). Now the hair and the hem of the garment I am sending along. May my lord investigate the matter!"[108] Inclusion of some personal token was particularly important when the dreamer was an unfamiliar person or when it was impossible for him to come to the royal court. The token may have functioned as a substitute. Malamat believes that they were meant to authenticate the dreamer's message, especially when the latter made demands of the king and it was important to refute charges of "fabricating" the gods' will.[109] Uffenheimer even maintains that the inclusion of a lock of hair or fragment of cloth had a magical significance, because they represented the person, and a stranger who possessed them had magical power over their owners and could even curse them through it.[110] In addition to the dispatch of these tokens, we also

---

105. These signs and portents are connected with the ways in which a prophet demonstrated that his prophecy was God-given. In Exodus 4:1–9, God turns Moses's staff into a serpent—a transformation that can be wrought only by supernatural forces. The Lord gives this power to Moses so that he will be able to persuade the people and Pharaoh that he is the emissary of God. Isaiah announces to Hezekiah that he will be saved from the Assyrian onslaught and that Jerusalem will not fall to Sennacherib's host. To reinforce the king's confidence in his recovery from his illness and his deliverance from Sennacherib, the prophet gives him a sign—the shadow of the gnomon, which has already descended, will climb back up the wall. This is a sign that, after it seemed that Hezekiah's last day had come, time will go backwards and Hezekiah will be only midway through his life. This sign was also relevant to the deliverance of the Kingdom of Judah and the people of Israel from the enemy threatening to annihilate them (Isa. 38:7–8).

106. Lewin, *The Psychology of Dreams,* p. 90.

107. *ARM* X:50; in "Akkadian Letters," trans. William L. Moran, *ANET,* 631; Moran, "New Evidence," pp. 38–40.

108. A 222; in G. Dossin, "Le Songe d'Ayala," *RA,* 69 (1975), pp. 28-30; Abraham Malamat, *Mari and Israel: Two West-Semitic Cultures* (Jerusalem: Magnes Press, 1991), p. 142.

109. Abraham Malamat, *Mari and the Early Israelite Experience* (Oxford: Oxford University Press, 1984), p. 95, n. 86.

110. On the scholarly debate on the significance of the inclusion of a personal token, see

find other ways of authenticating dreams in Mari.[111] A woman from the royal court, an advisor to the king, writes: "Let my lord have the *haruspex* look into the matter."[112] In another letter, a woman calls on the king to verify the vision of the *āpiltum* by divinatory means.[113] The same councilor referred to above, after a prophecy, admonishes the "*qabbatum* to be alert and not to enter the city without inquiring of the omens."[114]

In the next few pages we shall focus on responses to biblical dreams and attempt to determine whether the Bible provides guidelines for establishing whether or not they are prophetic.

Jacob's dream in Bethel is marked by an emotional response—astonishment that quickly gives way to fear. At first Jacob is surprised by the divine revelation: "Surely the Lord is present in this place, and I did not know it!" (Gen. 28:16). This amazement is itself surprising, because the Lord has already appeared to Abraham and Isaac, neither of whom evinced a similar response. Then the astonishment is replaced by dread: "He was frightened (וַיִּירָא) and said, 'How awesome (מַה נּוֹרָא) is this place!'" (v. 17). The fear, which is represented by the repeated use of the root .י.ר.א , once as a verb and once as an adjective, is a strong emotional reaction to the sanctity of the place: "This is none other than the House of God, and that is the Gate of Heaven" (v. 17).[115] Jacob is not afraid of punishment, as before his encounter with Esau: "Jacob was greatly frightened" (Gen. 32:8). His uneasiness at Bethel stems only from his sense of the sanctity of the place and nearness of God—"You shall venerate (תִּירָאוּ) My sanctuary, I am the Lord" (Lev. 26:2). At this stage Jacob's reaction

---

Benjamin Uffenheimer, *Ancient Prophecy in Israel* (Jerusalem: Magnes Press, 1984), pp. 29–33.

111. Malamat, *Mari and the Early Israelite Experience,* pp. 94–96; idem, "A Forerunner of Biblical Prophecy," pp. 46–47.

112. *ARM* X:94.

113. *ARM* X:81.

114. *ARM* X:80.

115. Jacob calls the place the "House of God" and the "Gate of Heaven." These two terms are quite different. The former refers to the place where God appears; the latter is the terminus of the angels' ascent to and descent from Heaven. Belief in this gate was widespread in antiquity. One of the epithets applied to the High Priest of Thebes in Egypt was "Opener of the Gates of the Heavens," and the name of the city of Babylon can be understood to mean "Gate of God." See Sarna, *Genesis,* p. 199. On the proximity of the House of God and the Gate of Heaven, see the Ugaritic parallels: M. Dahood and T. Penar, "Ugaritic-Hebrew Parallel Pairs," *Ras Shamra Parallels,* ed. L. R. Fisher, *AnOr* 49–51 (Rome: Pontifical Biblical Institute, 1972), p. 158, n. 137; J. S. Kselman, "The Recovery of Poetic Fragments from the Pentateuchal Priestly Source," *JBL* 97 (1978), pp. 161–162.

has nothing to do with the verbal message addressed to him by God in the dream.

This emotional reaction takes place during the night. Verse 18 proceeds to describe the ritual activity that Jacob performs the next morning.[116] He takes the stone that had been under his head "and set it up as a pillar and poured oil on the top of it" (v. 18).[117] In antiquity, there was a widespread belief that stones were the dwelling places of gods and spirits; the veneration of pillars may represent a survival of that belief. Later, stones symbolized the presence of the deity in a temple, and later still, served as a memorial to the deity's appearance in a particular place.[118] The prevalence of these beliefs may be the reason why the Torah banned such pillars.[119] We also read, however, about the erection of pillars as memorials to the dead.[120] The pillar is also used as a testimonial to the pact between Jacob and Laban (Gen. 31:45–54). A large stone is a memorial of the covenant between Israel and the Lord at Shechem: "And Joshua said to all the people, 'See, this very stone shall be a witness against us, for it heard all the words that the Lord spoke to us; it shall be a witness against you, lest you break faith with your God'" (Josh. 24:27). According to Sarna, this last verse is the key to understanding Jacob's action. The

---

116. The fact that in v. 16 we read "Jacob awoke" and in v. 18 we find "Jacob got up in the morning" is cited as supporting evidence by modern critics who hold to the documentary theory. They believe that v. 16 comes from J and v. 18 from E. A close reading of v. 16 (J), however, makes it apparent that the verse depends on vv. 11–12 (E), which is where we are informed that Jacob lay down and had a dream. What is more, Jacob's astonishment in v. 16 (J) that the Lord is present "in this place" (במקום הזה) must draw on v. 11 (E), in which we also have "a certain place" (במקום).

117. On sacred pillars in the Bible, see: C. F. Graesser, "Standing Stones in Ancient Palestine," *BA* 35 (1972), pp. 34–63, who distinguishes four functions: grave stele, contract stele, memorial stele, and cult stele ("to mark the sacred area"), which is found in Gen. 28:18; E. Stockton, "Sacred Pillars in the Bible," *ABR* 20 (1972), pp. 16–32.

118. Skinner, *Genesis,* p. 378. Houtman says that the stone is a cult object endued with divine power and representing God Himself. See C. Houtman, "What Did Jacob See in his Dream at Bethel? Some Remarks on Gen. 28:10–22," *VT* 27 (1977), p. 343; "Sacred Stones Sometimes Considered as the Dwelling of the God or Even the God Himself," see J. A. Fitzmyer, *The Aramaic Inscriptions of Sefire,* Bib. Or. 19 (Rome: Pontifical Biblical Institute, 1967), p. 90.

119. On the ban against pillars, see: Exod. 23:24, 34:13; Deut. 7:8, 12:3, 16:22; phrased as a prohibition against pillars and Asherah, see: 1 Kings 14:23 and 2 Kings 17:10; against pillars and idols, See: Lev. 26:1; Deut. 7:5 and 12:3; Micah 5:13.

120. Jacob erects a pillar for Rachel (Gen. 35:20); Absalom sets up one for himself because he has no children (2 Sam. 18:18).

stone that had been beneath his head is not only a marker; it is also a witness to the dream and to God's promises to Jacob.[121]

Another ritual activity performed by Jacob is his vow. It resembles others described in the Bible, such as those of Jephthah the Gileadite (Judg. 11:30–31), Hannah (1 Sam. 1:11), and Absalom (2 Sam. 16:8). In each case, someone makes a commitment that, if not fulfilled, will entail certain other actions on his / her part.[122] First comes a condition introduced by the word אִם "if"–in this case, God's protection–which sets forth the petition; this is followed by the commitment made by the person taking the vow. The conditions of Jacob's vow are symmetrically parallel to his commitments. It should be emphasized, however, that Jacob's vow is unique because God has already promised him (v. 15) everything he is asking for.[123] The vow, which is a reaction to the verbal content of his dream, refers to divine promises to him personally, but not to God's promises to the nation as a whole. Fokkelman, who noticed this, maintains that in general the patriarchs do not respond to divine promises focused on the distant future.[124] An echo of Jacob's action can be found in ancient Near Eastern literature, where vows are often associated with ritual demands made in dreams: the dreamer makes a vow within the dream

---

121. Sarna, *Genesis,* p. 199.

122. On biblical vows in general and Gen. 28:20–22, see L. R. Fisher, "Two Projects at Clermont," *UF* 3 (1971), pp. 27–31. The schematic structure of vows has ancient roots and can be found in ancient Ugaritic literature; see S. Parker, "The Vow in Ugaritic and Israelite Narrative Literature," *UF* 11 (1979), pp. 693–700, especially 698–99; T. W. Cartledge, *Vows in the Hebrew Bible and the Ancient Near East* (Sheffield, England: *JSOT* Press, 1992), pp. 166–175.

123. In Genesis Rabba 70:4, which deals with Jacob's vow, two interpretations are proposed. One maintains that the sequence of events has been inverted here and the theophany is in fact a response to Jacob's vow. In other words, first Jacob made his vow and only then did the Lord appear to him. According to the second interpretation, there is no condition here at all. Jacob merely says he will act in a certain way, *as a mark of gratitude to God,* after God has fulfilled all His promises. Benno Jacob holds that the real protasis of Jacob's vow is "if I survive." If this condition is not fulfilled, it does not mean that Jacob will not perform his vow, but that reality will have intervened and he will not be able to do so, because he will not have returned safe and sound to his father's house. In other words, the vow depends exclusively on the will of the Lord (B. Jacob, *Genesis,* pp. 191–192). Skinner noted that the conditions that Jacob sets in vv. 20 and 21a are compatible with v. 15. He lists three elements of Jacob's condition: (1) the Lord will be with Jacob; (2) the Lord will protect him; (3) he will return safe and sound to Canaan. He also notes the supplementary condition in v. 20, namely, if God "gives me bread to eat and clothing to wear." Cf. Judg. 11:30 and 2 Sam. 15:7–9. Jacob's vow must not be seen as bargaining with God, because he has already received everything that he asks for (Skinner, *Genesis,* p. 279).

124. Fokkelman, *Narrative Art in Genesis,* p. 75.

itself, in response to a divine promise that was also part of the dream.[125] In the present case, however, Jacob makes his vow after waking up. This is paralleled in the Ugaritic epic of Keret, where we read that El promised Keret the Princess Huray as his wife and gave him instructions for bringing her to his home. Keret sets out on his journey to 'Udm; en route, he vows as follows:

> As surely as Ashirat of the two Tyres
> And Elat of the Sidonians exists,
> If I may take Huray (into) my house,
> Introduce the lass to my court,
> I will give twice her (weight) in silver
> And thrice her (weight) in gold.[126]

In reaction to God's appearance in his dream, Abimelech acts at once and without hesitation to do precisely as he was instructed. First thing in the morning he summons all his servants, who are "greatly frightened" (Gen. 20:8) when he tells them about the dream. The Lord has punished Abimelech because of his "great sin," namely, adultery. The same idiom is found in Egyptian documents, as well as in an Akkadian document from Ugarit: "That woman has sinned a great sin against you," which evidently alludes to adultery.[127]

Abimelech acts at once to compensate Abraham for the damage to Sarah's reputation, giving him sheep and cattle and slaves.[128] The paired verbs "took" and "gave" (ויקח...ויתן) constitute a *hendiadys* expressing the actions of making a donation. The idiom is common in Hittite and Ugaritic gift documents.[129] Sarah also receives financial compensation for the slight to her reputation. As Samuel ben Meir (Rashbam, c. 1080–c. 1174) puts it, it is so "that people will not look at you disparagingly and say, 'Abimelech treated this woman wan-

---

125. Oppenheim, *Interpretation,* pp. 192–193.

126. J. C. L. Gibson, *Canaanite Myths and Legends,* second edition (Edinburgh: T. & T. Clark, 1978), pp. 87–88.

127. PRU IV, 139–140: 6–7; J. J. Rabinowitz, "The 'Great Sin' in Ancient Egyptian Marriage Contracts," *JNES* 18 (1959), 73; W. L. Moran, "The Scandal of the 'Great Sin' at Ugarit," *JNES* 18 (1959), pp. 280–281; J. Milgrom, *Cult and Conscience* (Leiden: Brill, 1976), pp. 132–133.

128. It should be emphasized that the gifts are lavished on Abraham when Abimelech sends Sarah back to him and are meant as compensation. This is different from the situation in chapter 12, where Pharaoh gives Abraham presents when he *takes* Sarah.

129. C. J. Labuschagne, "The *našû-nadānu* Formula and its Biblical Equivalent," in *Travels in the World of the Old Testament: Studies Presented to M. A. Beek,* ed. M. S. H. G. Heerman van Voss, Ph. H. J. Houwink ten Cate, and N. A. van Uchelen (Assen: Van Gorcum, 1974), pp. 176–180.

tonly,' because everyone knew that he took her in an honorable way and returned her against his will." The financial compensation to Sarah is referred to as "a covering of the eyes," that is, a ransom payment to cover over guilt.[130] In the Middle Assyrian Laws (Tablet A, section 22), we find that if a man takes a married woman on a business trip and does not know that she is married, he must take an oath to this effect and give two ingots of tin to her husband.[131]

It is true that there is no indication in our story that Abimelech took an oath to Abraham that he had not had relations with Sarah, but the Genesis Apocryphon from Qumran does seem to include one in the story of Abraham and *Sarai* in Egypt.[132] There Abraham recounts that Pharaoh took an oath to him: "To me [　]; and the king swore an oath to me that [he had] not [touched her?]. And then [they brought] Sarai to [me.] The king gave her [mu]ch silver and [go]ld; many garments of fine linen purple [and he laid them]" (column xx:30–31).[133] It seems plausible, then, that an oath was required of a man who had unknowingly kept company with a married woman, and that the compensation paid to her husband for the fact that his wife had been detained by another man for a certain period of time was common in the ancient Near East.[134] Abimelech's rapid return of Sarah and payment to Abraham indicate that he gave full credence to his dream. We find a similar reaction in the case of Laban, who also revises his plans after God appears to him in a dream and warns him not to harm Jacob. The next day Laban pays strict heed to the admonition (Gen. 31:24–29).

After his dream in the house of Laban (Gen. 31:10–13), Jacob, too, acts at once and without hesitation to implement the instructions he received in his

---

130. The literal sense of כסות עינים is a mask that covers the eyes. It should be compared to two similar expressions, the סתר פנים (face-mask) worn by an adulterer to conceal his identity (Job 24:15) and the מסוה (veil) that Moses places over his face to block the light radiating from it (Exod. 34:34). In the present verse, however, כסות עינים should not be understood literally, but as an idiom. See also B. A. Levine, *In the Presence of the Lord* (Leiden: Brill, 1974), p. 60, n. 18.

131. G. R. Driver and J. C. Miles, eds., *The Assyrian Laws* (Oxford: Clarendon Press, 1935), p. 392, 2: 105–111; G. Cardascia, *Les lois assyriennes* (Paris: Cerf, 1969), pp. 138–141.

132. J. A. Fitzmyer, *The Genesis Apocryphon of Qumran, Cave I,* second revised edition (Rome: Pontifical Biblical Institute, 1971), p. 67.

133. See also the Book of Esther, in which Ahasuerus lavishes presents on Mordechai and dresses him in garments of fine purple: J. Finkel, "The Author of the Genesis Apocryphon Knew the Book of Esther," in *Essays on the Dead Sea Scrolls in Memory of E. L. Sukenik,* ed. C. Rabin and Y. Yadin (Jerusalem: Hekhal Hasefer, 1961), pp. 178–179.

134. M. Weinfeld, "Sarah and Abimelech (Genesis 20) against the Background of an Assyrian Law and the Genesis Apocryphon," *Festschrift Delcore, AOAT* 215 (1985), pp. 431–435.

sleep. He summons his wives from home and recounts how El Bethel has appeared to him in a dream and commanded him to return to his homeland. As Nachmanides reads the passage, Jacob is trying to persuade them to accompany him. Jacob could not take his wives away from their father's house without their consent, because they were still part of that household.

The three-way conversation between Jacob and his wives echoes the earlier case of his mother: "They called Rebekah and said to her, 'Will you go with this man?' And she said, 'I will'" (Gen. 24:58). In both cases, the women must state their willingness to leave their father's house before the journey can be undertaken. He describes his dream to them in order to emphasize that this abandonment of their paternal homestead is a divine imperative and that they have an obligation to come with him. Rachel and Leah's response that they are like aliens in their father's house is tantamount to consent to leaving.[135] After the conversation with his wives, Jacob sets out immediately (Gen. 31:17); in other words, he does as he was bidden in the dream. Note that Rachel and Leah do not react to Jacob's dream vision of the rams, but only to the divine injunction to return to Canaan: "Now then, do just as God has told you." (v. 16). This omission buttresses the argument made above that our text conflates what were originally two separate dreams.

As after Jacob's dream at Bethel, a ritual response follows Solomon's dream at Gibeon (1 Kings 3:15). Solomon returns to Jerusalem and offers sacrifices before the Ark of the Covenant and makes a great feast for all his servants. The sacrificial rites link the end of the chapter with its beginning (1 Kings 3:4). Solomon did not hold a public feast when he ascended the throne, but only now, in the wake of the divine promise confirming him in his kingdom—ritual actions as a gesture to God to thank Him for the promises in the dream. Some scholars believe that the reference to שְׁלָמִים "peace-offerings" indicates a public banquet at which the content of the dream was made known to the assembled company.[136] A reading of the text, however, shows that it neither says that Solomon kept his dream to himself nor that he circulated its content to

---

135. The women's response gives us a realistic picture of their legal situation: they have no share in their father's estate. Laban has spent their dowry money, which should have been held in trust for them. According to ancient custom, the dowry did not become the property of the bride's father, but was held in escrow for her use (Von Rad, *Genesis,* p. 306). The technical terms חלק 'share' and נחלה 'inheritance' are also found in 2 Samuel 20:1 and 1 Kings 12:16, where they designate a rebellion against the king. On the significance of these terms in Akkadian and Ugaritic, see B. A. Levine, *Numbers 1–20, AB* (New York: Doubleday, 1993), pp. 449–450.

136. Gwilym H. Jones, *1 and 2 Kings* (Grand Rapids, Mich: W.B. Eerdmans, 1984), vol. 1: 128.

the general public. Garsiel, by contrast, maintains that the events in Gibeon are a gala to mark Solomon's coronation,[137] with the offering of sacrifices beforehand being an intrinsic part of this ceremony. The parallel celebration in Jerusalem, which is also accompanied by feasting and sacrifices in front of the tent of the Ark of the Covenant, are meant to be a political act, giving equal recognition to the cultic site in the capital and to that in the northern territory, as a way to bind the northern tribes to the royal covenant.[138]

Our examination of all these passages demonstrates that when a dream is prophetic, its meaning is absolutely clear to the dreamer, who responds with clear knowledge, a special frame of mind, or an overwhelming emotion. God appears to the dreamer in his sleep. The core of the dream is a verbal message, which is sometimes accompanied by visual scenes and always refers to the future. In some dreams, God comes to encourage the dreamer. In others, He cautions against harming a patriarch. In all cases, the dreamers' reactions indicate that they believe that God is indeed the source of their dreams and consequently proceed to do as He enjoined them.

Unlike prophetic dreams, God does not appear in symbolic dreams. In the next chapter, then, we shall attempt to determine whether the Bible considers symbolic dreams as messages from God and of external origin, or whether they echo the dreamer's repressed impulses and longings.

---

137. Moshe Garsiel, "King Solomon's Descent to Gibeon and his Dream," pp. 196–197 (Hebrew).

138. Some believe that the verse has gone through several stages of redaction and that in one of them Solomon's court scribes added the information that he returned to Jerusalem and made a banquet for all his servants to strengthen the affinity between Solomon's dream and the Egyptian royal novella. These scholars refer to the dream of Thutmoses IV, who when he returned to his capital told his courtiers and retinue about his dream. In a later stage, the words "stood before the Ark of the Covenant of the Lord" were added by the Deuteronomist editor, who wanted to downplay the embarrassing reference to Solomon's visit to Gibeon. See Jones, *1 and 2 Kings,* p. 128.

2

Symbolic Dreams

Although the ancients were unaware of the role of the subconscious as understood by modern psychology, the amora Rabbi Jonathan observed that "a person is shown only the thoughts of his own heart."[1] His colleague Rava added that people do not dream about something they cannot imagine while awake: no one dreams about a tree of gold or an elephant that can pass through the eye of a needle.[2]

Elsewhere in the Talmud, we read that a Roman emperor, seeking to test the wisdom of Rabbi Joshua ben Hanania, demanded that he tell him what the emperor was dreaming about at night. At the time, a war was raging between Rome and Parthia. Rabbi Joshua replied: "You will dream that the Parthians enslave you at hard labor and torment you and force you to herd loathsome animals using a golden crook." For the rest of the day the emperor could not stop thinking about the sage's answer. The result was that he did indeed dream precisely that.[3]

We also read about a conversation between Shahpour, the Parthian monarch, and the amora Samuel of Nehardea. The king asked Samuel, "Tell me, what will I dream tonight?" Samuel replied that he would dream that the Romans had come and captured him and forced him to grind date pits in a golden millstone. Once again the king thought about this answer all day and his dream that night was just what Samuel had foreseen.[4] All of these examples reflect the Talmudic belief that daytime thoughts and waking cares are the stuff of dreams.

In this chapter, we shall attempt to determine whether, according to the Bible, symbolic dreams have an inner psychological source, as the Talmud holds, or, like prophetic dreams, come from an external source—God. In sym-

---

1. BT Berakhot 55b.
2. Ibid.
3. BT Berakhot 56a.
4. Ibid.

bolic dreams, human beings see tableaux or actions that stand as *signs* and have a hidden meaning. Although the deity does not appear, we shall consider to what extent the hidden meaning contains a divine message.[5]

JOSEPH'S DREAMS

In the Joseph cycle, dreams come in pairs: Joseph's two dreams, the two dreams of the butler and the baker, and Pharaoh's two dreams. All of these play a weighty role in the Joseph stories. They are a major impetus in the plot; they link the individual episodes into a unified whole; and they create a palpable dramatic tension. Readers are eager to find out whether the dreams will come true.

Joseph's first dream (Gen. 37:5-7) begins with a harvest scene: Joseph and his brothers are binding sheaves of grain. Members of the family are pictured as farmers and the dream reflects their daily life as such. In verses 2 and 13, however, Joseph and his brothers are described as shepherds. The apparent contradiction actually fits with what we know about the Patriarchs. They were nomads or semi-nomads who herded livestock but also practiced agriculture (Gen. 26:12)–evidently in the process of transition from a fully nomadic life to a sedentary one.[6] After their arrival in Canaan, these shepherds lived on

---

5. The main difference between symbolic and prophetic dreams is that the Lord does not appear in the former; accordingly, the first part of prophetic dreams, in which the Lord summons the dreamer and identifies Himself, is not found in symbolic dreams. A number of scholars, including Richter, have described the external framework of symbolic dreams. Although he does not distinguish between prophetic and symbolic dreams, his model seems to be appropriate only for symbolic ones. It contains the following elements: 1. Announcement of the dream. 2. A call for attention, meant to increase listeners' suspense. 3. The scenes of the dream: (1) description and (2) outcome. 4. The meaning of the dream: a sentence that indicates the interpretation to be attached to the dream. 5. The symbol that appears in the dream and the meaning of the symbol. 6. The realization of the dream. On the structure of the dream, see Richter and also Gnuse, who applies Richter's model: Wolfgang Richter, "Traum und Traumdeutung im Alten Testament," *BZ* 7 (1963), pp. 215–216; Gnuse, *Dream,* pp. 92–101.

6. De Vaux notes that Isaac's agricultural adventures took place in Gerar, which is a cultivated agricultural district, whereas the story of Joseph belongs to the end of the Patriarchal period. According to him, the Patriarchs had not yet adopted a sedentary lifestyle. Closer examination reveals that the Patriarchs lived on the outskirts of cities, rather than in them, and concluded alliances with the city dwellers. The picture that emerges is of nomads in the midst of a process of sedentarization. In addition, the biblical tradition itself points to the significant difference between the lifestyle of the Patriarchs and of various nomadic groups. Isaac is the antithesis of Ishmael (Gen. 16:12 and 25:16–18), and Jacob of Esau (Gen. 25:27 and 27:39). The life of the Patriarchs is quite different from that of the Midianites or

the outskirts of settled districts, where their contact with the residents initiated that transition. In extrabiblical sources, too, we encounter nomads who also practiced small-scale farming.[7] Texts from Mari speak of shepherds who also harvested grain.[8]

Joseph's first dream is alive with action. Alongside naturalistic elements such as "... there (וְהִנֵּה) we were binding sheaves" we find occurrences that are not at all natural and are even supernatural: "... When (וְהִנֵּה) suddenly my sheaf stood up and remained upright." How can a sheaf stand up on its own? "... Then (וְהִנֵּה) your sheaves gathered around and bowed low to my sheaf" (Gen. 37:7).[9] Joseph's sheaf stands up in the center of the field; his brothers' sheaves encircle it and bow down. Nachmanides, David Kimḥi, and Don Isaac Abravanel all note that the content of the dream alludes to the future, when his brothers will bow down to him as part of an affair that involves grain. The meaning of the dream is quite clear.

The second dream (Gen. 37:9) recapitulates the first one.[10] The repetition reinforces the credibility of them both. In fact, Joseph will later interpret Pharaoh's second dream as meant specifically to buttress his first dream: "As for Pharaoh having had the same dream twice, it means that the matter has been determined by God, and that God will soon carry it out" (Gen. 41:32). Despite Joseph's powerful centrality and supernatural elements in both dreams ("...your sheaves ... bowed low to my sheaf" [Gen. 37:7]; "...the sun, the moon, and eleven stars were bowing down to me" [Gen. 37:9]), there are also fundamental differences between them. The first dream draws on Joseph's normal mundane environment; the second, on heavenly sights. In the first dream there are twelve brothers and twelve sheaves, and Joseph is represented by his own sheaf. In the second dream, there are only eleven stars, and Joseph

---

the Amalekites, with whom the Israelites came into contact somewhat later in their history. See R. de Vaux, *The Early History of Israel,* trans. David Smith (Philadelphia: Westminster Press, 1978), pp. 229–233.

7. Ibid., p. 230.

8. Sarna, *Genesis,* p. 265.

9. The adverb הִנֵּה is crucial to Joseph's dreams—introducing each of the three clauses of our verse, and similarly the two descriptive clauses in v. 9. The word expresses surprise and astonishment, and especially the dreamer's own amazement.

10. Some believe that Joseph's dream about celestial objects that bow down to him has an extrabiblical source and was interpolated into the story before its final editing. The dream of the sheaves is considered to be original and more appropriate to the story, because the idea that Joseph gave to Pharaoh—hoarding grain for the famine years—has affinities with the scene in which Joseph and his brothers bind the sheaves. See Ehrlich, *Traum,* p. 61; Donald B. Redford, *A Study of the Biblical Story of Joseph (Gen 37-50),* *VT* Sup 20 (Leiden: Brill, 1970), p. 70.

is not represented by his own star; the sun and moon, representing his parents, also appear. The second dream presents the physically impossible co-presence of sun, moon, and stars; moreover, Joseph's mother was no longer alive.[11]

Stars as representing human beings are a common motif in ancient literature and are mentioned in Genesis in the divine promises to the Patriarchs.[12] The image of heavenly bodies doing homage to an important person is also found in extrabiblical sources, such as in the dream of Nabonidus and in the dream of that king's chief astrologer.[13] There the reference to celestial objects represents an ascension to power. We should understand Joseph's dream in similar fashion.

There is no doubt that this pair of dreams points to Joseph's aspiration to dominate and rule his brothers. His brothers loathed him and he was not particularly fond of them. Jacob's love and preference for Joseph was the particular focus of their hatred, and to avenge himself on his brothers, Joseph used to bring Jacob bad reports of their conduct. Joseph longed to see his brothers bowing down to him, but because this yearning could not be fulfilled in the real world, he dreamt about it instead. Jacob could easily sympathize with Joseph's feelings and find in Joseph's dream an echo of the desires of his own youth. He had himself wrestled for the birthright with his brother Esau—and his dream at Bethel was an expression of his own aspiration for greatness and success in life. Hence it is not surprising to find that "his father kept the matter in mind" (v. 11).

Rivalry among brothers and the urge for power and dominion are frequent themes in Genesis: Cain and Abel, Isaac and Ishmael, Jacob and Esau, Ephraim and Manasseh.[14] In all these cases the younger brother excels and

---

11. B. Jacob, *Genesis*, p. 245. On the other hand, some believe that Gen. 37:10 (as well as 44:20) is a remnant of an ancient variant in which Rachel was still alive. As Driver put it: "J has mentioned her death in 35:19; perhaps E placed her death later" (Driver, *Genesis*, p. 222). Von Rad offers a similar hypothesis that ch. 37 comes from a different source (Von Rad, *Genesis*, p. 347-348). This conjecture, however, would entail that there be only 10 stars, not 11, since the dream scene would precede the birth of Benjamin.

12. C. H. Gordon, "The Patriarchal Age," *JBR* 21 (1953), p. 242. See also Genesis 15:15, 22:17, and 26:4.

13. Nabonidus was greeted by the moon, a star, and the planet Jupiter. "In my dream I beheld with joy the Great Star, the moon, and Marduk (i.e. the planet Jupiter) high up on the sky and it (the Great Star) called me by my name!" (see: "Babylonian and Assyrian Historical Texts," trans. A. Leo Oppenheim, *ANET*, 310). In another incident, an astrologer reported a dream in which he saw the Great Star, Venus, Sirius, the sun, and the moon, and foretold that he would be able to interpret it as a favorable omen for the king and his crown prince Belshazzar [YOS1, no. 39]. See Oppenheim, *Interpretation*, p. 205.

14. S. Thompson, *Motif-Index of Folk Literature* (Bloomington: Indiana University Press, 1955), V, 5:6; Donald B. Redford, *A Study of the Biblical Story of Joseph*, pp. 88–89.

overtakes his older sibling.[15] The same motif is found in extrabiblical sources, too: consider Bata over Anpu.[16]

But it is difficult to understand why Joseph aired the content of his dreams in public, since that only intensified his brothers' enmity. The best explanation is that his actions revealed his childish delight in lording over his temporarily discomfited siblings. We must remember that Joseph was a spoiled boy favored by his father. In this stage of Joseph's life, his conduct reflects foolishness rather than modesty and humility. As Arnold Ehrlich puts it:

> It is clear that Joseph was not speaking innocently when he told his dreams, but was purposefully informing his father and brothers that he had dreamt his dreams for them. If so, Joseph was not acting wisely by provoking his brothers' jealousy and his father's anger. He did so as the result of a divine decree, so that his brothers would hear his dreams and hate him even more and sell him. This teaches us that Joseph was not particularly wise; all his glory in Egypt was because the Lord was with him and made him successful.[17]

As far as the immediate context of the Bible is concerned, the meaning of the dreams relates directly to the dreamer Joseph and his immediate future. The midrash, however, sees another dimension in them, a hidden meaning fraught with implications for the distant future.

We were binding sheaves (אלומים) (Gen. 37:7).

You are gathering produce and I am gathering produce; yours is rotten while mine are upright: lo, my sheaf arose and stood upright.

Rabbi Levi said: You will make dumb idols (אלילים אלמים) before the calves of Jeroboam, as it says: "These are your gods, Israel" (Exodus 32:4).

---

15. Some note that David's story is similar to Joseph's. Like Joseph, he is the youngest in his family and a shepherd (1 Sam. 17:15); his father sends him to find out how his brothers are getting along (1 Sam. 17:17–18). The brothers rebuke him for his presumption. See Herbert Gordon May, "Pattern and myth in the Old Testament," *Journal of Religion* 21 (1941), p. 287; Redford, *Joseph,* p. 89.

16. Redford, *Joseph,* p. 88. In addition Redford mentions Horus over Seth. However, in his notes, he points to Griffiths' *The Conflict of Horus and Seth,* where we find: "In the Horus-Seth feud they are brothers, while in the Osiris-Seth feud Seth has become the paternal uncle of Horus and brother of Osiris. Seth is indeed often mentioned as the brother of Osiris. Only rarely is he described as the brother of Horus." See: J. Gwyn Griffiths, *The Conflict of Horus and Seth* (Liverpool: University Press, 1960), p.12.

17. Arnold B. Ehrlich, מקרא כפשוטו (New York: Ktav, 1969), p. 101.

Rabbi Aḥa said: You will conceal (להעלים) things concerning me before our father, saying: "A wild beast devoured him" (Gen. 37:33).[18]

The midrash relates to the dream in two different ways. It begins by quoting a verse, to which it appends a description of Joseph and his brothers gathering the harvest. The scene, which is related in the present tense, reviews and expands the biblical text while fitting perfectly into the dream. This interpretation refers to the text itself. In contrast, R. Levi and R. Aḥa have a different relationship to the text: they find allusions to the distant future and use the devices of paronomasia and metathesis to decipher the significance of the dream. R. Levi starts with the root א.ל.מ (on which אלומה 'sheaf' is formed) and derives two additional senses—"idol" (אליל) and "dumb" (אלם). R. Aḥa replaces the *aleph* with an *ayin* and uses the *hiph'il* construction to produce the verb "to hide." If until now the dream was interpreted as referring only to the dreamer (Joseph), now it has an additional level of meaning, with the emphasis on the brothers' future. This is a departure from the more usual method of dream interpretation, which referred exclusively to the dreamer's own future.[19]

THE DREAMS OF THE BUTLER AND THE BAKER

Daily life is also reflected in the dreams of the baker and the butler (Gen. 40:5-9 and 40:16). In their dreams, the two royal servitors are performing their normal functions in Pharaoh's court—namely, to guarantee the quality of the food and drink placed on the monarch's table (wine and bread symbolize all beverages and foods). What was the dereliction committed by the two? The text does not say, noting laconically only that they "gave offense to their lord the king of Egypt" (Gen. 40:1). The butler tells Joseph that in his dream he was serving wine to Pharaoh—handing the royal goblet to the king. The office of butler as described here is parallel to the Egyptian *wdpw* of the period 2000–1600 BCE and after that to the *wb3* or cupbearer of the New Kingdom (1600–1100 BCE).[20] The butler or cupbearer, the *wb3*, is sometimes called the *wʿb-ʿwy* 'pure hands.' Gardiner asserts that this expression relates to the prep-

---

18. Genesis Rabba 84:10.

19. On oneirocriticism and scriptural exegesis in GR 1012 see Maren Niehoff, "A Dream Which is Not Interpreted is Like a Letter Which is Not Read," *JJS* 43 (1992), pp. 69–71.

20. A. H. Gardiner, *Ancient Egyptian Onomastica* (London: Oxford University Press, 1947), vol. 1, pp. 43 and 44, on no. 122 *(wb3)*; J. Vergote, *Joseph en Égypte: Génèse ch. 37–50 à la lumière des études égyptologiques reécentes* (Louvain: Publications Universitaires, 1959), pp.

aration and serving of food to Pharaoh, especially wine and beer.[21] In Papyrus Leyde 348,10.5, we read *wbꜣ dp irp,* which means "cupbearer (or butler) who tastes the wine."[22] The butler, in addition to his eponymous role, also filled a political function. In wartime he accompanied Pharaoh; sometimes he was responsible for the palace and / or the royal treasury. Starting in the Nineteenth Dynasty, we encounter the "chief cook" and "chief butler" as members of diplomatic missions. Ramses III placed these ministers at the head of a list of his ministers and servants (Papyrus Harris I).[23] As for wine, as far back as the Old Kingdom it was stored in earthenware jugs imprinted with the origin of the wine. Under the New Kingdom, when people began to drink wine from painted cups, the name of the vintner was recorded.[24]

In his dream the butler sees vines, grapes, wine, and Pharaoh. All these are natural rather than imaginary objects, part of the real world. Some of the actions in his dream, by contrast, are quite unnatural. The vine develops with abnormal speed: "It had barely budded, when out came its blossoms and its clusters ripened into grapes."[25] Furthermore, in the real world one did not squeeze grapes directly into Pharaoh's goblet. Moreover, Pharaoh drank old wine, not grape juice.[26] (Of course, in the "time-lapse" scenario of the dream, the juice may have had time to ferment.) Unlike the rapid growth of the vine, the butler works slowly: "I took the grapes, pressed them into Pharaoh's cup, and placed the cup in Pharaoh's hand." It is interesting that in the Mesopotamian Book of Dreams, there are a number of dreams that incorporate goblets

35–40; K. A. Kitchen, "Cupbearer," in *The New Bible Dictionary,* ed. J. D. Douglas (Grand Rapids, Eerdmans, 1962), p. 283.

21. Gardiner, *Ancient Egyptian Onomastica,* p. 43.

22. A. H. Gardiner, *Late Egyptian Miscellanies* (Brussels: Éditions de la Fondation Égyptologique Reine Élisabeth, 1937), 137, line 1; R. A. Caminos, *Late Egyptian Miscellanies* (London: Oxford University Press, 1954), p. 498; J. Vergote, *Joseph en Égypte,* p. 36; Kitchen, "Cupbearer," *NBD,* p. 283.

23. "I made Egypt into many classes, consisting of: butlers of the palace, great princes. ..." (James Henry Breasted, *Ancient Records of Egypt* [New York: Russell and Russell, 1962], p. 200, section 402); J. Vergote, *Joseph en Égypte,* pp. 39–40.

24. Yehoshua M. Grintz, *The Book of Genesis* (Jerusalem: Magnes Press, 1983), p. 105 (Hebrew).

25. The Hebrew word אֶשְׁכּוֹל 'cluster' can now be connected with the Eblaite *aš-kà-lum* and *aš-qa-i-lu.* See M. J. Dahood, "Ebla, Ugarit, and the Bible," p. 279.

26. Ptolemaic temple texts describe unfermented grape juice squeezed by hand and cut with water as a refreshing beverage enjoyed by royalty. See S. R. Driver, "Joseph," in *A Dictionary of the Bible,* ed. S. Hastings. 2:772, (New York: C. Scribner's sons, 1902); Redford, *Joseph,* p. 205.

and the serving of wine: "If one gives him a full goblet, he will have a name and offspring. If one gives him wine, a friendly word; his days will be long."[27]

The baker is hesitant to tell his dream. Only after he has heard Joseph's favorable interpretation of the butler's dream and noted the points of contact between the two dreams does he open up to Joseph.[28] In the hope of obtaining a favorable interpretation, too, he begins, "In my dream, similarly" (Gen. 40:16).[29] According to Vergote, the Egyptian parallel to "baker" may be *rtḫty*.[30] Kitchen, however, believes that the term *sš wdḥw nsw* 'royal table scribe' is closer to the biblical expression.[31] The baker's dream is shorter than the butler's. Whereas the butler was active in his dream and actually served Pharaoh, the baker is passive and does nothing. He has three baskets (חֹרִי) on his head.[32] The baskets contain all manner of baked goods, fit for the royal table, but the birds are devouring Pharaoh's food. The baked goods and birds are realistic; what is imaginary is that the birds, by nature afraid to get close to human beings, are "eating out of the basket above my head" (v. 17). They keep eating for some time—another unrealistic touch.

The baker was responsible for Pharaoh's meals. The Harris Papyrus, which dates from the Twentieth Dynasty, lists about 30 types of bread that were used in the temples.[33] Erman and Grapow's dictionary of ancient Egyptian includes 38 kinds of cake and 57 kinds of bread that were unknown before the

---

27. Oppenheim, *Interpretation,* p. 279, lines x + 7, x + 8.

28. His colleague in this position is the Babylonian "chief of the guards," Nebuzaradan (2 Kings 25:8, Jer. 39:9).

29. The phrase "in my dream," which appears here for the second time, has a parallel in texts from Mari, *ina šuttiya,* which means "in my dream." See J. F. Craghan, "The ARM X 'Prophetic' Texts: Their Media, Style, and Structure," *JANESCU* 6 (1974), pp. 43–45; M. Weinfeld, "Ancient Near-Eastern Patterns in Prophetic Literature," *VT* 27 (1977), pp. 185–186.

30. J. Vergote, *Joseph en Égypte,* p. 37.

31. Kitchen, "Joseph," *NBD,* 658.

32. The meaning of חֹרִי is not certain. Some—including Rashi, Samuel ben Meir, Joseph Bekhor Shor, and David Kimḥi—believe it is derived from חוּר and means a "reed basket." Others—including Ibn Ezra, Sa'adia Gaon, and Nachmanides—derive it from חוּר 'white', i.e., "white bread." The latter opinion is bolstered by a text from Ebla in which we find *lú ḥa-ri,* meaning "baker of white bread." See M. J. Dahood's review of H. R. Cohen's *Biblical Hapax Legomena in the Light of Akkadian and Ugaritic,* Bib 62 (1981), pp. 273–274; idem, "Eblaite *ḥa-ri* and Genesis 40:16," *BibNot* 13 (1980), pp. 14–16; idem, "Eblaite and Biblical Hebrew," *CBQ* 44 (1982), p. 22.

33. P. Harris I, ed. W. Erichsen (Bibl. aeg. 5), 17a7–18a9 = James Henry Breasted, *Ancient Record of Egypt* (Chicago: The University of Chicago Press, 1906), pp. 134–136; Walter Wreszinski, "Backerei," *Zeitschrift für Ägyptische Sprache und Altertumskunde* 61 (1926), pp. 1–15; Vergote, *Joseph,* p. 37.

New Kingdom.[34] The Mesopotamian Dream Book, too, refers to cases in which people carry objects on their head: "If he carries dates on his head, sorrow. If he carries ... on his head, he will have riches. If he carries a mountain on his head, he will have no rival."[35]

According to Genesis 40:8, God provided Joseph with the interpretation of the two ministers' dreams. In any case, we can work with the assumption that dream interpretation relies on divine inspiration. This means that Joseph, moving from the imaginary world to the real world, was able to interpret the dreams after a close consideration and comparison of their details. In his interpretation, he repeats or reviews part of the dream: "Joseph said to him, 'This is its interpretation: The three branches are three days. In three days Pharaoh will pardon you and restore you to your post; you will place Pharaoh's cup in his hand, as was your custom formerly when you were his cupbearer'" (Gen. 40:12–13; similarly for the baker's dream, v. 18). Such word-for-word repetition is typical of dream tales in Mesopotamia and Egypt.

Joseph also relates to the numbers that appear in the dream. "Three" is a linchpin of both dreams. The butler sees *three* branches on the vine, which itself appears in *three* stages that rapidly succeed one another–budding, flowering, and finally producing ripe clusters of grapes. Then the butler performs *three* actions: he plucks the grapes from the vine, squeezes them into Pharaoh's cup, and places the cup in Pharaoh's hand. The word כוֹס 'cup' appears *three* times, as does the word "Pharaoh." In the second dream, the baker has *three* baskets on his head. There are *three* branches and *three* baskets, too.

In his interpretation of both dreams, Joseph deciphers this key number as meaning three days. How did Joseph know to make this equation? Abraham Ibn Ezra replies: "Perhaps יוֹם הוּלֶדֶת פַּרְעֹה[36] means 'the day on which he was born.' Today some kings make a feast on their anniversary and invite all their servants and give them presents; or perhaps the queen was pregnant." Nachmanides says that the rapidity with which the vine developed indicated that God was in a hurry to realize His purpose, and this is how Joseph understood that the three vines represented days rather than months or years. In extrabiblical sources we find that dream interpreters had to specify when the dream would be realized: "If [in his dream] he goes to Nittur, sorrow, well-be-

---

34. A. Erman and H. Grapow, *Wörterbuch der ägyptischen Sprache* VI (Berlin: Akademie-Verlag, 1950), p. 31; cited in Vergote, *Joseph en Égypte,* p. 37.

35. Oppenheim, *Interpretation,* p. 288, lines x + 13, x + 14, x + 15.

36. Although this phrase is almost always rendered as "birthday," the Hebrew construction is rather difficult and that sense not at all obvious; it is simply that no other plausible meaning suggests itself.

ing for one year" (x + 5).[37] Hence it is possible that in his interpretation of the dream Joseph was following the practice of the Mesopotamian oneirocritics.

On his birthday the king used to make a great banquet for all his servants, give them presents, and pardon prisoners.[38] The butler and baker wanted to be part of the festivities and accordingly dreamt that they were again serving the king, as in the past. The butler's dream is full of movement and action and attests to his diligence and meticulous attention to his work. He does not rely on others: he himself harvests the grapes, presses their juice, and serves the wine to Pharaoh. In contrast, not only is the baker reluctant to repeat his dream to Joseph, but he is totally passive in it. He stands there with the bread already baked but does not cover the basket to protect its contents from the birds or try to chase them away, leaving them to peck away undisturbed.[39] The birds' eating is the only activity in the dream. This is significant, because soon the birds will pick the flesh from the baker's corpse. The baker's inactivity alludes to his negligence, indolence, and inattention to his job. This difference between the two dreams may be what caused Joseph to interpret the butler's dream for life and the baker's dream for death. Of course, another possibility is that during the months that Joseph had spent with the two ministers, they had told him what was bothering them and unwittingly revealed significant details about themselves.[40]

The two ministers' dreams are realized very quickly—within three days—unlike Joseph's dreams, which were pending for many years. But the ministers' dreams are similar to Joseph's in that they refer exclusively to the dreamers themselves and have no national or religious content. The dreams provide readers with a glimpse into life at the royal palace and the Egyptian political

---

37. Oppenheim, *Interpretation,* p. 267, lines x + 5, x + 6; p. 268, lines x + 2; 277, line x + 15; J. J. M. Roberts, "On Signs, Prophets, and Time Limits: A Note on Psalm 74:9," *CBQ* 39 (1977), pp. 474–481.

38. Redford says that the king's birthday, like the god's birthday, was celebrated in Egypt in all periods. But we have no evidence for this predating the first century BCE. Celebration of the king's birthday was certainly customary in the Hellenistic period. Hence it is not surprising that the only evidence for it comes from the Rosetta Stone, where we read "birthday of the good god (the king)." As in our chapter, so too on Ptolemy's birthday a general amnesty was proclaimed. Redford adds that the celebration of the king's birthday became a popular festival under the Saites or perhaps the Persians. See Redford, *Joseph,* pp. 205–206; S. R. Driver, "Joseph," in *A Dictionary of the Bible,* ed. S. Hastings, 2:772 (N.Y.: C. Scribner's, 1902).

39. A bird of prey swooping down symbolizes danger. Abraham chases away the vulture and does not allow it to approach the sacrificial animals (Gen. 15:11). Because the baker does not chase the birds away, Joseph concluded that his fate was sealed.

40. Israel J. Gerber, *Immortal Rebels* (New York: Jonathan David, 1963), p. 217.

system, where the king is at once executive, legislature, and judge, adjudicating alone on matters of life and death. But in the Joseph cycle, the dreams function literarily as a catalyst for bringing Joseph to Pharaoh.[41] The butler does forget Joseph, only to remember him two years later when Pharaoh demands that someone interpret his dreams.[42] Significantly, the actions in the dreams of all three—Joseph, the butler, and Pharaoh—are supernatural, thus expressing the notion that even real world events are determined, not by natural and rational laws, but by a divine will that does not depend on natural law but directs events in the real world in the future.

PHARAOH'S DREAMS

Two years after the fateful birthday when Pharaoh pardoned one minister and condemned another, he himself has a pair of dreams. Initially they are related in the third person (Gen. 41:1-7), but when Pharaoh later recounts them to Joseph, he does so in the first person (Gen. 41: 17-23). The first dream takes place along the Nile,[43] and unlike those of Joseph and the two ministers, does not refer to his personal life and secret longings. Instead, it reflects the fundamental problems of Egypt, which focus on the Nile, cattle, and agriculture. The fact that Pharaoh is standing next to the Nile is symbolic, because the Nile has always been the lifeblood of Egypt.[44] The waters of the Nile have

---

41. The dreams unify the story and are the glue that hold its parts together. Without them, the story is no longer comprehensible. See: Redford, *A Study,* pp. 68–69, A. B. Ehrlich, *Randglossen zur Hebräischen Bibel I. Genesis und Exodus* (Leipzig: Heinrichs, 1908), p. 186.

42. The root ז.כ.ר 'remember' is important both in the present chapter and the next. It first appears when Joseph asks the butler to "think of me (זכרתני) when all is well with you again, and do me the kindness of mentioning me (והזכרתני) to Pharaoh, so as to free me from this place" (Gen. 40:14); it recurs at the end of the chapter, "Yet the chief cupbearer did not think of (ולא זכר) Joseph; he forgot him" (Gen. 40:23); and then it becomes the thread that links the next chapter with this one, after the magicians cannot interpret Pharaoh's dream: "The chief cupbearer then spoke up and said to Pharaoh, 'I must make mention (מזכיר) today of my offenses" (Gen. 41:9). On the signification of the verb, see B. S. Childs, *Memory and Tradition in Israel, SBT* 1/37 (Naperville, Illinois: A. R. Allenson, 1962), p. 15.

43. The Hebrew יאור is an Egyptian loan word. The Egyptian name for the Nile was *itrw* '(the) river', but the later spelling without the *t,* i.e., *irw* = Coptic *eioor,* is frequent. See T. O. Lambdin, "Egyptian Loan Words in the Old Testament," *JAOS* 73 (1953), p. 151; J. Černý, *Coptic Etymological Dictionary* (Cambridge [Eng.]; New York: Cambridge University Press, 1976), p. 48.

44. The preposition על is used after verbs to express towering above someone or something, as in Genesis 41:1, "Pharaoh stood by the Nile"—that is, above the water level.

always provided both drinking water and irrigation water. Its fish are an important food source.[45]

In the dream Pharaoh describes seven handsome and sturdy cows browsing in the reeds.[46] They are followed at once by seven scrawny cows who "stood beside the cows." Nachmanides notes: "Next to them and close to them, a sign that there would be no separation between the years of feast and the years of famine." Familiar figures on an Egyptian landscape, cows were the common pasture animal in Egypt, as sheep were in Canaan. The cows frequently swam in the Nile, whose banks were rich in pasturage, and it was only natural for them to browse there. Cattle were extremely important to the economy of Egypt in every period. They were used as draft animals as well as for milk and meat. Because of their economic importance, they played a significant role in religious life. The sky was sometimes depicted as a cow standing on its four legs, its body like a canopy over the earth, giving birth to the sun in the morning and swallowing it in its mouth at evening. A bovine goddess, Hathor, was worshipped in several districts and was one of the most important members of the Egyptian pantheon. She had many other forms, too, and was sometimes pictured as a woman with cow's ears.[47]

Verse 4 presents a strange description of how the gaunt cows devoured the fat ones.[48] Pharaoh, appalled by the unnatural sight, wakes up with a start. Cows are tranquil ruminants; here they were becoming cannibalistic carnivores and, most astonishingly, the weak and scrawny cows were devouring the healthy ones. What is more, when Pharaoh retells his dream to Joseph, he adds that this rich meal did not improve their appearance: "One could not tell

---

45. The Mesopotamian Dream Book contains many examples of people who fell into a river or crossed a river. "If he comes up from the river: good news." [45]: Oppenheim, *Interpretation,* pp. 287–288.

46. אחו *Aḫu* is another Egyptian loan word. Its original meaning was "land flooded by the Nile"; from there it came to mean "pasture land." From Egyptian the word passed into Hebrew and other Semitic tongues. See T. O. Lambdin, "Egyptian Loan Words in the Old Testament," p. 14; M. J. Dahood, "Northwest Semitic Notes on Genesis," *Bib* 55 (1974), p. 80. See the Ugaritic references for this root in B. Couroyer's review of Vergote in *RB* 66 (1959), p. 588; and Aramaic אחוה (= "its vegetation") in J. A. Fitzmyer, *Aramaic Inscriptions of Sefire, BibOr* 19 (Rome: Pontifical Biblical Institute, 1967), p. 47; W. L. Michel, *Job in the Light of Northwest Semitic, BibOr* 42 (Rome, Biblical Institute, 1987), 1:189–190.

47. It also seems that cow designated the word "year," but this signification is later, from the Hellenistic period. Redford, *Study,* p. 205; J. Janssen, "Egyptological Remarks on the Story of Joseph in Genesis," *JEOL* 5 (1955-56), p. 66.

48. "Seven was the number of fate. Seven represented the full number of blessings as well as curses" (A. Kapelrud, "The Number Seven in Ugaritic texts," *VT* 18 [1968], p. 497).

that they had consumed them, for they looked just as bad as before" (Gen. 41:21).

Pharaoh's second dream recapitulates and reinforces the first one. The phenomenon of double dreams is well known in the ancient Near East, as in the dreams of Gilgamesh and of Gudea.[49] Pharaoh describes seven solid and healthy ears of grain growing on a single stalk, followed by seven sere and windblown sheaves that swallow up the full ones. The former symbolize plenty; the latter, destruction.[50] The central motif in the dream is the ears of grain, which allude to an agricultural milieu. The dream is "populated" by natural objects that perform unnatural actions. In both dreams, the weak overcome the strong, a symbol that forebodes evil.

To interpret Pharaoh's dreams, Joseph follows the same method he used for the two ministers' dreams; that is, he links them with the personal situation of the dreamer and his life. The elements of the dreams—the cows, the ears of grain, and the Nile—are all associated with the economy of Egypt. There are three key points in Joseph's interpretation:

(1) *Pharaoh describes two dreams but Joseph treats them as one* ("Pharaoh's dream is one" Gen. 41:25) *because they had a single meaning.* Thus Joseph's approach differs from that of the magicians who tried to interpret two separate dreams: "None could interpret *them* for Pharaoh" (Gen. 41:8)

(2) *The number seven refers to years.* When he interpreted the ministers' dream, Joseph applied the key number—three—to days; but this time the key number refers to years. A year is the smallest unit of time in which the cycle of the seasons repeats itself. Paronomasia is conspicuous in his interpretation.[51] There is a play on words between שֶׁבַע 'seven' (Gen. 41:29), which is part of

---

49. "The Epic of Gilgamesh," trans. E. A. Speiser, *ANET*, 76–77, J. S. Cooper, "Gilgamesh Dreams of Enkidu: The Evolution and Dilution of Narrative," in *Essays on the Ancient Near East in Memory of Jacob Joel Finkelstein,* ed. Maria Jong Ellis (Hamden, Connecticut: Archon Books, 1977), pp. 39–44; J. H. Tigay, *The Evolution of the Gilgamesh Epic* (Philadelphia: University of Pennsylvania Press, 1982), pp. 82–93; on Gudea, see S. N. Kramer, *The Sumerians* (Chicago: The University of Chicago Press, 1963), pp. 137–140.

50. The "east wind" mentioned in the text (v. 6) is a warm and dry wind, known as the *hamsin* or *sirocco.* It is a common Bible symbol of destruction (Isa. 27:8, Hos. 13:15, Ezra 17:10). In Canaan it blows from the east, but in Egypt it comes from the south. In fact, in this passage the reference may be to a wind that blows from the Sahara Desert. See R. B. Y. Scott, "Meteorological Phenomena and Terminology in the Old Testament," *ZAW* 64 (1952), pp. 11–25.

51. Michael Fishbane, *Biblical Interpretation in Ancient Israel* (Oxford: Clarendon Press, 1985), p. 451.

the dream,[52] and שָׂבָע 'plenty', which appears in its interpretation and refers to the years of plenty and abundance.[53]

(3) *Drought and the River Nile are central components.* In his dream, Pharaoh stands alongside the Nile, the lifeblood of Egypt, and both the healthy and sickly cows come up out of its waters. Both good and evil come from the river. If fat cows emerge from it, it means that the river will provide Egypt with years of plenty; if thin cows emerge, the Nile is going to dwindle and dry up. If the gaunt cows, which must be hungry, do not graze, it means that there will be nothing to eat because there will be no pasturage. If the placid cow turns into a carnivore, it means that an uncommon phenomenon is at work, a famine so protracted that even peaceful animals will go mad and turn into predators. The second dream replaces the cows with ears of grain. The empty ears, an obvious sign of famine, swallow up the full ones. In fact, Pharaoh himself points Joseph to the solution. Describing how the thin ones swallow up the fat ones, he expresses his astonishment—"One could not tell that they had consumed them" (Gen. 41:21). Joseph understands the allusion: "No trace of the abundance will be left in the land because of the famine thereafter" (Gen. 41:31). The plenty that precedes the famine will have no effect on it: "All the abundance in the land of Egypt will be forgotten when the land is ravaged by famine" (Gen. 41:30). The gaunt cows and empty ears of grain symbolize the famine, just as the sturdy cows and full ears represent the bumper years.[54] We should recall that in his youth Joseph lived in Canaan and was familiar with famine—referred to in several episodes during the time of the Patriarchs (Abraham, Genesis 12; Isaac, Genesis 26).[55] Most important, Joseph's thir-

---

52. Egyptian religious art frequently depicts seven cows with a bull. Some have tried to use this to interpret the dream, but it seems more likely that it is a reference to the cows who support the dead Pharaoh in the afterlife. See J. Vergote, *Joseph en Égypte,* p. 56.

53. Similar wordplay is used by Amos, who sees a basketful of figs (קיץ) that allude to the end (קץ) of Israel (Amos 8:1–3).

54. Ruppert noted the parallel between פָּרָה 'cow' and the verb פ.ר.ה 'be fruitful'. See L. Ruppert, *Die Josephserzählung der Genesis* (Munich: Kösel, 1965), p. 71.

55. The stories about the famines in the times of Abraham and Isaac serve the proclivities of the biblical authors, whose literary and theological rationales we must keep in mind. Stories about Abraham's descent to Egypt, and Isaac's aborted attempt to follow in his footsteps, fall into the category of the actions of the fathers that prefigure those of the sons and presage the future descent to Egypt by Jacob and his sons, on account of famine, and their later exodus. The Egyptian exile of Jacob and his sons is part of the divine program first revealed to Abraham (Gen. 15:13–18).

teen years in Egypt taught him that the Nile rose in summer and subsided in
the autumn–and that an insufficient flood meant serious danger.[56]

Pharaoh's anxiety about famine seems to have been well founded, because
biblical, extrabiblical, and Egyptian sources all include the element of seven
lean years.[57] A Ptolemaic-era famine story is found on the Famine Stele,
which tells about events in the reign of the third-millennium king Djoser: "A
great misfortune had befallen the country: the Nile had not inundated the
land for seven years. Grain was scarce, seeds had dried up, and all food was
in short supply." Scholars have shown that this inscription actually dates from
the reign of Ptolemy V, specifically from the year 187 BCE.[58] Is the story a
reworking of an ancient tradition or a figment of its author's imagination?[59]
It is clear in any case that in the Ptolemaic period there was a tradition of
seven lean years. Gordon noted the motif of seven fat years and seven lean
years in Mesopotamia and Ugarit.[60] In the Epic of Gilgamesh, Anu, the god
of heaven, warns of an impending seven years of famine.[61] The Ugaritic story
of Aqhat mentions the seven-year failure of Baal, the god of rain and thun-
der.[62] A political alliance from the city of Sefire includes a variety of curses
against anyone who breaches the treaty, and one of them is seven years of
famine. In the Bible, the prophet Gad offers David the choice of a punishment
for conducting the census, including seven years of famine (2 Sam. 24:13).[63]

---

56. The book of Zechariah is aware of the fact that Egypt does not require rain because
the Nile rises and irrigates the fields. See also Deut. 11:10.

57. Stories about drought and famine derive from fertility myths, in which the drought
is the result of the death of a god or is caused by some vengeful spirit, by negligence on the
part of a deity, or by the inability of the god to prevent the famine (Redford, *A Study,* p. 98).

58. Ibid., pp. 206–207.

59. On the possibility that the text is based on an ancient source, see: "Egyptian Myth,
Tales, and Mortuary Texts, " trans. John A. Wilson, *ANET,* pp. 31–32.

60. C. H. Gordon, *Before the Bible: The Common Background of Greek and Hebrew Civilization*
(London: Collins, 1962), p. 69f and 88; idem, "Sabbatical Cycle or Seasonal Pattern?" *Orientalia* 22 (1953), pp. 79–81.

61. "Akkadian Myth and Epics," trans. E. A. Speiser, *ANET,* pp. 84–85, tablet
6:101–106.

62. "Ugaritic Myths, Epics, and Legends," trans. H. L.Ginsberg *ANET,* p. 153: "Seven
years shall Ba'al fail" (line 43).

63. The sources of the literary convention of famine are found in the execrations in Lev.
26:26ff. and Deut. 28:15ff. Famine is one of the curses repeated in both places. In Leviticus
we read: "When I break your staff of bread, ten women shall bake your bread in a single
oven; they shall dole out your bread by weight, and though you eat, you shall not be satis-
fied. ... You shall eat the flesh of your sons and the flesh of your daughters." (Lev. 26:26,
29). Cannibalism recurs in the same context in Deuteronomy 28: "You shall eat your own
issue, the flesh of your sons and daughters ... because of the desperate straits to which your

Thus it seems that seven was a marked literary convention in the ancient Near East.[64]

In sum, the dreams in the Joseph cycle present scenes from the daily lives of the dreamers and are filled with real world elements acting in unreal ways. At first glance it seems that the dreams are the fruit of the dreamers' own imaginations and a manifestation of their own desires and fears. But from the perspective of the biblical author, the dreams reflect a religious determinism according to which everything that takes place in life is ordained by God, in a world where human beings are powerless to alter the course of events. Whatever appears in a dream will take place in the future. The Joseph narratives, which begin with Joseph's own dreams, lead ultimately to their actualization: when the brothers come to Egypt to buy food they bow down to Joseph without knowing that he is their brother (Gen. 42:6 and 43:26). After Jacob's death they re-enact the dream once again, knowingly prostrating themselves before him and begging him to forgive their crime (50:18). The butler is restored to his post, the baker is hanged (40:21–22), and Pharaoh's dreams of seven fat and seven lean years (41:53–54) come to pass. When Joseph identifies himself to his brothers he says that their sale of him was the finger of God: "Now, do not be distressed or reproach yourselves because you sold me hither; it was to save life that God sent me ahead of you. ... God has sent me ahead of you to ensure your survival on earth, and to save your lives in an extraordinary deliverance. So, it was not you who sent me here, but God" (Gen. 45:5, 7–8). Events in Egypt are inevitable and foreordained by Divine Providence–by a God who does not appear directly, but who is above nature and whose latent presence and direction are felt everywhere.

---

enemy shall reduce you. He who is most tender and fastidious among you shall be too mean to his brother and the wife of his bosom and the children he has spared to share with any of them the flesh of the children that he eats" (Deut. 28:53–55). Imprecations of famine that will strike the Israelites are also found in Isa. 3:1 and 7, 8:21, 9:19; Jer. 11:22, 16:3–4, 21:7–9, 24:8–10, 29:17–18, 38:2, 42:15–17, 54:12–13; and Ezek. 4:16–17, 5:12–17, 12:16–19. In Leviticus 26:25–26, famine is one of a set of disasters that also includes war and pestilence. In Deuteronomy chapter 28, famine (vv. 23ff.) is mentioned along with pestilence (v. 21) and the sword (v. 25). This yoking of pestilence, war, and famine is found again only in Jeremiah (14:12, 21:7 and 9, et passim) and Ezekiel (5:12 and 17, 6:11–12, etc.). The three-fold scheme is also found in nonprophetic sources such as 2 Sam. 24:13 (1 Chronicles 21:12) and in Solomon's prayer at the dedication of the Temple (1 Kings 8:33–37).

64. See R. A. Carlson, *David, the Chosen King,* trans. Eric J. Sharpe and Stanley Rudman (Stockholm: Almqvist and Wiksell, 1964), p. 34; A. S. Kapelrud, "The Number Seven in Ugaritic texts," *VT* 18 (1968), pp. 494–499.

NEBUCHADNEZZAR'S DREAMS

Whereas the dreams in the Joseph narrative echo daily life and incorporate elements drawn from reality, the dreams of Nebuchadnezzar are strange and alien and invoke an imaginary world. The episode of the first dream occupies chapter 2 of Daniel. When Nebuchadnezzar forgets his dream, Daniel must first tell the king what he saw and only then interpret it for him. To moderns, forgetting one's dream is nothing unusual. Many people cannot remember what they dreamed the night before. According to Freud, the human mind often expresses in dreams taboo or infantile desires and impulses that in waking hours are repressed. In sleep, however, the censorship mechanism is less active, allowing those impulses to find expression—but only after being edited and camouflaged so that the dreamer does not recognize them fully. Upon waking, that mechanism regains its vigor and consigns the memories of the dream to utter or partial oblivion—although sometimes it imposes a reworking of sections that are remembered in order to make them correspond more closely to the real waking world and blur their origins.[65]

Because Nebuchadnezzar knows that he has had a dream but has forgotten its content, Daniel comes before him and describes it (vv. 31–35) and its meaning (vv. 37–45). The statue seen by the king had four segments, each made of a different metal. Daniel goes on to describe how the statue was shattered by a stone without human assistance. Nothing remains of the statue, but the stone became a mountain that filled the entire earth. Daniel interprets the four segments of the statue and its four metals as representing four kingdoms. During the time of the last one, the God of Heaven will establish a new eternal kingdom that will shatter all previous ones.

In the ancient world, the appearance of giant figures and statues in dreams was quite common. In the dream of Gudea we read: "In the dream, the first man—like the heaven was his surpassing [size], like the earth was his surpassing [size]."[66] In their dreams, the pharaoh Merneptah saw a giant statue of the god Ptah and Ptolemy Soter saw the colossus of the god Pluto in Sinope.[67] Herodotus (1.183) relates that in the Temple of Bel in Babylon there was "a figure of a man, twelve cubits high, entirely of solid gold." It should be em-

---

65. For a summary of the issue of forgetting dreams and ideas other than that presented above, see Isaac Lewin, *The Psychology of Dreams,* pp. 145–150.

66. Oppenheim, *Interpretation,* p. 245, section 8, no. 1.

67. Ibid., p. 251, section 8, no. 16 and 252, section 8, no. 21; John J. Collins, *A Commentary on the Book of Daniel* (Minneapolis: Fortress Press, 1993), p. 162.

phasized, however, that the statue seen by Nebuchadnezzar differed from all of these in that it represented the course of history rather than a deity.[68]

Two features of our story are especially noteworthy: the segmentation of the statue into four parts, and the interpretation that the four metals represent four kingdoms. We have seen that elements of dream stories are often found in extrabiblical sources. What sources did the author of Daniel know? Was the dream story his own invention or was he reworking older sources with which he was familiar? Many scholars have noted the coincidence between the metals that appear in the Book of Daniel—gold, silver, bronze, and iron—and Hesiod's stages in the moral decline of mankind, which are also symbolized by metals. The first, utopian stage, was the Age of Gold, followed by the ages of silver and bronze. Hesiod's fourth age—the Age of Heroes—is not identified with a metal. But the fifth age— his contemporary—returns to the paradigm and is referred to as the Age of Iron.[69] Evidently Hesiod adopted a scheme of four generations and four metals that already existed in the eighth century, but we know nothing about his putative source.[70]

Since the time of Meyer, scholars have been inclined to view this scheme as the result of Persian influence.[71] A passage in the Persian Zend-Avesta, which is a sort of midrash or homiletical exposition and expansion of the lost *Vohuman Yasn,* relates that Zarathustra asked Ahuramazda for eternal life. "Aûhzmazd showed the wisdom of all-knowledge unto Zaratuhst. Through it, he saw the trunk of a tree, on which there were four branches: one of gold, one of silver, one of steel, and one of iron mixed. Thereof he considered that he saw this in a dream."[72] Ahuramazda tells Zarathustra that the four branches represent four epochs of history, and each branch is identified with a different metal.[73] The resemblance to the Book of Daniel is unmistakable,

---

68. Ibid., p. 162.

69. See also Ovid, *Metamorphoses* 1.89–150; James A. Montgomery, *A Critical and Exegetical Commentary on the Book of Daniel, ICC l* (Edinburgh: T. and T. Clark, 1927), p. 188; Louis F. Hartman and Alexander A. Di Lella, *The Book of Daniel,* AB (New York: Doubleday, 1978), p. 146; Collins, *Daniel,* p. 162.

70. Collins, *Daniel,* p. 163, note 105.

71. Eduard Meyer, *Ursprung und Anfänge des Christenthums 1–2* (Stuttgart and Berlin: J. G. Cotta, 1923–1925), 2:189ff.; Montgomery, *Daniel,* p. 188; Collins, *Daniel,* p. 163, n. 110.

72. David Flusser, "The Four Empires in the Fourth Sibyl and in the Book of Daniel," *IOS* 2 (1972), p. 166.

73. "The trunk of a tree, which thou sawest, is the material existence, which I, Aûhzmazd, created. The four branches are the four periods which will come. That of gold is that when I and thou will hold a conference of religion, King Vištāsp shall accept the religion ..., that of silver is the reign of the king Artakhšīr the Kae. And that of steel is the reign of Khasrūy (Chosroe), son of Kawāt, of immortal soul. And that iron-mixed is the evil

especially since the fourfold division is applied to both kingdoms and metals.[74]

The scheme of four kingdoms is also found in Hellenistic and Roman sources. In a passage of Aemilius Sura, preserved by Velleius Patercilius (I, 6, 6), we find the kingdoms of Assyria, Media, Persia, and Macedonia, all of which were succeeded by Rome. The same four ancient kingdoms figure in the fourth Sibylline Oracle. That text divides world history into ten generations–six under the dominion of Assyria, two of Media, one of Persia, and one of Macedonia–again succeeded by Rome.[75] Swain says that the scheme, which derives from Persia, was originally tripartite, and the fourth kingdom was added only after the conquests of Alexander. He believes that the peoples of Asia brandished the scheme as propaganda in their struggles against Greece.[76] According to this hypothesis, the Jews received the scheme from the eastern lands, but replaced Assyria with Babylonia and substituted the kingdom of God for the perfect fifth monarchy. Nevertheless, nothing in the sources cited by Swain even hints at Asian hopes for a fifth kingdom. The fifth monarchy as the kingdom of God is the invention of the author of the Book of Daniel, who "Judaized" a concept that was alien to the spirit of Israel.[77]

The statue's golden head symbolizes the kingdom of Babylonia, over which Nebuchadnezzar reigns. In chapter 2 Daniel does not name the three kingdoms that will follow it and rule the world one after another, but most scholars believe that the four kingdoms of chapter 2 are the same as those in chapter 7–Babylonia, Media, Persia, and Greece.[78] In Daniel's last vision, which deals

---

sovereignty of the divs (wicked spirits), having disheveled hair, the seed of Aēsham, when thy tenth century will be at an end, O Spitāmān Zaratūhst" (ibid.).

74. There is a clear parallel between the mixed iron in the Persian text and the iron mixed with clay in Daniel. On the other hand, the Persian source has steel where both Daniel and Hesiod have bronze. It may be that the author of Daniel knew both the Hesiodic and the Persian schemes. According to Flusser, there is a slim possibility that he knew Hesiod directly from Greek sources, but it seems more likely that he knew him through the mediation of Oriental texts. The bottom line, he says, is that the author of the Book of Daniel found both schemes in Persian sources and merged them into one (ibid., p. 167).

75. Ibid., pp. 150ff., 159, n. 23.

76. J. W. Swain, "The Theory of the Four Monarchies: Opposition History under the Roman Empire," *CP* 35 (1940), pp. 1–21. Many scholars have accepted Swain's opinion, including: W. Baumgartner, "Zu den vier Reichen von Daniel 2," *THZ* 1 (1945), pp. 17–22; Harold L. Ginsberg, *Studies in Daniel* (New York: Jewish Theological Seminary of America, 1948), p. 5; Samuel K. Eddy, *The King is Dead: Studies in the Near Eastern Resistance to Hellenism,* 334–331 B.C. (Lincoln: University of Nebraska Press, 1961), p. 16; Flusser, "The Four Empires," p. 153.

77. Benjamin Uffenheimer, *The Vision of Zechariah* (Jerusalem: Kiryat Sefer, 1961), p. 170 (Hebrew).

78. Kaufmann, however, believes that the kingdoms in chapter 2 should be understood

with the Hellenistic kingdoms, there is an allusion to Rome as the successor to the wicked Greek empire.[79]

The view of Media and Persia as two successive kingdoms that inherited the Babylonian world-dominion one after another must be rejected as ahistorical.[80] Babylonia and Media divided the Assyrian empire between them and held sway simultaneously; Cyrus then conquered Media before he overran Babylonia. Darius is called "the Mede," but he is the king of Media and Persia, as is the Persian Cyrus. Daniel tells Belshazzar, the last Babylonian ruler, that his kingdom will be divided up among Media and Persia (5:28). In the reign of Darius the Mede, the kingdom was run in accordance with the "law of the Medes and Persians" (Dan. 6:9, 13, 16)–a united kingdom. This explains why the author of Daniel has nothing to say about the two intermediate kingdoms. As Uffenheimer explains, "The successive kingdoms are not

---

as four reigns rather than four sequential empires. Accordingly the first three refer to the monarchs of the Chaldean dynasty: Nebuchadnezzar is gold, Evil-Merodach silver, and Belshazzar bronze; the iron mixed with clay represents the united kingdom of Persia and Media, in which two nations shared control. It is difficult to accept this conjecture because it has no basis in the text, except possibly for the identification of Nebuchadnezzar with the golden head (v. 38). It also seems odd that the first three segments represent individual kings, while the fourth one stands for a full dynasty / kingdom. Furthermore, there is no foundation for a view of the kingdom of Persia and Media as an organic continuation of the Chaldean empire. See Y. Kaufmann, *Toldot*, 4, p. 429; A. Rappaport, "The Fourth Kingdom in the Book of Daniel," *Beth Mikra* 22 (1964), p. 15. For a summary of the arguments against understanding the dream in chapter 2 as referring to four kings and not to four kingdoms, see H. H. Rowley, *Darius the Mede and the Four World Empires in the Book of Daniel* (Cardiff: University of Wales Press, 1964), pp. 161–173; Menahem Haran, *The Biblical Collection* (Jerusalem: Magnes Press, 1996), p. 117.

79. "A consul will put an end to his insults" (Dan. 11:18); "ships from Kittim will come against him" (Dan. 11:30) [the Kittim are enumerated among the Greeks in 10:4]. The Apocrypha uses Kittim to mean the Romans. The author of the apocryphal Vision of Ezra explains that "the eagle I saw rising from the sea is the fourth kingdom that appeared in a vision to Daniel. ... But there was not revealed to him what I reveal to you now" (12:11–12). This may be understood as a change in the identification of the four kingdoms. For Daniel, they were Babylonia, Media, Persia, and Greece. In the apocryphal book, however, there is a suggestion that the fourth kingdom is Rome, and Media surrenders its place in the list. See also Josephus, *Antiquities* 10.10.4 and 209, who says that the Third Kingdom comes from the west and consequently should be identified with Greece; hence the fourth is Rome.

80. Rowley, *Darius*, pp. 6–8, 144ff. Ginsberg accepts Swain's explanation of the four kingdoms, namely, that the ultimate source for the faulty enumeration of the kingdoms in the Book of Daniel is the Persian formula of three kingdoms: Assyria, Media, and Persia. In the Hellenistic period, a fourth segment was added to the chain–Greece. The Jews, who took over this list, substituted Babylonia, as the annihilator of Judean independence, for Assyria, leaving the order Babylonia, Media, Persia, and Greece. Ginsberg, *Studies in Daniel*, pp. 5ff. See also Kaufmann, *Toldot,* vol. 4, pp. 424–427.

derived from historical experience but constitute an a priori concept inherited from his sources."[81] That is, the author attempted to explain history but identified only the first and fourth kingdoms, because his historical knowledge was vague and contradictory. The idea of four successive kingdoms was a fixed and sacrosanct tradition. Meyer, too, holds that the author of the Book of Daniel knew perfectly well that Media and Persia were the same kingdom, but used the ready-made scheme of the four periods and was unable to adapt it to fit the actual course of history. As a result, he introduced an artificial division of one epoch into two.[82]

Unlike the first three, the fourth kingdom merits a detailed description—just like the fourth beast in chapter 7. This kingdom, which is destructive and harmful (see 7:7 and chapter 8), is Greece. The iron legs symbolize the empire of Alexander, who conquered all the regions that had been under the control of the earlier kingdoms. The description of the legs (v. 41), which are part clay and part iron, represents the fission of the fourth kingdom.[83] According to the commentators, this alludes to the four-part division of Alexander's empire among the Epigonoi. The author of Daniel, however, was interested in the annals of the two successor kingdoms that competed to control Palestine—the northern kingdom of the Seleucids, centered in Syria, and the southern kingdom, the Egypt of the Ptolemies.[84]

Next comes "iron mixed with common clay; that means: they shall intermingle with the offspring of men" (v. 43) Some view this (as well as 11:6 and 17) as an allusion to the marriage alliances between the two royal houses— Antiochus II and Berenice (252 BCE), Ptolemy Epiphanes and Cleopatra, the daughter of Antiochus III (193–192)[85]—which failed to create peace between

---

81. Uffenheimer, *The Vision of Zechariah,* p. 168.

82. Eduard Meyer, *Ursprung,* vol. 2, pp. 189–190.

83. In v. 41, Daniel mentions a new detail ignored previously—the toes. When he describes the dream he mentions the statue's legs only; whereas in his interpretation he refers to " the feet and the toes." At first he mentions that "its feet [were] part iron and part clay (חסף)" (v. 33); whereas in the interpretation he goes into greater detail, referring to both "potter's clay" (חסף די פחר) and "common clay" or "mud" (חסף טינא).

84. The course of the internecine struggles among the Epigonoi and their kingdoms is reflected in the Book of Daniel. In chapter 7 the small horn damages the other ones. In chapter 8, the large horn is shattered and four smaller ones grow to replace it. In chapter 11, there is a reference to the dissolution of his empire after the death of Alexander (11:4), followed by a description of the protracted rivalry between the Ptolemies and Seleucids. Even the author's hopes depend on the outcome of the combat between the King of the North and the King of the South (11:40). See A. Rappaport, "The Fourth Kingdom in the Book of Daniel," p. 13.

85. H. H. Rowley, *Darius the Mede,* pp. 94–95. Ginsberg believes that the text refers only

them. Others believe that "offspring of men" means commoners rather than royal blood, and refers to mass intermarriage among members of different races. This is compatible with the historical facts: Alexander encouraged his soldiers to marry women from the Asian peoples with whom they came in contact.[86]

Unlike the four kingdoms, which are ephemeral, the fifth kingdom will last forever and will never be destroyed. It will be established by the God of Heaven, unlike the four kingdoms founded by earthly monarchs. It will "not be transferred to another people" but "will crush and wipe out" all of them (v. 44). The verse moves from negation—what will not be done to the fifth kingdom—to affirmation—what the fifth kingdom itself will do. Here Daniel does not state who will lead the fifth kingdom, but gives this information in his later vision (7:13–14). The stone that symbolizes the fifth kingdom is "the kingdom of Heaven" in Israel.[87] Sa'adia Gaon explains that the Kingdom of Israel is compared to a stone because of its "strength and force." The midrash expounds the passage as follows:

> What did he see? The King Messiah, as Daniel says: "A stone was hewn out, not by hands." R. Simeon ben Levi said: "This was the King Messiah." "And struck the statue": [and struck] every kingdom that worships idols. By what merit does he compare the King Messiah to a stone? By the merits of the Torah, because Israelites exhaust themselves studying and observing it, as it is said: "stone tablets" (Ex. 31:18). Another thing: By the merit of Jacob, about whom it is written "There, the Shepherd, the Rock of Israel" (Gen. 49:24). [Midrash Tanḥuma, *Terumah* 7]

Nebuchadnezzar's second dream is related in 4:7–15. It centers on a tree whose "top reached heaven" (cf. Jacob's dream in Bethel, "Its top reached heaven" [Gen. 28:12]), and its foliage extended to the ends of the earth.[88]

---

to the marriage of Antiochus II and Berenice (Ginsberg, *Studies in Daniel*, pp. 8–9); Hartman and Di Lella hold that it is not clear which marriage the text has in mind, or perhaps both of them (Hartman and Di Lella, *The Book of Daniel*, p. 149).

86. Montgomery, *Daniel*, p. 190.

87. St. Jerome takes the rock as Christ and the phrase "hewn out, not by hands" as a reference to the virgin birth. The New Testament writers frequently apply the image of a stone to Christ. See, for example, Mark 12:10–11, Matt. 21:42; Luke 20:17; 1 Peter 2:7 (alluding to Ps. 118:22 and Romans 9:33); 1 Peter 2:6 and 8 (alluding to Isa. 8:14 and 28:16). See Collins, *Daniel*, p. 171.

88. וחזותה לסוף כל ארעא Some render this as "it was visible [lit., 'its image (reached)'] to the ends of the earth," deriving from the root ח.ז.ה 'see' (e.g., Ps. 48:3). It makes more sense, however, to understand this noun here, as well as חזות (8:5 and 8), as meaning "branch" (סבך).

"Beneath it the beasts of the field found shade, and the birds of the sky dwelt on its branches; all creatures fed on it" (Dan. 4:9).[89] The tree symbolizes a king who has universal dominion; it represents the scope of his rule and the fact that he is the source of livelihood for all his subjects.[90] The beginning of verse 10 repeats the start of verse 7—"in the vision of my mind in bed." According to the nineteenth-century commentator Meir Leibush ben Yeḥiel Mikhel (the Malbim), this indicates that Nebuchadnezzar is starting to recount a *second* vision; i.e., the dream of the tree actually comprises two different visions: first, the vision of the great tree, with the animals and birds resting in its shade and on its branches (vv. 7–9), and then a separate vision of its being cut down, on instruction of the angel, and the replacement of its heart by that of a beast (vv. 10–14).

In other words, here is the dramatic turning point in the dream, at which the existing tree is destroyed. First there is a "holy Watcher coming down from heaven" (v. 10).[91] Then the watcher calls loudly to cut down the tree.

The roots ס.ב.כ and ח.ז.ה (as a by-form of 'hold') are used as parallel synonyms in Job 8:17: "His roots are twined (יסבכו) around a heap; they take hold (יחזה) of a house of stones."

89. Here תטלל is understood as "shade," relying on the many interchanges of *ṣade* in Hebrew and *ṭeṭ* in Aramaic. In Ezekiel we find a similar image: "All the beasts of the field bore their young under its boughs, and in its shadow lived all the great nations" (Ezek. 31:6). The sense of shadow also occurs in Neh. 13:19. On the other hand, the root צ.ל.ל also has the signification "sink," as in "they sank like lead in the majestic waters" (Ex. 15:10).

90. Cf. Ezek. 31:2–18.

91. והנה עיר וקדוש מן השמים יורד: Scholars have vacillated as to the meaning of the word עיר, which appears here and in v. 20 in the singular and in v. 14 in the plural form עירין. It seems to be derived from the root עור and mean "angel." This gloss suits the text, since עיר and קדוש can then be understood as a hendiadys. The use of עיר for "angel" is common in the apocalyptic literature, such as Enoch (1:5, 12:3, 14:10, etc.), as well as in Jubilees (4:22 and 7:21). Many medieval commentators followed the same path—including Abraham Ibn Ezra, Rashi, and David Kimḥi, who derived עיר from the root ע.ו.ר 'awake'; in other words, an angel is vigilant and never sleeps, as we read in Psalms: "The guardian of Israel neither slumbers nor sleeps (Ps. 121:4). The aggadists expounded the latter verse with reference to our passage: "Is there sleep above?! Heaven forbid, there is neither sleep nor sitting above. As the text has it, 'In the vision of my mind in bed, I looked and saw a holy Watcher coming down from heaven' (Dan. 4:10); and it is written 'This sentence is decreed by the Watchers' (ibid., 14). Whence we learn that there is no sleep in heaven." From this we may infer that an angel is a watcher at the gate and does not sleep. This idea is supported by Isaiah 62:6—"Upon your walls, O Jerusalem, I have set watchmen, who shall never be silent by day or by night"—and by the many "eyes" of the cherubs of the celestial chariot (Ezek. 1:18) Similarly, Zechariah refers to "the eyes of the Lord, ranging over the whole earth" (Zech. 4:10). The idea that angels do not sleep is also found in 1 Enoch 39:12. The term צופה 'watcher' is common in the apocryphal books: 2 Enoch 7:8; Jubilees 4:15; 1 Enoch 1:5 and 20:1; Testament of Reuben 5:7; Testament of Naftali 3:5.

This instruction is phrased in the imperative and is almost certainly addressed to the angels (cf. Isa. 40:1).[92] Here we have a transition from metaphor to reality.[93] From this point on, the text refers not to the tree (the vehicle) but to Nebuchadnezzar (the tenor), who will be bound in chains of iron and bronze and treated like a beast of the field. The irony is that Nebuchadnezzar, who imagined himself a superman, turns into a beast.[94] "He will be drenched with dew, and for seven years his human heart will be replaced by that of a beast."[95] In other words, given the biblical notion of the heart as the seat of intelligence, he will lose his wits. Sa'adia Gaon disputes the aggadic view that Nebuchadnezzar actually metamorphosed into an animal: "The truth is that his human form was unaltered; rather, his mind and perception were changed, as happened to Saul—'an evil spirit from the Lord began to terrify him' (1 Sam. 16:14); but nothing of his external appearance was changed."

Daniel was no less appalled than Nebuchadnezzar by the content of the dream. In his response, he repeats what Nebuchadnezzar said in verses 7–9, modifying it only slightly (for reasons of brevity, perhaps, or because it is the way of the Bible to vary phrasing and word order in such cases). The king will be expelled from human society, live with the beasts of the field, and eat grass. After Daniel proclaims this decree, he offers Nebuchadnezzar some advice—which makes the Talmudic sages wonder. "Is it conceivable that the righteous Daniel would offer such advice to Nebuchadnezzar the enemy of the Almighty?" (Tanḥuma ad loc.; also Exodus Rabba in slightly different form). The midrash replies: "Because he saw Israel as refugees in exile, dragged hither and thither and dying of hunger, he offered this advice out of mercy for them" (Tanḥuma and Exodus Rabba). Daniel counsels the king that, despite the evil decree issued against him, it is still possible to annul it by means

---

92. Hartman and Di Lella, *The Book of Daniel,* p. 172; Montgomery, *Daniel,* p. 195.

93. Hartman and Di Lella, p. 176.

94. ועם חיותא חלקה בעשב ארעא—that is, his lot is in the grass [i.e., fields], along with the beasts. Some (Sa'adia Gaon and the thirteenth-century R. Samuel ben Nissim Masnut) understand חלקה as referring to his food, that is, his food will be like that of animals, namely, grass. חלק is found in Aramaic with the sense of "portion" (as in "it is your portion and that of your children" [Lev. 10:13], which the Aramaic versions render as (חולקך וחולק בנך). See also the Aramaic Targum on Gen. 47:22.

95. Seven seasons (זמנים) will pass. The Aramaic word here is (עדנין), which means "times," "periods," or "seasons" (Dan. 2:8–12; 3:5–15; 7:12). But in this chapter (vv. 13, 20, 22, and 29, as well as in 7:25) it has, like the Hebrew מועד, the sense of "year": thus Rashi, Ibn Ezra, the Septuagint, and Josephus (*Antiquities* 10,10,6). Ginsberg sees this a Greek-based calque: in the classical period *chronos* meant both "time" and "year" (Ginsberg, *Studies in Daniel,* pp. 1–2).

of צדקה, which here has the meaning of beneficence or generosity.[96] The idea of giving charity to the poor appears in the midrash:

> He began saying to Daniel, "What do you advise me?"
>
> He said to him, "These poor people whom you have exiled from their country are hungry and thirsty and naked. Open your treasure-house to them and support them. Perhaps the dream will be alleviated, as it says—"May my advice be acceptable to you: Redeem your sins by beneficence and your iniquities by generosity to the poor; then your serenity may be extended." [Tanḥuma *Mishpatim* 4]

According to the rabbis, Daniel was punished for this action, despite his good intentions, and later lost his eminent position (BT Baba Batra 4a), as is shown by the episode of the lions' den.[97]

Daniel's interpretation indeed comes to pass. Verses 29–30 describe Nebuchadnezzar's expulsion from the company of civilized men, recapitulating verses 12–13, with the added detail that "his hair grew like eagle's [feathers] and his nails like [the talons of] birds." As Targum Yerushalmi explains, "He thought he was one of the forest beasts and consequently lived with them and did as they did; because of the length of time and surfeit of the black bile, he came to resemble them in his hairiness and long fingernails. And this is undoubtedly something wondrous." Don Isaac Abravanel, too, rejects the argument that Nebuchadnezzar actually turned into an ox:

> All this is foolishness and illusion. Nebuchadnezzar never turned into an ox. ... In miraculous fashion, ... though, ... the black bile came to dominate him, ... and he was revolted by human beings and ran away from them to live in the wilderness ... until his appearance and form were dimmed and his hair and nails grew very long and he ate grass like animals, because this is what those who live in the wilderness eat.... So too his mind was altered ... and he followed his appetites without concern for his intellect.[98]

As for extrabiblical sources, some cite a parallel in the story of the Babylonian

---

96. Here צדק does not have the standard meaning of צדק in the Bible but is related to the rabbinic צדקה 'charity'. On charity to the poor, see Tobit 4:7–11 and 12:8f; Ben Sira 3:29–4:10 and 29:8–13.

97. Some, on the basis of this midrash, associate ארכה with ארוכה 'healing' (as in Jer. 8:22). But it seems better to understand it, with Rashi, as referring to extension in time. Evidently there is an echo of the beginning of the chapter—"I, Nebuchadnezzar, was living *serenely* in my house"; Daniel's counsel was aimed at preserving this serenity.

98. *Ma'ayenei ha-yeshu'ah*, end of 5,5.

Job: "Like a she-*nâkim* or a *šûqû*-demon, he made my fingernails grow."[99] A similar description is also found in the tale of Ahiqar: "My nails were grown long like eagles'."[100] Some point to a parallel in the *Bacchae* of Euripides: Like Nebuchadnezzar, the Bacchae behave like animals; not only do they wear animal skins, they also suckle young fawns and wolf cubs.[101]

A parallel to Nebuchadnezzar's fate can be found in an Aramaic text from Qumran that deals with the prayer of Nabonidus (4QPrNab), the last king of Babylonia.[102] According to this document, Nabonidus spent seven years in Teima, afflicted by boils, as punishment for worshipping idols of silver and gold, wood and stone, believing them to be gods. He was cured, however, by a Jewish sage who worshipped the Almighty. The similarity in details between chapter 4 of Daniel and the Nabonidus prayer indicates that they are based on the same tradition. Nabonidus's abandonment of Babylon and protracted residence in Teima are a historical fact known from various Akkadian sources.[103] Evidently the author of the Book of Daniel replaced Nabonidus

---

99. Montgomery, *Daniel,* p. 244.

100. Ibid.

101. Norman W. Porteous, *Daniel* (Philadelphia: Westminster Press, 1965), p. 73; Montgomery, *The Book of Daniel,* p. 245.

102. D. N. Freedman, "The Prayer of Nabonidus," *BASOR* 145 (1957), pp. 31–32; L. F. Hartman, "The Great Tree and Nebuchadnezzar's Madness," in *The Bible in Current Catholic Thought,* ed. J. L. Mckenzie (New York: Herder, 1962), pp. 75–82; M. McNamara, "Nabonidus and the Book of Daniel," *ITQ* 37 (1970), pp. 131–149; J. T. Milik, "'Prière de Nabonide' et autres écrits d'un cycle de Daniel," *RB* 63 (1956), pp. 407–415; F. M. Cross, "Fragments of the Prayer of Nabonidus," *IEJ* 34 (1984), pp. 260–264; K. Beyer, *Die aramäischen Texte vom Toten Meer* (Göttingen: Vandenhoeck & Ruprecht, 1984), pp. 223–225; R. H. Eisenman and M. Wise, *The Dead Sea Scrolls Uncovered* (Rockport, MA: Element, 1992), pp. 66–73.

103. During his reign, Nabonidus spent a long period in the oasis of Teima. Because of his absence from the capital he could not perform the religious functions that were the responsibility of the king. Evidently his preference for the privacy of the oasis led to the rumors that he was seriously ill. See Hartman and Di Lella, *The Book of Daniel,* p. 178; "Babylonian and Assyrian Historical Texts," trans. A. Leo Oppenheim, *ANET,* pp. 312–315; C. J. Gadd, "The Harran Inscriptions of Nabonidus," *AnSt* 8 (1958), p. 88; Weisberg proposed that Nabonidus' actions were driven solely by political gain. According to him: " Nabonidus' actions in Teima are related to his position at Harran and Ur. His presence there was for a military purpose: to bypass the party of Babylonians who were against him and thereby minimize their clout, and then to outflank the Persians. The three cities Teima, Harran and Ur form a triangle which enabled Nabonidus to control the entire Babylonian empire and to extend its reach." See: David B. Weisberg, "Polytheism and Politics: Some Comments on Nabonidus' Foreign Policy," in *Crossing Boundaries and Linking Horizons. Studies in Honor of Michael C. Astour,* edited by Gordon D. Young, Mark W. Chavalas, and Richard E. Averbeck (Bethesda, Maryland: CDL Press, 1977), p. 555.

with Nebuchadnezzar, perhaps because the latter was more familiar to his contemporaries.[104]

Rudolf Meyer also notes that these texts, which both use the first person, derive from the confessions of Nabonidus, similar to what was found in inscriptions from Haran.[105] There is nothing in either the text from Qumran or the Nabonidus inscriptions to contrast the success or failure of the dream interpreters. This is found only in Daniel 4; hence we may see this element as meant to highlight the superiority and wisdom of Daniel over the Chaldean sages as well as the superiority of his God. That superiority is expressed at the end of the story when, after seven years, Nebuchadnezzar lifts his eyes to the heavens, toward the source of the voice; his reason is restored to him and he recites a psalm of thanksgiving. He expresses his wonder at the workings of the Creator and acknowledges the greatness of the Lord, whose sanctuary in Jerusalem he destroyed. Perhaps it is to this that Malachi was alluding: "For from where the sun rises to where it sets, My name is honored among the nations" (Mal. 1:11).

REACTION TO THE SYMBOLIC DREAM

In chapter 1 we discussed the dreamers' reactions to prophetic dreams. Here we shall consider how dreamers and listeners respond to symbolic dreams. As noted earlier, the Bible acknowledges that there are vain and meaningless dreams. The question, then, is: How can dreamers and listeners distinguish between those ordinary dreams that simply reflect one's private thoughts and emotions and those significant symbolic messages from God where the deity nevertheless does not appear?

The Bible does not report how Joseph reacted to his dreams; instead, we are told about the responses of his brothers and father. After the first dream, his brothers answered, "'Do you mean to reign (המלוך תמלוך) over us? Do you mean to rule (אם משול תמשול) over us?' And they hated him even more[106] for his talk about his dreams" (Gen. 37:8).[107] Here the motif of enmity returns for

---

104. It should be noted that aside from the reference to Nebuchadnezzar in chapter 1, which is anchored in a historical event, his character in the rest of the Book of Daniel has a distinctly legendary nature.

105. Rudolf Meyer, *Das Gebet des Nabonid* (Berlin: Akademie-Verlag, 1962), pp. 53–67.

106. ויוספו עוד שׂנא אותו (lit. "they continued to hate him): There may be a play on words here between ויוספו and יוסף (Joseph).

107. "His dreams"—even though we have so far been told about only one dream! The plural is surprising. For this reason David Kimḥi and S. D. Luzzatto believe that this is either

the third time (after vv. 4–5).[108] Ibn Ezra paraphrases the brothers' reaction in verse 8 as, "Will we make you king over us ['reign'] or will you dominate us ['rule'] by force?" Nachmanides, relying on Onkelos' Aramaic rendering, glosses it as, "Will you be king (מלך) over us or a governor (מושל) ruling us–for people bow down to both of them. You will never be king or governor over us"–that is, *king* and *ruler* are essentially synonymous because people must prostrate themselves before both. Although the brothers understood the dream to prophesy arrogance and control, nevertheless, at first they dismissed it as mere braggadocio.

Joseph also recounted his second dream to his father and brothers. According to Rashi, "After he told it to his brothers, he repeated it to his father in their presence."[109] Both times the brothers held their tongues, but their silence did not bode well. Jacob's response, by contrast, was fierce; he rebuked his son for–according to Rashi–needlessly provoking his brothers' hatred.[110] Jacob was trying to defuse the brothers' fury. Rashi continues:

> "Are we to come"–isn't your mother already dead? But [Jacob] did not know that this referred to Bilha, who had raised [Joseph] like a mother. From this our rabbis learned that there are no dreams without spurious elements; but Jacob was trying to get the brothers to dismiss the matter so that they would not envy him. This is why he said "Are we to come": just as there is no truth with regard to your mother, so it is all false.

In his rebuke, Jacob adds the words "bow low to you to the ground"–words not spoken by Joseph.[111] This prefigures future events, when all the brothers come to Egypt and bow down to Joseph (42:6, 43:26, 44:14). The brothers did not interpret the second dream, but Jacob did. Perhaps they were afraid to do so, or did not dare express its meaning in words. The fact that the dream

---

anticipation of another dream or an allusion to another dream that Joseph told his brothers but that was left out of our narrative.

108. The brothers hated Joseph even before he told them his dreams, for three reasons: (1) Jacob loved Joseph more than his brothers. (2) Joseph brought bad reports of their behavior to Jacob (v. 2). (3) Their father had given him a special coat–of the sort that princes were accustomed to wearing; Joseph's brothers saw it as a sign of their father's favoritism for him.

109. The Masoretic text of verse 10 is "he told it to his father and to his brothers," but "and to his brothers" is not found in the Septuagint, possibly because v. 9 already states that he had recounted the dream to his brothers.

110. A. A. Macintosh, "A Consideration of Hebrew gʻr," *VT* (1969), pp. 471–479, especially p. 474.

111. The extra words are an echo and reminder that Jacob prostrated himself before his brother Esau (Gen. 33:3).

was repeated terrified the brothers. Perhaps, as S. D. Luzzatto asserts, "They thought this was the meaning of the dream and believed it would come true in some fashion or other, since their father loved him more than his other sons and might appoint him to govern them."

After Jacob's rebuke, the narrator adds, "His brothers were jealous of him, and his father kept the matter in mind." This represents a new stage in the plot. Initially the brothers hated Joseph; but when, after the dream's repetition, they started to believe that their younger brother might indeed attain lofty office, their hatred was sharpened by envy—to the extent that they were ready to kill him. The irony, of course, is that with these murderous thoughts they sold him into slavery in order to keep his dreams from being realized. But it was precisely the sale that led to their fulfillment. Jacob, too, seems to have given credence to the dream; the fact that he "kept the matter in mind" suggests that he believed it would come true in the future; as Rashi glosses the phrase, he waited to see when it would come to pass.

In the dreams of the butler and baker, in contrast, we are told how the dreamers themselves reacted: "When Joseph came to them in the morning, he saw that they were distraught" (Gen. 40:6). Their faces gave them away, which is why Joseph asked, "Why do you appear downcast today?" (v. 7).[112] The ancient Egyptians believed that "sleep puts us in real and direct contact with the other world, where not only the dead but also the gods dwell. Dreams thus are a gift from the gods."[113] The theory and practice of oneirocriticism were considered to be a science in ancient Egypt. A particular dream might have various solutions, so only an adept in oneirocritical theory could interpret it, and an uninterpreted dream was considered to be a curse. The butler and baker, languishing in prison, did not have access to practitioners of this art, and their inability to understand the labyrinth of their dreams depressed and frustrated them.

Nachmanides understands the sequence of events differently, however: "They may have sent [a message] to some of the magicians in the morning or that there were other people with them in prison, but none of them could interpret it. Or perhaps they said, 'There is no one in the world who can interpret it truthfully because it is most arcane.'"

The same psychological reaction greets Pharaoh's dreams and Nebuchadnezzar's first dream. "Next morning, his spirit was agitated (ותפעם רוחו)" (Gen.

---

112. Lit. "Why are your faces bad?" For a Ugaritic parallel to this biblical idiom, see D. W. Young, "The Ugaritic Myth of the God Hōrān and the Mare," *UF* 11 (1979), p. 846. Young, however, read "Hōrān's face is loathsome" rather than " Hōrān looked sad."

113. Vergote, *Joseph en Égypte,* p. 48.

41:8); "In the second year of the reign of Nebuchadnezzar, Nebuchadnezzar had a dream; his spirit was agitated (וַתִּתְפָּעֶם רוּחוֹ), yet he was overcome by sleep." (Daniel 2:1).[114] This "agitation of the spirit" denotes excitement and terror. In Genesis, the Aramaic translators rendered it as ומטרפא רוחיה 'His spirit was confused *or* troubled.' Rashi added the gloss that his spirit "rang within him like a bell (פַּעֲמוֹן)"–in other words, he was in turmoil. Rashi also comments on the difference between the *niph'al* form in Genesis and the *hitpa'el* in Daniel: in the later case, he notes, "There were two blows, that he had forgotten the dream and that he did not know what it meant." We find the same idea in the Midrash Tanḥuma: "Pharaoh, who knew the dream but not its meaning, was troubled once. Nebuchadnezzar, who had forgotten both the dream and its meaning, had two troubles" (Tanḥuma *Miqqeṣ* 2). Pharaoh evidently rolled over and went back to sleep; but as for Nebuchadnezzar, "His sleep was interrupted" (v. 1).[115]

Thus Pharaoh and Nebuchadnezzar, both of whom had dreams they could not interpret, were overwrought and frightened.[116] Although Nebuchadnezzar's remarks to the magicians, exorcists, sorcerers, and Chaldeans (Dan. 2:3) indicate that he was bothered not only by the fact that he did not know the meaning of his dream, but also by the fact that he could not remember its content, Sa'adia Gaon tries to demonstrate that Nebuchadnezzar has not really forgotten his dream but merely wished to test the reliability of his wise men.[117] "For if he had forgotten [the dream], he would not have relied on their description of any particular dream and would have doubted it. They might have said something true and he would not know they were right." For Sa'adia, "knowing" the dream ("If you do not make the dream known to me" [v. 9]) means knowing its meaning.

In a similar context, the Talmud enumerates various actions that the sages recommended for those who had had unsettling dreams. One of these is

---

114. The basic signification of the root פ.ע.מ is "strike." See: Isa. 41:7, where it refers to a hammer blow, Judg. 5:28, the sound made by moving chariots; and Isa. 26:6, the sound made by marching men.

115. Most commentators agree that this is the meaning of ושנתו נהיתה עליו. Cf. Esther 6:1: "That night, sleep deserted the king." (Esther 6:1).

116. For a similar sense, see Ps. 77:5.

117. A similar idea is advanced by Flusser, who cites the account in Herodotus (1, 47) of the trial that Croesus king of Lydia (sixth century BCE) made of the Delphic and other oracles. Before he asked his important question, he sent them messengers to inquire, "What is the king of Lydia doing today?" According to Flusser, the author of the Book of Daniel did not understand that the king was really testing his councillors and accordingly altered the sense here. See Flusser, "The Four Empires," p. 156; Aage Bentzen, *Daniel* (Tübingen: Mohr, 1952), p. 23.

prayer. The dreamer should stand in the synagogue while the priests are pronouncing the Priestly Benediction and say as follows:

> Master of the World, I am Yours and my dreams are Yours. I have dreamt a dream and I do not know what it means. Whether I have dreamt for myself, or whether my friends have dreamt about me, or whether I have dreamt about others, if they are good, strengthen and reinforce them like the dreams of Joseph; if they require healing, heal them like the waters of Marah by Moses, like Miriam of her leprosy, like Hezekiah of his disease, and like the waters of Jericho by Elisha; and just as you turned the curse of the wicked Balaam into a blessing, so too turn all of my dreams to good.[118]

Another ritual mentioned by the Talmud is "rectifying a dream":

> Someone who has a dream and becomes depressed should go and rectify it before three men. What should he do? He should summon three men and say to them: "I have a dreamt a good dream." And they should answer him: "Indeed it is good and it will be good. The Lord will make it good; seven times may it be decreed for you from heaven that it be good, and it will be good."

Fasting is another response recommended in the wake of a distressing dream.[119] Because of the severity of the situation, the sages advised fasting on the day after the dream, even on the Sabbath, despite the provision of Jewish law that a public fast (except for the Day of Atonement) that falls on the Sabbath is deferred to the next day. On account of the sanctity of the Sabbath, Jews are commanded to spend the day in activities that are tranquil and pleasant; but if one is anxious and in a state of inner turmoil on account of a dream, he is permitted to fast on the Sabbath. However, because this Sabbath fast is a transgression of sorts, the person must later make amends by fasting *again* on a weekday.[120]

Another significant reaction, found in the stories of both Joseph and Daniel, is the monarch's generosity in rewarding the successful oneirocritic. After Pharaoh hears Joseph's interpretation of the dream and accepts his sage counsel, he appoints Joseph his viceroy: "He placed him over all the land of Egypt. Pharaoh said to Joseph, 'I am Pharaoh; yet without you, no one shall lift up hand or foot in all the land of Egypt'" (Gen. 41:43–44). Westermann notes

---

118. BT Berakhot 55b.
119. BT Sabbath 11a.
120. BT Berakhot 31b.

that Joseph's elevation by Pharaoh "is an event we can visualize in all details as very few others in the Bible. Every detail of the ceremony has been passed down to us in Egyptian representations, even down to the almost transparent linen garments. We can view the rings, the golden chains, and the war chariots in the museums."[121]

Nebuchadnezzar, too, remembers his promise to whomever interpreted his dream (v. 6) and names Daniel governor of Babylonia and prefect of all the wise men of the kingdom (Dan. 2:48). But Nebuchadnezzar displays another reaction, too: When he hears his dream interpreted he recognizes the primacy of the God of Israel, prostrates himself before Daniel, and ordains that an offering be set before him (vv. 46–47). As in the other stories in chapters 1–6, the Gentile ruler, initially presumptuous and self-confident to the point of challenging God, modifies his attitude and confesses his error. It is noteworthy that Nebuchadnezzar prostrates himself before Daniel–doing him divine homage, according to some. Abraham Ibn Ezra, for instance, says that "Nebuchadnezzar thought that Daniel was a god and wished to worship him." In the Malbim's reading, Nebuchadnezzar "suspected that there was a god within him, in the way of the ancients who used to impute divinity to everyone whom they saw as surpassing the natural course of nature." On the other hand, Sa'adia Gaon noted that there is no Torah prohibition against bowing down to human beings in a show of honor or respect. The Talmudic sages said that Daniel opposed Nebuchadnezzar's desire to offer sacrifices before him: "Daniel did not accept [the homage]; why? Just as idolators are punished, so too is the object of their devotion" (Genesis Rabba 96, 3).

Nebuchadnezzar's second dream, too, provokes a psychological response (Daniel 4:2). The author describes the king's trepidation in the wake of that dream. He is panic-stricken because it has a personal significance. His terror is expressed as "fright" and "alarm"–words that express a continuing state. The stark contrast between verses 1 and 2–the former describing Nebuchadnezzar as serene and flourishing, the latter as terrified in the wake of his dream–highlights the difference between the king's mental state before and after his dream.[122]

Just as the dream itself frightened Nebuchadnezzar, so its relation terrifies

---

121. Westermann, *Genesis 37–50,* p. 97.

122. Commentators have long tried to draw distinctions between the חֲלֶם 'dream', הרהרין 'thoughts', and חזוי ראשי 'visions of my head' of 4:2. Abraham Ibn Ezra glossed הרהרין as "mental musings" and חזוי ראשי as "images seen as if by the eyes," "because the eyes are in the head or because sight is in the brain." According to *Meṣudat David,* "הרהרין refers to my thoughts while I was sleeping on my bed–that is, the dream that is derived from one's thoughts; while the 'visions of my head' alarmed me, and this too designates a dream that

Daniel, as he discerns the meaning of the vision. Daniel is perplexed for an hour.[123] That is, Daniel was confused and upset by the dream and the fact that he had to tell the king what it meant. The roots used to express Daniel's reaction, ש.מ.מ. and ב.ה.ל, are often used as paired synonyms in the Bible: "The king shall mourn, the prince shall clothe himself with desolation (שְׁמָמָה), and the hands of the people of the land shall tremble (תִּבָּהַלְנָה)" (Ezek. 7:27). Daniel's hesitation about complying with the king's demand to interpret his dream is a clear indication that he views the dream as a sign from Heaven to Nebuchadnezzar and accordingly fears to interpret it for the king, who nevertheless tries to calm him.

Both Joseph and Daniel have no doubt that the monarchs' dreams come from God. "God has told Pharaoh what He is about to do" (Gen. 41:25); "God has revealed to Pharaoh what He is about to do" (Gen. 41:28); "But there is a God in heaven who reveals mysteries, and He has made known to King Nebuchadnezzar what is to be at the end of days. This is your dream and the vision that entered your mind in bed:" (Dan. 2:28; cf. also Dan. 2:45 and 4:21ff.). Thus the Bible acknowledges that the dreams of Pharaoh and Nebuchadnezzar are messages vouchsafed by God to the pagan kings. Neither Joseph nor Daniel interprets the dreams by virtue of their own abilities; instead, they merely give voice to the meaning that God has made known to them (Gen. 40:8, 41:16, 38–39; Dan. 2:17ff., 4:5, 6, 15).

In sum, the jealousy evinced by Joseph's brothers, the fear displayed by the Egyptian ministers and the two kings who could not decipher the message, and the honors and gifts showered on Joseph and Daniel after they interpret the monarchs' dreams all demonstrate that both dreamers and listeners considered both the symbolic dreams and their interpretations as heaven-sent messages foreshadowing the future.

And even though one might initially conjecture that dreams are spawned by the thoughts and passions of the dreamer himself, the symbolic visions are in fact riddles in which the Lord sometimes speaks (Num. 12:8). Most importantly, the Bible emphasizes that the finger of God draws the dreams and that He directs the one who analyzes them. This notion is encapsulated in Joseph's comments when he interprets the dreams of the ministers and of Pharaoh. Joseph repeatedly declares that he cannot interpret the dreams through his own wisdom; it is God who makes their meaning known to him (Gen. 40:8,

---

is seen in the brain, which is in the head. And he repeated the idea two and three times as a rhetorical device to reinforce and amplify the matter."

123. Rather than "perplexed," Rashi and St. Jerome both understand אשתומם to mean "was silent"; pseudo-Sa'adia renders it as "was silent and mute for an hour."

41:16, 38–39). The same applies to Daniel; the text of his book emphasizes that God revealed to him the content and meaning of Nebuchadnezzar's dream (Dan. 2:17) and that it is only through the spirit of God that is in him that he can interpret the king's dream (4:5–6, 15). For biblical authors, then, symbolic dreams come from the Lord, who causes dreams to be dreamt and interpreters to decipher their meaning.

Now that we have dealt with symbolic dreams that cannot be interpreted without the assistance of an expert, the next stage is to consider the actual interpretation of dreams, investigating the oneirocritics of ancient times, dream books, and the interpretation of dreams in the Bible and Talmud.

3

The Interpretation of Dreams

The interpretation of dreams has always been influenced by the prevalent theory about their sources. Because in antiquity it was assumed that dreams were divinely inspired and contained messages about the future, human beings took great pains to understand and interpret them. For that reason, it is not surprising that there were professional dream interpreters in the ancient Near East. Indeed, guidebooks for interpreting dreams are extant from both Egypt and Mesopotamia, complete with instructions and keys for interpretation. Clay tablets from Mesopotamia, most of them from the famous library of the Assyrian King Assurbanipal, discovered in Nineveh, present a collection of various signs and phenomena according to which the symbols and allusions could be deciphered and the dreamer's future could be predicted.

The methods used varied. Some relied on formal visual resemblance to the conditions or concepts they represented. Others marked the similarities to reality in sound or written form of dream elements. From Egypt, we have a portion of a hieratic papyrus (Chester Beatty) from the 12th Dynasty (19th–18th century BCE), published by A. Gardiner, as well as a demotic papyrus (Carlsberg) from the second century CE, which has been deciphered by A. Volten. It too lists various themes present in dreams and suggests ways to understand them.

As we have seen, both the Bible and the Talmud refer to dream interpretation. Joseph and Daniel interpreted dreams in the royal court. In Pharoah's Egypt, the court magicians were experts in that area. In Daniel the king calls in the "magicians, exorcists, sorcerers, and Chaldeans." In the Talmud we read about "24 dream-interpreters who lived in Jerusalem." In this chapter, then, we shall focus on those dream interpreters to determine who performed that function in the Bible and among various ancient peoples and what methods were used. In addition, we shall examine some of the extant dream-books from antiquity and determine whether such materials also existed in ancient Israel.

THE ETYMOLOGY OF פ.ת.ר AND ש.ב.ר

The root used to designate dream interpretation in the Joseph stories is פ.ת.ר 'explain, interpret': "And they said to him, 'We had dreams, and there is no one to *interpret* them.'" (Gen. 40:8).[1] The root appears in the Bible exclusively in the context of dream interpretation.[2] In Akkadian we find *pašāru* and פשר in late Hebrew and Aramaic. In the Book of Daniel we read: "Such was the dream, and... its meaning (פשרה) " (2:36 and 4:15). Elsewhere in Daniel, in chapter 5, there is a reference to deciphering a written sign, when King Belshazzar summons the wise men of Babylonia to tell him the meaning of the inscription on the wall: "and tell me its meaning (פשרה) " (5:7). At the end of that chapter, when Daniel comes to decipher the inscription for the king, he tells him that "this is the meaning of it (פשר מלתא)" (5:26).

The biblical idiom used in the Book of Daniel has a parallel in Akkadian, used with regard to the interpretation of texts associated with astrology and omen-reading. The identical Akkadian expression is *kî annî pišŭršu:* "indeed, this is its interpretation."[3] The phrase "interpret a dream" appears in biblical and late Hebrew as פתר חלום, in Aramaic as פשר חלם and Akkadian as *šutta pašāru*. Sperling pointed out that, though the late Hebrew פשר is well attested, it is never used in dream interpretation.[4]

All Hebrew sources, early and late, employ פתר. The similarity of Hebrew פתר and Akkadian *pašāru*, applied to dreams, extends beyond the meaning "interpretation." Oppenheim pointed out that *pašāru* cannot always be translated by the same English word. On the one hand, it may mean "reporting the dream," "interpreting the dream," or "removing the evil effect of a dream by magical means."[5] Note the following passage: "Dispeller of the heat, Lord of signs, possessor of the crown, dispeller of evil, negative and terrifying dreams and evil signs and portents."[6] The same nuance, "dispel," is applied to dreams expressed by the late Hebrew פתר. Note the advice of R. Yohanan:

---

1. *BDB* p. 837.

2. The verb פתר appears nine times in the Bible, all of them in Genesis chapters 40–41 (40:8, 16, 22; 41:8, 12 (twice), 13, 15 (twice). The noun פתרון is found another five times in the Joseph cycle in chapters 40 and 41 (40:5, 8, 12, 18; 41:11).

3. Oppenheim, *Interpretation,* p. 220; R. Thompson, *The Reports of Magicians and Astrologers of Nineveh and Babylon* (London: Luzacs, 1900), nos. 89, 176, and 256A.

4. Shalom David Sperling, "Studies in Late Hebrew Lexicography in Light of Akkadian," Ph.D. dissertation, Columbia University, 1973, p. 67.

5. Oppenheim, *Interpretation,* pp. 217–219.

6. Sperling, "Studies in Late Hebrew Lexicography in Light of Akkadian," pp. 68-69.

"If one sees a dream and is troubled by it, let him proceed to report it and (thus) dispel its evil consequences in the presence of three men."[7]

When we examine the nouns denoting interpretation, we find Hebrew פתרון, Aramaic פשר חלמא, and Akkadian *dīnu*. The Akkadian is different and therefore goes its own way. For the professional dream interpreter the Akkadian employs *šā'ilu(mupašširu)*, while the Hebrew has פותר חלומות and Aramaic has מפשיר. Consequently, Sperling maintains: "פתר is a form native to Hebrew while פשר is borrowed from Aramaic."[8] The late Hebrew פשר is related etymologically therefore to Aramaic פשר as well to Akkadian *pašāru*. However, it must be kept apart from Hebrew פתר. Sperling reached this conclusion based on semantic considerations. The following is his table, which summarizes the various uses of Akkadian *pašāru* and its correspondent in late Hebrew and Aramaic.[9]

	Akkadian	LH	Aramaic
"physical sense"	*pašāru*	pšr	pšr
"dispel anger"	*pašāru*	pšr	šdk
"dispel sorcery"	*pašāru*	bṭl	pšr
"absolve"	*pašāru*	pšr	šr'
"dissolve vow"	*pašāru*	ntr, prr, ptḥ	bṭl
"interpret dream"	*pašāru*	ptr	pšr
"to settle" (legal sphere)	*pašāru*	pšr	pšr

It appears that פתר corresponds semantically to Akkadian *pašāru* and Aramaic פשר–pertaining exclusively to dream interpretation. On the other hand, considering the semantic evidence in light of the etymological difficulties, it is obvious that the single semantic correspondence is fortuitous.

Another root used in the context of dream interpretation is ש.ב.ר, found in the account of the Midianite soldier's dream–"When Gideon heard the dream told and *interpreted*" (Judg. 7:15)–whose primary meaning is "break." The idea that breaking (or "cracking open") a dream is equivalent to interpreting it invites the metaphor of a dream as a sealed vessel that hides what is inside it; only when the vessel is shattered can the dream inside be revealed and understood.

Fishbane refers to a Mesopotamian parallel in which a dream is described

---

7. Ibid, 69; TB Ber., 55b.
8. Sperling, "Studies in Late Hebrew Lexicography in Light of Akkadian," p.91.
9. Ibid, p. 92.

by the priest of Ishtar.[10] When the priest describes the meaning of his epiphany he uses the expression *tabrīt mūši ša Ištar ušabrûšu,* or "the vision that Ishtar had revealed." According to Fishbane, the biblical form שברו is derived from the Akkadian verb *šubrû* 'to show or reveal in a dream or vision.'[11] In the biblical story, the Lord sends Gideon to the Midianite camp, where he overhears the soldier telling his dream to a comrade, who knows how to interpret it. There is a parallel between Gideon's overhearing the meaning of the dream and hearing a voice that predicts the future, a phenomenon known from the ancient east and designated *kledonomancy.*[12]

ANCIENT TERMS FOR DREAM INTERPRETERS

The Bible mentions the magicians and wise men of Egypt as experts summoned by Pharaoh upon waking from his dreams.[13] Scholars originally viewed the Egyptian priestly designation *ḥry-ḥb* as the source of the Hebrew word חרטום,[14] but others concluded later that its source was the form *ḥry-tp.*[15] Today some scholars maintain that the Hebrew word derives from *ḥry-tp ḥry-ḥb,* 'chief lector priest.'[16] Redford, for his part, thinks that the Bible borrowed the word via the demotic *ḥry-tm.*[17] Quaegebeur demurred and showed that the reading of the demotic form *ḥry-tm,* thought to be the late period

---

10. Michael Fishbane, *Biblical Interpretation in Ancient Israel* (Oxford: Clarendon Press, 1985), p. 456, n. 40.

11. Ibid., p. 457.

12. On the בת קול in rabbinic literature, see: D. Sperling, "Akkadian *egerrû* and Hebrew בת קול," *JANESCU* 4 (1972), pp. 63–74; S. Lieberman, *Hellenism in Jewish Palestine,* 2nd edition (New York: Jewish Theological Seminary, 1962), pp. 194–199.

13. On the term חרטום see: H. Kees, "Der sog oberste Vorlesepriester," *ZÄS* 87 (1962), pp. 119–139; K. Sethe, "Miszelle," *ZÄS* 70 (1934), p. 134; J. M. A. Janssen, "Egyptological Remarks on the Story of Joseph in Genesis," *JEOL* 14 (1955–56), 65f.; T. O. Lambdin, "Egyptian Loan Words in the OT," *JAOS* 73 (1953), pp. 145–155; Vergote, *Joseph en Égypte,* pp. 66–73; Yahuda thinks that the word consists of the two Egyptian words: *ḥry* (not *ḥry*) 'he that is upon or over something, chief', and *ḏm (ḏзm')* 'book, papyrus roll'–hence, "he who is over the books, writings," that is, someone who is learned in writings. See A. S. Yahuda, *The Language of the Pentateuch in its Relation to Egyptian* (London, Oxford University Press, 1933), p. 93.

14. James K. Hoffmeier, *Israel in Egypt* (Oxford: Oxford University Press, 1996), p. 88, n. 116.

15. Ibid., p. 88, n. 117.

16. Allan Gardiner, *Ancient Egyptian Onomastica,* p. 56; Jan Quaegebeur, "The Egyptian Equivalent of Ḥarṭummîm," in Sarah Israelit-Groll, ed., *Pharaonic Egypt,* p. 164; Hoffmeier, *Israel in Egypt,* p. 88.

17. Redford, *The Biblical Story of Joseph,* pp. 203–204.

vocalization of *ḥry-tp*, was mistaken. Relying on Ptolemaic- and Roman-era Greek texts from Egypt, Quaegebeur maintained that *tp* became *tb*, not *tm*. In addition, he pointed out that in the 13th century BCE, the vocalization of *tp* was *tb*, which accounts for the *ṭum* in the Hebrew חרטמים.[18] He also disputed Redford's late dating and held that the term might "just as well have been borrowed in earlier times."[19]

From the etymology we can deduce that one function of the חרטם was to deal with religious texts and rituals, and it is safe to assume that they were "experts" in magic and healing. Evidence of this is provided by two stories from the Westcar Papyrus[20] and the figure of Hor in the second demotic narrative of Setna-Ha-em-wese V,3ff.[21] The חרטומים were among those who had access to the House of Life, the highest Egyptian "university," where they taught mythology and dogma. In this institution they fixed the calendar and festivals, whence came their knowledge of mathematics and astronomy. They participated in religious ceremonies and chanted the liturgy for the dead and for Pharaoh. They knew the correct formula for embalming. On a more personal level, they tended to the king's coronation, interpreted his dreams, and warded off all lurking evil spirits and demons. They helped the king as he prepared for bed at night and got up in the morning. They also served as his physicians.[22]

The חרטומים are mentioned in the Bible in Genesis, Exodus, and Daniel. They are referred to as dream interpreters in Genesis (41:8 and 24). The Septuagint ascribes to them the function of dream interpretation or "interpreters (or prodigies)," whereas the Vulgate renders this as "interpreters of dreams." In Exodus (7:11 and 22; 8:3) the phrase חרטומי מצרים or חרטומים refers to the Egyptian magicians who attempted to emulate the spells worked by Moses and Aaron. Accordingly, here the Septuagint renders the term as "singers of incantations" and the Vulgate (except in 7:11) as "witches." The reference to wise men and sorcerers (מכשפים) alongside the חרטומים does not necessarily refer to different categories of experts, but may simply be a sup-

---

18. Quaegebeur, *Pharaonic Egypt,* pp. 166–169; Hoffmeier, *Israel in Egypt,* p. 88.

19. Quaegebeur, *Pharaonic Egypt,* p. 169.

20. S. Schott, ed. and trans., *Altägyptische Liebeslieder* (Zurich: Artemis-Verlag, 1950), pp. 176–180.

21. "Another Night, the librarian (?) Hor son of Pa-neshe came in these moments, he took his books and his amulets [to the place] in [which Pharaoh] was. He read to him writing, he bound (?) to him amulet to prevent" (F. L. Griffith, *Stories of the High Priest of Memphis* (Oxford: Clarendon Press, 1900), pp. 182ff.

22. Yehoshua M. Grintz, *The Book of Genesis* (Jerusalem: Magnes Press, 1983), p. 111 (Hebrew).

plementary gloss on חרטומים.[23] In Daniel, the חרטומים are mentioned along with אשפים (Dan. 1:20 and 2:2); they are also mentioned in parallel with the מכשפים and כשדים (ibid. 2:2, 10, 24 and 4:4). The power of the חרטומים and the other experts lies in dream interpretation (2:2 and 4:4); more generally, they are said to reveal mysteries (2:27 and 4:6). Daniel is given the title "chief of the חרטומים" (4:6 and 8:11) and in this capacity he interprets dreams. His ability to interpret dreams is because "the spirit of the holy gods is in him" (4:5 and 5:11).

The word חרטום is probably also found in Assyrian, in the form *hardibi,* which is closer to the Egyptian original than the Hebrew is. Oppenheim noted that the Assyrians used the services of Egyptian oneirocritics, who could be found in the royal court during the reign of Assurbanipal or even earlier. He reached this conclusion from his study of an Assyrian tablet[24] that provides information on five groups of personal names, each of which is followed by a summary and reference to the profession of the persons mentioned: those who administer oaths *mašmašu,* seers *bārû,* scribes, exorcists *kalû,* and ornithomancers *dāgil issūri.* All five groups seem to fall into the category of priestly experts. Next come two sets of foreign (Egyptian) names. The first three are *har-di-bi;* many others in the list are described as being "Egyptian scribes."[25] It seems likely that *har-di-bi* is parallel to the Egyptian *hry-tp.*[26] Other important evidence is found in a description of the booty and prisoners taken by Esarhaddon from Egypt. Among the professionals mentioned in the list is *har-di-(bi).*[27] Oppenheim notes that in Assyria and Canaan there was no technical term parallel to חרטום. This may be because the Egyptians were considered to be the specialists in dream interpretation, whereas astrology was the expertise of the Chaldeans. Great importance was attached to dreams in Assyria, but because the professional level of the dream interpreters was rather low, it was necessary to hire the services of Egyptian oneirocritics.[28]

There were three methods of dream interpretation in Mesopotamia: (1) intuitively, by an expert who tried to link the overt elements of the dream with what it alluded to; (2) by means of collections of dream omina; that is, the oneirocritic was a scholar of sorts who relied on dreambooks that collected dreams from the past in order to interpret the present dream; and (3) by

---

23. Roland de Vaux, *The Early History of Israel,* trans. David Smith (Philadelphia: Westminister, 1978), p. 304.

24. Oppenheim, *Interpretation,* p. 238.

25. Ibid.

26. Gardiner, *Ancient Egyptian Onomastica,* 1:56.

27. Oppenheim, *Interpretation,* p. 238; "Babylonian and Assyrian Historical Texts," Translator, A. Leo Oppenheim, *ANET,* p. 293.

28. Oppenheim, *Interpretation,* p. 238.

appealing to a deity; here the expert invoked magic to get the deity who was the source of the dream to interpret it for him.[29] The common belief was that a dream incorporated a message from the deity. Not only was it was very important to learn its meaning, but leaving it uninterpreted rendered the dreamer ritually impure. Moreover, to fully release the dreamer from the impurity that beset him, a ritual involved "transferring" the dream to a clump of mud, which was then thrown into the water where it dissolved and disappeared while prayers were recited.[30]

It should be emphasized that only the lower classes seem to have had recourse to oneiromancers; the upper classes relied on astrology, haruspicy, and nephelomancy. Even the professional designation "dream interpreter" is infrequent, restricted mainly to lists of uncommon words. Texts that describe dreams experienced by kings date only from the later rulers of the Chaldean (neo-Babylonian) dynasty of Babylon. Dreams are mentioned frequently in documents from the time of Assurbanipal, but these are always those of commoners whose dreams about the king were brought to the monarch's attention. Oppenheim believed that in Mesopotamia only the uneducated classes paid attention to their dreams.[31]

In Mesopotamian literature we encounter women as dream interpreters. The Sumerian god Tammuz lies down to sleep and has a nightmare. Waking up in a panic, he summons his wise sister Geštinanna, who interprets his dream for him:

> Bring my sister, bring! Bring my Geštinanna, bring my sister! Bring my scribe who understands tablets. Bring my sister! Bring my songstress who knows songs (?), bring my sister! Bring my wise one who knows the meaning of dreams, bring my sister![32]

It is interesting that the sister is referred to as "my scribe who understands tablets," which indicates that dream interpretation was already based on written texts. In the Epic of Gilgamesh his mother interprets his dreams for him. So too in the Hittite version of a Hurrian legend about the adventures of the hunter Keshshi, who had seven symbolic dreams. It is his mother who interprets his dreams. In the description of Gudea's dream, too, a woman is the oneirocritic, and she is referred to as "Ensi, priestess of the gods."[33]

---

29. Ibid., p. 221.

30. Ibid., p. 219; Sally Butler, *Mesopotamian Conceptions of Dreams and Dream Rituals* (Munster-Verlag,1998), pp. 180-181, 191.

31. Oppenheim, "Dream," *EMiqr* 3:148.

32. Oppenheim, *Interpretation,* p. 246.

33. Ibid., p. 245.

In Akkadian we find the term *šā'il(t)u,* which means "he who asks questions of the gods."[34] These persons were the ones who asked the gods questions and only they had the ability to understand the gods' answers. In a hymn to the god Shamash, the *šā'ilu* asks questions so that the deity will help him interpret a dream.[35] "In the cup of the seers, at the preparation of cedar thou causest the *šā'ilu* to hear the interpretation of dreams."[36] The *šā'ilu* asked questions while following the movements of oil in water in a vessel called a *mākaltu,* and on this basis interpreted the dream.

It is interesting that the cognate verb ש.א.ל 'ask' appears in the Bible, too, in association with dreams. In the story of the witch of Endor, we read: "And Saul inquired (וישאל) of the Lord, but the Lord did not answer him, neither by dreams nor by Urim nor by prophets" (1 Sam. 28:6). This verse contains both the verbs 'ask' שאל and ע.נ.ה 'answer'. In Akkadian, too, we find a similar linkage of *šā'il(t)u* with *apālu* 'answer'; the reference here may be to a diviner or prophet.[37]

Documents from Mari that refer to various types of prophets include two interesting designations for them: *āpilum* (fem. *āpiltum*) and *muhhûm* (fem. *muhhutum*). As for the first of these, the verb *apālu,* from which the participle *āpilum* is derived, means "to respond or answer."[38] In ritual texts this is the regular term for designating the god's response. Sometimes these people operated in groups, like the bands of prophets found in the Bible.[39] Documents from Mari indicate that the *āpilum* would declare the will of the deity without being asked a question. In other words, the prophecy of *āpilum* came at the initiative of the deity and did not require any mantic apparatus.[40]

---

34. Ibid., p. 221.

35. Ibid., p. 222.

36. Alfred Haldar, *Associations of Cult Prophets among the Ancient Semites* (Uppsala: Almqvist and Wiksells, 1945), p. 15; Oppenheim, *Interpretation,* p. 222.

37. Ibid.

38. Benjamin Uffenheimer, *Ancient Prophecy in Israel* (Jerusalem: The Magnes Press, 1984), p. 24; W. von Soden, *AHw* 1:56b–57a, s.v. *apālum;* Jean-Marie Durand, *Archives épistolaires de Mari I/1. ARMT* XXVI:1 (Paris: Editions Recherche sur les Civilisations, 1988), pp. 396-398.

39. Abraham Malamat, *Mari and the Bible: A Collection of Studies* (Jerusalem: Hebrew University, 1984), p. 72 (Hebrew).

40. Abraham Malamat, "History and Prophetic Vision in a Mari Letter," *Eretz-Israel* 5 (1958), p. 72. Oppenheim, however, notes two places in which the *āpilum* functioned as a diviner-priest, whose prophecies focus on interpreting the signs in the sacrificial animal. In these loci there is no connection with free and spontaneous prophecy. For a summary of the various opinions about the nature of the *āpilum,* see Uffenheimer, *Ancient Prophecy in Israel,* pp. 24–29.

In the Bible the word "answer" is usually referred to God Himself and not to his prophet, as in the Mari documents. Nevertheless, in practice in the Bible, too, it is the prophet who, as the spokesman of God, "answers"; sometimes this word does refer to him explicitly. "As soon as Samuel saw Saul, the Lord *answered* him, 'This is the man that I told you would govern My people'" (1 Sam. 9:17). Similarly, with regard to Jeremiah: "Thus you shall speak to the prophet: 'What did the Lord *answer* you? And what did the Lord speak?'" (Jer. 23:37). The idiom "a divine response," meaning the words of the Lord, appears once in the Bible, in Micah's prophecy (Micah 3:7). Micah also uses the verb "answer" when he refers to Balaam: "My people, remember what Balak king of Moab plotted against you, and how Balaam son of Beor answered him. ..." (Micah 6:5). Malamat hypothesizes that Balaam, who is not referred to as a prophet, belonged in the category of *āpilum* (to answer). Still, we are ignorant of the special circumstances in which the deity appeared to the *āpilum.* It seems likely, though, that the revelation was auditory and came in a vision.[41]

As for *muḫḫûm,* it is derived from a root that means "run amok, behave like an enthusiast." On Assyrian documents, written *maḫḫû(m),* it denotes one of the inferior temple servitors, who evidently had an ecstatic character. In Mari, the form *muḫḫûm* designates a physical or mental state. Malamat conjectures that this form is parallel to the Hebrew משוגע, which occasionally is used as a synonym for נביא (2 Kings 9:11, 29:26; Hos. 9:7). It is interesting that this term also appears in the context of dreams. In the dream (ARM X:50) mentioned in chapter 1, Addu-duri reports to the king about a dream she had. In so doing, she mentions the *muḫḫûm,* who conveyed a warning to Zimri-Lim not to go to war. Nevertheless, we should emphasize that due to the paucity of information we cannot determine the precise nature of these terms or how their missions were distinguished.[42]

Sometimes a *šā'ilu* 'priest' or *šā'iltu* 'priestess' is mentioned along with the *bārû* as experts who inquired of the deity.[43] They brought the word of the god and foretold the future. The fact that they are mentioned together in many places indicates that they had similar functions.[44] The *šā'ilu* was the chief expert in the interpretation of dreams, but it seems likely that the *bārû* was also

---

41. Ibid.

42. Malamat, *Mari and the Bible,* p. 72.

43. CAD S:I:109–112.

44. "A *bārû* by a vision did not decide the future, by incense a *šā'ilu* caused not by justice to radiate"; "a *bārû* by a vision guides him not aright. A *šā'ilu* by incense solves it not" (Haldar, *Associations of Cult Prophets Among the Ancient Semites,* p. 14); Guillaume identifies *šā'ilu* with *bārû:* "the *bārû* priests were sometimes called shailu, 'askers' or inquirers" (Alfred

involved. In an Assyrian letter we read that "he performs the *bārûtu*, he experiences dreams."[45] Some scholars believe that the specific function of the *šā'ilu* was oneirocriticism.[46] This is implausible, however, because the *šā'ilu* had other functions as well. For instance, we read of the *šā'iltu* who appealed to the god Assur with a difficult problem: "We shall ask here the *šā'iltu*-priestesses, the *bārîtu*-priestesses and the spirits of the dead (*etimmu*) and then Assur will threaten (?) you!"[47] An old Assyrian letter from Kültepe contains an appeal to a priestess in a case of illness: "We went to the *šā'iltu*-priestess and thus said the *ilum:* 'do not hold back my votive offerings!'"[48]

Sleeping in the temple was another method of oneirocriticism noted by Oppenheim. When the dream was arcane and could not be interpreted, the priest slept next to the "patient." Ostensibly, the priest was to have a dream in which he learned the interpretation of the patient's arcane dream.[49] Priests of this type are mentioned along with the *šā'ilu*, because their function was similar to that of the *šā'ilu*.

The term *šā'il(t)u* also seems to be found outside Mesopotamia. In a letter in Akkadian written by the king of Alashiya (Cyprus) to the king of Egypt, the latter is asked to dispatch a "*šā'ilu*-priest for eagles."[50] This professional predicted the future by studying the flight of birds and their cries. We should emphasize, however, that this method was not normally practiced in Mesopotamia.

TERMS FOR DREAM INTERPRETERS
IN THE BOOK OF DANIEL

In the Book of Daniel there is a list of the experts to whom the king turned with the demand that they interpret his dreams: חרטמים 'magicians', מכשפים 'sorcerers', אשפים 'exorcists', and כשדים 'Chaldeans'.[51] Just as Pharaoh called in the Egyptian magicians and wise men, so Nebuchadnezzar turned to his

---

Guillaume, *Prophecy and Divination Among the Hebrews and Other Semites* [London: Hodder and Stoughton, 1938], p. 40).

45. E. F. Weidner, "Aus dem Tagen eines assyrischen Schattenkonigs," *AfO* 10 (1935–36), 5:9.

46. Zimmerman, Dhorme, Frank, and Contenau all thought that dream interpretation was the specific function of the *šā'ilu* priests. See Haldar, *Associations of Cult Prophets*, p. 13.

47. Oppenheim, *Interpretation*, p. 221.

48. Ibid., pp. 221–222.

49. Ibid., p. 224.

50. Ibid.; EA 35:26.

51. Daniel 2:2.

specialists. The recourse to professionals to interpret dreams is also known from the courts of the kings of Assyria and Babylonia. All four types of experts mentioned in Daniel 2:2 appear in other verses, though not always in the same order. In 2:10 we have "magician, exorcist, or Chaldean," with the sorcerers left out. On the other hand, wise men and diviners (גזרין) are added to the list in 2:27.[52] The question, then, is what specific or unique functions were performed by the professionals we have enumerated? And what was their relationship, if any, to the interpretation of dreams?

Sorcerers

The מכשפים or sorcerers worked spells and enchantments. The Bible denounces them (Deut. 18:10, Mal. 3:5). The Hebrew כ.ש.פ is cognate with the Akkadian *kašāpu*, *kuššupu* 'bewitch, enchant' and its nominal derivatives *kišpu* 'magic, witchcraft' and *kaššapu/kaššaptu* 'magician, witch'.[53] The Arabic *kasafa* can mean both "grow" and "cut apart."[54] In Akkadian this root is used to denote black magic or magic to harm, whereas in Hebrew the distinction between black and white magic is not so clear-cut and we can say only that the feminine agent noun מכשפה connotes black magic. The Hebrew term מכשף does not encompass all the realms of activity of his Babylonian counterpart, such as raising the spirits of the dead, which in Israel was the domain of the אוב and ידעוני. It may be that the Bible's blurring of the boundaries between black and white magic stems from its opposition to all forms of sorcery.

In Mesopotamia, most of the cases in which sorcerers were involved had to do with social conflicts. Sorcerers and particularly female witches were the

---

52. There are in fact six different terms that appear in the Book of Daniel: wise men, exorcists, magicians, Chaldeans, diviners, and sorcerers. We find them as follows: Daniel 1:20–magicians and exorcists; 2:2–magicians, exorcists, sorcerers, and Chaldeans; 2:10–magician, exorcist, Chaldean; 2:27–wise men, exorcists, magicians, diviners; 4:4–magicians, exorcists, Chaldeans, and diviners; 5:7–exorcists, Chaldeans, and diviners; 5:11–chief of magicians, exorcists, Chaldeans, diviners; 5:15–wise men and exorcists. It is hard to reach any conclusions on the basis of this list. Driver maintains that there is a lack of clarity concerning the order of their appearance. "Wise men" seems to be a general designation that refers to all of them, although in 2:27 it appears alongside the others. See S. R. Driver, *The Book of Daniel* (Cambridge: Cambridge University Press, 1900), pp. 15–16.

53. *CAD* K:284.

54. Smith traces כשף to the Arabic *ksf* in the sense of "to cut" and explains it by that feature of Semitic religion in which worshippers cut themselves when appearing before a deity. He thinks the noun means "herbs or drugs shredded into a magic brew" (see Micah 5:11). See S. Robertson Smith, "On the Forms of Divination and Magic Enumerated in Deut. xvii. 10–11," *Journal of Philology* 14 (1885), p. 125.

allies of evil spirits, but did not always require the assistance of those spirits.[55] The *kaššap(t)u* could cause harm in several ways: by magic power in the evil eye of the *kaššap(t)u*, by evil words, and by noxious plants and potions whose influence was intensified by incantations. Sometimes the *kaššap(t)u* fashioned a small image of the person to be tormented from mud, flour, or metal and then tied this image in various sorts of knots, kept it away from water, or soaked it in enchanted water and fed it poisonous plants. All of this was done while incantations were being recited. The power of the *kaššap(t)u* was so great that he could stop up the mouths of the gods and prevent the afflicted person from asking help from the one who cast the spell.[56]

Exorcists

When the sufferer knew that his afflictions were the result of witchcraft—"a witch has bewitched me"[57]—he would use the white incantations of the "*maqlû* burning" series. He would appeal to the exorcist and through him to Marduk, to the gods of healing, or to his own personal divine patron. Sometimes he would call upon the gods in the heavens and earth and rivers to tear apart the incantation and redeem him from the witchcraft, which was considered to be a kind of sin. Sometimes he would himself recite incantatory phrases against the evil spirits or address his own body and limbs. He would use purgatives such as herbs, water, salt, oil, or as a ritual act he would prepare images of the witches and burn them along with symbolic objects. In order to achieve his request, he would say, "Burn my sorcerer and my witch! As for my sorcerer and my sorceress, speedily may their lives be extinguished! But me keep alive, so that I may praise thy greatness and sing thy glory."[58]

---

55. For a study on witchcraft see: Tzvi Abusch, *Babylonian Witchcraft Literature* (Atlanta: Scholars Press,1987).

56. It is interesting that the gods themselves, who know the source of the evil and the methods of combatting it, fight it with the aid of מכשפים. Because the evil does not depend on them but threatens them, too, they must have recourse to magical forces. In their wars among themselves the gods use incantations and magical materials. Magic is a lore that is used by evil spirits as well as by gods and human sorcerers. It is based on knowledge of the arcane forces that existed from primordial times and do not depend on the gods. See Yehezkel Kaufmann, *Toledot Ha' Emunah HaYisrae'elit* (Jerusalem: Bialik Institute, 1942–56), 1:354–356 (Hebrew).

57. Gerhard Meier, *Die assyrische Beschwörungssammlung Maqlû, AfO* 2 (Berlin: privately published, 1937), 1:127; on the *maqlû* ritual see: Tzvi Abusch, "An Early Form of the Witchcraft Maqlû and the Origin of a Babylonian Magical Ceremony," in *Lingering Over Words: Studies in Ancient Near Eastern Literature in Honor of William L. Moran,* ed. Tzvi Abusch, John Huehnergard, Piotr Steinkeller, 1-57.(Atlanta: Scholars Press,1990).

58. Maqlû 2:15–17; Sally Butler, *Mesopotamian Conceptions of Dreams and Dream Rituals,* 201.

When the sufferer did not know the reason for his afflictions, he would use the "*šurpu* burning" series, which included oaths that listed the types of transgressions the afflicted person might have committed, thereby causing his afflictions.[59] This suggests that the Babylonians assumed that the power of witchcraft and other forces that caused adversity were strengthened by sins that a person committed unintentionally or in a state of impurity. A person could atone for his sin through the *šurpu* ceremonies, which included confession and magical rites. We also read about a burning intended to purify individuals. The objects burned were thought to carry away the trangressor's sins and afflictions. Burning them could free the sufferer from his pain.[60]

The *šurpu* and *maqlû* series are linked with the Akkadian term *āšipu*, which is borrowed into Hebrew as אשפים. In the Hebrew portions of the Book of Daniel the form is אשף (1:20 and 2:2), whereas in the Aramaic sections we find אשף, אשפין, אשפיא (2:10 and 27, 4:4). Both the Hebrew and Aramaic forms, as stated, are borrowed from the Akkadian *āšipu* 'conjurer',[61] which denotes sorcerers who deal in white magic and are experts in the rites of counter-witchcraft and oaths.[62] The Septuagint uses μάγοι, the designation for the Persian priestly caste that specialized in witchcraft, to represent אשפים.[63]

In Mesopotamia, the *āšipu* used the *šurpu* and *maqlû* tablets.[64] They were the priests of Ea and Marduk, who performed their rituals in a piscine costume, because the fish was the totem animal of Ea. They guided sufferers in the ceremonies of counter-witchcraft and recited the appropriate formulas.

---

59. "Has he entered his neighbor's house? Has he approached his neighbor's wife? Has he shed his neighbor's blood? Has he carried off his neighbor's garment? Has he failed to relieve a poverty-stricken man? Has he driven out an upright man from his kinfolk? Has he broken up a close family?" (*ŠURPU* 2:47–53; for an English translation, see Isaac Mendelsohn, *Religions of the Ancient Near East* (New York: The Liberal Arts Press, 1955), pp. 213–214; a complete translation into English of the entire series can be found in Erica Reiner, *ŠURPU: A Collection of Sumerian and Akkadian Incantations,* AfO Beiheft 11 (Gratz: privately published by the editor, 1951).

60. Reiner, *ŠURPU,* p. 3.

61. *CAD* A:II:431.

62. The functions of the *āšipu* are different. He is the incantation-priest and exorcist who cleans taboos of uncleanness and removes bans, and he is the magician who chants the rites prescribed in such magical texts as the *šurpu, maqlû,* and *utukku* series. On the different functions of the *āšipu,* see: Michael S. Moore, *The Balaam Traditions,* SBLDS 113 (Atlanta: Scholars' Press, 1990), pp. 33–41; J. Laessøe, *Studies on the Assyrian Ritual and Series bīt rimki* (Copenhagen: Munksgaard, 1955). Cf. the review of Laessøe by W. G. Lambert, *Bibliotheca Orientalis* 14 (1957), pp. 227–230.

63. The term אשפים may be related to the biblical verb אסף in the sense of 'heal' (2 Kings 5:3).

64. Reiner, *ŠURPU,* 4.

While the ritual was in progress the sorcerer whispered in the ears of the beast about to be offered as a sacrifice. In addition to the priest there was also the *zammāru,* who accompanied the ritual by playing on musical instruments and reciting psalms in order to expel the baleful influence. "Fire-god, O mighty one exalted among the gods, who dost vanquish the wicked and the enemy, vanquish them [the witches] lest I be destroyed. Thou art my god, thou art my judge, thou art my helper, thou art my avenger."[65]

In addition, the *āšipū* also healed the ill who had been attacked by evil wizards.[66] They diagnosed the illness and predicted the fate of the patient—how long the illness would last, whether the sufferer would live or die.[67] To this end they relied on tablets that listed the symptoms of various diseases.

Hence it is possible that the reference to sorcerers and exorcists alongside the interpreters of dreams in the Book of Daniel should be understood against the background of the belief in the ancient Near East that dream interpretation included not only understanding the symbols in the dream but also exorcism of the evil forces associated with it.[68]

Chaldeans

The Chaldeans appear in Assyrian documents of the 9th century as inhabitants of southern Babylonia but later dominated the entire area.[69] In addition to "Chaldeans" as an ethnic designation in the Book of Daniel (5:30 and 9:1),[70] Babylonia is referred to as the "land of the Chaldeans" starting with that same period (Jer. 24:5, 25:12; Ezek. 1:3; 2 Kings 25:4). When "Chaldeans" are men-

---

65. *Maqlû* 2:15.

66. A. Leo Oppenheim, *Ancient Mesopotamia* (Chicago: University of Chicago Press, 1964), pp. 294 and 304: "Medical treatment at the Assyrian court and in important cases was under the direction of 'scientists.' They were *mašmaššu* and *āšipu* experts, trained in the lore of Eridu. ... They predicted the course of the disease from signs observed on the patient's body, and they offered incantations and other magic as well as other remedies indicated by the diagnosis."

67. E. K. Ritter, "Magic Expert (=Āšipu) and Physician (=Asû): Notes on Two Complementary Professions in Babylonian Medicine," in *Studies in Honor of Benno Landsberger on his 75th Birthday," AS 16* (Chicago: University of Chicago Press, 1965), pp. 299–321.

68. John J. Collins, *Daniel,* p. 156.

69. J. A. Brinkman, *A Political History of Post-Kassite Babylonia, 1158–722 BC* (Rome: Pontifical Biblical Institute, 1968), pp. 260–267.

70. R. Simeon Masnut wrote that "the Chaldeans did not have some special science like the other groups of wise men mentioned, but because the king was a Chaldean it was enough for them to be called by his name," that is, the other wise men mentioned here—magicians, exorcists, and sorcerers—belonged to other nationalities subject to Babylonia; these alone were referred to as Chaldeans because they belonged to the same people as Nebuchadnezzar.

tioned at the end of the list of those summoned to interpret Nebuchadnezzar's dream, the word is used as a technical designation. We should view them as professionals, since they were observers of the stars and constellations and experts in astronomy and astrology (Isa. 47:13). Indeed, in the Hellenistic age, "Chaldeans" became a synonym for astrologers and soothsayers.[71] Diodorus Siculus (first century BCE) described the Chaldeans and compared them to the Egyptian priests:

> But they occupy themselves largely with soothsaying as well, making predictions about future events, and in some cases by purifications, in others by sacrifices, and in others by some other charms they attempt to effect the averting of evil things and the fulfilment of the good. They are also skilled in soothsaying by the flight of birds, and they give out interpretations of both dreams and portents. They also show marked ability in making divinations from the observation of the entrails of animals, deeming that in this branch they are eminently successful.[72]

Abraham Ibn Ezra also conjectured that the Chaldeans mentioned in the present verse were knowledgeable about the constellations and expert in astrology. By contrast, Gersonides (Levi ben Gershom, known as Ralbag; 1288–1344) hypothesized that they cast lots to predict the future.[73]

Diviners

The noun גֹּזְרִין 'diviners' appears in this form only in the Book of Daniel, 2:27 and 5:11; the form with the definite article, גָּזְרַיָּא, is found in 4:4 and 5:7. It is interesting that the Septuagint did not translate the word but settled for transliterating it into Greek letters. The Vulgate renders it *aruspices,* which means "augurs" or "soothsayers," and the Peshitta does similarly. Some say that the word is derived from the verb גזר 'decree', because the גֹּזְרִין knew how to decree the course of the future by means of their words, thereby determining the lot of a human being. This sense is found in Job 22:28, "You will decree and it will be fulfilled."[74] The Akkadian verb *parāsu,* 'cut or slice', also has the sense of issuing a verdict. The noun *purussu,* derived from this verb, means the verdict both of the gods and of human judges.

In the Mishnah we find the phrase דַּיָּינֵי גְזֵרוֹת (rendered by Danby as "judges

---

71. Collins, *Daniel,* p. 137.

72. Diodorus Siculus 2.29; see also Strabo 16.1.

73. Divination by lots and haruspicy are mentioned in Ezekiel's prophecy about Nebuchadnezzar, where the king is said to have consulted תְּרָפִים and inspected the liver (Ezek. 21:26).

74. The verb גזר in this sense is also found in 4QPrNab 1:4.

of civil law": Ketubot 13:1) or גוזרי גזרות (BT Baba Qama 28b). On this basis, Sa'adia Gaon, in his commentary on the chapter, maintained that Nebuchadnezzar's גזרין were judges. Abraham Ibn Ezra, however, wrote that they were wizards whose words determined the fates of human beings.[75] Some say that they were stargazers (as in Isa. 47:13), who determined destinies from the stars. Another approach is reflected in the version of Symmachus, who defined them as "sacrificers," and in the Vulgate, which has them as "haruspices who read the livers and the inner organs of animals." This understanding can be supported by the Arabic *ğazzār* 'slaughterer, butcher'. Evidently we are dealing with diviners who based their utterances on their inspection of the remains of sacrifices.

Hence it may be that the term "wise men" comprises the exorcists, sorcerers, Chaldeans, and diviners, as is implied by 2:12–13, 18, 24, and other verses, where we read that Nebuchadnezzar was ready to liquidate all the wise men of Babylonia because they could not interpret his dream. A close reading of the Book of Daniel reveals that the author does not distinguish among these different specialties. Perhaps the king, distraught and angry, summoned all his wise men to help him understand his dream. It is also possible that the lack of distinction reflects the Bible's total rejection of magic and witchcraft, so that biblical authors are not precise in defining the functions of each of the professionals involved. Indeed, the חרטומים who are summoned to interpret Pharaoh's dreams in the Joseph cycle (Genesis 41:8 and 24) are mentioned alongside the sorcerers in the Book of Exodus.

DREAMBOOKS

Many peoples seem to have relied on dreambooks, which guided both experts and dreamers in their dream interpretation. As previously noted, from Egypt we have a fragment of a hieratic papyrus (Chester Beatty) from the 12th Dynasty (19th–18th century BCE), which was published by A. Gardiner, and a demotic papyrus (Carlsberg) from the second century CE, which was translated by Volten.[76] The first of these presents dreams in a table, arranged by

---

75. A. Dupont-Sommer, "Exorcismes et guérisons dans les écrits de Qoumrân," *Congress Volume*, Oxford 1959 VTSup 7 (Leiden: Brill, 1960), pp. 256–258, thinks the גזרין made decisions about spirits; J. Carmignac, "Un équivalent français de l'araméen *'gazir*,'" *RevQ* 4 (1963–64), pp. 277–278, derived it from "cutting off the way" for evil spirits.

76. A. H. Gardiner, *Hieratic Papyri in the British Museum*, Third Series, 1:9–23, Papyrus Chester Beady No. 3, 2, plates 5–8a, 12–12a (London: British Museum, 1935); Askel Volten, *Demotische Traumdeutung (PaP. Carlsberg XIII und XIV verso)*. (Copenhagen: Einar Munksgaard, 1942).

the type of fortune they allude to: dreams that bode well, followed by those that bode evil. The papyrus also categorizes people by type. The first are the "followers of the god Horus"; the second, the "followers of the god Seth."[77] The text describes the manners, expected life span, and physical appearance of those who follow the evil god Seth. They have red hair and are uncouth; they have a strong attraction to women; they are coarse and noisy when intoxicated; and they act aggressively toward their comrades.[78] The traits of those who follow the good god Horus are not extant, but this categorization is compatible with the modern notion that the content of dreams depends on a person's emotional make-up.

The dreamer is usually the only figure in the dreams found in the Chester Beatty Papyrus III. Sometimes he is active and sometimes passive. How well these dreams foretell the future depends on the oneiromancer's ability to interpret the dream correctly. The papyrus is written in the style of a medical text and the interpretations resemble diagnoses.[79] Dreams do not foretell events that are certain to take place in the future, but only events that are likely to happen if the prescription against "dream shock" does not cure the dreamer. Here too there is a parallel between "dream shock" therapy and modern psychology. The prescription has three parts: incantation, prayer, and a chemical concoction.[80] The dreams and their interpretations are presented in a fixed format. First comes the introductory formula, "if a man see himself in a dream," written once in each column. This is followed by a description of the dream—if a man did such and such in his dream, it is good (for him) and is a sign that something positive will happen to him; but if a man did something else in his dream it bodes evil (for him) and is a sign that something bad will happen to him. For example:

If a man sees himself in a dream:

(2:20) his mouth full of earth	good; eating (the possession of) his townsfolk.
eating donkey flesh	good; it means promotion.
eating crocodile flesh	good; (it means) eating the possessions of an official.
up a growing tree *(nht)*,	good; it means his loss *(nhy)*[81] of ...

---

77. Gardiner, *Hieratic Papyri*, p. 243.
78. Ibid., p. 20.
79. Sara Israelit-Groll, "Technical Language of Dream Interpretation," p. 73.
80. Ibid., p. 74.
81. Paronomasia.

looking at a window	good; the hearing of his cry by the god.(2:25)
rushes being given to him	good; it means the hearing of his cry.[82]

Sometimes the interpretation is unfavorable:

If a man sees himself in a dream:[83]

(7:25) his bed catching fire,	bad; it means driving away his wife.
waving a rag (?)	bad; it means his being mocked (?).
pricking himself through a thorn	bad; it means telling lies.
seeing the catching *(h3m)* of birds	bad; it means the taking *(nhm)* of his possession.
(8:1)	bad; ....
seeing his penis stiff *(nhtw)*	bad; victory *(nhtw)*[84] to his enemies.
sailing down a stream	bad; it means a life of bitterness (?)
being given a harp *(bnt)*	bad; it means something through which he fares ill *(bin)*.[85]

Oppenheim notes that the words "good" and "bad" were included in the Egyptian text to clarify the significance of the dream. They are not found in dreambooks from Mesopotamia, where the diviner understood whether the dream boded good or ill. Oppenheim concludes that we are dealing with a borrowing from Mesopotamia and that the words appeared in the Chester Beatty Papyrus III so that Egyptian readers would understand the meaning of the dream.

The most common methods of interpretation involved analogy, paronomasia, and actual resemblance between the content of the dream and waking reality. If the dreamer saw himself in a deep well, it meant he was going to be cast into a pit. If he saw white bread he would be given something that delighted him—an interpretation derived from the pun between *hd* 'white' and *hd* 'light up'. It was a bad omen if someone dreamt about birds being trapped, for it meant that his property would be taken from him—a pun on *h3m* 'catching' and *nhm* 'taking away'. There were also interpretations based on symbols.

---

82. Gardiner, *Hieratic Papyri in the British Museum,* p. 12.

83. Ibid., p. 17.

84. Paronomasia.

85. Paronomasia.

Someone who saw his face in a mirror would marry another woman, because a mirror symbolized a woman,[86] or because when a man looked in a mirror he saw another man and that other man symbolized a woman.[87]

Egyptian dream interpretation was sometimes based on a literal echo between the description of the dream and its interpretation. In the Egyptian dreambook we read that someone who killed an ox in his dream would kill his enemies; that someone who saw a dead ox would see his enemies dying; that if someone saw his mouth closed, the deity would eliminate something that he feared; that if someone cut his fingernails–the works of his hands would be taken from him. Only infrequently was there an antithetical echo, such as that a man who dreamt about his own death would have a long life.

Sometimes the same dream had contradictory interpretations–depending on the oneiromancer and his mood. If someone ate the flesh of an ox it was good; but in another passage the same dream was said to be bad. A dreamer who sailed with the current was said to be having a good dream; but elsewhere we are told that this was a bad omen. As we have seen previously, Joseph's dreams and their interpretation were of this sort, in which the interpretation was explicit in each case to the situation.

As we noted earlier, the dreambooks also included incantations and prayers. One prescriptive appeal to a deity resembles a prayer found in the Talmud (BT Berakhot 55b):

> To be recited by a man when he wakes in his own place. "Come to me, come to me, my mother Isis. Behold, I am seeing what is (?) far from me in my (?) city." Here am I, my son Horus, come out with what thou hast seen, in order that thy afflictions (?) throughout thy dreams may vanish, and fire go forth against him that frighteneth thee. Behold, I come that I may see thee and drive forth thy ills and extirpate all that is filthy. Hail to thee, thou (?) good dream that art seen <by> night (10,15) or by day. Driven forth are all evil filthy things that Seth the son of Nuth has made. (Even as) Re is vindicated against his enemies, (so) I am vindicated against my enemies.

> This spell is to be spoken when he wakes in his (own) place, there having given to him *pesen*-bread in (his) presence and some fresh herbs moistened with beer and myrrh. A man's face is to be rubbed therewith, and all evil dreams that [he] has seen are driven away.[88]

---

86. In contrast, "seeing his face in the water, bad; making free (?) with another life" (Gardiner, *Hieratic Papyri in the British Museum,* 18 (9, 20)).

87. Ibid., 22.

88. Ibid., 19.

Papyrus Carlsburg, by contrast, divides dreams into those of men and those of women. The dreams are arranged in sections according to various topics, including: what is said to the dreamer in his dream;[89] the beverage that he drinks (such as beer, wine, or water—for example, if a man drinks light beer good things will happen to him);[90] someone who sees himself eating excrement;[91] someone who is swimming with a man he does not know or who is swimming with his father, mother, and brothers.[92] The section that refers to the lascivious dreams of women is exceptional among the dreambooks of the ancient Near East. It includes the following:

18. If a horse couples with her, she will be violent with her husband;
19. If a farmer couples with her, then a farmer will give [...] to her.
20. If an ass couples with her, she will be punished for a great fault.
21. If a he-goat couples with her, she will die quickly.
22. If a ram couples with her, Pharaoh will be full of kindness to her.
23. If an animal couples with her, she will meet with a miserable fate.
24. If a wolf couples with her, craftsmen will do good things to her.
25. If a lion couples with her, she will see something beautiful.
26. If a crocodile couples with her, she will die quickly.
27. If a snake couples with her, she will take a husband who will be harsh to her and she will become ill.[93]

1. If she gives birth to a cat, she will have many children.
2. If she gives birth to a dog, she will have a boy.
3. If she gives birth to an ass, she will have an idiot child.
4. If she gives birth to a mouse, [ ] [to go] from here to god.
5. If she gives birth to a wolf [ ] in each house.
6. If she gives birth to a raven, she will have an idiot child.
7. If she gives birth to a crocodile, she will have many children.[94]

A Mesopotamian dreambook from the seventh century BCE consists mainly of broken tablets found in the famous library of Assurbanipal—only a few of which have been restored. A series of nine of them presents signs and portents. The first includes incantations to purge evil dreams, and the others enumerate signs for future events. Lists of dream signs have also been found

---

89. Volten, *Demotische Traumdeutung,* p. 95.
90. Ibid., 91, XIV, A.2.
91. Ibid., 97.
92. Ibid., 101.
93. Ibid., p. 87.
94. Ibid., 99, XIVF.

in Ashur, in Susa, and in Babylon; the series are referred to by their opening word, ^{d}Zaqiqu or "zephyr," the god of dreams. The dreams are classified by the key verb that appears in each of them, such as *ate, drank, met, travelled*–all based on activities of daily life. The section on eating refers to both cannibalism and coprophagy.

> If he eats meat he knows: peace of mind.
> If he eats meat he does not know: no peace of mind.
> If he eats human meat: he will have great riches.
> If he eats meat from a dead man: somebody will take away what he owns, [his] mind will [(not?)] be in peace.   [x + 15]
> If he eats meat from a corpse: [somebody] will take away what he owns, his mind [will (not?) be at pe]ace.
> If he eats his own entrails: his possessions [will   ].
> If he eats his own flesh: his property will [   ].
> With a disturbed mind he will live (lit. walk).[95]

The dreams on the tablet about travelling include descriptions of ascending to heaven and descending to the underworld. There are also dreams in which people fly.

> If a man flies repeatedly: whatever he owns will be lost.
> If a man takes off and flies (once): for a subject (MAŠ.EN.DÙ) (it means): loss of good things, for a poor man: loss of poverty, he will see his good wish(es fulfilled).
> If a man flies from the place he is standing on and (rises) towards the sky: to <this> man one will restore what he has lost.[96]

There are dreams about incest, about a man who has lost his teeth, about quarrels with family members, about receiving gifts, and so on. In this collection, one dream appears per line, in the format, "a man who in his dream did such and such, it is a sign for him that...."

As might be expected, the link between the interpretation and the dream is frequently tenuous and unfathomable. Nevertheless the interpreters evidently used three main methods. One was paronomasia: "(If a man in his dream) eats a raven *(arbu)*: income *(irbu)* will come in." "(If in his dreams somebody) has given him *miḫru*-wood, he will have no rival *(māḫiru).*"[97] The second method involved a conceptual association between the dream and the

---

95. Oppenheim, *Interpretation,* p. 271.
96. Ibid., p. 258.
97. Ibid., pp. 241 and 272.

interpretation: "(If in his dream somebody) has given him (perfume) oil: (it means) sweet words (and) pleasantness." Sometimes the link is quite clear: "(If a man in his dream) ascends to heaven: his days (on earth) will be short [   ]."[98] The third "method" involved pure superstition—there was no obvious link between the dream and its interpretation: "(If a man in his dream) has eaten the flesh of his hand: his daughter will d(ie)," followed by, "(if a man in his dream) has eaten the flesh of his foot: his son and heir (will die)."[99]

The dreambook also included tablets of incantations and rituals for purging oneself after a bad dream. As we have already noted, in Mesopotamia dream interpretation was not a matter only of assigning a meaning but was also required to avert evil. Dreams that were left uninterpreted made the dreamer impure; hence the ceremonies and prayers to remove the evil of the dream from the dreamer.[100]

In front of the lamp he shall ... a bundle of reeds ... the
hem of the right side of his (garment) he shall cut off and
hold it in front of the lamp. He shall say as follows:
"You are the judge, judge (now) my case: this dream
which during the first or the middle or the last watch of the night [5]
was brought to me in which you know but I do not know—
If (its content predicts something) pleasant, may its pleasantness not escape me—
If (it predicts something) evil, may its evil not catch me—
(But) verily (this dream) be not mine! Like this reed is plucked (from a bundle) [and]
Will not return to its (original) place and this hem was cu[t] from my garment [and]
[10]
Will not return to [my] garment after it has been cut off, this dream
Which [was brought] to me in the first or the middle or the last watch of night
Shall verily be not mine!" In front of the ... [   ]
He shall bre[ak] the reed into two [   ].[101]

This text is an appeal to the god Nusku to avert the evil of the dream. It is both a prayer and a set of rituals to insulate the dreamer from the bad dream.

---

98. Ibid.
99. Ibid., pp. 241–242.
100. Sally Butler, *Mesopotamian Conceptions of Dreams and Dream Rituals*, p. 191
101. Oppenheim, Interpretation, p. 298.

Lines 6 and 7, noted by Oppenheim, are a prayer requesting that any good dreams the dreamer may have forgotten do not disappear. This idea is echoed in the Talmud, where the dreamer asks the Lord to confirm and ratify any good dreams he has forgotten and to turn bad dreams into good ones.[102]

DREAM INTERPRETERS IN ISRAEL

The Bible does not include any dream interpretation books of the type known from ancient Egypt and Mesopotamia. Moreover, it presents no accounts of professional dream interpreters of the sort found among other nations. Nowhere in the Bible does a man of God interpret the dream of a poor man–both Joseph and Daniel interpret dreams for royalty in Gentile courts. Nevertheless, the Bible emphasizes that dream interpretation comes from God. Joseph was able to interpret dreams not through his own wisdom, but because the Lord vouchsafed their meanings to him: "Surely God can interpret! Tell me [your dreams]" (Gen. 40:8; see also 41:16, 38–39). Even though Daniel is a sage well versed in the laws of the Chaldeans and one of the leading savants of Babylonia, he too interprets dreams only by virtue of prophetic inspiration. God reveals the meaning of Nebuchadnezzar's dream to him in a nocturnal vision (Dan. 2:17). Similarly, it is thanks to divine inspiration that he is able to interpret Nebuchadnezzar's second dream (Dan. 4:5, 6, 15).

In the story of Gideon, the Lord gives him advance knowledge of his impending victory by means of a symbolic dream. Interestingly, however, it is a Midianite soldier who has the symbolic dream, not Gideon, who merely overhears its interpretation in the Midianite camp. Both the dreamer and the interpreter come from Midian and the peoples of the East, famous throughout the Bible for their wisdom. Thus here too the science of dream interpretation is seen to be a skill of non-Israelites.

Indeed, Kaufmann considers dream interpretation to be a magic art.[103] According to him, it was considered to be a special wisdom that revealed the will of the god by means of a special mantic sense or various strange omens. This stands in polar antithesis to the Israelite dream, where the Lord appears directly and speaks to the dreamer, who requires no intermediary in order to understand the dream. Nevertheless, the Bible does not absolutely dismiss riddle dreams and acknowledges their mantic value. According to Kaufmann, "The Bible tends to view dream interpretation itself as a prophetic Divine revelation and thereby to turn the riddle dream itself into a prophetic dream

---

102. BT Berakhot 55b.
103. Yehezkel Kaufmann, *Toledot*, p. 507–511.

that directly expresses the Word of God."[104] An angel interprets Zechariah's dreams and visions for him (Zech. 1:8, 2:1, 5:1). Similarly, an angel interprets the dream vision of the four beasts for Daniel (Dan. 7:1ff and 16ff). The visions of Amos (7:1–9 and 8:1–3) and Jeremiah (1:11–15 and 24:1–10) belong to the same category–the images serve as backdrops for the prophecies. The prophets do not understand the meaning of what they see until God reveals it to them. The biblical belief is grounded in the assumption that the Lord, who makes all decisions, heals the sick, and interprets dreams, is omnipotent.[105]

DREAM INTERPRETATION IN THE TALMUD

In the Talmudic period there seems to have been a guild of professional oneirocritics. Rabbi Benaa recounted: "There were 24 dream interpreters in Jerusalem. Once I had a dream and went to all of them. The interpretation given me by one was different from the interpretation of another, but all of them were realized. For all dreams follow the mouth."[106] Some dream interpreters would give a favorable interpretation if they received a fee, but an unfavorable one if not. It was said that Bar Hadya was a professional oneirocritic. Once Abaye and Rava had the same dream. Abaye paid Bar Hadya a gratuity, but Rava did not. They told him: In our dream someone read out to us the verse: "Your ox shall be slaughtered before your eyes, but you shall not eat of it" (Deut. 28:31). To Rava, Bar Hadya interpreted this to mean, "You will lose your wares and not enjoy your food from sadness." But to Abaye he said: "You will profit from your wares and will not enjoy your food out of happiness."[107]

The Sages had various views about dreams. We are told that when Mar Samuel, of the first generation of Babylonian Amoraim, used to awaken from a bad dream he would recite the verse from Zechariah: "Dreamers speak lies" (Zech. 10:2); but when he woke up after a good dream he would say, "Is it possible that dreams are meaningless? For it is written in the Torah: 'I speak with him in a dream' (Num. 12:6)."[108] We read (BT Yebamot 93b) that one of the Sages saw a broken reed in his dream. At first they were inclined to interpret this to mean that he had erred, on the basis of the verse: "You rely ... on ... that splintered reed of a staff" (2 Kings 18:21). But this view was rejected because it was also possible to interpret the dream favorably, on the

104. Ibid., p. 509.
105. Ibid., p. 510.
106. BT Berakhot 55b.
107. BT Berakhot 56a.
108. BT Berakhot 55b.

basis of another verse: "He shall not break even a bruised reed. ... He shall bring forth the true way" (Isa. 42:3)

The Sages attached symbolic meaning to dreams about prophets, kings, biblical books, and beasts and fowl. They said that if someone sees David in a dream, he should look forward to piety; if Solomon, he should look forward to wisdom; if Ahab, he should fear retribution. If someone sees the Book of Kings, he should anticipate greatness; if Ezekiel, he should expect wisdom; if Isaiah, he should expect consolation; and if Jeremiah, he should be concerned about retribution. If someone sees the Book of Psalms, he should expect piety; if Proverbs, he should expect wisdom; if the Song of Songs, he may hope for piety; if Ecclesiastes, he may hope for wisdom; if Lamentations, let him fear for punishment; and if someone sees the Scroll of Esther, he will have a miracle wrought for him.[109] The dream apparition of three Sages was considered to be especially significant. If one saw Rabbi (Judah ha-Nasi) in a dream, he could hope for wisdom; if Eleazar ben Azariah, he could hope for riches; if Rabbi Ishmael ben Elisha, he should fear punishment. There were also three disciples (scholars who never received ordination) whose appearance was significant. If one saw Ben-Azzai in a dream, he could hope for piety; if Ben-Zoma, he could hope for wisdom; if Elisha ben Abuya, he should fear punishment.[110] Dreams about beasts and fowl were good portents, except for the elephant, the monkey, and the hedgehog (because of their strange appearance, according to Rashi); similarly, all metals, fruits, and colors were favorable signs except for blue, which was the color of illness.

To interpret a dream one had to be an expert in the language: its words, adages, sounds, connotations, and idiomatic expressions. Some interpretations were based on verses from the Bible; others, on an associative link between the content of the dream and the interpretation. For example: "Someone who dreams about olive trees will have many sons,[111] for it is written, 'Your sons [shall be] like olive saplings around your table.' (Ps. 128:3)." Someone who dreamt that he had intercourse with his mother could expect to obtain understanding, after the verse, since it says, "Call understanding 'mother' " (Prov. 2:3).[112] Someone who dreamt that he had intercourse with a betrothed maiden could expect to acquire Torah knowledge, since it says, "Moses commanded us the Torah, an inheritance for the Congregation of Jacob" (Deut. 33:4).[113] Someone who dreamt that he had intercourse with his

---

109. BT Berakhot 57b.
110. Ibid.
111. Ibid. 57a.
112. Reading homiletically אם 'mother' instead of עם 'if'; ibid. 56a.
113. Reading homiletically מאורסה 'betrothed' instead of מורשה 'inheritance'; ibid.

sister could expect to attain wisdom, as in the verse, "Say to Wisdom, "You are my sister" (Prov. 7:4).[114]

There is also wordplay based on biblical verses. For example, if someone dreamt about barley (שעורים), he would be cleansed of his sins, in accordance with the verse, "Your guilt shall depart (וסר עוונך)" (Isa. 6:7).[115] If someone dreamt about a citron (הדר), it means that he would be honored (הדור) in the sight of his Maker, since it says: "The fruit of citron trees, branches of palm trees" (Lev. 23:40).[116] Another example: "If one sees palm trees in dreams, his iniquities will come to an end, as it says, 'Your iniquity, Fair Zion, is expiated' (Lam. 4:22)."[117] This interpretation is based on word play: תמרים 'palm trees' suggests תמו עונותיו 'rebels' [i.e. sins] are finished'. If one dreamt about a cat, if he lives in a place where the word for cat is שונרא, a beautiful song (שירה נאה) would be composed for him; if he lived in a place where the word was שנרא, he would suffer a change for the worse (שינוי רע). If one dreamt about an elephant (פיל), wonders (פלאות) would be wrought for him.

Some dream interpretations involved breaking a word into syllables. If someone dreamt about a palm frond (לולב), it meant that his heart (לו לב) [consonantally identical to] was one with his Father in Heaven.[118] Sometimes the allegory was clear: thus one who climbed on the roof would reach greatness, whereas one who fell from the roof would fall from greatness.[119]

These pages of the Talmud constitute a miniature dreambook. Note that most of the interpretations are favorable and that the few unfavorable interpretations serve chiefly to limit generally favorable interpretations. For example, if one dreamt about grapes: if they were white grapes, then whether or not it was the season when grapes ripened in the vineyard, it was a favorable omen. If they were black grapes, and if the dream took place in the growing season, it was still a good omen; only black grapes out of season were a bad sign.[120] One further example: "One of the disciples expounded before Rabbi Sheshet: 'If someone sees a serpent in a dream, his livelihood is guaranteed; if it bites him, [his livelihood] will be doubled; if he was killed, he will lose his livelihood.' Rabbi Sheshet corrected the disciple: 'If he dreams that he kills the serpent, all the more will his livelihood be doubled'."[121]

---

114. Ibid.
115. Ibid. 57a.
116. Ibid.
117. Ibid.
118. Ibid.
119. Ibid.
120. Ibid., 56b.
121. Ibid., 57a.

The Talmudic Sages believed that if an individual gave credence to the interpretation of his dream, it would be realized. Several times in the Talmud we find the adage: "All dreams follow the mouth."[122] In the Palestinian Talmud (Ma'aser Sheni 4:6) we read about a woman who told Rabbi Eliezer that she had dreamed that the doorpost of her house had broken. Rabbi Eliezer said this meant she would give birth to a son, which indeed occurred. Some time later she came to the house of study of Rabbi Eliezer with another dream. Because he was not there she recounted her dream to his disciples. They interpreted the dream to mean that she would give birth to a son but her husband would die. When Rabbi Eliezer returned and his disciples told him what had happened, he rebuked them sharply: "You have killed that man! For a dream follows its interpretation, as it is stated: 'And as he interpreted for us, so it came to pass' (Gen. 41:13)."

Elsewhere it is related that Rabbi Joshua ben Levi used to advise people that when they woke up after a dream they should quickly recite a biblical verse with positive implications that could be associated with the subject of the dream, before they had time to think of a verse with an inimical meaning. If you see a river, for example, you should get up and say: "I will extend to her prosperity like a stream" (Isa. 66:12), before you recall a negative verse such as: "For He shall come like a hemmed-in stream" (Isa. 59:19).[123] If you see a mountain in your dream, say, "How welcome on the mountain are the footsteps of the herald announcing happiness" (Isa. 52:7) to avoid thinking of "For the mountains I take up weeping and wailing" (Jer. 9:9).[124]

The Talmud incorporates quite a few sayings and opinions that reflect skeptical or credulous attitudes to dream interpretation: "Even though part of a dream comes to pass, not all of it comes to pass." "There is no dream without spurious elements."[125] "No good dream comes to pass in full and no bad dream comes to pass in full."[126] "Dreams make no difference."[127] There is a story that Rabbi Meir and Rabbi Nathan behaved improperly toward Rabban Simeon ben Gamaliel, the president of the Sanhedrin. "They were told

---

122. That a dream "follows the mouth" means that (1) the dream-interpreter has the power to cause the dream to be realized for good or evil; (2) that dreams resemble the symbolic acts of the prophets and are meant to make the vision conform to reality; (3) that this depends on the mouth of the dreamers and the words they use to describe the dream; (4) that the dream-interpreter can influence the dreamer—for example, a dream may move the dreamer to repentance.

123. BT Berakhot 56b.

124. Ibid.

125. BT Berakhot 55a.

126. Ibid.

127. BT Gittin 52a.

in their dreams to go and placate him. Nathan went; but Meir did not, saying, 'dreams are of no consequence.' "[128]

Other Sages, however, believed in dreams: "Three dreams come to pass: a dream of the early morning, a dream dreamed by a friend, and a dream that is interpreted within the dream, and some say also a dream that has been repeated."[129] Dream vows were considered to be valid: "Someone who dreams that he is excommunicated must be released by scholars. Someone who takes a vow in a dream must be released from it."[130] As previously noted, fasting to avert the effects of a bad dream is permissible even on the Sabbath (when fasting is forbidden), because a person who has had a bad dream is distraught and can have no greater Sabbath pleasure than this–because he believes that fasting will protect him.[131] We are told that once, in the House of Study, Rabbi Naḥman bar Isaac described the character of King Saul in a very negative light. After this he had recurrent nightmares. Trying to put an end to them he begged forgiveness, saying, "I abase myself before you, bones of Saul son of Kish." When the nightmares continued on the ensuing nights, he restated his apology: "I abase myself before you, bones of Saul son of Kish *king of Israel*"; only then did his nightmares cease.[132] A similar story is told about R. Ashi: once, during a discussion with his disciples about the image of King Manasseh of Judah, he told them that the monarch had been a great scholar but had sinned so grievously that he had no share in the World to Come. That night, King Manasseh appeared to R. Ashi in a dream and re-proved him: he, the king, was a greater scholar and more learned than the sage; but the attraction of idolatry is so strong that had R. Ashi lived in the time of Manasseh, he would have been no less a sinner than the king himself.[133] Some considered dreams to be a species of prophecy: Hananiah ben Isaac said explicitly that "a dream is a variety of prophecy."[134] BT Berakhot 57b says that "a dream is one-sixtieth part prophecy."[135] We read that R. Yossi ben Tanḥum from Kefar Agin, failing to heed the words of his father, who appeared to him in a dream, and also ignoring the warning of a fortune-teller, drowned after setting sail on an inauspicious date.[136]

128. BT Horayot 13b; see also Gittin 52a.
129. BT Berakhot 55b.
130. BT Nedarim 8.
131. BT Sabbath 11.
132. BT Yoma 22b.
133. BT Sanhedrin 102b.
134. Genesis Rabba 17:5.
135. BT Berakhot 57b.
136. JT Sabbath 2:6.

Whatever else, a dream has the capacity to make us aware of things beyond what we can perceive with our senses and intellect. Thus some Talmudic sages viewed dreams as auxiliary to waking thought and decision-making and believed that dreams have an internal source.[137] We read that Rabbi Meir suspected an innkeeper of being dishonest. During the night he had a dream that strengthened his suspicions. After that dream he kept an eye on his money and it turned out that his suspicions were justified.[138] R. Kahana, the disciple of Rav, once asked his master a particular question, but the latter had forgotten what he knew and could not answer him. That night R. Kahana had a dream, which he recounted the next morning to Rav. The content of the dream stirred Rav to remember the answer he had forgotten; that is, the answer was not in the dream, but it stimulated Rav's memory.[139]

Rava once vacillated concerning the solution of a halakhic problem; when he could not find an answer he said, "May I see the solution to this problem in my dream." In the event, however, he found the solution while awake and not in a dream.[140] In another case we hear of a man who had been sentenced to flogging by Rava. The man died under the lash and the Persian authorities wanted to punish Rava. During the night Rava's father appeared to him in a dream and told him to go sleep elsewhere. Rava did as his father bade and this saved his life. The next morning it was discovered that the bed in which he had originally been sleeping had been cut to ribbons.[141]

In a number of places in the Talmud we read about the indecision of Rabbi Zeira, who lived in Babylonia, with regard to immigrating to the Land of Israel. On the one hand he was attracted by the sanctity of the land, the religious precept to settle the land, and the opportunity of studying with the great Torah sages there. On the other hand, he knew that his teacher R. Judah, whom he esteemed greatly, was opposed to immigration to Eretz Israel. We read that his ultimate decision to make the move came in the wake of a dream that hinted that all of his sins would be forgiven if he did so.[142]

Thus these Talmudic Sages considered dreams to be an auxiliary tool for decision-making. They did not see dreams as obligatory, but as a datum to be

---

137. Isaac Lewin, *The Psychology of Dreams* (Tel Aviv: Dekel, 1980), p. 104.

138. BT Yoma 83b. It should be noted that Rabbi Meir did not always act in accordance with the content of his dreams and was consistent in his view that dreams were irrelevant for judicial decisions. This means that people must weigh the content of their dreams and decide whether to relate to them seriously or not.

139. BT Sanhedrin 82a.

140. BT Menahot 67a.

141. BT Ta'anit 24b.

142. BT Sabbath 41a, Ketubot 112a, Baba Metzia 85a.

weighed further after they awoke.[143] To them, dreams supplement and complement waking thought and have significance only for the dreamer, because they are the product of his or her heart and mind.[144]

In conclusion, dream interpretation was considered to be a magical art in Mesopotamia and Egypt. In the world of the Scriptures, however, only Joseph and Daniel are mentioned as dream-interpreters, and there is not a single biblical narrative in which a man of God interprets the dream of a commoner. The Bible explicitly notes that the interpretation of dreams comes from God (Gen. 40:8, 41:16, 38–39; Dan. 2:17, 4:6). Hence it is not surprising that the Scriptures do not incorporate dream interpretation literature of the sort found in Mesopotamia and Egypt. In Israelite belief, the Lord makes known His will to human beings through dreams, and there is no need for any intermediary to help them understand it.

The Talmud, however, seems to reflect the existence of dreambooks and presents a wide variety of opinions about the essence of dreams, from those who display a skeptical approach to their veracity to those who would place a good deal of reliance in them.

Thus far we have dealt with types of dreams and their interpretation. In the next chapter we shall consider whether the prophetic movement and wisdom literature rejected dreams or instead saw them as a legitimate link between human beings and their God.

---

143. Lewin, *The Psychology of Dreams,* p. 105.
144. Ibid.

4

Perceptions of Dreams in the Prophetic and Wisdom Literature

Although dreams are important in Genesis, the biblical corpus from 1 Kings 3 through Daniel 2 describes no specific ones–the prophets report their visions instead. Nevertheless, the prophets refer to dreams in a number of passages. Did they or didn't they allow that these experiences could be legitimate manifestations of the word of the Lord? Is there a prophetic consensus among them about their legitimacy or are there different shades of opinion?

Because we are dealing with a variegated literature produced by many authors over a long period of time, we would expect a proliferation of views on the subject as a matter of course. Some scholars have investigated chronological dimensions and literary genres as keys to interpreting the range of views. Ehrlich, for example, concluded that there is no correlation between historical periods and attitudes toward dreams. They are rejected in post-exilic passages (Zech. 10:2; Eccles. 5:6; Ben Sira 34:1–7, 40:5–7)[1] as well as in pre-exilic texts (Deut. 13:2–6, Jeremiah 23:25–32, 27:9–10, 29:8–9). In the later literature, however, we find a favorable attitude (Joel 3:1; Job 4:12–16, 7:13–14, 33:14–16; Daniel 2 and 3; 2 Mac. 15:11–16; Wisdom of Solomon 18:17–19; etc.).[2]

Gnuse, on the other hand, insists that literary genre is the important variable in this context:

Epic literature uses the dream report as a theological and literary device to foreshadow the unfolding plan of history for God's people. Likewise

---

1. In 34:5, Ben Sira writes about dreams: "Sorcery and divination and dreams are all vanity." There seems to be a verbal echo of Ecclesiastes here, but in the very next verse we are told that if dreams do not come from God, no attention should be paid to them. That is, we can see this as a favorable attitude toward dreams, if they come from God. In 40:5–7, however, dreams are an instrument through which God punishes the dreamer; this resembles what we find in Job 7:14 and 33:14–18. For various opinions about Ben Sira's atttitude toward dreams, see Gnuse, *The Dream Theophany of Samuel,* p. 103.

2. Ehrlich, *Traum,* pp. 169–170.

historical texts, which also contain created dream accounts, have a theological purpose for using this form. Prophetic texts, however, are critical of dreams because dreams infringe upon the exclusiveness of prophetic reception of the divine word. Wisdom texts criticize dreams as being ephemeral from the experiential standpoint of the common person. Finally, apocalyptic literature has a renewed fascination with the symbolic, bizarre, and mysterious phenomena, among which dreams are to be included by virtue of their often bizarre and monstrous imagery.[3]

Gnuse's opinion notwithstanding, we probably should not see Job 4:14–16, 7:13–14, and 33:14–16 as absolute rejections of dreams. It is worth noting that where there is a positive attitude toward the experience, the dream itself is described. When the attitude is negative, however, usually only the word "dream" appears with no specific description. In the pages that follow we shall examine those appearances of the word and determine whether each is meant to refer to a false prophecy, a fleeting experience, or a channel of communication. In so doing, we hope to convey a more nuanced view of the stance of ancient Israelite prophecy and the wisdom literature toward the phenomenon.

DREAMS AS FALSE PROPHECY

Jeremiah 23:25-32

I have heard what the prophets say, who prophesy falsely in My name: "I had a dream, I had a dream." [26] How long will there be in the minds of the prophets who prophesy falsehood–the prophets of their own deceitful minds–[27] who plan to make My people forget My name, by means of the dreams which they tell each other, just as their fathers forgot My name because of Baal? [28] Let the prophet who has a dream tell the dream; and let him who has received My word report My word faithfully! How can straw be compared to grain?–says the Lord. [29] Behold, My word is like fire–declares the Lord–and like a hammer that shatters rock! [30] Assuredly, I am going to deal with the prophets–declares the Lord–who steal My words from one another. [31] I am going to deal with the prophets–declares the Lord–who wag their tongues and make oracular utterances. [32] I am going to deal with those who prophesy lying dreams–declares the Lord–who relate them

---

3. Gnuse, *The Dream Theophany of Samuel,* p. 62.

to lead My people astray with their reckless lies, when I did not send
them or command them. They do this people no good–declares the
Lord.

This passage may be divided into three parts: vv. 25–27, vv. 28–29, and vv.
30–32.[4] The core, vv. 28–29, highlights the contrast between the lies of the
false prophets and the Lord's truth. Verses 25–27 and 30–32 provide the
backdrop and describe the contemptible deeds of the charlatans. While verses
25–27 describe their actions by means of rhetorical questions, vv. 30–32 are
phrased as a rebuke spoken by the Lord Himself.[5] The entire unit is marked
by symmetry and the recurrent use of identical or analogous expressions.[6]

The unit begins with the words of the false prophets who assert that the
Lord has appeared to them in a dream–"I had a dream, I had a dream" (v.
25). In response, Jeremiah demands to know how long the hearts and minds
of the false prophets will be full of deceit.[7] It is the false prophets who cause
the people to forget their God and emulate their ancestors, who followed
Baal.[8] Not only have the people forgotten their God (2:32, 3:31, 13:25, 18:15);
the false prophets intentionally cause them to do so.[9] The deeds of the false
prophets are no different than those of the prophets of Samaria, who spoke in
the name of Baal (v. 13).[10] The false prophets of Jerusalem are the heirs of

---

4. Robert P. Carroll, *The Book of Jeremiah* (Philadelphia: Westminster Press, 1986), p. 470.

5. "I am going to deal" three times over (לכן הנני על, הנני על) and again (הנני על) at the start of
each of these verses.

6. "Each other" (איש לרעהו) (v. 27) and "from one another" (איש מאת רעהו) (v. 30); "in the
minds" (בלב) (v. 26) and its evident parallel "their tongues (לשונם)" (v. 31); "the plan to make
My people forget My name, by means of [their] dreams (v. 27) and "to lead My people
astray with their ... lies" (v. 32). See also William L. Holladay, *Jeremiah 1* (Philadelphia:
Fortress Press, 1986), p. 642.

7. עד מתי היש (v. 26) is a single question–"how long will there be(?)"–with the interrogative
heh interpolated to reinforce the question. Such reinforcement and duplication can also be
found elsewhere in the Bible; for example: אחרי מתי עוד = "How much longer shall it be?" (Jer.
13:27), where the redundancy serves to emphasize the prophet's disappointment.

8. The association between earlier generations and Baal is a frequent motif in the Book
of Jeremiah. See 2:5–8, 9:13, and 16:11.

9. החושבים 'who plan' (v. 27): The *heh* functions as a relative pronoun whose antecedent
is found in the previous verse–the false prophets. Some commentators understand it to be
the interrogatory *heh;* for example, S. D. Luzzatto: "'How long will it be in the mind of the
prophets to make My people forget My Name.' The word החושבים has the interrogatory *heh,*
because he had broken off the train of thought in the middle." In any case, the meaning is
not that Israel will forget the name of the Lord but that Israel will no longer worship Him.

10. In v. 27 "Baal" is a code word that stands for prophets who addressed the people in
Baal's name: "the prophets prophesied by Baal" (Jer. 2:8). Hence the text has "Baal" in the
singular but with a plural sense.

those prophets.[11] But whereas in earlier generations false prophets spoke in the name of Baal, the false prophets of the present generation pretend to speak in the name of the Lord. They season their speech with expressions typical of true prophets, such as "declares the Lord" (v. 31).

If the false prophets insist on speaking to the people, they should directly say "I had a dream" so that the people will know that it is only a dream—it is well known that some dreams incorporate meaningless images. Verse 28 sets forth guidelines for preventing the deception, based on the verbs used. "Let the [false] prophet who has a dream tell the dream"; but let the true prophets "speak My word faithfully"(אמת). There is also a two-pronged metaphor that pits dreams and straw on one side and the words of the Lord and grain on the other.[12] "Straw" (תבן) here refers to the husks that envelop the kernels of grain and are eliminated at the start of threshing; "grain" (בר) means the kernel to which no refuse is attached. Because it is impossible to eat the grain when it is still mixed with straw, the latter must be removed.[13] Some scholars argue that in challenging the prophets to come forward and tell their dreams, Jeremiah shows that he did not reject dreams.[14] That is, dreams may be described in public, but only on condition that words are not put in God's mouth. This implies that Jeremiah acknowledges that these prophets knew the difference between speaking truth and speaking falsehood. Something similar is found in the Gemara (BT Berakhot 61b): "Rava said, 'people know in their hearts whether or not they are perfect righteous men.'"

The description of the deeds of the false prophets takes the form of a divine rebuke (vv. 30–32). The expression "I am going to deal with (הנני על) the prophets" appears at the start of three consecutive verses to emphasize that it

---

11. At the start of the chapter Jeremiah refers to the prophets of Samaria and the prophets of Jerusalem. His rebuke of the prophets of Jerusalem has an ethical and social character (23:14), whereas his rebuke of the prophets of Samaria is cultic (verse 13). Thus the unit merges the two indictments in the condemnation of the dreamer-prophets.

12. Verse 28 can be read as a test that the Lord sets for the false prophets; there is some resemblance with the competition between Elijah and the prophets of Baal on Mt. Carmel (1 Kings 18).

13. "The Sages asked, 'What do grain and straw have to with dreams?' Rabbi Johanan said, 'Just as grain cannot exist without straw, so dreams cannot exist without meaningless elements'" (BT Berakhot 55a). In other words, even though the prophetic dream and simple human dream have the same nature, in that both of them work through the imagination, they are distinguished in their essence. Prophetic dreams are already totally clean of straw and food for those with an intellect, whereas simple human dreams are like straw that grows with the grain, whose size is large and is food for beasts.

14. A. Guillaume, *Prophecy and Divination Among the Hebrews and Other Semites*, p. 218; J. P. Hyatt and S. Hopper, "Jeremiah," *IB* 5:993.

will indeed be so; each verse adds another reason why catastrophe will descend upon their heads. The false prophets have stolen the words of true prophets and reused them, uttering them lightly.[15] The difficult expression לקחו לשונם ("wag their tongues"?) occurs only here. Some interpret it to mean that they take their words (their tongues) and pretend that they are the words of the Lord by appending "declares the Lord" to them. Alternately, the sense may be that they speak smooth delusive language (לשון חלקות [cf. Is. 30:10, Ps. 12:3–4], with לקח by metathesis for חלק) of their own invention, rather than that which the Lord placed in their mouths. The false prophets use the idioms current with genuine prophets, including the signature phrase "declares the Lord," the typical formula used in the prophetic books to denote the words of the deity.[16] This is the only instance in the Bible of a verbal form of the root נ.א.מ; elsewhere we always find the noun נאום (which most English versions consistently render as an active verb).[17] Rashi and David Kimḥi both gloss וינאמו נאום to mean that the false prophets taught their tongues to proclaim their lies with the idiom נאום *YHWH* and to imitate the style of genuine prophets.

Verse 32 summarizes the seven previous verses. Jeremiah calls his adversaries "those who prophesy lying dreams." The indictment repeats his earlier charge (v. 13). He denounces the false prophets who tell their dreams and mislead the people through their "reckless lies"(שקריהם ובפחזותם). פחזות is a biblical *hapax legomenon,* evidently with the root sense of "reckless and immoral."[18] These prophets were not sent by the Lord and for this reason "do

---

15. Some believe that these false prophets are not humbugs who knowingly make themselves out to be prophets but genuine prophets who apply their talent for evil. That is, they reuse earlier prophecies that contain the genuine word of the Lord. This conjecture seems to be untenable, however, because the prophets of v. 30 are the same as those mentioned in vv. 28–38. The passage is bringing out the differences between the straw and the grain, between dreams and the word of the Lord, and between prophets and non-prophets; and the same applies to vv. 30–32. We must note, however, that Jeremiah has no word to apply to these impostors other than "prophet" (v. 26). See also A. R. Johnson, *The Cultic Prophet in Ancient Israel,* second edition (Cardiff: University of Wales Press, 1962), pp. 47ff.

16. The root נ.א.מ also has the sense of human speech, as in "I know what Transgression says (נאם) to the wicked" (Ps. 36:2).

17. There is no way to know whether the verb was in common use in Jeremiah's time. In post-biblical Hebrew, however, the verb is found as both נום and נאם, with the sense of "to speak or say." It is not clear whether the verb existed before the Book of Jeremiah or whether it created as ae result of this verse. On this see Holladay, *Jeremiah 1,* p. 645; M. Jastrow, *A Dictionary of the Targumim, the Talmud Babli and Yerushalmi and Midrashic Literature* (New York: Putnam, 1903), p. 887b, s.v. נום.

18. Zephaniah, too, says of Jerusalem that "her prophets are reckless (פחזים), faithless fellows" (Zeph. 3:4), that is, immoral and hypocritical. David Kimḥi explains the term as meaning "reckless," citing Judg. 9:4: "worthless and reckless fellows." The root פ.ח.ז is also

no good"– that is, they harm this people. Despite Jeremiah's threats he does not specify the punishment to be visited on charlatans–unlike 14:15, where he warns: "Those very prophets shall perish by sword and famine."

In summary, in this passage, which begins with the superscription "concerning the prophets," Jeremiah contrasts true prophets with polished orators out to deceive their audience.[19] According to Jeremiah, (1) they do not turn the people from backsliding–which is the chief mission of true prophets of the Lord; (2) they encourage the people to continue their attempts to throw off the Babylonian yoke and delude them into thinking that there will be peace, when in truth they can anticipate only calamity; (3) the Lord did not send them (vv . 21 and 32); (4) all their prophecies are invented; instead of encouraging the people to worship the Lord they consign His name to oblivion (v. 27) and (5) one of the ways employed by the false prophets to mislead the people was dreams, which, for true prophets, were legitimate manifestations of the word of the Lord. Echoing the evaluation found in Deuteronomy that associates dreamers with prophets who incite the people to worship idols (Deut. 13:2–6), Jeremiah bitterly denounces the dreamers and the dreams of false prophets. The passage contains no criticism of dreams that the Lord sends to His elect.

The date of the passage might well be from the fourth year of the reign of Zedekiah (chapters 27–29), when tension with the false prophets reached its peak [20] and King Jechoniah was making preparations to revolt against Nebuchadnezzar.[21] The people were imbued with the false hope that the yoke of Babylonia would soon be cast off and that Jechoniah and the other exiles would return to the Land of Judah, bringing the sacred vessels of the Temple with them.

Jeremiah 27:9-10

As for you, give no heed to your prophets, augurs, dreamers, soothsayers, and sorcerers, who say to you, "Do not serve the king of

---

found in cognate languages. In Arabic it means "to be haughty, boastful, reckless"; in Aramaic and Syriac, "to be wanton, lascivious." In rabbinic Hebrew the verb is used of rising passion (BT Nedarim 9b, Nazir 4b). See Sarna, *Genesis,* p. 333.

19. The false prophets who spoke in the name of Baal are called "the prophets of Samaria" (v. 13). This may be because Baal-worship was widespread in Samaria and people who had been intimate with the priestly circles in the temples of Ephraim came to Jerusalem after the destruction of Samaria in 721 BCE. The prophets of Samaria whom Jeremiah condemns evidently emerged from those groups.

20. J. Bright, *Jeremiah,* AB (Garden City, New York: Doubleday, 1965), p. 155.

21. See Jer. 27:16–20, 28:1–4, and 51:59.

Babylon." For they prophesy falsely to you–with the result that you shall be banished from your land; I will drive you out and you shall perish.

In these two verses and those that follow (12–15), Jeremiah rebukes the nations and King Zedekiah for believing that deliverance was imminent–a belief nurtured by the promises of prophets and augurs,[22] dreamers, diviners,[23] and sorcerers. According to Jeremiah, belief in their prophecies would lead to destruction and ruination. The only viable path available to Zedekiah and the nations was to accept the authority and yoke of the king of Babylonia.

Among the prognosticators enumerated by Jeremiah are חֲלֹמֹתֵיכֶם. Although this form usually means "your dreams," the Septuagint, Vulgate, and Peshitta all render it as "your dreamers." Its place in the list in verse 9 clearly indicates that they are correct: the word must denote an actor, parallel to the other actors mentioned here.[24] In fact, Rashi follows a similar path and avers that the term refers to "experts in dream interpretation." [25]

Jeremiah's declaration to the five nations stems from his recognition that it is the Lord who directs world history and that opposing Nebuchadnezzar means opposing the Lord. Just as Isaiah proclaims that the dominion of the Assyrians was temporary and would last only until they fulfilled the role the Lord had assigned them, so Jeremiah depicts Nebuchadnezzar as first and foremost the servant of the Lord and a tool in the hands of God. The prophets who encouraged the kings to rebel against Babylonia were lying, and here

---

22. קוסמים (here rendered "augurs," but elsewhere frequently "diviners") used magical means to extract information about a man's future from a god, especially by reading omens. They are associated with prophets in many passages; in Joshua 13:22 Balaam is referred to as a קוסם. In Micah 3:6 divination is mentioned as one of the occupations of prophets ("and it shall be dark for you so that you cannot divine [וחשכה לכם מקסם]). See further William I. Holladay, *Jeremiah 2* (Minneapolis: Fortress Press, 1989), p. 121.

23. The Bible provides no description of the methods of מעוננים 'soothsayers'. The term appears in the list of practices forbidden to the Israelites (Lev. 19:26 and Deut. 18:10, 14) and elsewhere, too, with a negative connotation (Isa. 55:3 and Micah 5:11). Some derive the word from עונה 'season' and explain it as designating a person who proclaims the appropriate time for some action. Rashi relates it to the soothsayer who says that today is good for a journey, tomorrow is good for trade, etc. (BT Sanhedrin 65b). Others derive the word from ענן 'cloud', i.e., a person who observes the clouds and predicts the future on the basis of their movements.

24. NEB suggests the vocalization חֹלְמוֹתֵיכֶם, a feminine participle with the meaning "dreaming women."

25. Andreas Resch, *Der Traum im Heilsplan Gottes: Deutung und Bedeutung des Traums im Alten Testament,* (Freiburg: Herder, 1964), p. 44.

Jeremiah presents the punishment that awaits those kings: "You shall be banished from your land; I will drive you out and you shall perish." The language echoes the warnings of retribution with which the Torah threatens Israel.[26]

The attitude towards dreamers here, then, is negative in the extreme, given that they are included in the same category as practitioners of the forbidden arts of divining, magic, and soothsaying.[27] And these verses underscore the apparent inability of Jeremiah's contemporaries to determine which prophet was telling the truth. Their perplexity and confusion are the result of actions by false prophets such as Hananiah son of Azur, who used the same vocabulary and idioms as Jeremiah and the other true prophets: "Thus said the Lord of Hosts, the God of Israel" (Jer. 28:2) and "Hananiah said in the presence of all the people, 'Thus said the Lord ....'" (ibid. v. 11).

Jeremiah 29:8-9

> For thus said the Lord of Hosts, the God of Israel: "Let not the prophets and diviners in your midst deceive you, and pay no heed to your dreams that you dream. [9] For they prophesy to you in My name falsely; I did not send them"–declares the Lord.

This passage is an excerpt from a letter dispatched by Jeremiah to the exiles in Babylonia. False prophets had arisen among them, assuring them that their residence would be only temporary and counseling them not to settle down in their new abode.[28] Accordingly, Jeremiah wrote to advise the exiles to build houses and plant gardens, to marry and have families. In the second half of the chapter Jeremiah warns the exiles specifically against the false prophets Ahab son of Kolaiah and Zedekiah son of Maaseiah, who tried to diminish the influence of Jeremiah's prophecies spoken in Judah. Another, Shemaiah the Nehelamite, denounced Jeremiah in messages he sent to the

---

26. "Amidst the various nations to which the Lord your God has banished you" (Deut. 30:1); '[you] shall perish among the nations" (Lev. 26:38).

27. The author may have drawn his material from Deuteronomy (18:10 and 14), where the roster of banned practitioners includes the קוסם, קוסמים, עונן, מנחש and מכשף. Here, though, prophets and dreamers are added to the list. This represents a double departure from Deuteronomy: (1) Moses refers only to Israelite prophets and dreamers, but Jeremiah to Gentiles as well; (2) Moses draws a sharp distinction between prophets and dreamers versus other illegitimate practitioners, whereas Jeremiah denounces all of them equally (Deut. 13:2–6 and 18:14–15).

28. Active among the exiles were persons who spoke in the name of the Lord and were considered to be prophets: "But you say, 'The Lord has raised up prophets for us in Babylon'" (Jer. 29:15). Cf. "I will raise up a prophet for them from among their own people, like yourself" (Deut. 18:18).

priests and people in Jerusalem.[29] In a letter to Zephaniah son of Maaseiah the priest, Shemaiah castigates him for not preventing Jeremiah from delivering his anti-revolt prophecies in the Temple precincts and for not punishing him for his prophecies (vv. 26–28). The chapter concludes with another epistle from Jeremiah to the exiles in Babylonia, in which he writes that Shemaiah and his offspring will not see the good things that the Lord will do for His people in the future.[30] These verses contain fierce criticism of prophets, diviners, and dreamers.[31] These three categories of prognosticators also appear in the list of foreign soothsayers (Jer. 27:9). Evidently this condemnation is part of Jeremiah's polemic against those who maintained that the exile would soon be over.[32] His call to the exiles contains the difficult expression חלמתיכם אשר אתם מחלמים, interpretation of which eludes scholarly consensus.[33] Perhaps we are dealing with dittography and should emend אתם<מ>חלמים to אתם חלמים 'that you dream', as the Septuagint (as well as the Vulgate and Peshitta) renders the verse.[34] In other words, the dreamers are

---

29. הנחלמי can be interpreted as referring to a place—i.e., Shemaiah from Nehelam (thus in the Aramaic Targum and by Rashi). But it can also be derived from חולם: David Kimḥi writes that he received this epithet because he had *dreams* that the exiles would soon return to Jerusalem.

30. Ezekiel, who lived in Babylonia, also had to contend with the false prophets there (Ezekiel 13). The punishment he predicted for them is similar to that decreed by Jeremiah for Shemaiah: "My hand will be against the prophets who prophesy falsehood and utter lying divination. They shall not remain in the assembly of My people, they shall not be inscribed in the lists of the House of Israel, and they shall not come back to the land of Israel" (Ezek. 13:9).

31. Some scholars believe that vv. 8–9 really belong after v. 13, because they interrupt the smooth flow from v. 7 to v. 10. But a close reading of the chapter discloses that vv. 8 and 9 reinforce the later verses, which state that the false prophets told the people that their stay in exile would be short. Accordingly Jeremiah admonishes and cautions the people against the false prophets who had not been sent by the Lord. See also Bright, *Jeremiah*, p. 208; J. A. Thompson, *The Book of Jeremiah* (Grand Rapids, Michigan: Eerdmans, 1980), p. 547.

32. Bright, *Jeremiah*, pp. 210–211. For the opposing view, see Robert P. Carroll, *The Book of Jeremiah*, p. 557, who says that the verse "simply warns against being deceived by prophets and dreamers." It seems, however, that we must take the verse in the context of the entire chapter.

33. Some suggest reading "the dreams which they dream" or "their dreams which they dream" (e.g., NJV, JB, RSV, Holladay, Condamin, Rudolph, and Bright). Others understand it as "your dream-interpreters"; see: Holladay, *Jeremiah 2*, p. 141. The consonantal text is consistent with a participle in either the *hif'il* or *pi'el*, which suggests a causative meaning; see J. Alberto Soggin, "Jeremiah 29,8b," *Old Testament and Oriental Studies, BibOr 29* (Rome: Biblical Institute Press, 1975), pp. 238–240; for a non-causative interpretation see *GKC*, §530.

34. *BDB*, 321.

the exiles themselves. The addition of diviners to prophets seems to be an attempt to fit the situation of the exiles into the pagan environment in which they were living—a world in which divining and dreams occupied a central role.

As in the previous chapter (27:9–10), here too dreams are mentioned in the same breath as false prophets and diviners and thus have a negative connotation. The key difference is that the dreamers here are Israelites. False prophets and diviners are causing the Israelites to have vain dreams.

Zechariah 10:2

For the teraphim spoke delusion, the diviners predicted falsely; and dreamers speak lies and console with illusions. That is why My people have strayed like a flock, they suffer for lack of a shepherd.

Some scholars are of the opinion that the first two verses of chapter 10 are a direct continuation of the end of chapter 9.[35] This was the opinion of the Masoretes, who inserted a section break after 10:2 but not before 10:1, thereby indicating their view that vv. 1 and 2 are the conclusion of the preceding prophecy (9:9–9:17). This also seems to be the view of Abraham Ibn Ezra. Chapter 9 concludes with the blessing of the land, whose fertility will make grain and wine abundant, so that the young men and women will be handsome and strong. The same topic, the fertility of the soil, opens chapter 10, with an appeal to the Lord to send end-of-season rain so that the land will be fertile.[36] Still, the second-person imperative at the start of v. 1, as well as its content, strongly suggests that this is a new unit rather than the continuation of the vision of salvation in 9:1–17. There is a tenuous thematic connection between the rain in 10:1, which provides the blessing of "grass in the fields for everyone," and the grain and wine mentioned at the end of the earlier

---

35. Charles Henry Hamilton Wright, *Zechariah and His Prophecies,* second edition (London: Hodder and Stoughton, 1879), pp. 265ff; Carol L. Meyers and Eric M. Meyers, *Zechariah 9–14,* AB (New York: Doubleday, 1993), p. 179.

36. It is not clear why the people should ask for rain at the end of the season, which is a sign of curse (1 Sam. 12:17–18; see also Mishna Ta'anit, end of chapter 1). Hence we should probably read, not בעת מלקוש 'in the season of the late rain' but בעתן[ו] ומלקוש 'in its season and late rain' (i.e., interpolating two *waws*), following the pattern of Deut. 11:14 and Jer. 5:24. Whereas MT has two terms that designate rain, מטר and מלקוש, the LXX adds a third term, πρόϊμον, which is usually rendered "autumn rains" or "early rains." This still appears in some English Bibles (*NEB*). The interpolation of these early rains was probably under the influence of the verse just mentioned (Deut. 11:14). Rain was of supreme importance in the land of Canaan, where the Israelites were dependent on the seasonal rains and not on springs, lakes, and rivers.

prophecy (9:17). In addition, v. 2 ends with the "lack of a shepherd," language that is echoed in v. 3. Note, however, that the shepherds of v. 3 are Gentile kings, whereas the reference in v. 2 is to the spiritual leadership of Israel. The most likely reading is that vv. 1 and 2 were a separate unit that was inserted into its present location by the editor in order to link the vision of salvation in 9:1–17 with the prophecy in 10:3–12.

In contrast to the bounty that the Lord showers on the earth as described in v. 1, in v. 2 the prophet highlights the lack of benefit from the *teraphim,* who were used to predict the future. Because the Lord alone brings rain and storms, these blessings are not to be sought from mortals, be they *teraphim,* diviners, or dreamers. It is interesting that Jeremiah, too, alludes to the contrast between the Living God, who gives rain, raises clouds, and sends thunderstorms, and the delusion and emptiness of idols (Jer. 10:12–15). Elsewhere he asks, "Can any of the false gods of the nations give rain? Can the skies of themselves give showers?" (Jer. 14:22).

The reference to *teraphim* and diviners in v. 2 has led a number of scholars to conclude that this prophecy is pre-exilic, dating from a period when the use of these techniques was widespread. We read repeatedly that the exile itself is punishment for these sins of Israel (for example, 2 Kings 23:24; Hosea 3:4).[37] It is more plausible, however, to conclude that the prophet was referring to sins of the past, not to idolatry in his own day.[38] Note, too, that the verbs are in the past tense: "The teraphim spoke delusion, the diviners predicted falsely." These are the misdeeds for which Israel was sent into the Assyrian exile. The verb דבר 'speak' appears here, as it does frequently in the prophetic books, to denote the true word of the Lord to His flock. The *teraphim,* by contrast, spoke delusion. Here the text was probably influenced by 1 Sam. 15:23, where we also have the association of קסם 'divination', עון

---

37. The *teraphim* were images used to foretell the future (on *teraphim* as instruments of divination, see Judg. 18:14 and Ezek. 21:26). Those who had recourse to *teraphim* were considered to have rejected the Lord (1 Sam. 15:23). Nevertheless, there were *teraphim* in Saul's own house (1 Sam. 19:13) and they were found throughout Israelite history (Hosea 3:4, 2 Kings 23:24). In 2 Kings 23:24 *teraphim* appear alongside the "fetishes" and "detestable things" that King Josiah destroyed. Some think that the *teraphim* were an image representing a primordial father, which explains their presence in the houses of Laban, David, Micah, and Hosea, where the text does not condemn them. Scholars are divided as to the root of the word. Some derive it from ר.פ.ה 'be limp, without energy'–i.e., something inert. Others assert that the root is ת.ר.פ 'decay, become foul', found in Aramaic and post-biblical Hebrew. It might also come from the Hittite *tarpi,* which means "spirit" or "demon." See also Meyers and Meyers, *Zechariah 9–14,* p. 186; Sarna, *Genesis,* p. 216; H. A. Hoffner, "Hittite Tarpis and Hebrew Teraphim," *JNES* 27 (1968), pp. 61–68.

38. Wright, *Zechariah and His Prophecies,* p. 267.

'delusion' (or 'iniquity'), and *teraphim*. The verse equates עָוֶן and שֶׁקֶר 'false-hood', both of which designate the deceptive messages reported to the peo-ple. There are many passages that link קֶסֶם and שֶׁקֶר (Jer. 14:14, 27:8–9, 29:9–10). This association between diviners and falsehood reflects the proph-ets' attitude towards diviners. In addition, the words *falsehood, predict* (חזה), and *diviners* link Zechariah with his predecessor Jeremiah, who used all of these terms (Jer. 14:14).

In the second half of the verse the prophet refers to dreams. Here חֲלֹמוֹת is the agent noun 'dreamers,' parallel to 'diviners' (Jer. 27:9); this is the under-standing of Targum Jonathan (נְבִיא שִׁקְרָא) and the Vulgate *(somniatores)*.[39] The verse says that the dreamers speak (יְדַבְּרוּ) in the imperfect—meaning that there were still dreamers who misled the people active in the prophet's time, whereas the careers of the *teraphim* and diviners were all in the past. The verb "speak," used of the *teraphim,* recurs here—as if to suggest that the messages of the teraphim and the dreamers are identical. Evidently Zechariah has in mind the false prophets who asserted that the Lord appeared to them in a dream and thereby deceived the people (cf. Jer. 23:25–29). Those who fore-told the future were supposed to comfort the exiles, but their words were empty.[40]

Because the people heeded these deceitful words and listened to those who attempted to comfort them (cf. Jer. 6:14), they strayed like a flock.[41] Indeed, "they suffer(?) for lack of a shepherd." Scholars have been hard put to explain this expression.[42] The root ע.נ.ה 'answer', when used without a following prep-ositional *bet* or *lamed*, has the meaning 'shout, cry' (Exod. 32:18; Deut. 21:7; Jer. 51:14). Rashi, David Kimḥi, and Abraham Ibn Ezra all glossed it here in

---

39. The Septuagint, however, renders the phrase, "dreams speak vanity." For arguments supporting חֲלֹמוֹת as a subject, see: W. Nowack, *Die kleinen Propheten,* HAT(Göttingen: Vandenhoeck und Ruprecht, 1903), pp. 295-96.

40. The combination of dreams and vanity is also found in Ecclesiastes: "For much dreaming leads to futility and to superfluous talk" (Eccles. 5:6).

41. A similar picture is found in the prophecies of Jeremiah: "My people were lost sheep: their shepherds led them astray" (Jer. 50:6). Jeremiah relates to the failure of the political leadership, whereas here it is a question of the absence of spiritual leadership. The word 'strayed' compares the people to a flock that has left its home pasture and been scattered (Jer. 23:1; see also Targum Jonathan on our verse). On the other hand, it should be noted that the verb generally refers to removing a stake or tent (cf. "My dwelling is pulled up and removed from me like a tent of shepherds (Isa. 38:12).

42. "Shepherd" refers to a Hebrew king in Jer. 23:1 and 50:6 and Ezek. 34:1. In Isa. 44:28 it applies to Cyrus; in Jer. 25:32 and Nahum 3:18 it designates other foreign mon-archs. See also Hinckley G. Mitchell, John Merlin Powis Smith, and Julius A. Bewer, *Haggai, Zechariah, Malachi, and Jonah,* ICC (New York: Charles Scribner's Sons, 1912), p. 288.

the sense of "submission," from the homonymous root ע.נ.ה that means "persecute, torture" in the *pi'el* and "suffer" in the *nif'al* (Isa. 31:4). Their interpretation suits the situation of the exiles living under foreign rule. It is no coincidence that this verb, which serves in the *pi'el* to denote the situation of those who occupy an inferior status in society (the stranger, the orphan, and the widow [Exod. 22:21–22]), is used here.[43] The prophecy refers to all of Israel and not only to the Northern Kingdom (see v. 6 and 7:14).[44] The author's use of יענו in the imperfect indicates that the references are to suffering that continues through his own time.

In sum, the linking together of *teraphim,* diviners, and dreamers in a single category creates a construct that represents Israel's lack of faith. The false prophets used all of these to foretell the future, and their dreams were unreal and devoid of content. Note that this verse resembles the passages we have considered from Jeremiah, who fiercely condemned the false prophets who used their divination and dreams to deceive the people. Like his predecessors Jeremiah and Ezekiel, Zechariah rails against the absence of spiritual leadership and attacks the "shepherds" who only led the people astray.[45]

Deuteronomy 13:2-6

> If there appears among you a prophet or a dream-diviner and he gives you a sign or a portent, [3] saying, "Let us follow and worship another god"—whom you have not experienced—even if the sign or portent that he named to you comes true, [4] do not heed the words of that prophet or that dream-diviner. For the Lord your God is testing you to see whether you really love the Lord your God with all your heart and soul. [5] Follow none but the Lord your God, and revere none but Him; observe His commandments alone, and heed only His orders; worship none but Him, and hold fast to Him. [6] As for that prophet or dream-diviner, he shall be put to death; for he urged disloyalty to the Lord your God—who freed you from the land of Egypt and who redeemed you from the house of bondage—to make you stray from the

---

43. Meyers and Meyers, *Zechariah 9–14,* p. 193.

44. Wright, *Zechariah 9–14,* p. 270; Mitchell, Smith, and Bewer, *Haggai, Zechariah, Malachi, and Jonah,* p. 287.

45. We should emphasize that we have referred only to the appearances of the word חֲלוֹם in Zechariah. In Zech. 1:1, however, we read that the visions came to the prophet at night. Is the reference perhaps to visions that came in the form of a dream? Does this refer only to the first vision, or to the entire book of visions? To know whether these visions describe dreams we must treat each one separately. On what is common to Zechariah's visions and dreams, see Uffenheimer, *The Vision of Zechariah,* pp. 61–63, 84–85, and 139–145.

path that the Lord your God commanded you to follow. Thus you will sweep out evil from your midst.

This passage, from the section presenting regulations regarding those who incite to idolatry (Deut. 13:2–19), refers to Israelite prophets and dream-diviners.[46] "Among you" emphasizes that prophecy is restricted to Israel. The text repeatedly distinguishes prophets from dream-diviners (vv. 2, 4, 6), but the nature of the distinction is not clear. Ehrlich, for example, conjectured that these dream-diviners constituted a sub-genus of foreign prophets.[47] He also believed that the sign referred to was merely the dream and its interpretation.[48] Nachmanides followed a similar path: "'The Lord your God is testing you' refers to the portent that the Lord showed him in his dream or in his *kihun.*"[49] The words of incitement, too, "Let us follow and worship another god," may be part of the message conveyed by the dream. Recall that in the ancient Near East dreams often conveyed ritual instructions, as in the case of Gudea, who was told to build a temple to Ningirsu.

According to the text, the prophet or dream-diviner will announce a sign or portent whose subsequent fulfillment will prove that one should comply with his call to worship other gods.[50] Ostensibly the realization of the sign or portent would be a tempting indication that the prophet was speaking the word of God. Nevertheless one must not heed him, because the content of his words constitutes ipso facto proof that they are not a divine decree. Actually, the Lord is tempting Israel by making the prophet's prediction come

---

46. The prophet himself has his status defined in a special law (Deut. 18:16–18), the meaning of the law indicates that there is a linguistic proximity between it and Deut. 13:2–6: נביא 'prophet' בקרבך 'in your midst', קום 'arise'. According to this law the source of the prophecy are words that the Lord places in the prophet's mouth. But what is interesting is that in this law dreams do not appear as a method of communication between the Lord and prophets. By contrast, see Numbers 12:6.

47. Ehrlich, *Traum,* p. 161.

48. Ibid.

49. Nachmanides glosses the term *kihun* or *kahin* in his commentary on v. 2: "The souls of some people contain a mantic power by which they know future events. He does not know whence it comes to him but he secludes himself and the spirit enters him so that he says, 'the future will be such for that person'; the philosophers call this *kahin.*

50. "Sign" and "portent" are the terms for the wonders that prophets worked to prove the divine origin of their messages to the people. The signs and portents that Moses performed are a very good example of this (Exod. 4:1–9). Similarly, the old prophet shattered the altar in Bethel as a sign that his proclamation of its destruction would come to pass (1 Kings 13:3, 5), and Isaiah made the shadow of the gnomon go backwards (Isa. 38:7–8). See also Num. 16:28–29 and 1 Kings 18:36. On miraculous signs in biblical belief see Kaufmann, *Toledot,* 1:473–475; Uffenheimer, *Ancient Prophecy in Israel,* pp. 284–287.

true. He wants to test the people and see whether their love for Him is so steadfast that not even a miraculous sign or portent can persuade them to accept the words of the prophet.

Even though the instigator in question is not a true prophet and the Lord did not send him, the passage refers to him as a *prophet.* The term "false prophet" is a later coinage, found in the Septuagint and Talmudic literature. The passage in Deuteronomy calls on the people not to listen to "that prophet" and not to examine whether there is some substance to what he says—there is no doubt that everything he says is falsehood of his own invention, aiming at evil, and that the sign or portent was worked by sorcery or stratagem and not by mantic power. The same caveats apply to the dream-diviner, who did not have a dream at all but invented his tale in order to deceive.

Clearly the realization of the sign or portent is not the most important criterion and should not impress the people. The prophet or dream-diviner has urged disloyalty to the Lord, making proclamations that are tantamount to a call to revolt against Him. The noun סרה is really much stronger than "disloyalty"; it is related to סורר ומורה 'wayward and defiant' (Deut. 21.18), or may indicate that he turns away (סר) from the truth—in other words, tells lies. S. D. Luzzatto noted that Jeremiah used the noun in the connotation of speaking falsehood (Jer. 28:16 and 29:32); so, evidently, does Isaiah (59:13b). This seems to be its sense in the present verse, too, with reference to the lies told by the prophet or dreamer.[51] Whereas v. 4 admonishes the people not to heed the words of the prophet or dream-diviner, v. 5 is a call to obey the word of God, as is stated explicitly later: "The Lord your God will raise up for you a prophet from among your own people, like myself; him you shall heed" (Deut. 18:15).

The fulfillment of the sign or portent given by false prophets has long exercised the commentators. In Sifre on this verse and in the Talmud (BT Sanhedrin 90a) we read: "Rabbi Yose the Galilean said, 'See how the Bible penetrated to the bottom of the intention of the idolaters, to whom it gave dominion; do not listen to them even if they make the sun and moon and stars and constellations stand in their places, … for the Lord is testing you.' Rabbi Akiva said, 'Heaven forbid that the Holy One Blessed be He should stop the sun and moon and stars and constellations for idolaters! He speaks only through someone who was formerly a true prophet but then became a false

---

51. The cognate Akkadian expression "speak *sartu* [or *sarrātu, surrātu*]" means both "tell lies" and "propose disloyalty" (Jeffrey H. Tigay, *Deuteronomy: The JPS Torah Commentary:* [Philadelphia: Jewish Publication Society, 1996], p. 367, n. 20).

prophet.'"[52] Commentators have recoiled from the possibility that a false prophet could work wonders and attempted to explain the phenomenon in various ways. Ibn Ezra explained that these signs and portents are symbolic but perfectly natural events, as in Isa. 20:3 and other passages. Nachmanides believed that the reference is to persons endowed with supernatural powers who exploit them to work a sign or portent, pretend to be prophets, and on the strength of this urge the people to worship idols. Maimonides (Moses ben Maimon, known as Rambam, 1130–1204) in his code, in the chapter entitled "Laws of Idolatry and Customs of the Gentiles" (1:1), explained the train of reasoning that can lead people to think that God wants them to serve other gods in addition to Himself:

> In the days of Enosh, the people fell into gross error, and senseless was the counsel of the wise men of that generation. Enosh himself was among those who committed the error. The error was this: They said that in view of the fact that God created the stars and celestial spheres to guide the world, setting them on high and honoring them, and they are His ministering servants, they deserved to be praised, glorified, and honored. It is the will of God, blessed be He, that we glorify and honor anyone who is glorified and honored, just as a king desires that respect be shown those who stand and minister before him, since this is an indirect way of honoring the king himself. When this notion entered their mind, they began to build temples in honor of the stars and offered sacrifices to them, praising and glorifying them in speech and prostrating themselves before them, in order to win the favor of the Creator, according to their wrong thinking.[53]

Nachmanides applies a similar explanation to the worship of other gods:

> Now this man who calls himself a prophet and gives instruction to worship idols, in accordance with the plain meaning is a prophet of idolatry, who says that the image of Peor sent me to you, for he is god, and commanded that you serve him in such and such a fashion. This is the type referred to later as well—"any prophet … who speaks in the name of other gods—that prophet shall die" (Deut. 18:20)—because anyone who prophesies in the name of other gods is doing so to serve them, because they are his gods, and he is mentioned there along with

---

52. See Reuven Hammer, *Sifre on Deuteronomy* (New Haven: Yale University Press, 1986), 137:84.

53. Maimonides, *Mishneh Torah,* "Idolatry and Heathenism" 1:1, trans. Philip Birnbaum (New York: Hebrew Publishing Company, 1944), p. 30; Tigay, *Deuteronomy,* p. 367 n. 22.

the false prophets. But the implication of what our sages said is that the prophet mentioned here is speaking in the name of the Lord and says that the august Lord sent me to have you worship Peor because he was His partner in the work of creation, or that he is greater than all gods before him and He wants you to worship him. They said that even if they tell you to worship idols for only a single hour–for example, they say worship Peor today only and you will succeed in such and such a thing, for such is the will of the august Lord–they deserve death, and this too is the plain meaning of the Scripture.

Here Nachmanides offers two interpretations: that the inciter is a consciously idolatrous prophet, or that he has been misled to believe that the Lord sent him to tell the people to worship some other god and accordingly showed him a sign "in his dream or *kihun.*"

In sum, the above suggests that the Book of Deuteronomy does not necessarily repudiate the phenomenon of dreams. What it does reject are false prophets who use dreams for propaganda purposes and divert the people from the correct path. Ehrlich explains that the verse is directed against the professional diviners of the ancient world; true prophets, however, can receive divine revelation.[54] Gnuse maintains that the verses in Deuteronomy reflect the popular vacillation and uncertainty about how to identify a true prophet. The passage, he feels, presents a theological criterion for such identification. In his view, the rejection of dreams is a direct result of the association between dreams and false prophets: "Dreams are not rejected as a possible means of revelation but one must be very critical of them."[55]

DREAMS AS FLEETING EXPERIENCES

Isaiah 29:7-8

Then, like a dream, a vision of the night, shall be the multitude of nations that war upon Ariel, and all her besiegers, and the siegeworks against her, and those who harass her. [8] Like one who is hungry and dreams he is eating, but wakes to find himself empty; and like one who is thirsty and dreams he is drinking, but wakes to find himself faint and utterly parched–so shall be all the multitude of nations that war upon Mount Zion.

These verses are the conclusion of a unit that begins with 29:1, beginning with

54. Ehrlich, *Traum,* p. 162.
55. Gnuse, *Dream,* p. 86. N. 99.

the exclamation "ah!" (הוי) and ending with "so shall be the multitude"(כן יהי המון). It is subdivided into three parts (vv. 1–3, 4–6, 7–8). Because the passage begins with הוי we naturally expect it to be an admonitory prophecy. In v. 7, however, and even before that, in v. 5, we realize that in fact the prophet is describing deliverance. The background is the siege of Jerusalem, here denominated "Ariel."[56] The great drama presented to readers describes the helplessness of the city under siege (vv. 4 and 5). Jerusalem will be brought so low the prophet compares it to someone who is wallowing in the dust, oppressed, its voice like a ghost's.

Some believe that the siege described here is historical; the Bible reports at least four sieges of Jerusalem—during the reign of Ahaz (734 BCE; Isa. 7), by Sennacherib during the reign of Hezekiah (701 BCE, Isa. 22 and 36–37), and by Nebuchadnezzar in 598 and in 587 BCE.[57] This motif is also found in Jeremiah, Ezekiel, and Zechariah.[58] On the other hand, the picture of the armies of many nations encamped about Jerusalem, as found in this chapter, is devoid of any historical basis. Here in Isaiah 29 there is no indication of the identity of the besiegers, how long they will invest the city, what will cause their downfall, and what will happen afterwards. This is quite different from the verses about Sennacherib's downfall at the gates of Jerusalem (9:1–4; 10:25–34; 37:33–38), which is an historical event.

The Ariel prophecy turns on a motif that is found in various avatars in the prophetic literature and the Psalms. It focuses on the eve of the redemption at the end of days, when all the nations of the world assemble to make war on Jerusalem and conquer it, only to meet a sudden overthrow. There is no particular historical underpinning to the motif. It takes shape as a result of the recurrent sieges of Jerusalem during the First Temple Period, and the ability of the city to withstand them strengthened the popular belief in its immunity (Isaiah 26). It seems likely that Sennacherib's failure to conquer Jerusalem in

---

56. Many scholars have tried to explain the derivation of "Ariel" and there is little consensus among them. The name appears in the Bible in various forms: (Isa. 29:1–7; 1 Chron. 11:22; Ezek. 43:15 [qere]); אראל (2 Sam. 23:20), אראיל (Ezek. 43:15 [ketib]), הראל (ibid.), and אראלם (Isa. 33:7), with the plural suffix *mem*; we also find אראל in the Mesha Stone (l. 12). In Ezekiel 43:15–16 the context is ritual and the reference is to part of the Temple, and the dimensions of the אראיל are reported. Among the glosses offered for the word are (1) one of the important ritual vessels in the Temple; (2) angel; (3) the Temple, Mount Zion, or all of Jerusalem; (4) a large lion. On this matter see at length, H. G. May, "Ephod and Ariel," *AJSL* 56 (1939), pp. 44–69; W. F. Albright, *Archaeology and the Religion of Israel* (Baltimore: Johns Hopkins Press, 1942), pp. 151 and 218; N. H. Tur-Sinai, "Ariel," *EMiqr* 1:558–560.

57. John D. W. Watts, *Isaiah 1–33*, WBC vol. 24 (Waco, TX: Word, 1985), p. 381.

58. R. de Vaux, "Jérusalem et les prophètes," *RB* 73 (1966), pp. 481–509; J. H. Hayes, "The Tradition of Zion's Inviolability," *JBL* 82 (1963), p. 424.

the year 701 BCE helped crystallize this belief, which thereafter lost its association with reality and took on an eschatological character. It is also possible that it evolved only after the destruction of the Temple and the Babylonian exile.[59] That is, the city itself was destroyed but the faith in its strength was transmogrified and merged into notions about the end of days.

In contrast, these eight verses feature a theological theme that recurs frequently in the Book of Isaiah—namely, that Jerusalem, the City of David, will not escape justice. The Lord will employ foreign armies to punish it, standing behind the enemies and directing their actions. Whereas previously the nations fought against the city and the Lord defended it, here it is the Lord who has brought the foe to the gates of Jerusalem.[60] All of a sudden, however, the Lord will intervene and deliver the city. His appearance is described as "roaring, and shaking, and deafening noise, storm, and tempest, and blaze of consuming fire" (v. 6).[61] The Lord will punish the enemies and they will vanish.

The foes, it is said, will be like "fine dust and flying chaff" (v. 5); the siege itself will be like a dream or vision of the night—unreal. Like a dream, it will prove to have been ephemeral; the enemies of Jerusalem will vanish.[62] Here dreams are equated with nocturnal visions (v. 7). According to David Kimḥi, "What a man sees in his dream is called a vision even though it is not a prophecy." The author also compares the enemies to those who are hungry and thirsty and who dream about food and drink, only to wake up and find no food or water to be had. The enemies anticipated the downfall of Jerusalem, but their imagined future passes away like a dream. In sum, Isaiah here treats dreams as products of the imagination and uses them as a metaphor for something devoid of content. There is no hint here of the notion that dreams come from the Lord.

Job 20:8

He flies away like a dream and they cannot find him; he goes away like a night vision.

---

59. The post-exilic texts that employ this motif are Ezekiel 38–39, Joel 4, and Zechariah 12 and 14. The dates of the other texts (Isaiah 25:6–8; 29:1–8; Psalm 46) are unclear and there is no agreement as to whether they are pre- or post-exilic.

60. Marvin A. Sweeney, Rolf P. Knierim, and Gene M. Tucker, eds., *Isaiah 1–39* (Grand Rapids, Michigan: Eerdmans 1996), pp. 375–376.

61. According to BT Sanhedrin 94a, Sennacherib's soldiers were consumed by fire like Nadab and Abihu the sons of Aaron, whose souls were incinerated within them while their bodies were left unmarked.

62. Some see the image in v. 8 of the enemies themselves as dreamers as a gloss, added by a later editor, on the descriptions in vv. 5–6.

In vv. 7–9, Zofar says about wicked people what Job says about people in general, and this is in fact the crux of the argument between Job and his friends. Job asserts that God created man weak. His friends, for their part, counter that this weakness is a punishment for human sins. The language of this verse resembles Ps. 73:20 and Isa. 29:7, where the wicked and the enemies disappear with the light of day. Here this image is applied to the wicked, who will vanish just as dreams and nocturnal visions do—hence dreams and night visions are parallel and equivalent, as in Job 7:14. According to Clines, "The night vision is here certainly a dream, though in 4:13 it seems to be a waking vision."[63] As for "they cannot find him," the subject must be supplied from the agent-participle רֹאָיו 'those who see him' in v. 7.

In other words, the case of the wicked is like that of a dream, which cannot return and be seen again. וְיִדַּד 'he goes away' (root נ.ד.ד) in the second half of the verse is parallel to יָעוּף 'he flies away' in the first half; for the parallelism compare "like a sparrow wandering (נוֹדֶדֶת) from its nest" (Prov. 27:8) and "when the sun comes out, they fly away (וְנוֹדַד)" (Nahum 3:17). The form יִדַּד is a *hof'al* of a פ"נ verb, not conjugated as a gemmate. The verb is deponent–passive form with an active sense–like נֶעְלַם 'disappear.' The idea is that just as dreams and night visions are devoid of content and have no substance, so too nothing will remain of the wealth and strength of the wicked. A similar idea is found in Egyptian literature, where dreams are "a figure for things that are fleeting, illusory, or even deceptive."[64] In the Instruction of the Vizier Ptahhotep we find the simile, "a short moment like a dream."[65] Elsewhere we read, "A dream is transient, a fleeting thing, so it is used as a figure for things that last a short while: 'He goes quickly like a dream.'"[66]

Ecclesiastes 5:2,6

> Just as dreams come with many matters, so does the voice of a fool with much speech. ... [6] For much dreaming [leads to] futility and [to] superfluous talk. Fear God.

Some see v. 2 as a marginal gloss that has crept into the text, because the verse seems to interrupt the harmony of the chapter.[67] Such was the interpretation of Jastrow, who said that v. 2 actually belongs with v. 6 and joins the two

---

63. David J. A. Clines, *Job 1–20*, WBC 17 (Dallas, TX: Word Books, 1989), p. 486.

64. H. Grapow, *Die Bildlichen Ausdrücke des Ägyptischen* (Leipzig: Hinrich's, 1924), p. 140.

65. Miriam Lichtheim, *Ancient Egyptian Literature* (Berkeley: University of California Press, 1973), 1:68.

66. Ibid., 3:51.

67. George Aaron Barton, *The Book of Ecclesiastes* (New York: Scribner's, 1909), p. 123.

verses while deleting parts of them.[68] Perhaps v. 2 was inserted because v. 3 also mentions fools. If so, we should note that כסיל 'fool' appears in the first section of this unit (in 4:17), where Ecclesiastes admonishes against joining the fool in his thank-offering. Similarly, דברים 'speech, words' appears in 5:1. In fact, כסיל and דברים are key terms in this unit, which runs from 4:17 to 5:7 and contains many recurring words, including "God" seven times, "vow" five times, "words" or "speech" four times, and "fool" three times.

Verse 2 is expressed as a simile: just as dreams are full of many items that have no connection, the fool's utterances are many and confused. Ecclesiastes calls on wise men to be careful. Just as dreams contain many matters but few genuine ideas, so too the fool utters many words—with little meaning. Rashi interpreted the verse in a similar vein: "It is the way of dreams to come with many thoughts that people examine and contemplate during the day, and it is the way of the fool's utterances to contain many words, and by saying so much he makes foolishness issue from his mouth and never stops sinning. Accordingly I say, let your words be few." The implication, however, is that dreams come from the dreamer's own psyche and do not have an external origin.

The idea that there is nothing substantial in dreams is repeated in v. 6. Abraham Ibn Ezra understands the first part of the verse as repeating v. 2. In fact, scholars have yet to come up with a plausible solution to the grammatical problems that v. 6 poses. All agree that the first half—"for many dreams and futility, like superfluous talk"—is elliptical and that the predicate must be supplied by conjecture. Targum Jonathan adds "do not give credence" to all these things, and Rashi accepts this. The *waw* prefixed to דברים הרבה is best understood as the comparative *waw*, as in v. 2; that is, there is nothing substantial in either dreaming or talk. It is possible, though, that the *waw* has replaced a *bet*, and the sense is that there are many dreams and much futility in superfluous words, and the use of רב 'many' is an intentional echo of v. 2. Still another possibility is that the missing predicate is "pay no attention" (as in 7:21) or "keep your mouth from rashness" (as in 5:1). Barton suggested inverting the word order so that "words" precedes "futility / vanities" and reads: "For in a multitude of dreams and words are many vanities."[69] Wright, after reviewing the various proposed emendations, suggests inserting a prefix *bet* before "words," even though this reading too is difficult, and then renders: "For in the multitude of dreams are also vanities, and in many words also."[70]

---

68. Morris Jastrow, *A Gentle Cynic* (Philadelphia: Lippincott, 1919), pp. 216–217.

69. Ibid., p. 125.

70. Charles Henry Hamilton Wright, *The Book of Koheleth* (London: Hodder and Stoughton, 1953), pp. 363–364.

Gordis tries to maintain the received text and proposes, "In spite of all dreams, follies and idle chatter, indeed fear God."[71]

According to the midrash *(Ṣemaḥ David 2, Yᵉmot ʿolam)*, one who has bad dreams or visions that cause him to be afraid should immediately proceed to prayer, repentance, and charity. But vows are unnecessary, because it is possible to give charity without one. According to the Italian Renaissance commentator Obadiah Sforno, if someone wants to make a vow because he was terrified by bad dreams and the like, the vow is unnecessary; it is enough to fear God, and this will avert the calamity. Evidently the advice to fear God is the core, since this is how the entire book concludes: "The sum of the matter, when all is said and done: Revere God and observe His commandments! For this applies to all mankind" (Eccles. 12:13).

Verse 6, then, repeats the theme of the maxim in v. 2: Excessive words are like many dreams and vanities. Dreams are empty and have no substance (cf. Zech. 10:2, "Dreamers speak lies and console with illusions"). Qoheleth compares the words of the fool to dreams: just as dreams are chaotic and insubstantial, the fool's words are confused and meaningless, vain and futile. It follows that Qoheleth does not ascribe any religious meaning to the phenomenon and does not believe that it contains any message whatsoever concerning the dreamer's future. In sum, he views dreams as exclusively personal experiences, unlike the prophetic literature, which assigns them a role in public life. Oppenheim, like Qoheleth, identifies in v. 2 the rationalist view characteristic of the wisdom literature and offers an extrabiblical parallel from a text from Kuyunjik: "Remove [wo]e and anxiety from your heart (literally: from your side), [wo]e and anxiety create (only bad) dreams."[72]

Psalm 73:20

> As one does a dream after waking, O Lord, in the city [*or* when You are aroused] You despise their image.

Psalm 73 deals with the classic theme of the wisdom literature: God's conduct of the world and the thorny problem of theodicy. The chapter asks the twin questions—why evil besets the righteous and why the wicked prosper—and then answers them. The verse we are considering compares the wicked to a dream that vanishes when one wakes up. The Lord is called on to despise the wicked.[73] The word צלמם relates to the wicked, who are only the image of a

---

71. Robert Gordis, *Koheleth: The Man and His World* (New York: JTS, 1951), p. 239.

72. Oppenheim, *Interpretation,* p. 227; K 1453: 18–19.

73. RSV omits the word "Lord" and reads, "They are like a dream when one awakes,

shadow and not substantial.[74] The wicked will evaporate as dreams do, and will be abased and demeaned in the sight of all the people of their city. Some conjecture that בָּעִיר is not "in the city" but an elided form of the *hif'il* infinitive בְּהָעִיר, from the root ע.ו.ר 'arouse oneself, awake'.[75] If we accept this interpretation the two parts of the verb have parallel verbs–מהקיץ 'awake' and בְּהָעִיר 'arouse'; these two roots are used together in Ps. 35:23. This interpretation is certainly appropriate here: the first hemistich would then refer to waking up after a dream, after which the dreamer, now awake, discovers the nullity of the wicked. The poet's attitude toward dreams, then, is dismissive. They are a transient phenomenon devoid of substance, and so are the wicked, who will vanish.

Psalm 126:1

> A song of ascents. When the Lord restored the fortunes of Zion–we were like dreamers [*or* we saw it as in a dream].

This psalm, which has six verses, is divided into two equal sections of three verses each. The first begins with "When the Lord restores the fortunes of Zion," the second with "Restore our fortunes, O Lord." The first verse ends, "We saw it as in a dream," and the last verse of the first part, "We rejoiced." Some of the verbs in the first half are in the perfect; all those in the second half are in the imperative or the imperfect. That is, the psalmist begins with thanksgiving for past bounty and then switches to a petition for the future. The poet may be uttering a prayer in the lines, "You have begun to deliver us, now complete what you have begun." It is also possible to read the entire psalm as thanksgiving for past salvation and construe the hortative שׁוּבָה 'restore' in v. 4 as describing past action. Yet another possibility is that the

---

on awakening you despise their phantoms." Kraus emends "Lord" to איננו 'is not', with the sense of "disappear," and renders the verse, "like a dream upon awakening, they have disappeared" (Hans Joachim Kraus, *Psalms 60–150*, trans. Hilton C. Oswald [Minneapolis: Augsburg, 1989], p. 83). It is hard to accept these emendations, because vv. 18–20 are a single unit in which the poet is saying that the success of the wicked is an illusion and ultimately they will perish. Already in v. 18 there is a description of how the Lord "rewards" the wicked by means of flattery and deceit. Verse 20 continues this line of thought and calls on the Lord to reveal the nullity and contemptibility of the wicked before all.

74. According to the Septuagint, צלמים refers to their image, and it renders: "As the dream of one awakening, O Lord in Your city You will despise their image."

75. J. L. Crenshaw, *A Whirlpool of Torment* (Philadelphia: Fortress Press, 1984), p. 105; J. J. Stewart Perowne, *The Book of Psalms*, vol. 2 (Andover: Warren F. Draper, 1882), p. 22. This reading seems to go back as far as David Kimḥi, who cites it in his father's name but does not accept it himself.

entire psalm is future-oriented; in other words, that the gerund בְּשׁוּב in v. 1 means, "When the Lord at some time in the future restores the remnant to Zion," then will we say, "We saw it in a dream"; in this view, the imperfects in v. 2 (יִמָּלֵא and יֹאמְרוּ) have a future sense.

Commentators and scholars have long wrestled with the phrase שִׁבַת צִיּוֹן 'the fortunes(?) of Zion.' Some say that the reference here is to the exiles who returned (שָׁבוּ) to Zion from captivity (שְׁבִי). The returnees prayed to the Lord to bless the produce of their land so that they could settle down on the estates to which they returned. This reading can be supported from Jeremiah 48:46–47: "Woe to you, O Moab! The people of Chemosh are undone, for your sons are carried off into captivity, your daughters into exile. But I will restore the fortunes (וְשַׁבְתִּי שְׁבוּת) of Moab in the days to come—declares the Lord" (Jer. 48:46–47). In this context it is clearly possible to understand that the Lord is promising to bring home the Moabite captives of v. 46. Following this line, Psalm 126 refers to the return of the Jews from the Babylonian captivity. Another interpretation is that שׁוּב שִׁיבָה[76] is like שׁוּב שְׁבוּת and should be understood in the light of Ps. 14:7—"When the Lord restores the fortunes of His people (בְּשׁוּב ה' שְׁבוּת עַמּוֹ)"—where it clearly denotes a return to the former favorable situation and has nothing to do with exile and captivity.[77] In the same vein we have "The Lord restored (שָׁב שְׁבִית [קרי: שְׁבוּת]) Job's fortunes ... and the Lord gave Job twice what he had before" (Job 42:10). An identical expression with a similar signification could be found in the text of the Aramaic treaty found at Sefire from the middle of the eighth century CE, where the spelling שיבת indicates that it comes from the root שׁ.ו.ב 'restore' and not from שׁ.ב.ה 'take captive'. In other words, the text of the Psalm has to do with the restoration of the Israelites' fortunes and not with their return from captivity.[78]

Some allege that כְּחוֹלְמִים 'like dreamers' should be rendered as "were healthy" or "were healed," drawing on "You have restored me to health and revived me" (וְתַחֲלִימֵנִי וְהַחֲיֵינִי) (Isa. 38:16; see also Job 39:4), where the root ח.ל.מ has this sense. This notion is common in the prophetic books, where Israel's afflictions are compared to a disease and its deliverance to healing (Hosea 6:7 and frequently in Jeremiah). In fact, the Aramaic Targum renders our verse as "like sick persons who have been healed." Strugnell follows the same path:

---

76. Taking שִׁיבה as derived from שׁ.ו.ב, like ביאה and קימה from ב.ו.א and ק.ו.מ (Lam. 3:63).

77. Charles Augustus Briggs and Emily Grace Briggs, *The Book of Psalms, ICC* (Edinburgh, T. and T. Clark, 1907), 2:455–456.

78. Mitchell Dahood, *Psalms III: 101–150, AB* (Garden City, NY: Doubleday, 1970), p. 218; Fitzmyer, *The Aramaic Inscriptions of Sefire*, Biblica et Orientalia 19 (Rome: Pontifical Biblical Institute, 1967), pp. 119–120.

"Then we were as men who had been/were healed."[79] This rendering is compatible with reading the psalm as referring to the restoration of fortunes, which clearly parallels recovery from illness. It also sees "dream" as quite inappropriate here, because the speakers are praying and waiting for deliverance and have no reason to believe they will not succeed.

On the other hand, "dream" is compatible with the idea that the psalm deals with the return of the exiles from Babylonia. The people's joy in their deliverance is so great that all their past troubles now seem to have been an insubstantial nightmare. Another possible interpretation is that the idea of returning from exile seemed dreamlike and unbelievable to them—and that the Psalmist holds dreams to be an image of the vacuous and unreal.[80]

DREAMS AS CHANNELS OF COMMUNICATION

Joel 3:1

> After that, I will pour out My spirit on all flesh; your sons and daughters shall prophesy; your old men shall dream dreams, and your young men shall see visions.

Some see this verse as a direct continuation from the end of the previous chapter. People will praise the name of the Lord and will no longer be shamed, because He is in their midst.[81] Further, because the people have been told about the plenty that is to follow the plague of locusts, the prophet goes on to speak of a key tenet in the faith of Israel—namely, the advent of a great and terrible day when all the nations who have harmed Israel will be punished. Even though the Babylonians will come to occupy their land, and other peoples will subjugate them and put an end to their greatness, they need not fear, because the time will come when the Lord will judge all of their enemies and proclaim the righteousness of His people Israel.

The prophecy will be fulfilled in the distant future; והיה אחרי כן 'after that' is a transitional formula synonymous with 'in the days to come' (lit., 'at the end of days'; Isa. 2:2 and Micah 4:1).[82] The expression refers to all the prophecies

---

79. J. Strugnell, "A Note on Psalm 126, 1," *JTS* 7 (1956), pp. 239–243.

80. Dahood offers another interpretation; for חולמים he would read חול-מ-ים 'sand from the sea' (Dahood, *Psalms III: 101–150*, p. 219).

81. Arvid S. Kapelrud, *Joel Studies* (Uppsala: A. B. Lundequist, 1948), p. 126.

82. On the other hand, אחרי כן by itself is also used with respect to actions that take place immediately (Exod. 11:1, 1 Sam. 24:6). By contrast והיה is used in the prophetic books to allude to the distant future; see Isa. 7:21, Jer. 17:24, Ezek. 38:10, Hos. 1:5, Amos 8:9, and Zech. 13:2.

in chapters 3 and 4 to be fulfilled after the previous promises have been realized.[83] Rashi and David Kimḥi understand it to designate the Messianic Era, when the Lord will pour his spirit on all flesh.[84] And this pouring of the spirit of the Lord will turn all Israel into prophets.[85]

The spirit is not under human control; it is given by God in order to endow human beings with life[86] or to allow a person to accomplish great deeds.[87] Here it will enable people to prophesy. Compare Moses's words to Joshua: "Would that all the Lord's people were prophets, that the Lord put His spirit upon them!" (Num. 11:29). Joel's ideal is similar—namely, that all Israel will be prophets. Prophecy, the vocation of rare individuals, will in the future be the lot of the entire people of Israel. All existing barriers—gender, age, and social status—will be removed.

Some inquire as to the meaning of the idea that the spirit will be poured "on all flesh (בָּשָׂר)": Is the reference to (1) all human beings and animals (as in Gen. 6:13 and 17, 7:15); (2) only animals (ibid. 7:21); (3) all human beings of all races (Gen. 6:12, Isa. 40:6, Jer. 25:31, Zech. 2:17); or (4) only Israel (Jer. 12:12)? Kapelrud believes that the reference is only to the people of Israel, on the basis of the analogy with Ezekiel: "For I will pour out my spirit upon the House of Israel" (Ezek. 39:29).[88] Wolff points out that in the previous chapter the word of the Lord was addressed specifically to the people of Israel (2:19), and thereafter it is said that the Lord is present among Israel. A reference to other nations appears only in chapter 4.[89] Similarly, David Kimḥi also limits the verse to Israel, whose merit is such that the Holy Spirit can rest on them—"on all flesh among Israel, just as it says elsewhere, all flesh, referring not to all animals but only to human beings." Finally, Don Isaac Abravanel says that although all human beings of all nations will recognize the greatness of the Lord, only Israelites can reach the prophetic degree described in the verse.

The mention of "your sons and daughters" indicates that the verse refers to

---

83. Hans Walter Wolff, *Joel and Amos,* trans. Waldemar Janssen, S. Dean McBride, Jr., and Charles A. Muenchow (Philadelphia: Fortress Press, 1977), p. 65.

84. For the basic signification of the root שׁ.פ.כ, see Exod. 4:9 (pouring water), Gen. 9:6 (shedding blood), etc. Similar to the metaphor of pouring spirit, found here, is the idiom of pouring out the heart (Ps. 62:9, Lam. 2:19), or the soul (1 Sam. 1:15, Ps. 42:5).

85. In a similar story in 1 Sam. 10, we read how the Spirit of the Lord descended upon Saul and caused him to prophesy. In other words, the Spirit of the Lord causes people to make prophetic utterances.

86. Isa. 42:5; Ps. 104:29–30; Ezek. 37:14. See also Wolff, *Joel and Amos,* p. 66.

87. Judg. 6:34 and 14:36.

88. Kapelrud, *Joel,* p. 131.

89. Wolff, *Joel and Amos,* p. 67.

the future; this is why the younger generation appears first.[90] By contrast, the second part of the verse–"your old men shall dream dreams, and your young men shall see visions"–creates a parity between old and young.[91] There seems to be no particular correlation between the categories of persons–sons, daughters, old men, and young men–and the type of experience attributed to each.[92] Redemption will come to all of Israel as a gift from God. The pouring of the spirit of the Lord on Israel is a sign of the renewal of relations between the Lord and his people, as we have already read: "I am in the midst of Israel" (Joel 2:27). On the other hand, David Kimḥi in his commentary quotes Maimonides (*Guide of the Perplexed* 2:36) to the effect that not every man can be a prophet. Not even the appropriate study and preparation are a guarantee of success, for prophecy depends on whether a person has been endowed with the natural qualities and disposition for it.

Joel's attitude toward dreams is positive, unlike Jeremiah's attack on the false prophets who exploited dreams for purposes of propaganda and deceit. Jeremiah's rejection of dreams is foreign to Joel, who was evidently more influenced by the Pentateuch, which was canonized during his period, and which relates to dreams as a positive phenomenon.

Job 4:12-16

> To me a word came in stealth; my ear caught a whisper of it. [13] In thought-filled visions of the night, when deep sleep falls on men, [14] Fear and trembling came upon me, causing all my bones to quake with fright. [15] A wind passed by me, making the hair of my flesh bristle. [16] It halted; its appearance was strange to me; a form loomed before my eyes; I heard a murmur, a voice.

Eliphaz is one of the seven Gentile prophets enumerated in the Talmud (BT Baba Batra 15b). It is not by chance that in the verses under consideration he describes a dream, a vision of the night that resembles, in both theme and

---

90. Some believe that "your sons and daughters" actually denotes all the inhabitants of Judah, whereas "old men" and "young men" refer to the entire male population, because the elders had an honored social status and made the decisions, while the young men served in the army. See James L. Crenshaw, *Joel, AB* (New York: Doubleday, 1995), p. 166.

91. Malbim (Meir Leibush ben Jehiel Mikhel, 1809–1879), on the other hand, does read the verse as making a distinction between the old and the young. The older people, who reach maturity before the redemption, will see dreams, which is a lower level of revelation. The younger men, by contrast, though born before the redemption, reach maturity only after the start of the Messianic Era. They will see visions, which belong to a higher level, albeit still lower than full prophecy.

92. This is also the opinion of Ehrlich, *Traum,* p. 140, n. 5.

language, the descriptions of the epiphanies experienced by Elijah (1 Kings 19) and Isaiah (chapter 21). Eliphaz, however, had neither a prophetic revelation nor a theophany in which the Lord appeared in His full glory, but only a mysterious vision.

Eliphaz's recital moves from the explicit and familiar to the arcane. In v. 7 he tells his audience to "remember now" what is well known to everyone. In v. 8 he continues with what "I have seen"–that is, information that may not be known to all, but has been made available to him. Then he relates what no man can know unless it is revealed in a mysterious vision–how the word of the Lord was vouchsafed to him in stealth.[93] Rashi, picking up on this use of the root ג.נ.ב, reminds us that the words of the Lord came to the Hebrew prophets openly, whereas "the Holy Spirit is not made manifest to pagan prophets in public."

Eliphaz continues that his ear caught (only) a שֵׁמֶץ of the vision. The meaning of שֵׁמֶץ is uncertain. Some say it means "small part";[94] others, "whisper." The author may have had both denotations in mind. That is, Eliphaz is saying that he was not worthy to have the entire secret revealed to him, but only part of it, and even what was said was said in a whisper.

Eliphaz refers to his experience as a "vision of the night"–night being the time "when deep sleep falls on men." The word *dream* is not mentioned; but given the poetic context it is only natural that appropriate lyrical terminology be used. In any case, nocturnal visions are mentioned alongside (Isa. 29:7, Job 33:15), or in parallel to (Joel 3:1 and Job 20:8) dreams in other passages. Here Eliphaz uses three terms: בִּשְׂעִפִּים 'thoughts', חֶזְיֹנוֹת 'visions', and תַּרְדֵּמָה 'deep sleep', in what seems to be a series of reversed Chinese boxes. Deep sleep is the appropriate state for the establishment of a link between human beings and God; the Lord Himself is the cause of this state. The word תַּרְדֵּמָה appears in the story of the covenant between the pieces (Gen. 15:12), the creation of Eve (Gen. 2:21), David's nocturnal penetration of Saul's camp and refusal to harm the sleeping king (1 Sam. 26:12), and in the context of Divine revelations vouchsafed to prophets (Isa. 29:10, Job 33:15). In all these passages the word refers to a state of deep sleep:[95] "When deep sleep falls on people" is a formula to indicate the hour of the revelation. The poetic word

---

93. Compare 2 Sam. 19:4.

94. Some scholars explain שמץ as a "small part" (thus the rendering in Targum Jonathan and the Peshitta); for this meaning, see Ben Sira 10:10 and 18:32. This gloss is supported by E. Dhorme, *A Commentary on the Book of Job*, trans. Harold Knight (London: Nelson, 1967), p. 59. It is hard to accept this view, however, because it seems to be incompatible with the verb applied to שמץ in Job 26:14–"the mere whisper that we *hear* of Him."

95. In Jonah 1:5–6 the word is used ironically: Jonah has fallen asleep, not to establish

שְׂעִפִּים designates the thoughts that run through a person's head in sleeping visions.[96] Evidently Eliphaz, sunk in a deep sleep, had visions in which he saw himself engrossed in thought, and it was in that state that a mysterious and terrifying vision came to him.[97] Eliphaz was stricken by fear even before the revelation, a fact that the verse notes twice. This fear, which is a sign of the proximity of something from another world,[98] caused him to tremble physically (this too is mentioned twice), his bones "quaking with fright" (in biblical symbolism, the bones represent the entire body).[99] Thus Eliphaz's fear is the same as Abraham's *before* the Lord appeared to him in a vision. With dreams, the fear is experienced only afterwards (Gen. 20:8 and 28:17).

At the start Eliphaz feels a wind blowing on him—an indication of the imminence of the revelation. This wind makes the "hair of his flesh" stand on end.[100] The bristling of the body hair is a psychological phenomenon motivated by fear. Nevertheless, some believe that the letter *sin* should be a *samekh*—סערה 'storm' instead of שׂערה 'hair'; rearranging the hypothetically corrupt text then yields the common idiom רוח סערה 'stormwind'.[101] Tur-Sinai, too, notes the frequent biblical parallelism of wind and storm (Ezek. 1:4, 12:11, 13; Ps. 55:6, 148:8; and in parallel Isa. 41:16; so too Targum Jonathan).[102]

After relating his psychological reaction, Eliphaz attempts to describe what it was that stood before him. He is not very explicit, because it was a figure that defied description in human language. Eliphaz could not really make out the image. He heard a דממה 'silence' that was also a voice, because the voice was not of this world; it was not heard, like other voices, but perceived in some mysterious way that cannot be described in words. Some, however, under-

---

contact with God but to run away from Him. See Robert Gordis, *The Book of Job* (New York: Jewish Theological Seminary, 1978), p. 49.

96. שׂעפּים appears in the same sense in Job 20:2; the form שׂרעפּים is also found in Ps. 94:19 and 139:20. See Samuel Rolles Driver and George Buchanan Gray, *The Book of Job*, ICC (Edinburgh: T. and T. Clark, 1950), p. 45; Gordis, *Job*, p. 48. N. H. Tur-Sinai, *The Book of Job* (Jerusalem: Kiryat Sefer, 1957), p. 81, maintains, however, that here שׂעפּים means specifically alarming thoughts rather than thoughts in general.

97. Tur-Sinai glossed the word שׁמץ in 12:20 as "fear"—"and my ear took fright thereof"—thereby creating a parallel fear in vv. 12 and 14. See Tur-Sinai, *Job*, pp. 80–81.

98. Cf. Dan. 10:7.

99. Driver and Gray, *Job*, p. 45.

100. Cf. the Assyrian phrase, the specter "which makes the hair of my body to rise and of my skull to stand on end" (Dhorme, *Job*, p. 51).

101. Habel, p. 115.

102. Tur-Sinai, *Job*, pp. 82–83; Gordis, *Job*, p. 42, rendered this verse as "a storm made my skin bristle." See also Anton C. M Blommerde, *Northwest Semitic Grammar and Job*, Biblica et Orientalia 22 (Rome: Pontifical Biblical Institute, 1969), p. 40.

stand דממה to mean "murmur"[103] (as in 1 Kings 19:12), and gloss דממה וקול as a hendiadys that designates a soft murmuring sound.

Eliphaz refers to his experience as a "vision of the night," but it strongly resembles a dream, with elements of sleep and voices in it. And even though Eliphaz was terrified, he did not reject the phenomenon. On the contrary, his nocturnal vision served as a channel of communication between God and Eliphaz–parallel, some say, to the experience of Gilgamesh:

> Sleep, which is shed on mankind, fell on him.
> In the middle watch, he ended his sleep.
> He started up, saying to his friend:
> "My friend, didst thou not call me? Why am I awake?
> Didst thou not touch me? Why am I startled? Did not some god go by?
> Why is my flesh numb? My friend, I saw a third dream,
> and the dream that I saw was wholly awesome!
> The heavens shrieked, and the earth boomed,
> [Day]light failed, darkness came.
> Lightning flashed, a flame shot up...."[104]

Job 7:13-14

> When I think, "my bed will comfort me, my couch will share my sorrow,"
> [14] you frighten me with dreams, and terrify me with visions. ...

These verses expand and supplement vv. 3 and 4, which describe Job's agony and the sleeplessness caused by his extreme pain. At first he had hoped to find comfort from his friends (2:11); but the magnitude of his afflictions spawned a wish that the Lord sever the thread of his life that he may find relief in death (3:10).[105] Because his request for final surcease is not granted, his only remaining hope is to find comfort in sleep[106]–but even in repose he is assaulted by dreams and visions that frighten and terrify him. Job's dreams

---

103. Tur-Sinai says that the blank here is that after the storm, for which he finds support in Psalm 107:29; Tur-Sinai, *Job*, p. 83.

104. "Akkadian Myth and Epics," trans. E. A. Speiser, *ANET*, p.83; Gilgamesh 5:4:7–17; Oppenheim, *Interpretation*, p. 216; Clines, *Job 1-20*, p. 131.

105. Even though Job desires death, he never even hints at the possibility of suicide. In fact, the case of Ahithophel in 2 Sam. 17:23 is the only instance in the whole Bible of premeditated suicide. When Saul falls on his sword (1 Sam. 31:4), it is in order not to fall into the hands of the Philistines.

106. In Deut. 3:11, the word ערש is used literally for "bed," whereas here it is a metaphor for sleep.

are symptoms of his emotional and physical state (vv. 4–5, 11ff.);[107] in fact, a parallel motif can be found in a Mesopotamian work about the sufferings of the righteous man.[108]

God appeared to Job in dreams and visions. The two terms are used in parallel, and both are associated with terror: with regard to his dreams, that terror is expressed by the word וחתתני; with regard to the visions, by תבעתני, a root found in the third person feminine in 9:34 and 13:21.[109] Some say that these dream terrors were a symptom of his leprosy.[110] In any case, they extended his daytime afflictions. The terror they caused notwithstanding, dreams and visions represented a legitimate instrument for communication between the Lord and Job. Rather than a cruel assault by God, they seem to have been more of a conduit by which the Lord exhorted Job not to sin.

Job 33:14-16

> For God speaks time and again–though man does not perceive it–[15] in a dream, a night vision, when deep sleep falls on men, during slumbers on their beds. [16] Then He opens men's understanding, and by disciplining them leaves His signature.

Elihu is telling Job not to complain that God does not respond to human beings, as Job did, for example, in chapter 9: "If [man] insisted on a trial with Him, He would not answer one charge in a thousand" (Job 9:3).[111] According to Elihu, God speaks to human beings in several ways, but they usually do not know that what they have perceived is the word of God.[112] Elihu was

---

107. Ehrlich, *Traum,* p. 146.

108. (47) My strength is gone; my appearance has become gloomy"; (54) "when I lie down at night, my dream is terrifying" (W. G. Lambert, *Babylonian Wisdom Literature,* pp. 32–33).

109. The root ב.ע.ת. 'terrify suddenly' in the *pi'el* is characteristic of the language of Job; see 3:5, 9:34, 13:11, 21, 15:24, 18:11, 33:7. Elsewhere in the Bible it is found in 1 Sam. 16:14–15; 2 Sam. 22:5, Isa. 21:4; and Ps. 18:5.

110. Driver and Gray, *Job,* 72.

111. It is interesting that Elihu, too, uses the expression "one in a thousand" (אחד מני אלף) (33:23), which suggests that he is relating specifically, inter alia, to Job's remarks in chapter 9.

112. ישורנה 'perceive': Translators and commentators disagree about this word. The Targum rendered the root ש.ו.ר in the sense of "see," as in Balaam's prophecy: "As I see them from the mountain tops, gaze on them (אשורנו) from the heights," (Num. 23:9). By contrast, the Peshitta and Vulgate have "not repeating"; that is, God speaks once and does not repeat what He has said. But this reading is at odds with what follows, which is that God does repeat what He says. In any case, "seeing" is here meant metaphorically, with the sense of "understanding." See K. Budde, *Das Buch Hiob,* second edition, (Göttingen: Vandenhoeck and Ruprecht, 1913), p. 207.

evidently influenced by Eliphaz's remark about dreams (4:12), and he quotes it almost word for word (4:13). The verse reiterates that there is a parallel between a dream and a night vision, as found in 20:8, and also that of dreams and visions, in 7:14. During dreams people are asleep, as the verse emphasizes twice: "When deep sleep (תרדמה) falls on men, during slumbers (תְּנוּמוֹת) on their beds." In Ps. 132:4 there is a parallel between sleep and slumber. For the plural form תְּנוּמוֹת, compare Prov. 6:10 and 24:33.

During sleep the Lord illuminates the hidden and tells human beings what they should do. "Then he opens men's understanding" is, literally, "uncovers men's ears"; the same idiom, גילה את אוזנו של, is found in "the Lord had *revealed... to* Samuel" (1 Sam. 9:15) and in " I thought I should *disclose the matter to you*" (Ruth 4:4).[113] The Assyrian parallel, *uzna puttu*, means "open the ears," that is, "say" or "make known."[114]

In dreams God sends reproof and counsel, as reflected in the expression ובמסרם יחתם, "by disciplining them leaves His signature." There may be a double meaning here, both מוסר 'reproof' from the root י.ס.ר. and מוסרות 'yoke' from the root א.ס.ר, so that the sense is that he imposes the yoke of his commandments on human beings.[115] Abraham Ibn Ezra explained that when the Lord speaks with human beings in dreams He rebukes them and then seals the verdict against them. Nachmanides wrote that the afflictions described in the verse bear the signature of the Lord Himself. Evidently the meaning is that dreams pass away but leave their imprint–which is the seal or signature of God–on the soul. Some suggest emending the text to read וּמוֹרָאִים יְחִתֵּם, 'He frightens them with terrors'.[116] Others read וּמַרְאִים יְחִתֵּם 'He frightens them with visions', relying on the Septuagint rendering "in visions of terror."[117] If we accept this emendation the text is identical to 7:14, where Job speaks of dreams and visions with which the Lord terrified him–although Elihu adds that they did not deter Job from sinning.

The author of Elihu's speech evidently drew on a literary tradition that he knew from Genesis 20.[118] Rashi was the first to note the similarity between

---

113. Cf. also 1,Sam. 20:2, 12, 13; 2 Sam. 7:27.

114. Dhorme, *Job,* p. 494.

115. Cf. "He seals their fetters" (Ps. 2:2) or "He seals their instruction." See Gordis, *Job,* pp. 374 and 375; Driver and Gray, *Job,* pp. 287–288.

116. D. Bernhard Duhm, *Das Buch Hiob* (Leipzig and Tübingen: J. C. B. Mohr, 1897), p. 159; G. Hölscher, *Das Buch Hiob* (Tübingen: Mohr, 1952), p. 80.

117. Driver and Gray, *Job,* p. 288; Marvin H. Pope, *Job,* p. 250; Dhorme, *Job,* p. 495. H. H. Nichols, "The Composition of the Elihu Speeches," *AJSL* 27 (1910–11), p. 156, stayed closer to the Septuagint and read "appearances of terrors."

118. For the similarity between Abimelech's dream and this verse see J. M. Husser, *Le*

the first half of v. 16 and the dream of Abimelech king of Gerar. The Lord appeared to Abimelech in a dream and warned him to release Abraham's wife Sarah. As a result, Abimelech was spared a grave sin. According to Rashi, dreams are the first channel through which God creates a link with human beings. The second channel is presented in the second half of this verse; that is, the Lord will afflict and punish a person who does not heed His words as conveyed in a dream. This idea is intimately connected with v. 14, where we read that God speaks to human beings in two ways. If a person does not heed the word of the Lord in the dream he will hearken to the pain. Thus affliction is another form of communication. But is it plausible that people must suffer before they obey the Lord? An answer is suggested in Prov. 3:11–12: "Do not reject the discipline of the Lord, my son; do not abhor His rebuke. For whom the Lord loves, He rebukes, as a father the son whom he favors." The Lord chastises only those whom He loves, those whose deeds are important to Him. God is like a Father who seeks his child's welfare. But the child must be prepared to hearken to the father's voice, and this cannot happen until the child's rebellious spirit has been broken.

In sum, through dreams God reveals hidden messages to people and instructs them as to what they should do, using language of reproof and counsel.

SUMMARY

In the biblical prophetic and wisdom literature we find three different attitudes towards dreams: (1) The first attitude links them to false prophets–those who pretended to be true prophets and who diverted the people from the straight path and from its God. This attitude is conspicuous in Jeremiah, who castigates the prophets of Samaria and the prophets of Jerusalem. The core of his rebuke is aimed against the prophets of Jerusalem who, though they spoke in the name of the Lord, delivered the message "The Lord has said: 'All shall be well with you'; and to all who follow their willful hearts they say: 'No evil shall befall you'" (Jer. 23:17). Instead of rebuking the people, these prophets misled them and encouraged them to throw off the Babylonian yoke. Of salient importance to our study is that these false prophets claimed that the Lord had appeared to them in dreams, which were the source of their prophecies and proclamations. Hence it is clear that Jeremiah shares the negative evaluation of Deuteronomy, which views dreamers as prophets who incite the people to idolatry (Deut. 13:2–6). Zechariah, too, sees dreams as the

---

songe et la parole: Étude sur le rêve et sa fonction dans l'ancient Israel, BZAW 210 (Berlin: De Gruyter, 1994), pp. 221–222.

brainchildren of dreamers and their messages merely products of the dreamers' inner reflections. Since this negative attitude focuses on denunciation of false prophets, it is not an absolute rejection of dreams as a legitimate channel for Divine revelation.

(2) The second attitude considers dreams as metaphors for the insubstantial and imaginary—inner fabrications whose sources lie in the human psyche. Dreams satisfy yearnings and fantasies that are not fulfilled during waking hours. This attitude is prominent in Isaiah 29:7–8 and in Psalm 73:20, where what we dream about at night turns out to be quite insubstantial in the light of morning. Ecclesiastes also took this approach, ascribing no religious significance to dreams and denying that they contain any message about the future. He equates them with words of fools, full of confusion and devoid of substance.

(3) The third attitude is positive: Joel refers to the Messianic Age, in which the Lord will pour his spirit on all flesh. His prophecy includes the dreams of elders. A positive attitude can also be found in the Book of Job. Even though Job reiterates that the Lord terrifies him and afflicts him in his dreams, it is patent that dreams are used as authentic channels of communication between man and God.

*

The objection to dreams may be rooted in Israelite prophecy's rejection of determinism. Whereas Jeremiah and Ezekiel emphasize that the fate of human beings depends on their conduct, biblical dream sequences are marked by the view that everything that is going to happen has been preordained and that everything is known in advance. The Lord warns Abimelech in a dream not to touch Sarah; God cautions Laban to do nothing to Jacob, whether for good or evil; and the angel tells Jacob to go back to his homeland. In dreams of the Joseph cycle, every event in human in life is predetermined by God and human beings cannot alter or amend the course of events. When Joseph unmasks himself to his brothers, he tells them, "Now, do not be distressed or reproach yourselves because you sold me hither; it was to save life that God sent me ahead of you" (Gen. 45:5); "God has sent me ahead of you to ensure your survival on earth, and to save your lives in an extraordinary deliverance. So, it was not you who sent me here, but God" (Gen. 45:7–8). What happened had to happen.

Samuel says to Saul: "Moreover, the Glory of Israel does not deceive or change His mind, for He is not human that He should change His mind" (1 Sam. 15:29). What God has determined is immutable. Earlier in the same chapter, however, the Lord told Samuel: "I regret that I made Saul king"

(v. 11)."[119] This transition from determinism to free choice and repentance is clearly articulated in Amos. At first we find, "Can two walk together without having appointed it? (Amos 3:3). Later, however, he says, "Hate evil and love good, and establish justice in the gate; perhaps the Lord, the God of Hosts, will be gracious to the remnant of Joseph" (Amos 5:15). Repentance *may* change the divine mind. Finally though, he declares twice that "the Lord relented concerning this. 'It shall not come to pass,' said the Lord" (Amos 7:3, 6).

A similar view is articulated by Jonah: "I know that You are a compassionate and gracious God, slow to anger, abounding in kindness, renouncing punishment" (Jonah 4:2). Subsequently, after the people of Nineveh repent: "God renounced the punishment He had planned to bring upon them, and did not carry it out" (Jonah 3:10).

Thus far our attention to dreams has focused on the root ח.ל.מ. But a study of the Bible indicates that the distinction between dreams and visions, and between divine revelations to persons waking or sleeping, is not always clear-cut. What is more, sometimes words like מַרְאָה 'vision' and חֲלוֹם 'dream' are used in parallel (Num. 12:6); elswhere, חֲלוֹם in the construct depends on חִזָּיוֹן (Job 33:16). In the next chapter we shall consider the words מַרְאָה and מַחֲזֶה, both usually rendered "vision," and investigate whether they designate dreams. To this end we shall consider them both as terms and as phenomena—what they mean, and whether the stages we have identified in dreams are also found in visions.

---

119. נחמתי, a *nifʿal* from the root נ.ח.מ, means "I regret" or "I have changed my mind"—an example of how the Torah speaks in human language (BT Berakhot 31b). One who changes his mind is frequently distressed by the vacillation: "And the Lord regretted (וינחם) that He had made man on earth, and His heart was saddened" (Gen. 6:6).

5
Visions

The line of demarcation between dreams and visions, or between God's appearance to a sleeper in a dream and genuine revelation to a waking person, is not clear and distinct in every case.[1] Maimonides writes: "None of them see a prophetic vision, but only a dream in a nocturnal vision, or in daytime after they fall into a trance, as it says: 'I make Myself known to him in a vision, I speak with him in a dream' (Num. 12:6)."[2] In other words, the prophets experienced their revelations in nocturnal dreams or during the day, after falling into a trance, so that, in effect, all prophecies came in dreams. According to Maimonides, prophecy is not merely foretelling the future; in the prophecy, God reveals Himself to the prophet and charges him with a mission. This revelation may be accompanied by an image or vision, or only with speech. In addition, the various revelations in the Bible differ as to degree and level,[3] with the lowest level represented by the dreams recounted in Genesis.

In the present chapter we shall study the use of the two Hebrew words מֶחֱזֶה and מַרְאֶה to determine whether there is any link between them and dreams. Do visions and dreams describe the same phenomena? To answer this and

---

1. Weisman, for example, notes that the literary roots of visions are the various types of dreams in the Bible. In his article he deals with the types of visions found in the Book of Amos. The first pair is a dream-vision, in which God shows Amos the vision, who uses his physical senses to understand its meaning and respond to it (7:1–4). He compares this type with Joseph's dreams (Genesis 37:5–10), but notes the fundamental differences between them. The second pair is when the person does not understand the meaning of the symbols and must have it interpreted by God or some emissary. The prophetic visions closest to this type are the visions in Jeremiah (1:11–14), the double vision in Jeremiah 24, and Amos 7:7–8 and 8:1–2. To this he compares the dreams of Pharaoh's ministers (Genesis 40) and Pharaoh's own dreams (Genesis 41). In the last type of vision, God Himself appears and proclaims His message directly. In this respect it resembles the "theological (prophetic) dream." See Ze'ev Weisman, "Paradigms and Structures in the Visions of Amos," *Beit Mikra* 39 (4) (1969), pp. 40–57.

2. Maimonides, *Mishneh Torah* 7:2.

3. *Guide of the Perplexed* 2:45.

other questions we will study these words from their terminological and phenomenological aspects.

THE ETYMOLOGY OF THE VERB ה.ז.ח

The word מַחֲזֶה[4] appears only four times in the Bible (Gen. 15:1, Num. 24:4 and 16; Ezek. 13:7) and is generally rendered in English as "vision."[5] The noun is derived from the root ה.ז.ח 'see', which some believe is borrowed from Aramaic.[6] In that language we have the form חֲזָה, which means "see, perceive with the eyes" and refers both to the eyes and to supernatural visions of various kinds.[7] In Arabic, *ḥazā* means "prophesy as an augur" only; *ḥāzin* is "seer." Accordingly, some derived it from the proto-Semitic *ḥzw. Later, however, scholars encountered the Ugaritic verb *ḥdy* and the Arabic parallels *ḥaḍā* 'guard' and *ḥaḍā* 'sit opposite'. There seems to be no semantic difficulty in associating the senses of "opposite" and "see" because the evolution from the former to the latter is quite plausible. The problem is that Hebrew *z* represents proto-Semitic *ḍ* as well as *z.* Hence it is possible that in southern Canaanite *ḥzy* = "see" and *ḥdy* = "see" were both used until they merged after the assimilation of *ḍ* to *z.* Thus חָזָה is etymologically related to both proto-Semitic roots.[8]

In addition to the root ה.ז.ח, biblical Hebrew has the root ה.א.ר, with the same sense of "see." The question is whether these roots are really synonymous or can be distinguished in some fashion. A survey of the biblical uses of the verb חזה and its derivatives indicates, in fact, that it is a technical term denoting chiefly the Lord's revelation to prophets.[9] Its use in other contexts is extremely rare.[10]

---

4. We also have the form מֶחֱזָה, which means "light, place of seeing, window"; cf. וּמֶחֱזָה אֶל מֶחֱזָה 'windows facing each other' (1 Kings 7:4,5). See *BDB,* 303.

5. Ibid.

6. A. Jepsen, "Chāzāh," in *TDOT* 4:281; Ludwig Koehler, ed., *Lexicon in Veteris Testamenti Libors* (Leiden: Brill, 1951), p. 284, says that חזה is the Aramaic equivalent for the Hebrew ראה.

7. *TDOT* 4:281–282; *BDB,* 302.

8. J. Blau, "Notes on the Vocabulary of the Bible," in *Sefer Yosef Braslavi* (Jerusalem: Qiryat Sefer, 1971), pp. 439–440 (Hebrew).

9. From the root ה.ז.ח we have the nouns חָזוֹן, חִזָּיוֹן, חָזוּת and חֹזֶה. The nouns חָזוֹן and חִזָּיוֹן denote the prophets' experience of divine revelation (Ezek. 7:26; 2 Sam. 7:15). The words of God are transmitted in this revelation (Ps. 89:20; Job 4:12–13 and 33:14–16). Both חָזוֹן and חִזָּיוֹן take place at night, as indicated by the idiom "nocturnal vision" (see Isa. 29:7; Job 33:15, 20:8, and 4:13). Sometimes the Bible states explicitly that חָזוֹן and חִזָּיוֹן are associated with sleeping, as in "In a dream, a night vision, when deep sleep falls on men, while they slumber on their beds" (Job 33:15; cf. 4:13). What is more, חָזוֹן appears in parallel with חֲלוֹם 'dream': "Then, like a dream, a vision of the night (Isa. 29:7; cf. Dan. 1:17); as does חִזָּיוֹן (Job

On the other hand, the root ר.א.ה refers to both normal sight and to super-natural vision: "I beheld (וָאֶרְאֶה)the Lord" (Isa. 6:1). There are, however, con-texts in which it is impossible to distinguish חזה from ראה: Ps. 58:9 and 11 (cf. Jer. 20:12; Micah 4:11; Isa. 33:20.)[11] It seems that, over time, the original concrete sense of these verbs was blurred until they became the normal ab-stract terms to denote a prophetic experience; accordingly we find them used with reference to prophetic experiences where there was no element of vi-sion; for example, "The word that Isaiah son of Amoz prophesied (חזה)" (Isa. 2:1; cf. Amos 1:1, Micah 1:1, Isa. 13:1, and Hab. 1:1). In Ezekiel 1, the ex-pression "I saw visions of God" (v. 1) is parallel to "the word of the Lord came to" (v. 3). In Genesis 46:2, the expression "a vision by night" refers to a divine revelation that is exclusively auditory. Thus whereas the root ר.א.ה refers to both normal and supernatural sight, ח.ז.ה has a more restricted meaning and refers chiefly to revelations to prophets, at night or during a trance, that in-clude a divine message.

Because the root ח.ז.ה and its derivatives are associated with divine revela-tions to prophets, it seems plausible that the noun מַחֲזֶה is used in similar con-texts. In fact, this noun appears only four times in the Bible; its use in the Pentateuch is rare because all the occurrences of forms of the root ח.ז.ה are in the prophetic books. The concatenation of "the word of the Lord"[12] and "in

---

33:15, 7:14, 20:8; Joel 3:1). On the basis of these passages, some believe that a חָזוֹן lacks the element of theophany or a visual element that must be interpreted. Accordingly, although a חָזוֹן includes the words of God and appears by night, it differs from a dream. In the Book of Daniel, by contrast, חָזוֹן includes the element of sight: "While I, Daniel, was seeing the vision" (Daniel 8:15). In the Aramaic sections of Daniel (chapters 2–6), the verb חֲזָה has the primary signification 'see'. This is clear in 3:25, 27 and 5:5, 23. In chapters 2 and 4 the verb refers to the pictures that the dreamer sees in his sleep (2:26, 4:2; 2:31, 34, 41, 43, 45; 4:6, 15, 17, 20). What is more, in Daniel we have the form חֶלְם חֶזְוֵי which refers to seeing in a dream; compare "in my other dream, I saw" (Gen. 41:22)). *TDOT* 4:282–284.

10. The root ח.ז.ה also denotes "seeing God," i.e., theophany. Accordingly in Exodus 24:11, we read that the elders of Israel "beheld (וַיֶּחֱזוּ) the God of Israel." The notion of seeing God occurs in several verses in Psalms: "I shall behold You in the sanctuary (Ps. 63:3); "Then I, justified, will behold Your face (Ps. 17:15); see also Ps. 11:7, 27:4, and 46:10. Some-times the Lord himself is the subject of the verb חזה: "His eyes behold, His gaze searches mankind" (Ps. 11:4); "Your eyes will behold what is right" (Ps. 17:2). God's sight is associ-ated with the idea that the Lord scrutinizes human beings, "sees through" them and knows what is within them. A similar idea is found in Ex. 18:21, where Moses is told to "seek out (תֶחֱזֶה) from among all the people capable men to serve as judges: Jethro is counseling Moses to scrutinize–see through–them in order to choose the appropriate people. It may be that a similar idea is found in Prov. 22:29 and 29:20.

11. *TDOT,* 4:289.

12. This very common expression for prophetic revelation occurs only twice in

a vision" (Gen. 15:1) is characteristic of prophetic revelations. In Gen. 20:7, Abraham is specifically referred to as a prophet. Compare, too, Gen. 18:17, "Now the Lord had said, 'Shall I hide from Abraham what I am about to do'" and Amos 3:7, "Indeed, my Lord God does nothing without having revealed His purpose to His servants the prophets." In addition to this verse, the word מַחֲזֶה appears in the Pentateuch in Num. 24:4 and 16, when the divine afflatus enters Balaam.

THE ABRAHAMIC COVENANT (GENESIS 15)

In Genesis 15:1, God appears to Abram in a vision (בַּמַּחֲזֶה). The traditional commentators differed as to whether the word *vision* in v. 1 refers to the entire chapter (David Kimḥi) or whether two separate but consecutive divine revelations are described here (Abraham Ibn Ezra). Samuel ben Meir, by contrast, held that the promises to Abram were made at different times and the chapter recounts two different events that did not take place one after the other. Many modern scholars believe that the chapter combines two different sources.[13] But the multiple-source thesis is untenable for this chapter, as shown by the extreme variation of scholarly opinions as to the assignment of its parts to the various sources.[14]

With regard to content, the chapter clearly has two parts.[15] The first part, vv. 1–5, comprises the promise of a son and the promise of many offspring. The second, vv. 7–21, adds the promise of the land. The revelation in the first

---

Genesis—here and in v. 4 (A. A. Dillman, *Genesis,* trans. W. B. Stevenson [Edinburgh: T. & T. Clark, 1897], 2: 56).

13. Vv. 1–6 E, vv. 7–21 J (cf. Wellhausen) or interwoven E in 1b, 3a, 5, 11, 12a, 13a, 14, and 16, with the rest J. See J. Wellhausen, *Die Composition des Hexateuchs und der historischen Bücher des Alten Testaments* (Berlin: Reiner, 1899; repr. Berlin: Walter de Gruyter, 1963), p. 21; M. Noth, *A History of Pentateuchal Traditions,* trans. with an introduction by Bernhard W. Andersen (Englewood Cliffs, NJ: Prentice Hall, 1972), p. 28, n. 85, pp. 200–201, n. 544; E. A. Speiser, *Genesis,* pp. 114–115; John Skinner, *Genesis,* pp. 276–277; J. A. Emerton, "The Origin of the Promises to the Patriarchs in the Older Sources of the Book of Genesis," *VT* 32 (1982), p. 17.

14. N. Lohfink, *Die Landverheissung als Eid: Eine Studie zu Gn 15* (Stuttgart: Verlag Katholisches Bibelwerk, 1967), p. 24, n. 1, p. 27, nn. 7 and 8; Moshe Anbar, "Abrahamic Covenant, Genesis 15," *Shnaton* 3 (1978), pp. 34–52. According to Anbar, the chapter is the end-product of the merger of separate stories, the first in vv. 1–6 and the second in vv. 7–21. He holds that each story is an independent creation inspired by ancient sources. Their original date of composition is evidently the end of the First Temple period; their merger took place at the start of the exile, in order to blend into a single text the ceremonial promises of a son, many offspring, and the land.

15. Sarna, *Genesis,* pp. 111–112.

part certainly takes place at night: "He took him outside and said, 'Look toward heaven and count the stars, if you are able to count them.' And He added, 'So shall your offspring be.'" (Gen. 15:5). In the second part, the revelation takes place at sunset or twilight: "As the sun was about to set, a deep sleep fell upon Abram, and a great dark dread descended upon him" (Gen. 15:12); and subsequently, "when the sun set and it was very dark ..." (Gen. 15:17). Hence the promise of offspring took place at night, when Abram was awake, whereas the promise of the land took place when Abram was asleep or in a deep trance.

Van Seters, Hoftijzer, Snijders, Rendtorff, and Westermann have all noted the unity of the chapter,[16] as did Sarna, who noted the intimate connection between its two parts—especially the motifs of the promise of offspring and the promise of the land, which are associated and interwoven through the end of Genesis.[17] A close reading of the chapter reveals that the two sections have a parallel structure and that each consists of three parts: (1) a promise by God (vv. 1 and 7–8); (2) Abraham's expression of doubt and worry (vv. 2 and 8); and (3) another promise by God, expressed in words and a symbolic act (vv. 4, 9, and 21). In both sections, God begins his speech with the words "I am" (vv. 1 and 7), and Abram replies, "O Lord God" (vv. 2 and 8)—a rare conjunction of the divine names in the Bible. In addition, the keywords "offspring" (vv. 3, 5, and 13), "inherit" (vv. 3, 4 [twice], 7, and 8), and "take/bring out" (vv. 5 and 7), appear in both parts of the chapter. The same applies to many of the idioms that appear in both chapter 15 and the previous chapter. All of this strengthens the argument for the unity of chapter 15.[18]

---

16. "There seems to be no need to dispute any longer that the text, in spite of a certain awkwardness of style, is a unity" (John Van Seters, *Prologue to History* [Louisville, Kentucky: Westminster/John Knox Press, 1992], p. 249); idem, *Abraham in History and Tradition* (New Haven: Yale University Press, 1975), pp. 249–250. For the literary unity of chapter 15, see also: J. Hoftijzer, *Die Verheissungen an die drei Erzväter* (Leiden: Brill, 1956), pp. 17–55; L. A. Snijders, "Genesis XV, The Covenant with Abraham," *OTS* 12 (1958), pp. 261–279; R. Rendtorff, "Genesis 15 im Rahmen der theologischen Bearbeitung der Vätergeschichten," *Werden und Wirken des Alten Testaments: Fs. C. Westermann*, ed. R. Albertz, H. P. Müller, H. W. Wolff, and W. Zimmerli (Göttingen: Vandenhoeck and Ruprecht, 1980), pp. 74–81; Westermann, *Genesis 12–36*, pp. 250–257; John Ha, *Genesis 15: A Theological Compendium of Pentateuchal History* (Berlin: Walter de Gruyter, 1989), pp. 43–57.

17. On the promise of offspring and the land, see Gen. 12:2 and 7, 13:14–16, 16:6–7, 24:7, 26:3–4, and 28:3–4 and 13–14.

18. Chapter 15 is full of words and idioms that appear in the previous chapter; this strongly suggests a link between the two chapters. "Fear not" (v. 1) links up with the previous chapter, in which Abram overcame the four kings, a victory for which he may perhaps fear revenge. The Lord's statement, "I am a shield (מָגֵן) to you" (v. 1) reminds us of Melchizedek's "And blessed be God Most High, Who has delivered (מִגֵּן) your foes into your hand" (Gen.

The opening of the chapter—"The word of the Lord came to Abram in a vision"—is a typical introductory formula for divine messages to prophets.[19] Subsequently we have the Lord's encouraging promise, "Fear not, Abram, I am a shield to you."[20] "Fear not," in its various grammatical forms, appears some 80 times in the Bible as a formula of encouragement and comfort. Its sense is made clear by the expressions that accompany it: "I am a shield to you" (Gen. 15:1); "for I am with you" (Gen. 26:24); "I will be your help" (Isa. 41:13); "for I will redeem you" (Isa. 43:1).[21] Similar formulas are known from the ancient Near East. The prophecies to Esarhaddon begin with the expression "fear not," after which we find "I will go before you," "I will protect you," and so on.[22] Similarly, the god appears to King Zakir of Hamath and Lu'ath and says: "Do not fear, for I have made you a king, and I shall stand by you and deliver you from [all these kings who] set up a siege against you."[23]

In the dialogue between Abram and the Lord, the latter promises Abram both an heir and many offspring.[24] Here Abraham is wide awake. The Lord takes him outside and tells him to look up and count the stars.[25] This revelation is both visual and aural. Direct and unmediated, it is typical of the age of the Patriarchs.[26] Sarna, discussing the topic of revelation, says that it is difficult

---

14:20). The Lord concludes a covenant (ברית) with Abram, while in the previous chapter we were introduced to Abram's allies (בעלי ברית) (14:13). The Amorites, who in chapter 14 are Abram's allies (14:13), are to be dispossessed of the land (vv. 16 and 21). Abram's slave is Damascene Eliezer (15:2), while in chapter 14 we read about how Abram pursued the four kings to north of Damascus (14:15). For other linguistic echoes that point to the link between the two chapters, see Sarna, *Genesis,* p. 112.

19. Cf. 1 Sam. 15:10; 2 Sam. 7:4; 1 Kings 12:22, 16:1, 17:2 and 8, 18:31, and 21:17.

20. The image of a shield is common in Psalms. Particularly close to our verse is Psalm 3:4, "But You, O Lord, are a shield about me."

21. E. W. Conard, "The 'Fear Not' Oracles in Second Isaiah," *VT* 34 (1984), pp. 143–145.

22. "(15) [Esarhad]on, king of the countries, fear not!"; (20) "I shall lie in wait for your enemies, I shall give them to you. I, Ishtar of Arbela, will go before you and behind you" ("Akkadian Oracles and Prophecies," trans. Robert H. Pfeiffer, *ANET,* 449–450).

23. "Canaanite and Aramaic Inscriptions," trans. Franz Rosenthal, *ANET,* p. 655; J. C. Greenfield, "The Zakir Inscription and the Danklied," *Proceedings of the Fifth World Congress of Jewish Studies* (Jerusalem: World Union of Jewish Studies, 1969), 1:182–183.

24. The motif of the promise of a son also appears in Judg. 13:2–5; 1 Sam. 1; 2 Kings 4:8–17; and Luke 1 and 2. It is also found in the Ugaritic stories of Keret and Aqhat, where we read about childlessness, the promise of a son, and the birth of a son.

25. The stars as representing an immense number can be found in the promises in Gen. 22:17 and 26:4; cf. Ex. 32:13; Deut. 1:10, 10:22, and 28:62; Neh. 9:23.

26. Claus Westermann, *The Promises to the Fathers,* p. 120; idem, "The Way of the Promise through the Old Testament," in B. W. Anderson, ed., *The Old Testament and Christian Faith* (New York: Harper, 1963), pp. 200–224.

to know whether the scene described here is a real event or a dream theophany.[27] Those who opt for the latter option note the nighttime setting of the vision, which can be inferred from verse 5.[28] According to them, the stars are seen during the dream. David Kimḥi, in his commentary on vv. 5 and 12, writes: "He took him out of his tent in a prophetic vision. ... This is like 'He brought me in visions of God to Jerusalem' (Ezek. 8:3). ... Everything was in a prophetic vision, for it was all one vision on a single occasion." Nevertheless we should note that the examples he cites took place in "visions of God" and by "the spirit of the Lord."

In the dialogue between the Lord and Abram, the former introduces himself as "I am the Lord" (v. 7)–the first time this formula appears in the Bible.[29] It is interesting that in prophetic dreams, too, we have found that God identifies and introduces Himself; for example, in Jacob's dreams at Bethel–"He said, 'I am the Lord, the God of your father Abraham and the God of Isaac'" (Gen. 28:13)–and in Laban's house–"I am the God of Bethel" (Gen. 31:13). The formula "I am So-and-So" is also found in other traditions of the ancient East.[30] The dialogue between the Lord and Abram reminds us of the dialogue in Abimelech's dream: God's opening statement (verse 1b), the address to God in a question that is really a complaint (vv. 2–3), and the divine reply that explains His position (vv. 4–5).

Some go further and suggest, on the basis of Abram's request for a son and heir, that this is an incubation dream.[31] A similar petition is found in Ugaritic texts that are considered to describe incubations. In the story of the dream of King Keret, the deity appears and asks why he is weeping. Keret replies, "What need do I have of silver and gold? ... Let me beget sons. ..."[32] In reply,

---

27. Sarna, *Genesis,* p. 113.

28. J. Skinner, *Genesis,* p. 278; Ehrlich, *Traum,* pp. 36 and 39. On p. 36 Ehrlich refers to this as a vision, but on p. 39 as a dream.

29. Compare the use of the similar formula, "The Lord appeared to Abram and said to him, 'I am El Shaddai'" (Gen. 17:1)); "The Lord appeared to him and said, 'I am the God of your father Abraham'" (Gen. 26:24); "And He said, 'I am God, the God of your father'" (Gen. 46:3).

30. O. Kaiser, "Traditionsgeschichtliche Untersuchung von Genesis 15," *ZAW* 70 (1958), pp. 107–126.

31. Julian Obermann, "How Daniel was Blessed with a Son," *Supplement to the Journal of the American Oriental Society* 66 (2) (New Haven: American Oriental Society, 1946), p. 28.

32. "What need (have) I (of)
silver and yellow metal, (even) gold,
a share of his estate perpetual,
slaves, three horses (and) chariot(s)
from the stables of the son of the slave-girl?

the god tells him how he can find a woman who will bear him sons. Some compare Keret's petition with Abram's request here: "What can You give me, seeing that I am childless" (Gen. 15:2). In another story in the Aqhat saga, Daniel provides the gods with food and drink for six days; on the seventh day he is vouchsafed a response from Baal, who in turn petitions El, who conveys to Daniel his blessing of the birth of an exemplary son.[33] Note, however, that in contrast to Daniel's ritual preparations and Keret's tears, Abram does nothing. The Lord appears to Abram at His own initiative. Nor does the text in Genesis specify the location of this epiphany.

The second dialogue between the Lord and Abram occupies verses 7–21.[34] This colloquy focuses on the promise of the land to Abram's descendants, a promise accompanied by a ceremonial slaughtering of animals. God instructs Abram to take a three-year-old heifer, a three-year-old she-goat, a three-year-old ram, a turtledove, and a young bird. Abraham cuts them in pieces (except for the bird) and places the pieces in parallel rows. The animals listed in v. 9 were precisely those offered in Israelite sacrifice.[35] Moreover, according to Leviticus 1:17, a sacrificial bird is not cut up or separated into pieces, but merely torn open.[36] According to the retelling of this scene in the Book of Jubilees (chapter 14), Abram built an altar, offered sacrifices, and sprinkled the blood on the altar. A ceremony parallel to that in our chapter is found in Jeremiah 34:17–19, but there only a calf is used.[37] As noted, cutting up the animals connotes a sacrificial offering, and so does the age of the animals. A three-year-old animal was considered to be the most desirable offer-

---

So do thou give (me) what is not in my house:

Give me the wench Hury

(the most) gracious progeny of thy first-born."

See G. R. Driver, *Canaanite Myths and Legends* (Edinburgh: T. and T. Clark, 1956), p. 33.

33. Obermann identifies this as an incubation. See, however, Margalit's criticism of this interpretation: Julian Obermann, "How Daniel was Blessed with a Son," p. 10ff.; B. Margalit, *The Ugaritic Poem of Aqhat, BZAW* 182 (Berlin and New York: De Gruyter, 1989), pp. 260–266.

34. Verse 7 begins with "Then He said to him," in order to provide continuity between the two halves of the chapter.

35. See Leviticus 1.

36. There is disagreement about the word גוזל. In addition to our verse, it appears only in Deuteronomy 32:11, where it refers to a young eagle. Apparently here the reference is to a dove, because we also have the common idiom blank. Genesis Rabba 44:17, Targum Onkelos, Septuagint has a pigeon. For a parallel, see Leviticus 1:14, 5:7 and 11.

37. On the Jeremiah text, see P.D. Miller, Jr., "Sin and Judgment in Jeremiah 34:17–19," *JBL* 103 (1984), pp. 611–613.

ing in ancient Israel and the Near East.[38] In Greece, too, it was the custom to offer three-year-old animals at covenant ceremonies.

In contrast to the view that Abram's actions allude to the offering of sacrifices, some argue precisely the opposite.[39] Here we have no altar and no mention of the sprinkling of blood, as is found in Exodus 24:8. Furthermore, the "sacrificial" animals are neither eaten nor burned. Their carcasses serve only to define an alley through which God passes. Linguistically, too, the terminology of this chapter is not the same as that of the sacrificial regulations of the Priestly Code. There the term carcass (פגר) does not appear, and the second type of bird is specifically a pigeon (בן יונה), not a "young bird" (גוזל). Nor does the Priestly Code emphasize a requirement for three-year-old animals. Several questions remain, nevertheless, such as why precisely the animals of the Israelite sacrificial ritual are involved here, and why Abram did not rend the bird.

The facts that Abram cut apart the animals that were used in sacrifice and that he slept while the Lord conveyed a message to him have led a number of scholars to conclude that the text is describing an incubation.[40] But this conjecture must be rejected: it is the Lord who tells Abram to slaughter and split the animals; in incubation ceremonies the sacrifice is offered at the dreamer-petitioner's initiative. Eichrodt, on the other hand, believes that here Abram is depicted as a seer in quest of divine guidance. This is why he offers sacrifices and follows the flight of birds. These actions have ancient Babylonian origins. The author of Genesis himself no longer understands their full significance; evidently with the passage of time these customs had been forgotten or had sunk into oblivion.[41]

Parallels to the covenant ritual described here can be found in treaties from the second and first millennia BCE. In one of the Mari letters, the idiom whose

---

38. Where the Masoretic text of 1 Sam. 1:24 reads "with three bulls," the Septuagint (and 4qsam^a) have "with a three-year-old bull." The Septuagint version seems to be preferable because we subsequently read that only one bull was slaughtered (verse 25). See F. M. Cross, "A New Qumran Biblical Fragment Related to the Original Hebrew Underlying the Septuagint," *BASOR* 132 (1953), pp. 15–26. Rattner, however, thinks the MT is correct: R. Rattner, "Three Bulls or One: Reappraisal of 1 Sam 1:24," *Bib* 68 (1987), pp. 98–102.

39. Sarna, *Genesis,* p. 114; B. Jacob, *The First Book of the Bible,* p. 101; B. A. Levine, *In the Presence of the Lord,* SJLA 5 (Leiden: Brill, 1974), p. 37, n. 93.

40. Anton Jirku, "Ein Fall von Inkubation im AT," *ZAW* 33 (1913), p. 153; C. Gordon, *Ugarit and Minoan Crete* (New York: Norton, 1966), p. 25; Obermann, *Daniel,* p. 28; Julius Wellhausen, *Der Text der Bücher Samuelis* (Göttingen: Vandenhoeck and Ruprecht, 1871), pp. 21–22.

41. Walter Eichrodt, *Theology of the Old Testament* (Philadelphia: Westminster, 1961), 1:302, n. 2.

literal meaning is "kill a donkey foal" actually has the sense "conclude a covenant."[42] When the donkey foal was slaughtered, a dog and she-goat were also brought, reminiscent of the three animals cut apart by Abram. The extrabiblical texts indicate that in addition to the slaughter of animals, there was also an imprecation. In a treaty of the seventeenth century BCE from Alalakh, between Yarimlin and Abban, Abban conveyed the city of Alalakh to his vassal Yarimlin. The text reads (11.39–42): "Abban placed himself under oath to Yarimlin and had cut the neck of a sheep (saying): (Let me so die) if I take back that which I gave thee."[43] With our chapter in mind, note not only the slaughtering of animals but also that it is the stronger party that binds itself under threat of punishment. The implication is that God binds himself by sanctions if He does not fulfill the conditions of His promise to Abram.

The cutting apart of animals is also found in two treaties of the eighth century BCE. We will cite one of them here.[44] The well known Sefire inscription reports on a treaty between Bir-Ga'yah, king of KTK, and Matı''el, king of Arpad. The treaty alludes to a violation by Matı''el and adds: "[Just as] this calf is cut in two, so may Matı''el be cut in two, and may his nobles be cut in two! [And just as] a [ha]r[lot is stripped naked], so may the wives of Matı''el be stripped naked."[45] According to the treaty, the slaughtering of an animal

---

42. Cutting up animals was an integral part of the covenant ceremony, as we find in the Mari letter: "I went to Ašlakka and they brought me a young dog and a she-goat in order to conclude a covenant [literally, "kill a donkey foal"] between the Haneans and the land of Idamaraṣ. But, in deference to my Lord, I did not permit [the use of] the young dog and the she-goat, but (instead) had a donkey foal, the young of a she-ass, killed, and thus established a reconciliation between the Haneans and the land of Idamaraṣ." See M. Held, "Philological Notes on the Mari Covenant Rituals," *BASOR* 200 (1970), p. 33; Weisberg points to the similarity between the splitting of Tiamat and the Biblical Covenant Between the Pieces as recorded in Gen 15 and Jeremiah 34. See: David B. Weisberg "Loyalty and Death: Some Ancient Near Eastern Metaphors," *Maarav* 7 (1991), pp. 264-266.

43. D. Wiseman, "Abban and Alalakh," *JCS* 12 (1958), p. 129; M. Weinfeld, "The Covenant of Grant in the Old Testament and in the Ancient Near East," *JAOS* 90 (1970), p. 196; idem, "The Loyalty Oath in the Ancient Near East," *UF* 8 (1976), pp. 400–401. Compare the translation by McCarthy, who believes that slaughtering animals was part of the treaty, but not an imprecation: "Abba-An is under oath to Yarimlim and also he cut the neck of a lamb. (He swore): I shall never take back what I gave thee." See D. J. McCarthy, *Treaty and Covenant, AnBib* 21 (Rome: Pontifical Biblical Institute, 1963), p. 185.

44. The second example comes from the curses in the vassal treaty of Esarhaddon, king of Assyria: "Just as male and female kids and male and female lambs are slit open and their entrails fall down upon their feet, so may the entrails of your sons and daughters roll down over your feet" (trans. D. J. Wiseman, "The Vassal Treaties of Esarhaddon," *Iraq* 20 (1958), pp. 69–72; see also the translation by E. Reiner, *ANET*, 359).

45. J. A. Fitzmyer, *The Aramaic Inscriptions of Sefire, BibOr* 19 (Rome: Pontifical Biblical

when the covenant was concluded was a magical act accompanied by imprecations that threatened one party with dire punishment should it violate the conditions of the pact.

A biblical parallel to the Covenant between the Pieces appears in the Book of Jeremiah.[46] There, according to the text, during the Babylonian siege of the city the nobles of Jerusalem set their slaves free, only to force them back into servitude later. The prophet complains bitterly about this: "I will make the men who violated My covenant, who did not fulfill the terms of the covenant which they made before Me, [like] the calf which they cut in two so as to pass between the halves: The officers of Judah and Jerusalem, the officials, the priests, and all the people of the land who passed between the halves of the calf shall be handed over to their enemies, to those who seek to kill them. Their carcasses shall become food for the birds of the sky and the beasts of the earth" (Jer. 34:18–20). We may infer that someone who passes between the pieces subjects himself to the punishment of being rent in two should he violate the agreement.[47] A comparison of the extrabiblical texts reviewed above with the passage from Jeremiah indicates their affinity, because all include both imprecations and the slaughter of animals. On the other hand, the element of the curse is absent from Genesis 15. Another difference is that in the Covenant between the Pieces it is the Lord who passes between the halves of the carcasses, whereas in Jeremiah He is the guarantor of the covenant. Finally, in contrast to the self-imprecation of the ancient Near Eastern treaties, chapter 15 concludes with a divine promise to Abram.[48]

Institute, 1967), pp. 14–15 and 56–57. See also "Canaanite and Aramaic Inscription," trans. F. Rosenthal, *ANET,* 660.

46. On this Jeremiah text, see P.D. Miller, Jr., "Sin and Judgment in Jeremiah 34:17–19," *JBL* 103 (1984), pp. 611–613.

47. In Genesis God is a party to the covenant, as shown by the fiery furnace that passes between the pieces. In Jeremiah, by contrast, He is the guarantor of the covenant (v. 18).

48. The fact that the curses of the vassal treaties are replaced by a divine promise to Abram has led scholars to conclude that this chapter is modeled on a second type of treaty known to us from the ancient Near East–the grant treaty. In grant treaties, the ruler took upon himself a unilateral obligation toward his servant, granting land to him and his offspring in return for their loyal service. There are no curses against either party in this kind of treaty. Instead, the imprecation is directed at anyone who violates the treaty and deprives the servant of what the king has granted him. The treaty is meant to protect the rights of the servant who received the grant, while the curse is directed against any third party who might try to violate the treaty. This model is also found in the Bible, with Abraham and David. Both are granted land and a dynasty. On this, see at length M. Weinfeld, "The Covenant of Grant in the Old Testament and in the Ancient Near East," *JAOS* 90 (1970), pp. 184–203; S. E. Loewenstamm, "The Divine Grants of Land to the Patriarchs," *JAOS* 91 (1971), pp. 509–510.

After all the preparations for the covenant ceremony, which must have taken some time, Abram stands and waits. Birds of prey swoop down on the carcasses and Abram chases them away.[49] The appearance of the birds may be a sign that forebodes evil, as we find later (vv. 13–16); here Abram chases away the evil sign. In Egyptian art, the falcon was the totem bird of, among others, the god Horus, with whom the pharaoh was identified.[50] The fact that Abram chases the bird away may allude to the future conflict in Egypt. The Israelites will be enslaved in Egypt but will depart from that country with vast possessions. Another possibility is that the descent of the birds of prey is a warning sign that the corpse of anyone who violates the covenant will be left as carrion for beasts and fowls. It may also be meant to inform Abram that foes will indeed attempt to prevent the fulfillment of the covenant, but the Israelites will be able to overcome them if they hold firm to the covenant. In this reading, the slaughtered animals symbolize the Israelites, and Abram is defending his offspring against attacks by their enemies.[51]

The biblical author proceeds to describe how the sun was about to set; as night approached, a deep sleep fell upon Abram.[52] Moreover, when the deep sleep falls on Abram, the verse also notes the "dark dread" that besets him (v. 12b). His fear is the same as that which plagues Eliphaz when the Lord appears to him in a deep sleep: "A word came to me in stealth; my ear caught a whisper of it. In thought-filled visions of the night, when deep sleep falls on men, fear and trembling came upon me, causing all my bones to quake with fright" (Job 4:12–14). The message to Abram relates to the future; its theme is both national and personal. For 400 years his offspring will be aliens, enslaved and persecuted, for God has decreed that the Israelites will be subjugated in Egypt. Only after three generations in that country will the fourth generation return to Canaan. On the personal level, Abram is told, "You shall

---

49. The Hebrew word עיט does not indicate a species of bird but is a generic term for birds of prey; in the Bible, birds of prey can symbolize the Gentile nations. See Ezek. 17:3 and Zech. 5:9.

50. Sarna, *Genesis,* p. 117.

51. G. J. Wenham, "The Symbolism of the Animal Rite in Genesis 15: A Response to G. F. Hasel," *JSOT* 19 (1981), pp. 61–78; *JSOT* 22 (1982), pp. 134-137.

52. For תרדמה as "deep sleep," see Gen. 2:21, Job 4:13 and 33:15–16. In the last of these, the word is associated with dreams: "In a dream, a night vision, when deep sleep falls on men, while they slumber (בתנומות) on their beds. Then He opens men's understanding, and by disciplining them leaves His signature (Job 33:15–16); and cf. Isa. 29:10. See also *BDB,* 922. J. Hartley, *Book of Job, NICOT* (Grand Rapids: Eerdmans, 1988), p. 112, suggests that תנומה refers not to a deep natural sleep but to a "stupor that God causes to fall upon a person, blocking out all other perceptions, in order that the person may be completely receptive to the divine word."

go to your fathers in peace; you shall be buried at a ripe old age" (v. 15); that is, he will not witness the start of their servitude with his own eyes, nor even its incipient causes. His descendants, however, will have to wait outside the land until the fourth generation, when the sin of the Amorites reaches its full measure. After Abram hears this message, the text returns to the present time: the sun has set and the darkness of night begins; in this blackness Abram sees a smoking furnace or oven[53] and a flaming torch that passes between the pieces of the slaughtered animals. These symbols are the emissaries of the Lord and signs of His presence.[54]

The cut-up animals and untouched bird have preoccupied commentators. An echo of this can be found in the midrashic homilies that seek to allegorize the scene. Particularly evident is the influence of the paradigm of the four kingdoms found in the Book of Daniel.[55] One such commentary is that of Nachmanides on verse 12:

> "A great dark dread descended upon him": They expounded this as an allusion to the servitude of four kingdoms. For the prophet found in his soul *dread.* And after that came *darkness,* and after that the darkness was *great,* and after that he felt that it was descending upon him, like a burden too heavy to bear.
>
> They said: *Dread*–this is Babylon; *darkness*–this is Media, who darkened the eyes of the Israelites with fasting; *great*–this is the kingdom of Antiochus; *descended upon him*–this is Edom (Rome).
>
> And all of this was relevant to Abraham, for when the Holy One, blessed be He, made a covenant with him to give the land to his descendants as an eternal possession, He told him, like one who leaves aside a part of his gift, that four kingdoms would subjugate his descendants and rule in their land–if they transgressed against him.

---

53. The idiom "smoking furnace" has no parallel elsewhere in the Bible. Parallels are found, however, in a series of oaths against witches from Maqlû, where we read, inter alia: "I sent out against you repeatedly a 'going' [i.e., lighted] oven (*āliku tinūru*), a fire that has caught"; cf. Maqlû II, line 19; see also W. von Soden, "Zum akkadischen Wörterbuch 89–96," *Orientalia* 26 (1957), p. 127. It is possible that here too we have an ancient oriental image that had been forgotten by other biblical authors.

54. At the revelation on Sinai, smoke and fire appear with the Lord (Ex. 19:18 and 20:18). During the journeys of the Israelites in the wilderness, a pillar of cloud by day and a pillar of fire by night accompanied their camp (Exodus 13:21). On the links between the revelation at Sinai and the Covenant between the Pieces, see Van Seters, "Confessional Reformulation in the Exilic Period," *VT* 22 (1972), pp. 448–459.

55. See Genesis Rabba 44:14.

After that, He made known to him another exile, which they would suffer first, namely, the Egyptian exile.

David Kimḥi saw the cut-up animals as the nations and the bird as Israel. That is, God showed Abram not only what would happen to him and his descendants in the near future but in the distant future, until the end of the generations and the Messianic era. The predatory birds would persecute the dove throughout the generations of the exile. All these nations who harmed Israel would be rent apart and cut into pieces; they would oppose and fight one another until they disappeared, and so too would be divided in their creeds and beliefs. But this is not the case with Israel, whose Torah and faith are not separated; they will remain one nation. All of this is symbolized in the vision, in that "he did not cut up the bird."

As for the nature of the experience described here, denominated מַחֲזֶה 'vision', the question is whether it is a nocturnal vision or a daytime experience, a waking vision or a dream. It seems most plausible that we have here a description of a single revelation that lasted for more than a full day. According to v. 5, Abram was awake during his conversation with the Lord, for he goes outside, looks up at the heavens, and counts the stars; this indicates that it was night. After his colloquy with the Lord, Abram cut up the animals and the bird of prey descended on the carcasses. The preparations for the covenant ceremony took many hours and occupied the entire day after the Lord instructed Abram what to do.

When the sun set, a deep sleep fell upon him and he had a dream in which the Lord conveyed to him His promise of the land. In his dream, Abram saw the cut-up carcasses and the flaming torch passing between them. In other words, what he sees in the dream is a direct continuation of the external waking reality.[56] This reality is thereby understood to have symbolic meaning for the future and to herald events that flow from Abram's merits in the past. In classical prophecy, there is only an associative link between external reality and the vision, and additional elements are mixed into the latter. Here, however, the vision is a reproduction of waking reality. It is not a prophetic vision, however, because the notion of an assigned mission is still missing. Abram's theophany, then, has two stages: in the first stage he is awake, but in the second he is dreaming. Perhaps his revelation is called a מַחֲזֶה because it emphasizes that a חוֹזֶה –a pact–was signed and sealed between him and God.

---

56. Benjamin Uffenheimer, "Genesis 15," in *Studies in Bible Dedicated to the Memory of Israel and Zvi Broide,* ed. Jacob Licht and Gershon Brinn (Tel Aviv: Tel Aviv University, School for Jewish Studies, 1976), p. 21.

THE BALAK–BALAAM PERICOPE (NUMBERS 22-24)

The word מַחֲזֵה appears twice in the Balaam pericope, and the two verses are almost identical. In Num. 24:4: "Word of him who hears God's speech, who beholds visions from the Almighty (מַחֲזֵה שַׁדַּי יֶחֱזֶה) prostrate, but with eyes unveiled." And in Num. 24:16: "Word of him who hears God's speech, who obtains knowledge from the Most High, and beholds visions from the Almighty, prostrate, but with eyes unveiled." Before we attempt to gloss these difficult verses and the word מַחֲזֵה as it appears in them, we should consider several themes of the pericope that are relevant to the phenomenon of dreams in general.

When the story begins, the Moabites are panic-stricken on account of the Israelites' conquest of the neighboring kingdoms of Siḥon and Og. Balak son of Zippor, king of Moab, invites Balaam son of Beor to come and curse Israel. Goldziher, followed by J. Pedersen, noted a number of parallels between the figure of Balaam and the "men of God" of ancient Arab society, of which, in the pre-Islamic period, there were two types: the seer (šā 'ir) and the priest (kāhin). Goldziher noted the similarity between Balaam and the šā 'ir, the poet-seer who went out before a battle to curse the enemy, while at the same time praising the men of his own tribe and encouraging them to victory.[57] The poem of derision and bravado, comprising many short apothegms, was known as a hijā'. The Arabs believed that the šā 'ir, who was in contact with the higher forces, endowed the hijā' with magical power. While there are no explicit curses in Balaam's aphorisms, Balak says to Balaam: "Come then, put a curse upon this people for me, since they are too numerous for me; perhaps I can thus defeat them and drive them out of the land. For I know that he whom you bless is blessed indeed, and he whom you curse is cursed." (Num. 22:6). The Arabic hijā' is paralleled by the maxims of the ancient bards (Num. 21:27). We know that before the battle of Badr Muhammad summoned a poet to curse his enemies. The custom among the Bedouin, too, was to summon a kāhin or soothsayer to curse the enemy.[58] But Balaam resembles the Arab poets in two respects only—his capacity to curse and bless. It should also be

---

57. I. Goldziher, *Abhandlungen zur arabischen Philologie* 1 (Leiden: Brill, 1896), pp. 19–25; A. Guillaume, *Prophecy and Divination among the Hebrews and other Semites* (London: Hodder and Stoughton, 1938), pp. 224ff.; J. Pedersen, "The Role Played by Inspired Persons among the Israelites and the Arabs," in H. H. Rowley, ed., *Studies in Old Testament Prophecy* (Edinburgh: T. and T. Clark, 1950), pp. 127–142.

58. Theodor H. Gaster, *Myth, Legend, and Custom in the Old Testament* (New York: Harper and Row, 1969), p. 303.

noted that whereas the Arabic bard railed against the enemy, Balaam addresses Balak.

The first allusion to dreams in this story comes in Balaam's response to Balak's emissaries: "He said to them, 'Spend the night here, and I shall reply to you as the Lord may instruct me. ...' God came to Balaam ... (Num. 22:87–9).[59] Rashi comments: "The Holy Spirit descends upon him only at night, as for all prophets of the nations: for example, Laban in a nocturnal dream, as it says, 'But God appeared to Laban the Aramean in a dream by night' (Gen. 31:24)." Maimonides (*Guide of the Perplexed* 2:41) categorizes the Lord's appearance to Balaam as the first form of prophecy. He continues, however:

> The phrase, 'And Elohim (an angel) came to a certain person in a dream of night' does not indicate a prophecy, and the person mentioned in that phrase is not a prophet. The phrase only informs us that the attention of the person was called by God to a certain thing, and at the same time that this happened at night. ... Note and consider the distinction between the phrases, 'And Elohim came,' and 'Elohim said,' between 'in a dream by night,' and 'in a vision by night.'

When God appears to Balaam, he tells him how to respond to Balak's invitation: "You must not curse that people, for they are blessed" (Num. 22:12). Here God imposes a mission on Balaam—to refrain from speaking. Note that the dialogue between God and Balaam is reminiscent of the dialogue between the Lord and Abimelech in the latter's dream.

After the Lord instructs him not to curse the Israelites, Balaam dismisses Balak's ambassadors. The king, however, believes that it is merely Balaam's honor that is at issue and accordingly sends a second delegation of higher-ranking officials to flatter the prophet. Balaam, thinking that it may be possible to bend God's will, tells them, "So you, too, stay here overnight, and let me find out what else the Lord may say to me (v. 19)." This echoes the method of the soothsayers, who would repeat their actions again and again until they at least received a favorable response from the deity.[60] Thus God makes a second nocturnal visitation to Balaam. As in the first dialogue, here too the text reports that "that night God came to Balaam" (Num. 22:20).[61] As

---

59. Some would see this as alluding to an incubation dream, but this conjecture has no solid foundation.

60. Xenophon (Anabasis 6.4.19) sacrifices three times on each of two or three consecutive days in the hope that "the victims may turn out favorable to us" (Jacob Milgrom, *Numbers: The JPS Torah Commentary* [Philadelphia: The Jewish Publication Society, 1990], p. 189).

61. According to Josephus, here the idea was to change God's mind out of anger and

we saw in chapter 1, similar language is used in dream revelations to other Gentiles: "But God came to Abimelech in a dream by night" (Gen. 20:3); "But God came to Laban the Aramean in a dream by night" (Gen. 31:24). In all three cases when God appears to Gentile prophets, the message refers to the future of a person(s) mentioned in the dream, but the connection with the dreamer himself is limited.

Unlike Abimelech and Laban, Balaam has two revelations dealing with the same topic. As we saw in the previous chapter, repetition is typical of dreams (those of Joseph and Pharaoh, for example) and emphasizes the authenticity of the message. Although God initially forbade Balaam to go with the men and subsequently permitted him to accompany them, both times the crux of the divine message is "You must not curse that people." The second dream emphasizes the potency of God's message; compare: "As for Pharaoh having had the same dream twice, it means that the matter has been determined by God, and that God will soon carry it out" (Gen. 41:32).

At this point, we should mention the inscription discovered at Deir 'Alla in Transjordan, recounting the story of Balaam. What is important for us is that the description of the revelation there is identical to that in the Pentateuch: "Lo, the gods came to him at night and [spoke to] him." So too is the description of what follows—"And Balaam arose the next day"—which parallels the biblical "Balaam arose (ויקם) in the morning" (Num. 22:13, 21).[62] This is not a normal biblical locution, the standard idiom is וישכם. Also noteworthy is that the Deir 'Alla inscription refers to Balaam as a seer of God, and in 24:4 and 16 he calls himself one "who beholds visions from the Almighty"—where in both cases the verb is חזה.

Another important element involves the construction of the altars. Balaam asks Balak to construct seven altars and prepare seven bullocks and seven

---

then to dispatch Balaam with hostile intent (*Antiquities of the Jews* 4:107). Wellhausen, however, sees the two dialogues between Balaam and God as coming from two independent sources: J. Wellhausen, *Die Composition des Hexateuchs und der Historischen Bucher des Alten Testaments,* p. 110.

62. On the Deir 'Alla inscriptions, see for translation: J. Hoftizer and G. van der Kooij, *Aramaic Texts from Deir 'Alla* (Leiden: Brill, 1976); otherwise J. A. Fitzmyer, "Review of Aramaic Texts from Deir 'Alla," *CBQ* 40 (1978), pp. 93–95; J. A. Hackett, *The Balaam Text from Deir 'Alla* (Chico, CA: Scholars Press, 1984); P. K. McCarter, "The Balaam Text from Deir 'Alla: The First Combinations," *BASOR* 239 (1980), pp. 49–60; M. Weinfeld, "The Prophecy of Balaam in the Inscription from Deir 'Alla (Sukkoth)," *Shnaton* 5–6 (1982), pp. 141–147; B. A. Levine, "The Deir 'Alla Plaster Inscriptions, *JAOS* 101–102 (1981), pp. 195–205; idem, "The Balaam Text from Deir 'Alla: Historical Aspects," *Biblical Archaeology Today* (Jerusalem: Israel Exploration Society, 1985), pp. 326-339.

rams for sacrifice.[63] The idea is to offer a bullock and ram on each altar, in hopes of getting the Lord to put words in his mouth.[64] Balak and Balaam perform this action three times. Because the use of multiple altars in a single ceremony is not documented elsewhere in the Bible, it is clear that this is a foreign custom, where each altar is dedicated to a different deity.[65] Balak must stand next to the sacrifices while the diviner goes in quest of prophetic signs, and thus for every altar (see vv. 6, 15, and 17), Weinfeld finds a Mesopotamian parallel: the *āpilū* uttered their prophecies while the person on whose behalf the sacrifice had been offered stood nearby.[66] We know from the Bible of the requirement that the public be present when sacrifices are offered. According to the Mishnah, "How can a man's offering be offered if he does not stand by it?"[67] It seems from the details of the biblical story that here we have something similar to the custom of the *bārû* priests, who built altars and offered sacrifices on them before beginning their magical rites.[68] In addition, the *bārû* priests and the *āšipu* included their "client" in their rituals. The priest held the client's hand during the ceremony. "The person who brought the sacrifice had to hold the sheep while the priest offered the sacrifice."[69] The person who brought the sacrifice had to spread his hands in prayer and prostrate himself on the ground.

The moves from Bamoth Baal (v. 41) to Sedehzophim (23:14) and after that to Rosh Peor[70] stemmed from the assumption that the location of the cere-

---

63. Rashi notes that the Patriarchs had built a total of seven altars—four by Abraham (Gen. 12:7 and 8; 13:18, 22:9), one by Isaac (ibid. 26:5), and two by Jacob (ibid. 33:20 and 35:7).

64. Abraham Ibn Ezra noted the significance of the number seven in the liturgical calendar: the seventh day is the Sabbath, the seventh week brings the festival of Shavuot, the seventh month is Tishrei, the seventh year is the sabbatical year, and the seven sprinklings of blood in the Temple on the Day of Atonement. The sacrifices that the Lord enjoined Job's friends to offer also consisted of seven bullocks and seven rams (Job 42:8).

65. "At dawn, in the presence of Ea, Shamash, and Marduk, you shall erect seven altars, you shall set seven censers of cypress, you shall pour the blood of seven sheep." See Milgrom, *Numbers,* p. 194; cf. Virgil, *Aeneid* 6:38–39.

66. M. Weinfeld, "Ancient Near Eastern Parallels in Prophetic Literature," *VT* 27 (1977), pp. 186–187.

67. Mishna Ta'anit 4:2.

68. S. Daiches, "Balaam, a Babylonian Bārû?" *Assyriologische und Archaeologische Studien Herman von Hilprecht gewidmet* (Leipzig: J. C. Hinrichs, 1909), pp. 60–70.

69. Benjamin Uffenheimer, *Ancient Prophecy in Israel,* p. 47; H. Zimmern, *Beiträge zur Kenntnis der Babylonischen Religion* (Leipzig: J. C. Hinrichs, 1896–1901), 100:11 and 68:73–74.

70. Elsewhere (21:20), this last is designated הפסגה 'the peak'. This may be one of the peaks of the Abarim range (21:11), which rises above the Israelite camp. The place has not

mony had magical significance.[71] Because Balaam was supposed to curse Israel, he had to see all the people, so that none of the magic force of the imprecation would be lost. Perhaps Balak believed that the setback at Bamoth Baal was due to a deficiency in the ritual and that Balaam's view, of cardinal importance for magical acts, had been impaired. Hence the monarch repeated the same actions and preparations as before. He may also have believed that a change of place might bring a different message from God, in accordance with the adage, "a change of place changes luck."[72]

Another possible significance of the move to Sedehzophim, to the top of the peak there,[73] is that Sedehzophim is, literally, an "observation point" for stargazers or ornithomancers.[74] The Phoenicians called astrologers "watchers of the sky."[75] In other words, Balaam goes to a high place in order to observe the stars or the flight of birds.[76] In this he again resembles the Babylonian *bārû,* who practiced an inductive mantic prophecy that was fundamentally rational, since it was based on the examination of signs and portents. Despite the points of contact with the *bārû,* Daiches' total identification of Balaam as one should be rejected. The description of Balaam incorporates both popular and legendary elements. All the same, the underlying model evidently is the Babylonian *bārû* diviner.[77] It should be remembered that the character of Balaam as depicted in his aphorisms is not identical with the character described in the story itself. Whereas in the first part of the story, Balaam is a diviner summoned by the king of Moab to curse Israel, in his last two utterances he is a kind of prophet-seer—one who can act only in accordance with the will of God, as he repeatedly emphasizes (24:13, 22, 8, 11, 38; 23:3, 6, 12, 26).[78]

yet been identified but there was a temple of Baal there (Num. 25:3, Hosea 9:10). This is the chief subject of chapter 25. The Neofite version reads here "idols of Peor," evidently influenced by that temple. See Milgrom, *Numbers,* p. 201.

71. We learn about the importance of the location of the rituals conducted by the *bārû* priests from the designation "the place where destiny is determined," the place of the judges (Zimmern, *Beitrage,* 96:1–6).

72. BT Rosh Hashana 16b.

73. According to Targum Jonathan and Targum Onkelos, פסגה simply means "height"; but the Septuagint sometimes renders it as a proper noun.

74. Milgrom, *Numbers,* p. 198; Gaster, *Myth,* p. 305.

75. Gaster, *Myth,* p. 305.

76. The Hebrew word מצור, with the sense of "observation point," is cognate to the Akkadian *maṣṣartu* 'celestial observatory'. The two roots appear side by side in Habakkuk: "I will stand on my watch, take up my station at the post (מצור), and wait to see (ואצפה) what He will say to me" (Hab. 2:1).

77. Jacob Liver, *Studies in Bible and Judean Desert Scrolls* (Jerusalem: Bialik, 1971), pp. 363–364 (Hebrew).

78. Milgrom, *Numbers,* p. 473.

After the ritual ceremonies, we are told twice that Balaam went in quest of the divine word. Twice, too, we read that "God manifested Himself (וַיִּקָּר) to Balaam" (Num. 23:4, 16).[79] The sense is of וַיִּקָּר is of an involuntary, "chance" (מקרה) encounter. The verb is associated with Israelite prophetic revelations only twice (Ex. 3:18 and 5:3), when Moses is describing his revelation to Pharaoh.[80] Evidently, it specifically designates a divine revelation to Gentiles, whose prophecies–despite all their rituals and magical ceremonies–are purely a matter of chance and coincidence. Rashi notes: "וַיִּקָּר, with the sense of being provisional, of disgrace, of impurity and nocturnal emission; that is, with difficulty and infamy. He appeared to him by day only to make known His affection for Israel"–that is, He appeared to him at night. Nachmanides, however, writes:

> God manifested Himself to Balaam–because this man did not reach the degree of prophecy, it is recounted in this language, namely, that the divine word came to him now by chance, to the glory of Israel. This is why it says "God came to Balaam," because this expression is not used for prophets, but for one who is not of that degree, and so too "God came to Abimelech," "God came to Laban the Aramean." It may be that what it means is that the divine will comes in speech from the Most High to minds that are dreaming, because Balaam too falls in the day and a deep sleep and opening of the eye fell upon him.

Going off alone in search of divine revelation is also found in Mesopotamian sources.[81] Some believe that Balaam goes off for a similar reason. A related possibility is that he goes off to observe the flight of birds or movement of the clouds in order to divine God's will and forecast the future. We have evidence from Mesopotamia of the use of observation of combat between birds and their cries as portents of the future. Some maintain that Balaam goes off to work magic rites. This reading relies on emending the obscure word שְׁפִי to כשפים, yielding "and he went in quest of enchantments."[82] But evidently שְׁפִי is in fact the singular of שפיים 'high hills'.[83] Each time Balaam and Balak climb

---

79. The subject of the two verbs "did" and "offered up" is the same. It is Balak who offers the sacrifice; see "your / his offering" in vv. 3, 6, 15, and 17. Evidently the words "Balak and Balaam" in v. 2b are an interpolated gloss (Gray, *Numbers,* p. 342).

80. The Bible uses the root ק.ר.ה for divine revelation (Ex. 3:18 and 5:3). The same root *(q.r.y)* appears in an inscription from South Arabia with the meaning of a divine revelation (Gaster, *Myth,* p. 305).

81. Daiches, "Balaam," pp. 63–64.

82. Gray, *Numbers,* p. 343.

83. See also: "like searing wind from the bare heights (שפים) of the desert" (Jer. 4:11);

to an elevated spot from which they can make visual contact with the Israelites, so that, as they believe, the curse will assail them.[84]

Balaam's repeated attempts to enter into communion with God by offering sacrifices point to the difference between him and Israelite prophets. The latter never chased after prophecy. In fact, they often declined the mission imposed upon them by God (Ex. 3:4; Jer. 1). Balaam, by contrast, actively endeavors to receive a prophetic message and relies on magical means to achieve it. But when God does indeed appear to Balaam: "And the Lord put a word in Balaam's mouth" (Num. 23:5), the Sages visualize that "word" in concrete terms: "Rabbi Eliezer said, 'an angel'; Rabbi Jonathan said: 'a hook.'"[85] According to the first opinion, the Lord placed Balaam under the supervision of an angel who did not allow him to curse Israel (thus Rashi). Another interpretation is that an angel entered his mouth and settled down in his throat, so that whenever Balaam opened his mouth to speak it was the voice of the angel that came out.[86] According to Rabbi Jonathan, who says that God put a hook in his mouth, whenever Balaam tried to curse Israel He would pull on the hook and close his mouth so that he could not say anything.[87] In any case, both the Midrash and the Bible emphasize Balaam's total dependence on God's will and whatever word He might put in his mouth. Although it seems that Balaam would be very happy to curse Israel in return for a large reward, from the outset it is plain that his mouth is not his own, and he never attempts to act counter to the divine will.

From his previous attempts Balaam understood that not only was the Lord unwilling for him to curse Israel; in fact, He wanted him to bless them. As the text has already hinted (22:20), Balaam is merely an instrument of the Lord to achieve this end. Hence, in reference to the third time, we read that "Balaam... did not, as on previous occasions, go in search of omens" (Num. 24:1).[88] In other words, in his earlier attempts Balaam had sought to observe

---

"Spoilers have come upon all the bare heights of the wilderness" (Jer. 12:12); "And the wild asses stand on the bare heights" (Jer. 14:6); similar is "Raise a standard upon a bare hill (הר נשפה)" (Isa. 13:2).

84. See Ezek. 6:1.

85. BT Sanhedrin 105b.

86. Midrash Tanḥuma 12, Numbers Rabba 20:18.

87. "*And He put a word in his mouth:* What is this putting? What does the text omit when it says, 'Return to Balak and speak thus'? When he heard that he was not allowed to curse, he said, 'Why should I go back to Balak and wound him?' But the Holy One, blessed be He, put a bridle and bit in his mouth, like a person who harnesses an animal with a bit to lead it wherever he wants, and told him, 'You will return to Balak even against your will'" (Rashi on Num. 23:16).

88. Gray believes that we should not infer from this verse that previously Balaam had

the omens in order to know the future. When he opened his mouth this time, however, the divine afflatus penetrated him, and he spoke his piece from divine inspiration.[89]

The expressions "word of the man whose eye is open (שְׁתֻם הָעָיִן)," "who beholds visions from the Almighty," "prostrate, but with eyes unveiled," which introduce both his third and fourth oracles, are very difficult and have long troubled the commentators. Rashi understands שְׁתֻם הָעָיִן on the basis of the Mishnah: "If a Gentile helped an Israelite to take jars of wine from one place to another, and the presumption is that the wine was watched, it is permitted; but if the Israelite had told the other that he would be gone, [the wine is forbidden] if [he was gone] time enough for the other to bore a hole (וְיִשְׁתֹּם) and stop it up, and for the clay to dry" (Mishnah Avoda Zara 5:3). There Rashi glosses the verb as "will open, as in שְׁתֻם הָעָיִן (Num. 24), which means 'open.'" Thus Rashi understands שְׁתֻם הָעָיִן to mean "open-eyed," that is, someone who has good vision.[90] If we accept this interpretation, the expression is synonymous with "eyes unveiled" גְּלוּי עֵינָיִם in the second half of the verse and there is no contrast. The Samaritan rendering and Targum Onkelos both follow this line. If the two phrases are synonymous, the meaning may be that that he sees divine visions when in a trance. Others understand שְׁתֻם to be like סָתֻם 'closed, sealed' (as in Lam. 3:8). That is, Balaam failed to perceive the Lord's appearance to him or was physically blind and the Lord opened his eyes so that he could see the angel.[91] This reading is somewhat problematic, however, because the implication of 22:41 and 23:13

---

practiced magical rites because the text does not state so explicitly. On the other hand, the verse can be read as a sort of flashback; that is, it fills in a detail omitted previously (Gray, *Numbers*, p. 343).

89. Here and later Balaam introduces himself and declares that the source of his utterance is the Lord (v. 4). A similar formula appears in David's introduction of himself, followed by reference to the divine source of his song: "The utterance of David son of Jesse, the utterance of the man set on high, the anointed of the God of Jacob, the favorite of the sons of Israel: The spirit of the Lord has spoken through me, His message is on my tongue" (2 Samuel 23:1–2).

90. Morag notes that the root 'שתם' is a hapax in the Mishna, too, and that its sense clearly has to do with boring a hole and perhaps with making a small crack. In Aramaic the root has a similar sense; קוּלָא שְׁתִימָא is a vessel that has been tapped (JT Avodah Zarah 5:4). It may be that שְׁתֻם הָעָיִן has to do with Balaam's appearance; that is, that one of his eyes was like a hole or narrow crack. Despite this deficiency in his physical vision, he had spiritual vision, whence the expression, "who beholds visions from the Almighty, prostrate, but with eyes unveiled." But this explanation seems far-fetched, because nothing in the text contrasts physical vision and spiritual vision. See S. Morag, "Layers of Antiquity: Some Linguistic Observations on the Oracles of Balaam," *Tarbiz* 50 (1980/1981), pp. 12–14.

91. Milgrom, *Numbers*, p. 203; BT Nedarim 31a and Sanhedrin 105a.

is that Balaam must be able to see Israel in order to curse them—as is suggested, too, by his oracle (23:9). It is also difficult to explain the contrast between the conjectural "closed eye" of the first half of the verse and "open eye" of the second half.

Verse 4—"Word of him who hears God's speech, who beholds visions from the Almighty, prostrate, but with eyes unveiled"—is echoed by the Deir 'Alla inscription, whose superscription reports that Balaam son of Beor was "a man who saw the gods," and later says that "he saw a vision like a burden of God." The verse hints that Balaam's experience includes both visual and aural elements. Rashi says that "the plain meaning is like the Targum—that He appears to him only at night when he is lying down. And the homiletic meaning is that when He appeared to him, he did not have the strength to stand on his feet and fell on his face because he was uncircumcised and it was loathsome for him to have an epiphany when standing upright." According to Targum Onkelos, God appeared to him when he was in his bed at night. Abraham Ibn Ezra held that "the sense of both 'hear' and 'behold' is through sorcery, and it seems plausible that it is a prophecy in a dream as in the words of Eliphaz, 'A form loomed before my eyes; I heard a murmur, a voice' (Job 4:16)."

In the Bible, the root נ.פ.ל 'fall' (rendered "prostrate" above) is often associated with sleep, as in "a deep sleep fell upon Abram" (Gen. 15:12)[92] which was also in a מַחֲזֶה. As for the second half of the verse, Ibn Ezra commented that "even though he was sleeping, he saw with his eyes, as in '[I was asleep,] but my heart was wakeful' (Cant. 5:2)—that is, he saw with his inner eye and the revelation took place in a dream." We have already noted two places in the Book of Job where the root נ.פ.ל is associated with dreams and sleep—"In thought-filled visions of the night, when deep sleep falls on men" (Job 4:13, 33:15). According to Levine, "prostrate, but with eyes unveiled" means that Balaam sees the vision in a dream, but with his eyes open.[93] Alternatively, conjectures Levine, the reference may be to a form of hypnosis in which a person falls into a deep sleep or trance but the eyes remain open. Some believe that the character of Balaam

---

92. The root נ.פ.ל generally has the sense of "fall, descend, be defeated." See: Esther 6:13; Isa. 30:25; Ezek. 30:4; 2 Sam. 2:23; etc. It has other senses too, including "take to one's bed" (Ex. 21:18). Because it also denotes bowing down (2 Sam. 19:19), Milgrom sees its use here as indicating that Balaam honors and worships the Lord; he finds support for this reading in other verses (Gen. 17:13 and Josh. 5:14). According to him, Balaam is in control of his senses—the text states that he sees and hears—and not in a trance (Milgrom, *Numbers*, p. 203). According to Targum Jonathan, falling on his face means that he is too weak to stand up because of the intensity of the prophetic experience (cf. Isa. 8:11 and Ezek. 3:14).

93. Baruch A. Levine, "The Righteousness of the Lord," *Eretz Israel* 20 (1970), p. 210 (Hebrew).

incorporates charismatic-ecstatic elements, reminiscent of the god-gripped who are open-eyed and clear-sighted in their ecstasy. The phrases "visions from the Almighty," "prostrate, but with eyes unveiled," and "the man whose eye is open" are not technical terms referring to a magical rite but evidence that ecstatic elements have been woven into the figure of Balaam.[94] Levine also suggests that Balaam had several different experiences: "He had visions both sleeping and waking."[95] This interpretation is compatible with our conclusion about Abram's vision. There, as we saw, there were two stages, the first to Abram when awake, the second after he had fallen into a deep sleep. With both Abram and Balaam, too, the theophany is preceded by a ritual ceremony.

MOSES AS A UNIQUE PROPHET
(NUMBERS 12:6–8)

> And He said, "Hear these My words: When a prophet of the Lord arises among you, I make Myself known to him in a vision [בַּמַּרְאָה], I speak with him in a dream. [7] Not so with My servant Moses; he is trusted throughout My household. [8] With him I speak mouth to mouth, in a vision [וּמַרְאֶה] and not in riddles, and he beholds the likeness of the Lord. How then did you not shrink from speaking against My servant Moses!"

According to v. 8, the Lord speaks to Moses in a מַרְאֶה (*aleph* with a *segol*), whereas to other prophets He makes himself known in a מַרְאָה (*aleph* with a *qamaṣ*). In other words, there is a difference between how God appears to Moses and how He appears to other prophets. The difference in the vocalization evidently stems from both exegetical and theological considerations. Nevertheless, some modern scholars maintain that the vocalizations are equivalent and the difference artificial, late, or superfluous.[96] Grammatically, מַרְאָה is a feminine noun, and מַרְאֶה masculine. But the difference in gender is no basis for a difference in meaning, since similar pairs can be found throughout the Bible.

Verse 6 reports that God appears to His lesser prophets in מַרְאָה and in dreams, which are inferior forms of revelation. מַרְאָה is parallel to "dream." The vocalization should not be changed; the whole point of the passage is the difference between the prophetic modes of Moses on the one hand and of Miriam and Aaron on the other. To emphasize this difference, v. 7 adds that Moses is

---

94. Uffenheimer, *Ancient Prophecy in Israel,* p. 51.

95. Levine, "The Righteousness of the Lord," p. 210.

96. A. Margaliot, "Numbers 12: The Nature of Moses's Prophecy," *Beit Miqra* 81(2) (1980), p. 141, n. 22.

the Lord's trusted servant. Verse 8 further clarifies this unique status: the Lord speaks to Moses face to face (lit. "mouth to mouth") recapitulating Ex. 33:11: "The Lord would speak to Moses face to face, as one man speaks to another."[97] Again: "Never again did there arise in Israel a prophet like Moses—whom the Lord singled out, face to face" (Deut. 34:10). Moses is unique in that the Lord speaks to him directly, face to face, and nothing interposes between them when the Lord addresses him.[98] What is more, Moses sees clearly, and does not need to have the meaning of his vision explained to him. By contrast, the מַרְאָה, the dream-riddle vouchsafed to other prophets, requires interpretation and explanation.

Targum Onkelos approached the matter differently. The מַרְאָה of Moses and the מַרְאָה of the other prophets differ not in gender but in number.[99] Onkelos rendered the מַרְאָה of the other prophets with a masculine plural noun, but the מַרְאָה of Moses in the singular, i.e., "sight." This may be because the former is related to multiple prophets and the latter to Moses alone; or he may have been influenced by the midrashic and aggadic tradition that the prophets delivered their utterances through the medium of nine mirrors מַרְאָה, whereas Moses saw through only a single mirror (Leviticus Rabba 1:14, ed. Margolioth, p. 31).[100]

In the Septuagint, the difference between the other prophets' מַרְאָה and Moses' מַרְאֶה is that the former is translated as "vision" but the latter as "concrete vision." Nevertheless, the הַמַּרְאֶה הַגָּדֹל of the burning bush (Ex. 3:3) is rendered by the same word (with the appropriate change in grammatical form) as the מַרְאָה of the other prophets in Numbers. This may simply indicate that Numbers and Exodus were translated by different hands.

The rabbinic midrashim on this verse do not see any difference between מַרְאָה and מַרְאֶה. According to Leviticus Rabba, 1:14 (ed. Margolioth, pp. 30–32):

> Rabbi Judah says, 'All the prophets saw through nine mirrors, as it is

---

97. The image here is that of a royal court where only the highest-ranking officials have free access to the monarch. Those who enjoyed this privilege were referred to as those "who saw the king's face" (see 2 Kings 25:19; Esther 1:14).

98. Even though Moses is close to God, he does not actually see God's face: "He said, 'you cannot see My face, for man may not see Me and live'" (Ex. 33:20). Hence the expression "face to face" does not mean that a person sees the face of his friend, but that there is a direct and immediate relationship between the two parties. Verse 21 adds that Moses "beheld" the Lord only after He had passed. See Baruch A. Levine, *Numbers 1–20, AB* (New York: Doubleday, 1993), pp. 341–342.

99. Athalya Brenner, "מַרְאָה and מַרְאֶה," *Beit Mikra* 83(4) (1980), pp. 373–374 (Hebrew).

100. See also BT Sanhedrin 97b and Sukka 45b.

written, "like the vision of the vision I had seen, like the vision I had
seen when I came to destroy the city, and visions like the vision that I
had seen by the Chebar Canal. Forthwith, I fell on my face" (Ezek.
43:3).[101] But Moses saw through only one mirror–"in a vision and not
in riddles" (Num. 12:8).' Our sages say that all the prophets saw through
a clouded mirror, as it says, 'When I spoke to the prophets, I granted
many visions [and spoke parables through the prophets]' (Hosea 12:11).

This homily is based on the principle that prophetic sight is like looking in a
mirror (מַרְאָה) that distorts the image somewhat. Moses looked through only a
single mirror, whereas the other prophets saw an image that had been
reflected nine times, so that the image was greatly distorted. The midrash
glosses all the uses of מַרְאָה in the sense of mirror but recognizes no distinction
between מַרְאָה and מַרְאֶה.[102]

The classical commentators–Rashi, Rashbam, Abraham Ibn Ezra, Joseph
Bekhor-Shor, and Nachmanides–ignored the difference of vocalization and
grammatical form between the other prophets' מַרְאָה and Moses' מַרְאֶה. Although they did remark on the difference between his prophecy and theirs,
nothing they write suggests that they were relying on the variant vocalization;
nor does it seem to have been significant for Maimonides (*Guide of the Perplexed* 2:41–45).[103] The first exegete to refer to the difference in vocalization
was Baḥya ben Joseph ibn Paquda (second half of the eleventh century), who
wrote that both מַרְאָה with a *qamaṣ* and מַרְאֶה with a *segol* mean "glass mirrors."
The difference is that the image reflected in a מַרְאֶה is blurred and distorted,
whereas that seen in a מַרְאָה is much truer. He reaches these conclusions on
the basis of remarks by the Talmudic sages. Isaac ben Moses Arama
(1420–1494), the author of *Aqedat Yiṣḥaq*, also noted the difference in vocalization. He maintains that whereas מַרְאָה means "mirror," מַרְאֶה refers to what is
seen directly with the eye.[104]

In Daniel 10, the form מַרְאָה appears four times: twice in v. 7 and again in
vv. 8 and 16. According to verse 8: "So I was left alone to see this great vision
(המראה הגדלה הזאת)" (Dan. 10:8). This is the only locus where מַרְאָה is certainly
of feminine gender (as shown by the gender of the modifying adjectives). The

---

101. R. Judah reaches the number of nine mirrors by adding up each occurrence of
"vision" ("visions" = 2) and "seen" in this verse.

102. מַרְאָה with the sense of "mirror" is found only once in the Bible: "He made the laver
of copper and its stand of copper, from the mirrors of the women who performed tasks at
the entrance of the Tent of Meeting" (Ex. 38:8).

103. Amos Hakham, "The מַרְאֶה of Moses versus מַרְאָה," *Sefer Gevaryahu,* ed. B. Z. Luria
(Jerusalem: Kiryat Sefer, 1989), vol. 1, pp. 64–65.

104. Ibid., p. 65.

text may indicate that there is a difference between Moses's vision of the burning bush (Ex. 3:3), which is הַמַּרְאֶה הַגָּדֹל הַזֶּה in the masculine gender, and Daniel's vision. It is interesting that when Daniel describes the מַרְאָה he says, "I heard him speaking; and when I heard him speaking, overcome by a deep sleep, I lay prostrate on the ground" (Dan. 10:9). In other words, here מַרְאָה clearly designates a dream. We must emphasize, however, that at the beginning of the chapter (v. 1) the same experience is referred to as a מַרְאֶה.[105] Hence it seems that the Masoretic text and vocalization are not consistent in marking the variations in the texts of Daniel and Ezekiel. In chapter 8 it is the form מַרְאֶה that occurs in vv. 16 and 27, and it seems likely that when Daniel sees this מַרְאֶה he is asleep—"When he spoke with me, I was overcome by a deep sleep as I lay prostrate on the ground" (Dan. 8:18). Perhaps here מַרְאֶה designates the images that Daniel saw in his dream.

This ambiguity is also found in Ezekiel. The beginning of that prophet's career is when "the heavens opened and I saw visions (מַרְאוֹת) of God" (Ezek. 1:1).[106] In Ezekiel, the singular form is always vocalized מַרְאֶה with a *segol* (11:24 and many others places; and in the construct, with a *sere* in 43:3). The Masoretes did not hesitate to equate Ezekiel's מַרְאֶה with Moses' מַרְאֶה, even though they did distinguish Moses' מַרְאֶה from Samuel's מַרְאָה. Elsewhere we have "He brought me, in visions (בְּמַראוֹת) of God, to the Land of Israel, and He set me down on a very high mountain, near which there seemed to be the outline of a city to the south (Ezek. 40:2; cf. Ezek. 8:3). Here the prophet may be describing a dream, as Rashi avers: "He did not take me there but showed it to me as if I were there."

JACOB'S VISION (GENESIS 46:1–5)

בְּמַרְאֹת הַלַּיְלָה in the plural occurs in Gen. 46:2. Here Jacob / Israel stops off in Beer Sheba on his way to Egypt and offers sacrifices, after which the Lord appears to him in a vision by night.[107] The text does not explain why Jacob

---

105. Brenner, "מַרְאֶה and מַרְאָה," p. 374, says that the formal difference between מַרְאֶה and מַרְאָה does not necessarily indicate a difference in meaning, and notes that in Daniel 10 they are used to designate the same vision.

106. To confuse matters further, מַרְאוֹת is the plural of both מַרְאָה and מַרְאֶה.

107. Similar stories are found in the second section of the Book of Genesis—the Patriarchal cycle (chapters 12–36). By contrast, sacrifices and theophanies are absent from the third part of the book, the Joseph cycle (chapters 37–50). Hence Westermann is of the opinion that the story in its present form belongs to the Patriarchal cycle: Klaus Westermann, *Genesis 37–50*, trans. John J. Scullion (Minneapolis: Augsburg, 1986), p. 154.

stopped to pray in Beer Sheba.[108] Perhaps he was afraid to continue his journey because of his frailty and advanced age. Perhaps he was anxious about
leaving Canaan to settle elsewhere, because his father Isaac had been forbidden to do so (Gen. 26:2).[109] More likely Jacob stopped in Beer Sheba in order
to seek divine blessing for his emigration. A close reading of Genesis reveals
that the Patriarchs often interrupted their journeys in order to pray (Gen.
12:8–9 and 28:18). Here, though, we read about a sacrifice to God.[110] The fact
that Jacob offered his sacrifice before the Lord appeared to him, rather than
afterwards, suggests that here we have an incubation: Jacob offered sacrifices
and requested divine assistance; as a result, the Lord appeared to him and
encouraged him.[111] Moreover, Jacob's arrival at the site of the revelation is not
described as a matter of chance. It seems plausible that he was aware of the
sanctity of the site. Josephus's description of the incident reinforces this
view:[112]

> Halting at the Well of the Oath, he there offered sacrifice to God; and
> fearing that by reason of the prosperity prevalent in Egypt his sons would
> be so greatly enamored of settling there ... and furthermore that having
> taken his departure into Egypt without God's sanction his race might be
> annihilated; yet terrified withal that he might quit this life before setting
> eyes on Joseph—these were the thoughts which he was revolving in his
> mind when he sank to sleep. Then God appeared to him and called him
> twice by name. ... Encouraged by this dream, Jacob with greater ardor
> departed for Egypt along with his sons and his sons' children.[113]

---

108. Beer Sheba is mentioned as the place where Isaac was born, where Abraham
planted a tamarisk tree to indicate his tie to the Land of Canaan (21:33), where he returned
from Mount Moriah (22:19), and from where Jacob set forth on his long trek to Haran
(28:10).

109. In fact, according to Jubilees 44:3, Jacob invited Joseph to come visit him in Canaan.

110. The sacrifice is referred to as זבח, a term associated only with Jacob (Gen. 31:54), as
distinguished from עולות (Gen. 22:2 and 20:8). The difference between the two rituals is that
only a small portion of a זבח is burned on the altar and most of the slaughtered animal is
eaten in a festive meal (Sarna, *Genesis*, p. 312).

111. Some believe that the sacrifice may have been a thank-offering, expressing Jacob's
gratitude that Joseph was alive (Sarna, *Genesis*, p. 312). Some say that Jacob offers a sacrifice
to the God of his father Isaac in order to stress that even though his father has died, he
remains bound to God in the present and the future. Despite the fact that he is leaving for
a foreign land, this bond remains fast and will not be loosed at the borders of Canaan (Jacob,
The First Book of the Bible, p. 309).

112. Gnuse, *Dream*, p. 70, n. 63.

113. Josephus, *Jewish Antiquities*, trans. H. St. J. Thackeray (Cambridge, Massachusetts:
Harvard University Press, 1930), 2: 170–176.

This theophany was in a "vision by night." It is extraordinary, because God does not otherwise appear in the Joseph cycle (but is active only behind the scenes). Even though מַרְאֹת 'visions' is derived from root ר.א.ה. 'see', there is nothing visual here: the Lord merely speaks to Jacob.[114] The plural form is the plural of generalization,[115] like the plural form of in Gen. 37:8 and Dan. 2:1, where the reference is to a single dream.[116] The revelation takes place at night. As Lichtenstein notes, the idiom "vision by night" parallels "dream by night" (Gen. 20:3 and 31:24). To support his view that Jacob's "vision" is really a dream, he cites the Akkadian phrase *tabrīt mūši*, which means "nocturnal revelation" and is used synonymously with *šuttu* 'dream'.[117] The revelation itself has three parts: (1) a description of God's appearance; (2) the message; (3) the response to the message.[118] The structure is identical with that of prophetic dreams (see above, chapter 1).

Jacob's theophany begins with a divine summons: "God called to Israel in a vision by night: 'Jacob! Jacob!' He answered, 'Here'" (Gen. 46:2).[119] This summons is identical to that at the start of Jacob's dream in the house of Laban: "And in the dream an angel of God said to me, 'Jacob!' 'Here,' I answered" (Gen. 31:11). Its purpose is to prepare Jacob for the message. The double vocative is followed by Jacob's reply to the Lord, the laconic "Here [I am],"[120] which indicates both humility and alacrity. As in prophetic dreams, here too the Lord introduces Himself: "I am God, the God of your father" (Gen. 46:3); similarly, God introduces Himself in Jacob's other two dreams (28:13 and 31). The author uses this invocation of the divine name to echo 46:1, which reports that Israel sacrificed to the God of his father Isaac. The repetition of God's name here highlights the close relations between God and Jacob.

---

114. In Ezekiel, the phrase "visions of God" occurs several times (Ezek. 1:1, 8:3, 40:2). Although the associated verb indicates that sight is involved–"I saw visions of God" (Ezek. 1:1 and 43:3), there are also aural elements (Ezek. 1:24, 8:5, 40:4, 43:6).

115. Moshe Greenberg, *Ezekiel 1:20,* AB (Garden City, NY: Doubleday, 1983), p. 41; Westermann, *Genesis 37–50,* p. 155.

116. In both passages, the Septuagint and Peshitta have "dream" in the singular.

117. M. Lichtenstein, "Dream Theophany and the E Document," *JANESCU* 1–2 (1969), p. 46, n. 4.

118. Westermann, however, sees a different three-part structure: (1) introduction (v. 2); (2) instruction (v. 3a); (3) promise (vv. 3b–4) (Westermann, *Genesis 37–50,* p. 155).

119. We find a double vocative also with regard to Samuel (1 Samuel 3:11), Moses (Exodus 3:4), and Abraham (Genesis 22:11).

120. Abraham's responds with the same idiom, when God addresses him at the start of the binding of Isaac pericope (Gen. 22:1) and again when he is about to slaughter his son (22:11).

The message to Jacob relates to his future; it begins, "Fear not to go down to Egypt."[121] The expression "fear not" appears earlier, in the Lord's words to Abram (Gen. 16:1) and to Isaac (26:24) and recurs later, addressed to Moses and subsequently to almost every important figure in the Bible. This formula is considered to be the hallmark of what is known as the "salvation prophecy."[122] The Lord's prior appearances in dreams have been intended to encourage Jacob, and this time it is no different. The Lord's promise to Jacob includes the pronouncement that his offspring will be a great nation. This continues the earlier pledges to the Patriarchs about the number of their descendants.[123] They will grow into nationhood in Egypt; accordingly their sojourn in that country will be protracted, as part of the divine program (Gen. 15:13–16).[124] This passage is unique in associating the sojourn in Egypt with the multiplication of his offspring. What we have here is a sort of flash-forward–so that the personal message acquires a national character as well.[125]

In His message to Jacob, the Lord says, "I Myself will go down with you to Egypt, and I Myself will also bring you back" (v. 4). Boundaries do not exist for the Lord; just as He protected Jacob in Mesopotamia (Gen. 31:13) and in Canaan (35:3), so too He will protect him in Egypt. This verse provides the basis for the concept of the exile of the Shekhinah (Divine Presence). As the Mekhilta notes, the verse indicates that when the Israelites went down to Egypt, the Shekhinah went with them.[126] Commentators do not agree whether the promise made in the second half of the promise–"I Myself will also bring you back"–is personal or national in character. Some believe that

---

121. The formulaic "fear not" appears three other times in Genesis: 16:1, 21:17, and 26:24. Conrad identifies four stages in Jacob's theophany here: (1) God identifies Himself; (2) the promise, "Fear not"; (3) the reason for fear–the descent to Egypt; (4) and the promise that Jacob's offspring will become a great nation and that Joseph's hand will close his eyes (E. W. Conrad, "The 'Fear Not' Oracles in Second Isaiah," *VT* 34 (1984), pp. 143–145.

122. H. Gressmann, "Die literarische Analyse Deuterojesajas," *ZAW* 34 (1914), pp. 287ff.; A. de Pury, *Promesse divine et légende cultuelle dans le cycle de Jacob,* pp. 223ff.

123. Gen. 17:20, 18:18, 21:13 and 18; Ex. 32:10; Num. 14:12.

124. On the realization of the promise to Abraham, see Ex. 1:7.

125. Note that vv. 3 and 4 recapitulate what is said in Genesis 15:13–16, which also speaks about the descent to and exodus from Egypt. Westermann holds that the verses here and in Genesis 15 are a later expansion meant to link the Patriarchal age with the Exodus. Because both chapters convey a personal message and have similar content, Westermann believes that they may very well be the work of the same editor (Westermann, *Genesis 37–50,* p. 157).

126. "Wherever Israel was exiled, the Divine Presence was exiled with them" (BT Megillah 29a).

it refers to Jacob only, because it is phrased in the singular and addressed specifically to him. Jacob will die in exile; accordingly, Rashi, Rashbam, and Abraham Ibn Ezra understand God's promise to refer to Jacob's burial in the Cave of Makhpelah. It seems preferable, however, to read the promise as both personal and national. Jacob himself will return to Canaan to be buried in his ancestral tomb (Gen. 47:29 and 50:5–13). Later, his descendants too will return to the Promised Land. Their return to Canaan will be the fulfillment of the promise of a great nation: if Jacob's descendants do not return to Canaan they will assimilate into the Egyptian people. Joseph Bekhor-Shor noted the double meaning of the verse: "I will bring back your body to be buried in the tomb of your ancestors and your offspring to give them the Land of Canaan."

The reaction to the message conveyed in the revelation is that "Jacob set out from Beer-Sheba" (Gen. 46:5). We are told that, perhaps because of his advanced age and weakness, he required his sons' assistance: "The sons of Israel put their father Jacob ... in the wagons that Pharaoh had sent to transport him." The verb קוּם–here rendered "set out"–normally denotes action (e.g., Gen. 21:32 and 24:10); here, though, it may merely indicate the end of the theophany.[127] Finally, the episode ends with the report that the sons of Israel journeyed to Egypt with all their families; that is, they accepted God's message to Jacob.

The bottom line is that a revelation in "a vision by night" is identical, in both form and content, to God's earlier appearances to Jacob in dreams. Each time Jacob sets out for another country, God appears to him in a dream and encourages him. The earlier dreams, like this "vision," are associated with a holy site. The format of all the various epiphanies is the same, beginning with God's introducing Himself and continuing with a message of encouragement. This is manifested by the phrase "Fear not," God's promise to remain with Jacob (46:4 and 28:15), and the promise to return him to his homeland (46:4, 28:15, and 31:13).

GOD'S APPEARANCE TO SAMUEL (1 SAMUEL 3)

Further evidence for the affinity of dream and מַרְאָה / vision is provided by 1 Sam. 3:15: "Samuel was afraid to report the vision to Eli" (1 Sam. 3:15). The story of God's appearance to Samuel in chapter 3 is the direct sequel to the first two chapters of the book. Samuel's birth, in the wake of his mother's prayer and vow at Shilo (chapter 1), leads to his vocation as a spiritual leader

---

127. Sarna, *Genesis,* p. 313.

in Israel, as do his growth and education in the sanctuary in chapter 2. Just as his mother consecrated him to the Lord, now the Lord consecrates him to his mission. Both consecrations take place in the sanctuary, with the theophany of chapter 3 elevating Samuel to the status of a prophet and announcing the disasters that will befall the House of Eli.

Although Samuel hears God's voice, he is different from other prophets, as many scholars have noted: the Lord does not impose a mission on him, nor instruct him as to what he must do in the future—details prominent in the consecrations of Isaiah, Jeremiah, and Ezekiel.[128] Accordingly, on the basis of a comparison with dreams from Mesopotamia, some have assigned chapter 3 to the genre in which a deity appears to an individual in a dream and only tells him what is going to happen without telling him what to do.[129]

The account of the Lord's appearance to Samuel begins by marking the hour and the setting: "The lamp of God had not yet gone out" (1 Sam. 3:3),[130] suggesting that the voice called to Samuel around daybreak (cf. v. 15–"Samuel lay there until morning"). The lamp is mentioned in order to explain why Samuel ran to Eli's couch: the voice that called came from inside the sanctuary of the Lord, which was lit up—but Samuel saw no one there. Thus the narrator presents the background for the revelation, which is to take place next to the Ark of the Lord, the very core of the priestly ritual.[131]

The ancients were gravely perplexed by the fact that Samuel was "lying down in the temple of the Lord (בהיכל ה')‎ where the Ark of God was."[132] How

---

128. Isaiah 6; Jer. 1:4–10; Ezek. 1–3. Compare also the commissions to Moses (Exodus 3), Gideon (Judg. 6:11–17; and Jehu (2 Kings 9:5–10). Some scholars, however, believe that the story is nevertheless a consecration to prophecy. See Moshe Elat, *Samuel and the Foundation of Kingship in Ancient Israel* (Jerusalem: Magnes Press, 1998), p. 30, n. 76.

129. Ibid., p. 30; Robert Gnuse, "A Reconsideration of the Form-critical Structure of I Samuel 3: An Ancient Near Eastern Theophany," *ZAW* 94 (1982), pp. 379–390; idem, *The Dream Theophany of Samuel,* pp. 133–152.

130. The lamp here is evidently the candlestand on which the oil lamps were placed. In the Pentateuch, the candelabrum is also referred to as a "lamp" (Ex. 27:20 and Lev. 20:2). The lamp burned before the ark and was accordingly called the "lamp of God." In the Pentateuch, we find that the Israelites were commanded to keep a lamp burning before the Lord from evening to morning (Ex. 27:11). The lighting of the lamp was considered to be a sacred ritual.

131. Yaira Amit, "The Story of Samuel's Consecration to Prophecy in the Light of Prophetic Thought," *Moshe Goldstein Volume,* ed. B. Z. Luria (Jerusalem: Society for Bible Research, 1987), p. 31 (Hebrew).

132. L. W. Batten, "The Sanctuary at Shilo and Samuel's Sleeping Therein," *JBL* 19 (1900), pp. 29–33. Batten believes that Samuel was sleeping where the Ark was located and that he was a watchman, as Joshua had been. It should be remembered, however, that the verse notes that Samuel was lying down in the sanctuary. Within the sanctuary there were

could a non-priest lie down in a holy place where only priests serve, and then only in an upright posture (see Deut. 18:5)? Accordingly some have taken the prepositional *bet* to mean, not "in," but "next to or near" the sanctuary–a common usage.[133] Evidently Samuel was lying down in a chamber adjoining the sanctuary, from which it was possible to see the Ark, the focus of divine revelation.[134] In Samuel 3, the word היכל 'sanctuary' refers to a structure that contains a number of rooms.[135] Samuel and Eli were not sleeping in the same room; later we also read that Samuel opened the doors of "the House of the Lord," as the sanctuary is called both here and in 1:7. In both Ugaritic literature and the Bible, the terms house (בית) and sanctuary (היכל) are frequently used interchangeably.[136] The fact that the Ark of God stood in the Holy of Holies suggests that the voice that called to Samuel originated from the Holy of Holies.

The revelation itself builds up step by step. Three times the Lord calls Samuel. Three times Samuel thinks that it is Eli who is summoning him, goes to him, and states his willingness to do his bidding.[137] After the third time, Eli understands that it is the Lord who is speaking and tells Samuel how to reply. The text makes it clear that Samuel did not expect the Lord to appear to him, but some see the repeated summons as an artistic device meant to heighten the suspense. Be that as it may, here we have a contrast between the naiveté of the young Samuel and the slowness of Eli, who should have known that it was a divine revelation and should himself have been the object of the theophany.[138] Samuel finally responds to the Lord's summons by saying, "Here

---

a number of rooms, since Samuel and Eli did not sleep in the same room, and what is more, the text notes that it was a building with doors (verse 15).

133. For example, "Abimelech ... encamped at [i.e., outside or near] Thebez (בתבץ)" (Judg. 9:50); "Israel was encamping at [i.e., adjacent to] the spring (בעין) in Jezreel" (1 Sam. 29:1).

134. S. R. Driver, *Notes on the Hebrew Text and the Topography of the Books of Samuel*, second edition (Oxford: Clarendon Press, 1966), p. 42.

135. היכל is derived from the Akkadian *ekallu* 'palace', which is in turn a borrowing from the Sumerian é. g a l 'large house'. With this sense it is also found in Northwest Semitic, including both Ugaritic and Hebrew.

136. U. Cassuto, "Biblical Literature and Canaanite Literature," *Tarbiz* 14 (1942), p. 6.

137. Gnuse, *Dream*, p. 156, says that the three-fold summons is a literary motif found in other cultures and offers a number of examples thereof.

138. There are many contrasts in this story: Eli, the blind priest, ultimately understands but does not see, while Samuel does not understand, but will eventually hear and see. Eli lies in his place and Samuel lies in the sanctuary. Samuel has not previously known the Lord, while the sons of Eli are described as not knowing the Lord (1 Sam. 2:12).

I am," the normal response in dreams (Gen. 31:11 and 46:2), though it also is found in waking revelations (Gen. 22:11).

The fourth time the Lord calls Samuel, the author, unlike the previous times, describes the appearance of the Lord: "The Lord came, and stood there" (1 Sam. 3:10). In other words, He comes to the place where Samuel is lying down and appears to him there,[139] calling to mind the Lord's appearance to Jacob in a dream at Bethel: "And the Lord was standing" (Gen. 28:13). The image that God is standing alongside the dreamer is also found in extrabiblical sources, as we saw in chapter 1.

For both Jacob and Samuel the revelations come in holy places, Bethel and Shiloh. But in Samuel's case, "came" indicates that the Lord journeyed as it were from his sanctuary to the place where Samuel was lying. The verb "come" is also associated with dreams (Gen. 20:3 and 31:24).[140] "The Lord came, and stood there" may indicate that this time Samuel beheld an image in a prophetic vision; this is why the text reads "stood there (וַיִּתְיַצֵּב) " as in the story of Balaam, when "an angel of the Lord placed himself (וַיִּתְיַצֵּב) in his way as an adversary" (Num. 22:22) (thus David Kimḥi; cf. "The Lord came down in a cloud; He stood (וַיִּתְיַצֵּב) with him there" [Ex. 34:5]). This time, Samuel does answer the Lord, but not in the terms Eli had told him to use: "If you are called again, say, 'Speak, Lord, for Your servant is listening.'" (1 Sam. 3:9). Samuel does not refer to the Lord by name. David Kimḥi comments: "Because he was still afraid to mention the name in a prophetic vision." Rashi, however, says that "[Samuel] said, 'Perhaps it is a different voice.'" Evidently Samuel found it difficult to digest the fact that the Lord was addressing him.

In Malamat's opinion, the fact that the Lord summoned Samuel four times on the same night is of great importance.[141] He refers to a dream from Mari (ARM XIII, no. 112), in which a deity appears to a lad in a dream and warns him against building a house. The lad does not tell anyone about the dream, and the next night the god appears in another dream with the same message. Malamat believes it was only after the dream was repeated that the lad became convinced of the divine origin of the message. In Samuel's theophany, the divine summons occurs four times during the same night before Samuel discloses the message to Eli. In both cases the repetition of the dream is intended, according to Malamat, to persuade the dreamer that it was authentic,

---

139. So too with Moses: "The Lord came down in a cloud; He stood with him there, and proclaimed the name Lord" (Ex. 34:5).

140. It should, however, be emphasized that both "come" and "stand" are associated with waking revelations; see, for example Amos 7:7 and 9:1 and Ex. 19:9.

141. A. Malamat, *Mari and the Bible*, pp. 78–79.

given that both dreamers were young, had no prior experience of divine revelation, and were thus unable to evaluate it.

The Lord's message to Samuel relates to the future and to the fate of the House of Eli (vv. 11–14).[142] The body of the prophecy begins with the announcement, "I am going to do in Israel ..." (1 Sam. 3:11) What he is going to do, however, is not made explicit until the next episode, which recounts the capture of the Ark, the destruction of Shiloh, and the rout of the Israelites. The unfinished prophecy creates a sense of impending doom, but we are merely told that the doom is so intense that "both ears of anyone who hears about it will tingle"–a picturesque image for the gravity of the catastrophe. Later prophets employ the same verb with regard to the destruction of the First Temple (2 Kings 21:12, Jer. 19:3). When the disaster actually occurs, Eli realizes that the Lord has truly spoken.

Eli's sin was that, despite his knowledge of his sons' misdeeds, he did not deter or hinder them.[143] As David Kimḥi wrote, "Even though he [admonished] his sons, this was when he was old and they were not afraid of him. But when they began their misdeeds and he could have prevented them and argued with them forcefully, he did not do so." The prophecy concludes with an oath phrased in the negative. Even the sacrifices and meal-offerings that normally atone for sins against God will be of no avail; they cannot atone for the iniquity of the house of Eli. Some view this as measure for measure, since Hophni and Phineas were priests who offered sacrifices and meal-offerings.[144] This prophecy, although brief, is crucial, because it is addressed by the Lord to Samuel and highlights his rise as a prophet. The prophecy also serves as the introduction to the next chapter, which recounts the Philistines' capture of the Ark of the Lord, as well as the deaths of the sons of Eli–and of Eli himself.

The words "Thus and more may God do to you" (v. 17) are an adjuration

142. This prophecy has already been delivered in 2:27–36. Here, however, the Lord reveals to Samuel the actual catastrophe that will befall the House of Eli.

143. The misdeeds of Eli's sons are described as "his sons cursed themselves" (1 Sam. 3:13). The classical exegetes understood "themselves" to be a scribal emendation introduced out of respect for the Lord, instead of the original "cursed Him." According to Rashi, "what should have been written is 'they curse Me'; but the text was emended out of respect for the Almighty." Another possibility is מקללים 'curse' should be understood in the sense of מקילים 'make light of'; in other words, they did not actually curse God, but treated Him with disdain. As Rashi wrote, "every curse signifies disrespect and disdain."

144. David Kimḥi, "He said this because they were priests who offered sacrifices and meal-offerings; that is, their priesthood will avail them nothing before Me. This punishment is measure for measure: they sinned by dishonoring the offerings, and their punishment is to have no atonement through offerings."

in which "thus" stands for some evil that is stated explicitly elsewhere. Over time, oath-takers tended to omit the curse and retain only this formula. The idiom appears only in the books of Samuel, Kings, and Ruth.[145] Eli refers to Samuel fondly as "my son," and the latter replies, quickly and modestly, "Here I am." Samuel does tell Eli everything the Lord had said to him. Eli responds, "He is the Lord; He will do what He deems right" (v. 18)–that is, Eli accepts the divine decree against himself and his house and does not question the Lord's justice.[146] Thus the section begins with *do*–"I am going to do in Israel such a thing" (v. 11)–and ends with *do*: "He will do what He deems right." The conclusion indicates Eli's faith in the Lord and Samuel's devotion and loyalty to Eli.

Some compare the Lord's appearance to Samuel with the inscription of Sargon recounting his biography before he became the king of Akkad, when he served Uzrababa, the king of Kish.[147] That inscription describes Sargon's dream, which is similar in many ways to Samuel's theophany.[148] The deity informs Sargon of the impending doom of his master. Both Sargon and Samuel serve in a temple and experience their dreams there. Both react with fear, and as a result both masters become aware of the theophanies. Although both revelations announce the end of the reigns of the ruler whom they serve–and the rulers press the servitors to learn the content of the revelations–a major

---

145. 1 Sam. 14:44, 20:13, 25:22; 2 Sam. 3:9 and 35, 19:14; 1 Kings 2:23, 19:2, 20:10; 2 Kings 6:31; Ruth 1:17. See Driver, *Samuel*, pp. 44–45.

146. David says something similar: "I am ready; let Him do with me as He pleases" (2 Sam. 15:26); see also 2 Kings 20:19 and Isa. 39:8.

147. Moshe Elat, *Samuel and the Foundation of Kingship*, pp. 30–31.

148. 12 At that time, the cupbearer, in the temple of Ezinu,
    13 Sargon, lay down not to sleep, but lay down to dream.
    14 Holy Inana, in the dream, was drowning him [Urzababa] in a river of blood.
    15 Sargon, screaming, gnawed the ground.
    16 When King Urzababa heard those screams,
    17 He had them bring him [Sargon] into the king's presence.
    18 Sargon, come into the presence of Urzababa, (who said):
    19 "O cupbearer, was a dream revealed to you in the night?"
    20 Sargon replied to his king:
    21 "O my king, this is my dream which I will have told you about:
    22 There was a single young woman, she was high as the heavens, she was broad as the earth,
    23 She was firmly set as the [bas]e of a wall.
    24 For me, she drowned you in a great [river], a river of blood."
    25. [   ] U[rzab]aba chewed his lips, became seriously afraid.
See translation: J. S. Cooper and W. Heimpel, "The Sumerian Sargon legend," *JAOS* 103 (1983), p. 77.

difference between the two is that Eli submits to the decree while Uzrababa endeavors to get rid of Sargon, who threatens his position.

Whatever the literary analysis of Samuel's theophany, the question remains whether this revelation in a vision is the same as a revelation in a dream. Did Samuel dream while he was sleeping? Or was this a waking epiphany? Those who hold for the second option maintain that he must have been awake, since each time he heard the voice calling him he ran to Eli. Furthermore, he engages in a dialogue with the Lord and the word *dream* does not appear in the text.[149] On the other hand, the latter omission is irrelevant if all the indications of dreams are present. In addition, a colloquy between the dreamer and the deity is found in both Abimelech's and Solomon's dreams. As for Samuel's running to Eli, it can be argued that he kept waking up to do so and then fell asleep again.

Some scholars do believe that Samuel's was a dream theophany.[150] Hertzberg, for example, notes the verb שכב 'lie down', which he believes connotes sleep.[151] The text says that Samuel was lying down each time the Lord called him (vv. 3, 5, and 9)–and the root ש.כ.ב appears seven times in the story. Even after he receives the oracle we read that Samuel lay there until the morning (v. 15). Hence it may be that he fell asleep after the Lord called him by name and that the revelation took place when he was asleep.[152] It should be noted that שכב occurs twice in the account of Jacob's dream at Bethel: before the revelation–"he lay down in that place" (Gen. 28:11)–and then in the Lord's promise to Jacob–"the ground on which you are lying" (Gen. 28:13). On the other hand, one can argue that שכב does not necessarily indicate sleep, and that Samuel was recumbent but fully awake during the revelation. Similarly, Samuel's repetition of the response that Eli had dictated to him calls into question the idea that this is a dream. It is implausible for a person who receives instructions when awake to repeat them precisely when

149. Henry Preserved Smith, *A Critical and Exegetical Commentary on the Books of Samuel,* ICC (New York: Scribners, 1899), p. 27; John Mauchline, *1 and 2 Samuel,* NCB (London: Oliphants, 1961), p. 59; Andreas Resch, *Der Traum im Heilsplan Gottes: Deutung und Bedeutung des Traums im Alten Testament,* pp. 111–112; Yaira Amit, "Samuel's Consecration," p. 32.

150. Ehrlich, *Traum,* p. 47; L. H. Brockington, "Audition in the OT," *JTS* 49 (1948), p. 5, n. 2; Gnuse, *Dream,* pp. 140–152; Oppenheim, *Interpretation,* pp. 188–190.

151. There is ample evidence of this. See 1 Sam. 26:5 and 7; 2 Sam. 4:5 and 7, 11:9 and 13.

152. H. W. Hertzberg, *1 and 2 Samuel Commentary,* trans. J. S. Bowden (Philadelphia: Westminster, 1964), p. 42.

asleep.[153] On the other hand, as noted previously, Samuel does modify what Eli told him to say.

Some say that the fact that Samuel was lying down in the sanctuary of the Lord indicates that this was an incubation dream.[154] In the ancient Near East, one way to try to receive a divine message in a dream involved going to a place deemed sacred and sleeping there. Here, though, Samuel did not go to the sanctuary; he lived there[155] by virtue of his assigned task, which was to guard the sacred place. Moreover, the text does not describe any preparations for an incubation. Indeed, Samuel is quite astonished each time God calls him and thinks that it is Eli who is summoning him.[156] At the same time, Eli does not originally comprehend that it is the Lord who is calling the lad. Hence we must reject the opinion that this is an intentional incubation.[157]

Another element found here that some associate with dreams is the divine summons to the dreamer. In our text, Samuel is called three times: Jacob, too, is called in his dream (Gen. 31:11), and again when God appears to him in a vision by night (ibid., 46:2). In extrabiblical sources too, the deity calls the dreamer by name. Oppenheim cites a text in which the priest of the goddess Ishtar of Arbela was sleeping, only to be awakened, like Samuel. "He woke up with a start and Ishtar made him see a nocturnal vision."[158] According to Oppenheim, the summons by name had a single objective, which was to prepare Samuel for God's appearance to him in a dream.[159] He understands the experience of the priest of Ishtar in the same fashion.[160] Oppenheim also

---

153. T. H. McAlpine, *Sleep, Divine and Human, in the OT, JSOT* Suppl. 38 (Sheffield: *JSOT* Press, 1987), pp. 61–62; Resch, *Traum,* p. 112.

154. W. Eichrodt, *Theology of the Old Testament,* vol. 1, trans. James A. Baker (Philadelphia: Westminster, 1961), p. 105; Anton Jirku, "Ein Fall von Inkubation im AT (Ex 38:8)," *ZAW* 33 (1913), p. 153; Theodor H. Gaster, *Thespis, Ritual, Myth, and Drama in the Ancient Near East* (New York: Schumann, 1950), p. 271; H. J. Kraus, *Worship in Israel: A Cultic History of the Old Testament,* trans. Geoffrey Buswell (Richmond: John Knox, 1965), pp. 110 and 175.

155. Smith, *Samuel,* pp. 27–28, says that this is not an incubation but something quite similar.

156. R. W. Klein, *1 Samuel* (Waco, TX: Word, 1983), p. 32.

157. Ehrlich, *Traum,* pp. 45–48. According to him, only 1 Kings 3:4 contains legitimate references to incubation rites; T. H. Gaster, "Dreams: in the Bible," *Encyclopedia Judaica* 6:208, rejected the idea of incubation; Smith, *Samuel,* pp. 27–28; Klein, *1 Samuel,* p. 32.

158. " Akkadian Oracles and Prophecies," trans. Robert H. Pfeiffer, *ANET,* p. 451; Oppenheim, *Interpretation,* p. 249.

159. Ibid., p. 190.

160. In Akkadian, the revelation is called *tabrīt mūši* and translated as "nocturnal vision." Oppenheim says that one must be careful when translating this phrase and that it may be a poetic idiom for "dream." The precise meaning, however, remains unclear (ibid., pp. 201 and 205).

refers to the motif of wakefulness, also found in the Greek world, where the god would address the sleeper and ask him, "Are you asleep?[161]

Accordingly Oppenheim believed that the dream is "a sui generis state of consciousness, a hovering between the eclipse of sleep and the stark but dull reality of the day."[162] To buttress his view, he cites the Egyptian word *ršw.t* 'dream,' which is not only etymologically connected with a root meaning "to be awake," but is also written with the determinative representing an opened eye. Oppenheim thus believes that there was an element of wakefulness in dreams. Gnuse, who follows Oppenheim, asks: "Is the dreamer awake, semi-conscious, or asleep and yet dreaming that he is conscious? This is unanswerable, but we cannot exclude these experiences from the category of dream because the recipients seem awake, as some commentators do with the Samuel experience."[163]

To summarize, our survey of the terms מַחֲזֶה and מַרְאָה has taught us that they are similar to the phenomenon designated by the word חֲלוֹם 'dream'. We find the term מַחֲזֶה in the Lord's appearance to Abram–the Covenant between the Pieces–and in the Lord's appearance to Balaam. These מַחֲזֶה theophanies have two stages: in the first the recipient is awake, and in the second he is asleep, in a dreamlike state. There are ritual actions associated with both. The message in Abram's vision is both personal and national and relates to the future; the message conveyed to Balaam is also national–it refers to the future of Israel.

The term בְּמַרְאֹת הַלַּיְלָה occurs in the Lord's appearance to Jacob before he went down to Egypt (Gen. 46:1–5), and the language here is identical to that used when the Lord appears in dreams. In addition, this epiphany seems to fall into the category of incubation dreams. The message in the מַרְאָה vision also relates to the future and has both a personal and national dimension–in fact, the personal message resembles that of the other dreams in which God encourages Jacob before he sets out on a journey. Finally, the Lord also appears to Samuel in the sanctuary in Shiloh in a מַרְאָה 'vision'. Here, as we have seen, the description of the revelation is linguistically identical to the description of God's appearance in dreams, and the message relates to the future in more than a personal way–the tragic doom of the House of Eli. Finally, Samuel's reaction to the vision, too, is like other reactions to dreams in the Bible.

Thus far we have dealt with the types of dreams and visions in the

161. Ibid., p. 189.
162. Ibid., p. 190.
163. Gnuse, *Dream*, p. 145.

Bible–prophetic and symbolic. We have considered the interpretation of symbolic dreams in Israel and the relationship between Israelite prophecy and dreams. Here we have considered the terms מַרְאָה and מַחֲזֶה. In the last chapter we will consider, on a broader scale, the literary and didactic functions of dreams in the Bible–that is, what they are meant to teach and why they were included in Scripture.

6

The Intent of the Dream Stories

Biblical narrative, which in the main is a historical recitation, is characterized by a simple and flowing style, devoid of rhetorical ornamentation. Irrelevant details are omitted. The story-tellers, who had a fixed and unwavering world view, sought to present the facts themselves in an objective and realistic fashion. Their proclivity for brevity and restraint allows readers to focus on those actions that lead to the climax of the tale and draw their own conclusions.

This brevity provided the midrashic homilists with many opportunities for filling in background and lacunae. Subsequently, the biblical redactors, too, had clear and fixed goals. When they selected from among the many tales and folk legends dealing with the patriarchs, judges, and kings that circulated among the people, they took only those appropriate to their objectives and reworked and revised them to suit their purposes. Thus the stories of the Bible have a common ethical and religious bent. They are intended not to give pleasure but to enlighten and educate. Rhetorical flourishes are out of place, and the basic narrative unit is relatively short, uniform, and lucid. Each has a definite beginning and end and usually leads into the next incident.[1] To whom were they addressed? What are they meant to teach? Why were they included in the Holy Scriptures? To consider these questions, we shall focus on four specific narratives: Jacob's dream at Bethel, the Joseph cycle, Solomon's dream at Gibeon, and the dreams and visions in the Book of Daniel.

JACOB'S DREAM AT BETHEL (GENESIS 28:10-22)

When God appeared to Jacob, the latter said: "This is none other than the abode of God." (Gen. 28:16) He added in his vow: "And this stone, which I have set up as a pillar, shall be God's abode."(v. 22) Some see Jacob's words as reflecting the situation in the period of the Judges, when there was an Israelite sanctuary near Bethel. In fact, some scholars link the sanctuary near

---

1. S. D. Goitein, *Bible Studies* (Tel Aviv: Yavneh, 1963), pp. 13–40.

Bethel with Jacob. Hermann Gunkel, for example, sees the Bethel story as a ceremonial legend that accounts for the holiness attributed to the sanctuary and explains the origins of its associated rituals–for example, why the Israelites anointed stones with oil, and gave tithes there.[2] In Genesis we read about other sites of primitive ritual such as Penuel, Shechem, Beer Sheba, and Beer-lahai-roi, where the text notes the presence of sacred wells and trees and where the Patriarchs felt God's presence and worshipped.

Problems arose in a later period, however, when the Israelites no longer had a keen sense of divine presence in these places and began to seek reasons for the rituals associated with them. In most cases, the standard answer was that God had appeared to the Patriarchs there, and a particular ritual was conducted to commemorate that theophany. Gunkel notes that often in the history of religion, ritual and ceremonial legends appear and evolve as religious sentiments dim. In the case of Bethel, because God appeared to Jacob, whose head lay on a stone when he beheld the celestial ladder, the site was sanctified and the stone became a temple.[3]

Skinner agrees. According to him, the story comes to explain the anointing of the stone and giving of tithes. Like Gunkel, Skinner believes that sites such as Bethel were sacred even before the Patriarchal age–going back to the primitive forms of Semitic religion within Canaanite culture. Hence it is difficult to know to what extent the legends associated with them were transferred to the Patriarchs and to what extent the Patriarchs themselves developed these traditions.[4]

Von Rad also believes that the narrative is intended to clarify its association with the stone and to explain how Bethel became a famous cultic site.[5] According to the text, Jacob erected the pillar and anointed it with oil. Hence it is possible that pilgrims of later generations behaved similarly and anointed the stone. According to Von Rad, ritual legends characteristically recount the first performance of the cultic act, by way of grounding its legitimacy. When the pilgrims brought their tithes to Bethel they were participating in Jacob's vow and identified themselves with him (see Amos 4:4). Hence Jacob's vow indicates: (1) the Lord's first appearance and summons to Jacob; (2) that it was

---

2. Herman Gunkel, *The Legends of Genesis*, trans. W. H. Carruth (Chicago: Open Court, 1907), pp. 30–33.

3. Ibid., p. 33.

4. John Skinner, *A Critical and Exegetical Commentary on Genesis, ICC* (New York: Charles Scribner's Sons, 1910), pp. 12–13.

5. Gerhard Von Rad, *Genesis: A Commentary*, trans. John H. Marks (Philadelphia: Westminster Press, 1972), p. 285.

Jacob who built the later altar; and (3) that it was Jacob who initiated the giving of tithes at this site.[6]

Sarna does not accept the association of the building of the sanctuary at Bethel with Jacob.[7] If the story focused on ritual, he argues, we might expect it to mention a prayer or altar. Neither of these elements appears in the text; nor, in this context, does the expression "house of God" (vv. 17 and 22) mean a temple. He also notes that whereas Abraham and Isaac built altars after God appeared to them, Jacob did not–although he did construct an altar after his return to Canaan from Haran–but this is not a temple. Nevertheless, the text clearly associates the original sanctity of Bethel with Jacob–a link that, as we shall see, endured for many centuries.

Bethel is first mentioned in Genesis 12:6, where we read that Abraham, when he first arrived in Canaan, built altars at two important locations, one near Shechem and the other between Bethel and Ai. Later we are told that Abraham "invoked the Lord by name"–that is, proclaimed his new faith–in the vicinity of Bethel (v. 8). When Abraham returned from Egypt the text again notes that he encamped near Bethel and again invoked the Lord by name there. The Lord did not appear to Abraham at that site. Nor is it certain that the Bethel mentioned in the Abraham stories is identical with the place where Jacob later spent the night and experienced his epiphany–which (Gen. 28:10-22) comprises the next mention of Bethel. Verse 17 of that narrative presents a homiletic interpretation of the name: "This is none other than the abode of God, and that is the gateway to heaven." After that we read, "He named that site Bethel; but previously the name of the city had been Luz" (v. 19).

In the narrative of Jacob's return from Padan Aram and journeys in the land of Canaan we again find references to Shechem and Bethel. In 35:7 we are told that Jacob named the place where he had his dream "El Bethel." Later we read, "Jacob gave the site, where God had spoken to him, the name of Bethel" (v. 15). The reference is evidently to a particular spot between Bethel and Ai, near the town of Bethel, and not to the Canaanite city itself, as the text underscores.

The later history of Bethel makes it clear that an ancient tradition was associated with the site. Although the sanctuary there was deemed holy for many generations, especially among the northern tribes, Bethel was first mentioned as a central national and religious site in the period of the Judges. Because of the presence there of the Ark of the Lord, tended by Phineas the

---

6. Ibid., p. 286.

7. Sarna, *Genesis,* p. 398.

grandson of Aaron (Judg. 20:18–28), the Israelites were in the habit of going there to inquire of the oracle of the *urim* (Judg. 20:18 and 27) and to pray, fast, and offer sacrifices (Judg. 20:26 and 21:2–4). Bethel seems to have been important for both civilian and military reasons. Not only was it a major pilgrimage site (1 Sam. 10:13), but the roads to Bethel are mentioned in stories from the period of the Judges (Judg. 20:30 and 21:9), and two thirds of Saul's army bivouacked there (1 Sam. 13:2).

Later, after Solomon built the Temple in Jerusalem and made it the central sanctuary for all Israel, the importance of the site waned. When the kingdom split after Solomon's death, Jeroboam established cultic centers in Bethel and Dan to serve as alternatives to Jerusalem. Bethel was selected both for its traditional sanctity and for its geographic location, which made it easy to divert Jerusalem-bound pilgrims to it. In the period of Elijah we read of the presence of a band of prophets there (2 Kings 2:2–3). It is interesting that Elijah and Elisha, who fought against Baal worship, seemed to evince no opposition toward the shrine in Bethel. Nowhere in the Bible do we find any allusion to their displeasure with the place. Only the later tradition, reflecting the Deuteronomic centralization of the cult at a single location, recounts the story of the man of God from Judah who came to rebuke Jeroboam as he was about to present an offering on the altar at Bethel (1 Kings 13). The prophet Ahijah of Shiloh also rebuked Jeroboam, delivering the following message in the name of the Lord: "You have gone and made for yourself other gods and molten images to vex Me" (1 Kings 14:9).

In the eighth century BCE, Amos and Hosea issued strong denunciations of Bethel. The latter referred to it as בֵּית אָוֶן (house of delusion). Amos, who was active in the northern kingdom, directed his shafts against the cultic practices of its sanctuaries in general and against Bethel in particular (Amos 3:14, 4:4, 5:5–6, and 9:1). Hosea's opposition was even fiercer; he rejected the Bethel cult as idolatrous, a treasonous breach of the covenant between the Lord and Israel (Hos. 4:15, 5:8, 8:5, 10:5–6, 8, and 15, and 13:2).

Bethel seems to have been sacked in the national catastrophe of 722/21 BCE, when the Kingdom of Israel fell to the Assyrians. The prophets understood this calamity to represent the utter defeat and punishment of the pagan cult; according to Jeremiah, "And Moab shall be shamed because of Chemosh, as the House of Israel were shamed because of Bethel, on whom they relied" (Jer. 48:13). Nevertheless, the sanctity of Bethel was not obliterated, and the local priesthood survived for another century (2 Kings 17:28). The cultic center at Bethel was finally eradicated by King Josiah of Judah as part of his religious reforms (2 Kings 23:15; 1 Kings 13:1–5). According to 2 Kings 23:15, Josiah destroyed the high place of Bethel and defiled the altar with the bones of corpses. The city was burned and totally destroyed by the Babylonians shortly before 587 BCE.[8]

As noted, the prophet Hosea was bitterly opposed to the Bethel cult and considered it to be engaged in idolatry. He even gave a negative twist to the local traditions associated with the name of Jacob (Hos. 12:4–5 and 13). Nevertheless he acknowledged that the Lord appeared to Jacob at Bethel and promised a blessing to him and to his descendants. The tradition of the theophany was thus authentic and ancient: Hosea would not have repeated the story if the tale was a later tradition to which various elements were added in order to make it suit the spirit of the age.[9]

Bethel had a long and ancient history predating the Patriarchs. Originally a Canaanite holy site, it is identified with the village of Beitin, located about 10.5 miles north of Jerusalem at an elevation of 2,886 feet above sea level. Many archeological excavations in the area have revealed that there was an altar at the crest of the hill before 3500 BCE and that a temple was built there in the nineteenth century BCE. Hence there is no doubt that Bethel was a sacred Canaanite site before and during the Patriarchal age.[10]

The name Bethel is also found in Ugaritic—*bt il*—and in Akkadian—*bīt ili.* El was the chief god of the Canaanite pantheon. Thus it represents the familiar form for temple names—the word בַּיִת 'house' followed by the name of the deity honored there. We can compare Beth-Anath (Josh. 19:38), Beth-Azmaveth (Ezra 2:24), Beth-Baal-Berith (Judg. 9:4), and others. In all of these cases the name of the sanctuary was applied to the nearby urban settlement.[11]

The expression "El Bethel" appears twice in Genesis. When Jacob recounts to his wives his dream about the rams who are mounting the sheep, he says that the angel of God told him: "I am the God of Beth-el [אָנֹכִי הָאֵל בֵּית אֵל], where you anointed a pillar" (Gen. 31:13). In the account of his return to Canaan from Padan Aram we read: "There he built an altar and named the site El-Bethel" (Gen. 35:7).

---

8. Later we read that the returnees from Babylonia who came with Zerubbabel included 223 persons from Bethel and Ai (Ezra 2:28 and Neh. 7:32). According to Nehemiah 11:31, Bethel and the surrounding villages were one of the places settled by the Benjaminites who returned from exile. In the Hasmonean period Bethel was fortified by Bacchides, the general of Demetrius Soter (1 Macc. 9:50). The last mention of Bethel is that Vespasian conquered it during the Great Revolt (Josephus, Antiquities 13:1.3; Wars 4:9.9).

9. Sarna, *Genesis,* p. 399.

10. J. Kelso et al., "The Excavation of Bethel (1934–60)" *AASOR* 39 (Cambridge: American School of Oriental Research, 1968).

11. Sarna, *Genesis,* p. 399.

The question is whether the expression "El Bethel" should be taken as alluding to a Canaanite deity worshipped under the name "Bethel."[12] There is in fact abundant evidence for the cult of a deity named Bethel whose name was derived from the holy site. In Jeremiah 48:13, for example, the prophet parallels the Moabite deity Chemosh with Bethel. The verse indicates that the Israelites prayed to that deity. In a treaty between the Assyrian king Esarhaddon and King Ball of Tyre from the seventh century BCE, in which the gods are called upon to curse anyone who violates the pact, Bethel appears among the list of deities invoked.[13] As a theophoric element, it is also found in personal names in Babylonia from the time of Nebuchadnezzar to that of Darius II. Later, around the year 400 BCE, the Jews of Elephantine in Egypt were familiar with deities like Eshem-Bethel, Herm-Bethel, and Anath-Bethel.[14] Among their personal names we find Bethel-Nathan, Bethel-Aqob, and so on. In Ugaritic texts the expression *bt il* appears a number of times, but in several places it is clear that the meaning is merely the "house of El."

Whether it is ever the name of a particular deity is a matter of scholarly debate.[15] Additional evidence has been uncovered in a Greco-Syrian text from the dedication of an oil press in 223 CE, found at Kfar Nebo. It includes the name of the god *Sumbétylos* along with two other gods.[16] Hence there is no doubt that the Semitic pantheon in general and the Canaanite pantheon in particular included a deity known as Bethel. We may conjecture that it was the veneration for temples that led people to consider the sanctuaries to be deities in their own right. The house of the father of the gods, El, was a prime example.

On the basis of this evidence some scholars have hypothesized that Genesis 31:13 refers to a deity called "Bethel" and indicates that the cult of this god existed among the Israelites' ancestors. Accordingly, they have emended the

---

12. Cf. Genesis 28:17 and 22, 32:20; 1 Sam. 10:3; Amos 3:14 and 5:5; Hos. 10:8 and 15; and Zech. 7:12. In the last of these we should read it as a personal name. See J. P. Hyatt, "A Neo-Babylonian Parallel to *Bethel-Sar-Eṣer,* Zech. 7:2," *JBL* 56 (1937), pp. 387–394.

13. "May Bethel and Anat-Bethel deliver you to a man-eating lion,"see: "Akkadian Treaties from Syria and Assyria,"Translator. Erica Reiner, *ANET,p.* 534(iv); see also J. P. Hyatt, "The Deity Bethel and the OT," *JAOS* 59 (1939), p. 82.

14. Ibid., pp. 84–85. According to Hyatt, חרמביתאל, אשמביתאל and ענתביתאל are to be taken as names of double deities.

15. Ibid., p. 87; W. F. Albright, "The North-Canaanite Poems of Al'êyân Ba'al and the 'Gracious Gods'," *JPOS* 14 (1934), p. 136; H. L. Ginsberg, *The Ugarit Texts* (Jerusalem: Vaad Halashon, 1936), pp. 82f. In contrast, see M. H. Pope, *El in the Ugaritic Texts,* VTSup 2 (Leiden: E. J. Brill, 1955), pp. 59ff., who denies any reference to Bethel in the Ugaritic pantheon.

16. Hyatt, "The Deity Bethel in the Old Testament," p. 86.

text to read, "I am the God El-Bethel [אנכי האל אל בית אל],"[17] or "the god *who appeared to you* in Bethel."[18]

We should note, however, that the divine name used in the story of Jacob's dream at Bethel is "Elohim" or "Elohei (the god of) your father." In addition, the idea that Bethel is the name of a god can be rejected because the conjunction "where" occurs twice in Gen. 31:13–"I am the God <of> Beth-el, *where* you anointed a pillar and *where* you made a vow to Me"–proving that "Bethel" is a place name.

It is almost certain, however, that the Canaanites worshipped the head of their pantheon, who was named El, in the city of Luz, and that they called his temple "Bethel"–the "House of El"–and this designation was transferred to the city. Hence it is possible that the Patriarchs and their descendants considered El-Bethel to be their own deity, too, similar to El Elyon, Creator of Heaven and Earth, who was the tutelary god of Shalem (Gen. 14:18 and 22), and used "Bethel" as an epithet for the Lord. This is hinted at in the tradition that Abraham built an altar to the Lord there (Gen. 12:8 and 13:3) and in the memory that Jacob erected a pillar there, vowed that it would become a house of God (Gen. 28:15–22), and named the place Bethel (Gen. 28:19). The site, already sacred to the Canaanites, remained holy to the Israelites.

If this was so, with the passage of time it seems that the tradition shared with the cults of the neighboring peoples blurred the uniquely Israelite lineaments of the site near Bethel. The ritual there acquired a form that was more appropriate for the ancient Canaanite tradition. This was particularly conspicuous when Jeroboam installed a golden calf there. A calf, after all, is a young bull, and in Ugaritic writings a bull is the totem of the Canaanite El.

From all this we may conclude that Jacob's dream at Bethel has two main objectives: to explain how Bethel came to be a holy site; and to rupture the Canaanite associations with Bethel. Even though the area is referred to as "a place," which in fact means "a *sacred* place" (and indeed the place was sacred for the Canaanites), Jacob arrives there only by chance. He discerns no holiness in the site, as is attested by his reaction after his dream: "Surely the Lord is present in this place, and I did not know it!" (Gen. 28:16).

The stone on which Jacob rests his head is unremarkable. It has no intrinsic sanctity or magical power. It has one purpose only, to serve as a marker of the divine revelation to Jacob. But to sever all pagan associations with Bethel, the author emphasizes the Tetragrammaton. It is YHWH who stands by Ja-

---

17. Abraham Ibn Ezra, David Kimḥi, S. D. Luzzatto.

18. See the Aramaic versions and the Septuagint; the same approach is followed by Skinner, Speiser, and Westermann in their commentaries on the verse.

cob and identifies Himself as the God of his fathers. After the dream, too, Jacob himself emphasizes the name YHWH. Further, when Jacob returns from Mesopotamia he instructs the members of his household to discard their foreign gods, purify themselves, and change their clothes before they approach the place (Gen. 35:2). In short, the biblical author ignores the pre-biblical sanctity of the place. And the authentic holiness of Bethel derives only from the theophany that Jacob experienced there.[19]

THE DREAMS IN THE JOSEPH STORIES
(GENESIS 37-50)

Joseph's story, in the version we have, is a single unit constructed with sophisticated narrative harmony, quite different from the individual short tales that make up the patriarchal cycle. Except for chapters 38 and 49, Genesis 37–50 is a single unit, a novella whose plot advances steadily to its climax, when Joseph makes himself known to his brothers. Dreams are an inseparable part of that novella and play a crucial role in the development of the plot. From the time that Joseph relates his dreams to his brothers, readers ask themselves if, when, and how the dreams will come true. According to Redford, nothing would remain of the story of Joseph were we to excise the dreams from the text.[20] They anticipate future events and prepare readers for the astonishing developments that soon occur.

The theological perspective of chapters 37–50 is totally different from that of the stories of Abraham and Jacob. There is nothing about cult centers here, nor does the author mention a covenant or promise. Whereas the stories of the Patriarchs emphasize their segregation from the various nations inhabiting Canaan, Joseph mixes with the Egyptians and even marries an Egyptian woman. The Lord does not appear to him and does not intervene directly in his life. Instead, all his deeds are directed by a universal notion of good and evil. Indeed, the author does not directly mention the name of God.

Joseph's dreams and the dreams of the Patriarchs vary widely as well. The Patriarchs' dreams are prophetic; God appears to them and acquaints them directly with His words and promises of present and future blessings. By contrast, the dreams of the Joseph cycle are symbolic. God does not appear in them and an expert is required to unravel their meaning.

A close reading of the Joseph cycle, however, shows divine providence directing events from behind the scenes. Accordingly, when Joseph searches

---

19. Sarna, *Genesis,* p. 400.

20. Redford, *A Study,* pp. 68–71.

for his brothers in the countryside, he encounters "a man" who knows exactly where they are (Gen. 37:15); a convoy of merchants en route to Egypt passes just as the brothers are wrestling with their brother's fate. God helps Joseph in Potiphar's house and subsequently in prison. And God's name is on Joseph's lips at the decisive moments in his life: when Potiphar's wife attempts to seduce him (39:9); when he interprets the dreams (40:8 and 41:16); when he interrogates his brothers (42:18); and when he finally reveals himself to them and says, "So, it was not you who sent me here, but God" (Gen. 45:8).

The background details in the Joseph stories indicate that the author was familiar with Egyptian culture; but it is no easy matter to determine the historical period described. Although the story, in its present format, does not resemble any specific tale, many motifs link it with extrabiblical literature. The biblical account of Joseph and Potiphar's wife recalls the Egyptian "Story of the Two Brothers," in which the wife of the older brother attempts to seduce the younger brother, who spurns her.[21] And Joseph's ascent, as a foreigner, to a high position in Egypt is similar to that of a certain "Tûtu," whose name appears on a pillar found at Tel el-Amarna.[22] Tûtu lived during the reign of Amenhotep IV (Akhenaten) and held many offices, which included the king's first servitor in the Temple of Aten, the king's first minister in a boat, the supervisor of the treasury of the Temple in Amarna, and the "highest mouth" in the entire land of Egypt. It is interesting that the wall paintings in his tomb at Tel el-Amarna show how Tûtu was appointed to his positions by Pharaoh. We see him having a gold chain placed on his neck, leaving the palace, mounting a chariot, and traveling in it while the people prostrate themselves before him.[23] All of this recalls what happened to Joseph (Genesis 41:41–43). Similarly, in the Harris Papyrus, which dates from the twelfth century, we read about a Hurrian from Syria, named Irsu, who became a prince of Egypt and to whom the entire country paid tribute.[24] Another Semite, named Yanhamu, became the governor of Canaan and Syria under Akhenaten (1353–1335 BCE). His name is mentioned in the Amarna Letters;

---

21. "Egyptian Myth and Mortuary Texts," trans. John A. Wilson, *ANET*, pp. 23–25.

22. N. G. Davies, *The Rock Tombs of El-Amarna*, vol. 6 (London: Egypt Exploration Fund, 1908), pp. 7–15, plates xix–xx.

23. Roland de Vaux, *The Early History of Israel*, trans. David Smith (Philadelphia: Westminster Press, 1978), p. 299; Wenham, *Genesis 16–50*, pp. 395–396.

24. De Vaux, *The Early History of Israel*, p. 300. The name Irsu means "the one who made himself." He is identified with Siptah, the last Pharaoh of the Nineteenth Dynasty. Another view is that Irsu usurped the throne between the Nineteenth and Twentieth Dynasties. Malamat identifies him with the Cushan-Rishathaim mentioned in Judg. 3:7–11. See A. Malamat, "Cushan Rishathaim and the Decline of the Near East about 1200 B.C.," *JNES* 13 (1954), pp. 231–242.

it is possible that inter alia he was in charge of the cereal stores.[25] Yet another, Ben Ozen, who came from somewhere east of the Sea of Galilee, attained the post of royal herald or marshal at the court of Merneptah (1224–1214 BCE).

As noted above, the signet ring, fine garments, and golden chain Pharaoh gave Joseph at his investiture are described in detail in Genesis 41:41-43. Significantly, the words 'ring' and 'fine linen' are borrowed from Egyptian.[26] And the placing of a golden chain around Joseph's neck is a well-known Egyptian ceremony attested to by many wall paintings. These three elements also appear in Assyrian sources, where we read how Ashurbanipal appointed Necho as vassal king of Egypt: "I clad him in a garment of multicolored trimmings, placed a golden chain on him [as the] insigne of his kingship, put golden rings on his hands."[27] In Esther, too, Mordecai receives a ring from Ahasuerus and leaves the palace in "royal robes ... and a mantle of fine linen."[28] In Daniel, we read that the Chaldean king Belshazzar clothed Daniel in purple, placed a golden chain on his neck, and proclaimed that he should rule as one of three in the kingdom (Dan. 5:29).

Scholars disagree about Joseph's precise title and status. Some, including the Egyptologists Vergote and Kitchen, believe that he was the vizier.[29] Others are of the opinion that he was merely the minister of agriculture.[30] The problem with the term "vizier" is that the corresponding Hebrew expression

---

25. J. A. Knudtzon, *Die El-Amarna-Tafeln* (Allen: Otto Zeller Verlagsbuchhandlung, 1964), 85, 22ff.; 86, 15–16; De Vaux, *The Early History of Israel,* p. 299; *The Amarna Letters,* ed. and trans. William L. Moran, (Baltimore: John Hopkins University Press, 1992), 85, 156; 86, 158. For Amarna personal names see Richard S. Hess, "Amarna Personal Names" *Dissertation Series 9 American Schools of Oriental Research* (Winona Lake: Eisenbrauns, 1993), pp. 82-84.

26. שֵׁשׁ is an Egyptian word that also appears once in Proverbs (31:22) and several times in Exodus (Chapters 27, 29, 36, 38, and 39), in connection with the vestments of the High Priest. Later Biblical books, such as Esther and Chronicles, use בּוּץ, found in Aramaic and Akkadian, instead, and this word was later taken over into Greek. The members of the tribe of Judah included "the families of the linen factory (בֵּית־עֲבֹדַת הַבֻּץ) at Beth-ashbea" (1 Chron. 4:21); Hiram the master artist of Solomon's Temple was "skilled at working ... in fine linen (בּוּץ)" (2 Chron. 2:13), whereas Oholiav and Bezalel, the artisans of the sanctuary in the desert, were "endowed with the skill to do ... work ... in fine linen (שֵׁשׁ)" (Ex. 35:35). See Vergote, *Joseph en Égypte,* p. 119; Grintz, *The Book of Genesis,* pp. 114–115; A. Hurvitz, "The Uses of שֵׁשׁ and בּוּץ in the Bible and its Implications for the Date of P," *HTR* 60 (1967), pp. 117–121.

27. A. Leo Oppenheim, "Babylonian and Assyrian Historical Texts," trans. A. Leo Oppenheim, *ANET,* p.295.

28. See Esther 3:10, 6:8, and 8:2. On the comparison with Esther see: J. A. Loader: "Esther as a Novel with Different Levels of Meaning," *ZAW* 90 (1978), pp. 417–421.

29. Vergote, *Joseph en Égypte,* pp. 102–114; Kitchen, "Joseph," *NBD,* p. 658.

30. W. A. Ward, "The Egyptian Office of Joseph," *JSS* 5 (1960), pp. 144–150, esp. 150.

"in charge of my court (*or* over my house [עַל בֵּיתִי])," which parallels the Egyptian phrase *mr pr* 'master of the palace', refers to the person responsible for the royal palace or administrator of the royal domains; this job placed him on a lower rung than the "vizier." De Vaux counters that in Israel the "steward" who was "in charge of the palace" (1 Kings 16:9; Isaiah 22:15 and 19–20), occupied a more important position than the equivalently named functionary in Egypt.[31] Accordingly, when the author refers to Joseph as "master of the palace" he is using the Hebrew equivalent for the Egyptian vizier.

Some scholars have tried to use the difficult verb יִשַּׁק as a key to unlocking Joseph's post: Pharaoh tells Joseph, "You shall be in charge of my court, and by your command shall all my people be directed (יִשַּׁק כָּל עַמִּי)" (Gen. 41:40). Onkelos and Rashi associate it with "the one in charge of my household (וּבֶן מֶשֶׁק בֵּיתִי)"(Gen. 16:2) and inferred that Joseph was responsible for the sustenance of the people of Egypt. By contrast, Rashbam and Abraham Ibn Ezra associated יִשַּׁק with the root נ.ש.ק: "He will be vigorous with weapons of war to go out against the enemies." Sperling emends יִשַּׁק to יֵשֵׁב 'sit' and renders, "at your command all my people shall sit" (i.e., obey).[32] Egyptologists, however, gloss יִשַּׁק as related to נשיקה 'kiss', noting that the Egyptian idiom "kiss the earth" means "render homage"; thus, "according to your commands shall all people kiss [the earth in submission]."[33]

Other details, such as the officials of the royal house and the story of the prisoners in the royal prison and the arrangements there indicate that the author was intimately acquainted with the structure and operations of the Egyptian royal court. The names Potiphar, Potiphera,[34] Asenath,[35] and

---

31. R. De Vaux, *Ancient Egypt,* pp. 129–131.For a comprehensive overview of the term "minister over the royal house" see N. S. Fox, *In the Service of the King,* pp. 81–96

32. S. D. Sperling, "Genesis 41:40: A New Interpretation," *JANESCU* 10 (1978), pp. 113–119.

33. K. A. Kitchen, "The Term nšq in Genesis xli.40," *ExpTim* 69 (1957), p. 30; Vergote, *Joseph en Égypte,* pp. 96–97; Von Ed. König, "Die sprachliche Gestalt des Pentateuch in ihrer Beziehung zur ägyptischen Sprache," *JBL* 48 (1929), p. 342; Redford, *A Study,* p. 166, n. 4. Cohen, by contrast, suggests that means "seal the mouth," hence "kiss" or, as here, "be silent, submit to." J. M. Cohen, "An Unrecognized Connotation of nšq peh with Special Reference to Three Biblical Occurrences," *VT* 32 (1982), pp. 416–424.

34. Potiphera is the same in form as Potiphar in Genesis 39:1; the latter is merely an abbreviated variant of the former, with loss of the final ayin. Potiphera means "the one whom Ra has given"; see Kitchen, "Potiphar," *NBD,* p. 1012; Westermann, *Genesis 37–50,* p. 36; Hamilton, *The Book of Genesis, Chapters 18–50,* p. 508; see also Midrash Rabba 86:3: "Potiphar is Potiphera." On the basis of the Hebrew the aggadists expounded the name Potiphar as "because he used to fatten calves (שהיה מפטם עגלים) for idol worship; Potiphera, because he used to uncover himself (פורע עצמו) for idol worship."

35. Asenath means "she belongs to the Goddess Neith," or "she belongs to her father,"

Zaphenath-paneah[36] also point to an Egyptian milieu, as are the description of the agrarian reform and the fact that the priests' estates were exempt from taxes.[37] Finally, with the embalming of the bodies of Jacob and Joseph, the 70 days of mourning correspond to the Egyptian embalming period, and the lifespan of 110 years attained by Joseph was the Egyptian ideal.[38]

As for the date of composition of the Joseph cycle, Redford points out that the patriarchs are mentioned throughout the Bible, but not Joseph. The omission of Joseph's name indicates that the stories were not known at a time when the books of the Bible had already been written down. In other words, the Joseph cycle dates from the exilic period and was interpolated into the Patriarchal period in order to explain the Israelites' descent to Egypt.

One of the touchstones for determining the date of its composition are the names that appear in it. Some have related them to the Nineteenth Dynasty, the time of Moses; others would date them as late as the Saite and Persian periods.[39] A more plausible theory is that of Schulman, who concluded that "the Egyptian names, all of which are of approximately the same date, argue for the writing of the stories to be dated to a time when these names were in current usage, to the time of the late Twenty-first to Twenty-second Dynasties, which corresponds in historical biblical chronology to the period of David and Solomon."[40] The author's broad knowledge of Egypt suits the period when there were regular contacts between Israel and Egypt, around the year

---

or "she belongs to you" (fem. sing.; that is, to a goddess or to her mother). Such names are well-documented in the Middle Kingdom and Hyksos periods (2100–1600 BCE); see Kitchen, "Asenath," *NBD*, p. 94.

36. Scholars do not agree about the meaning of Zaphenath-paneah. The popular view was that it means, "God speaks and he lives" or "The god said: he will live." See G. Steindorff, "Der Name Josephs Saphenat-Pa'neach," *ZÄS* 27 (1898), pp. 41ff.; idem, "Weiteres zu Genesis 41,45," *ZÄS* 30 (1892), pp. 50ff.; Redford, *A Study*, pp. 230–231. Vergote and Kitchen pointed out that this name is more appropriate for a newborn child than for an adult. They also noted that the name Zaphenath-paneah is found only in a later period (1100–500 BCE). Accordingly, Vergote understood it as meaning "the man who knows things" (*Joseph en Égypte*, p. 142); whereas Kitchen understood it as "(Joseph) who is called 'Ip-'ankh" (*NBD*, p. 1353).

37. Redford, *A Study*, p. 238.

38. On the number 110, see D. Spanel, *Through Ancient Eyes: Egyptian Portraiture* (Birmingham, Alabama: Birmingham Museum of Art, 1988), p. 25; in Israel, by contrast, 120 is the ideal age attained by Moses (Deut. 31:2 and 34:7).

39. For the Mosaic period, see Vergote, *Joseph en Égypte*, pp. 141–150. For the later date, see Redford, *A Study*, pp. 228–231. For a general survey of the dating of the Joseph stories, see Gary A. Rendsburg, *The Redaction of Genesis* (Winona Lake, Indiana: Eisenbrauns, 1986), pp. 119–120.

40. A. R. Schulman, "On the Egyptian Name of Joseph: A New Approach," *SAK* 2

900.[41] Nothing in the text points to a later date. When Pharaoh's daughter wed Solomon, a retinue of courtiers escorted her to Jerusalem, where it is likely that they told the locals about their country.

Some of David and Solomon's royal clerks may have been Egyptian or borne Egyptian names.[42] Solomon had commercial contacts with Egypt (1 Kings 10:29), and his men were frequent visitors to that country. The flight of Ben-Hadad the Edomite (1 Kings 11:17–24) and of Jeroboam after his abortive revolt are extreme examples of the normal relations of Egypt and Israel. The close ties with Egypt and the presence of Egyptians at the king's court may explain the detailed backdrop of Egyptian culture in the Joseph cycle.

That assumption is buttressed by the royal expropriation of land initiated by Joseph. A less drastic method was rejected by Samuel when the people asked him for a king (1 Sam. 8:13–16).[43] The fact that expropriation is rejected in Samuel but accepted in Genesis suggests that the stories were written in different periods. Moreover, in Solomon's time the Israelite state was on the road to becoming an empire. The state bureaucracy was based on the Egyptian model and the royal court needed more land. Special taxes were imposed to support the king and his household, and a large work force was drafted to build the Temple and various public-works projects. Perhaps this inspired the thought that the Egyptian system of land tenure was preferable.[44]

Mazar notes that the milieu and the ethnic and sociopolitical picture reflected in the stories of the Patriarchs seem to fit into the end of the period of the Judges and the beginning of the kingdom.[45] The *Sitz im Leben* of the stories, some of them based on folk legends from the nomadic age, belongs to a period only one or two generations before the great historiographical work received its first written form. The nature and tendency of the Joseph cycle,

---

(1974), pp. 235–243, especially p. 243; for a similar view see De Vaux, *The Early History of Israel,* pp. 387–388; Rendsburg, *The Redaction of Genesis,* p. 119.

41. A. Malamat, "Aspects of the Foreign Policies of David and Solomon," *JNES* 22 (1963), pp. 1–17; Rendsburg, *The Redaction of Genesis,* p. 119.

42. De Vaux, *The Early History of Israel,* p. 310.

43. I. Mendelsohn, "Samuel's Denunciation of Kingship in the Light of the Akkadian Documents from Ugarit," *BASOR* 143 (1956), pp. 17–22.

44. De Vaux, *The Early History of Israel,* p. 307; K. H. Henry, "Land Tenure in the Old Testament," *PEQ* (1954) pp. 5–15. On p. 13 Henry writes that the Joseph story reflects an Israelite situation. In contrast, see A. Alt, "Der Antiel des Königtums an der sozialen Entwicklung in den Reichen Israel und Juda," *Kleine Schriften zur Geschichte des Volkes Israel* 3 (1959), pp. 348–372; he says that the Genesis description does not apply to any period in the history of Israel.

45. Benjamin Mazar, "The Historical Background of the Book of Genesis," in *Canaan and Israel* (Jerusalem: Mossad Bialik, 1974), p. 136 (Hebrew).

as well as the significant place allotted to Joseph among his brothers, the transfer of the birthright from Manasseh to Ephraim, and the many anachronisms
strengthen the conjecture that the traditions and motifs were woven and developed in the highlands of Ephraim in the twelfth and eleventh centuries and
received a sophisticated literary form no earlier than the end of the eleventh
century BCE.[46]

We should remember that Israelite literature reached impressive heights in
the period of David and Solomon.[47] The composition and redaction of the
Book of Genesis is one of these high points. Among the other works written
at the same time are the stories of David (2 Sam. 9–20 and 1 Kings 1–2) and
parts of the story of Samuel. A comparison of Genesis with 2 Samuel 11–15
reveals the link between these works; Benno Jacob noted many similar idioms
in the two.[48] Cassuto also noted this fact and read Genesis 20:1–18, which
deals with Abimelech's seizure of Sarah, as a parallel story to the capture and
return of the Ark by the Philistines.[49] These similarities are no coincidence.
On the contrary, they indicate that Genesis and parts of Samuel were written
during the same period, the reigns of David and Solomon.[50]

Von Rad argues that the Joseph cycle, written during the reign of Solomon,
depicts the ideal figure of the wise courtier.[51] Joseph is a God-fearing, humble,
tolerant, and tactful person, possessed of the ideal traits of Egyptian and Israelite wisdom literature. The absence of any ritual etiology (*Heilsgeschichte*) or
divine revelation, on the one hand, and the emphasis on the directing providence of God, which disrupts human plans, on the other, leads Von Rad to
conclude that the *Sitz im Leben* belongs to the wisdom literature.[52] He further
notes that the consummate virtues with which Joseph is endowed are also on
display in the *Wisdom of Amenemope*–further evidence of an Egyptian influence on the Joseph cycle.

---

46. Ibid., pp. 142–143.

47. Rendsburg, *The Redaction of Genesis,* p. 119, n. 27.

48. B. Jacob, *Das Erste Buch der Tora: Genesis* (Berlin: Schocken, 1934), pp. 1048–49;
Rendsburg, *The Redaction of Genesis,* p. 120.

49. U. Cassuto, *A Commentary on the Book of Genesis: From Noah to Abraham* (Jerusalem:
Magnes Press, 1964), p. 341.

50. R. Alter, *The Art of Biblical Narrative* (New York: Basic Books, 1981), pp. 117–120.
Alter points to the connection between 1 Samuel 18 and Genesis 39 and 1 Samuel 19 and
Genesis 31; W. Brueggemann, "David and his Theologian," *CBQ* 30 (1968), pp. 156–181;
Rendsburg, *The Redaction of Genesis,* p. 120.

51. Gerhard von Rad, "The Joseph Narrative and Ancient Wisdom," *The Problem of the
Hexateuch and Other Essays,* trans. E. W. Trueman Dicken (New York: McGraw Hill, 1966),
pp. 292–300.

52. Ibid.

Crenshaw, on the other hand, rejects Von Rad's hypothesis and notes the importance of divine Providence in the Joseph stories. God, who directs matters, hides His will from evil men and sets their wicked schemes to naught–revealing His plans only to Joseph, His chosen one. This theme is totally foreign to Israelite or Egyptian wisdom literature, in which no person knows the ways of God and the plans of even righteous individuals are stymied.[53] Further, he notes, the figure of Joseph is not really compatible with the ideal man of Israelite and Egyptian wisdom literature. He does not control his emotions (Gen. 45:2 and 14, 50:1 and 17), is supremely tactless when he tells his brothers about his dreams, and later treats them with excessive severity. Finally, nothing in the story deals with Joseph's education: he is chosen as the king's counselor purely on the basis of his spiritual attributes.

The Joseph cycle as we have it was evidently written with a single goal: to explain the Israelites' descent to Egypt. Its main motif, from beginning to end, is that descent and the subsequent re-ascent to Canaan–both engineered by divine providence. Initially the brothers *lower* Joseph into the pit; then they *raise* him from the pit in order to sell him to the Ishmaelites, who take him *down* to Egypt. When the bitter news is brought to Jacob, he cries out, "I will *go down* mourning to my son in Sheol" (Gen. 37: 35). At the start of the next chapter, Judah *goes down* from his brothers (38:1). At the beginning of chapter 39, we read that Joseph was taken *down* to Egypt, from the Ishmaelites who took him *down* there. After Potiphar's wife accuses Joseph of attempting to rape her, he is again *lowered* into a pit, from which he is *raised* up in order to appear before Pharaoh.

Because of the famine, the brothers *go down* to Egypt to buy food, and when they *go back up* to Canaan and tell their father what happened to them in Egypt and that the lord of that land wishes to see Benjamin, Jacob refuses, saying, "My son must not *go down* with you, for his brother is dead and he alone is left. If he meets with disaster on the journey you are taking, you will send my white head *down* to Sheol in grief" (42:38). The severity of the famine changes Jacob's mind; in the end he agrees to send Benjamin and the brothers *go down* to Egypt a second time. When the brothers *come back up*, they bring the news that Joseph is alive and his invitation to Jacob: "*Come down* to me without delay" (45:9). Jacob hesitates to leave the land of Canaan, but the Lord appears to him and tells him, "Fear not to *go down* to Egypt, ... I Myself will *go down* with you to Egypt, and I Myself will also bring you *back up*" (46:3–4). Next we read that Jacob and all of his household *went down* to Egypt. Joseph

---

53. J. L. Crenshaw, "Method in Determining Wisdom Influence upon 'Historical' Literature," *JBL* 88 (1969), pp. 135–137.

comes up to meet his father and tells him that he will *go up* to Pharaoh and inform him of his family's arrival.

After Jacob's death, Joseph and his brothers *go up* to Canaan to bury him there, and then *go back down* to Egypt. Before his death, Joseph tells his brothers, "I am about to die. God will surely take notice of you and *bring you up* from this land to the land that He promised on oath to Abraham, to Isaac, and to Jacob" (50:24). Finally, he makes the Israelites take an oath, saying, "When God has taken notice of you, you shall *carry up* my bones from here" (50:25). Thus the story concludes with an allusion to the *ascent* of Joseph's bones and of all the Israelites to the Chosen Land.

The story at the same time shows how divine Providence steers human actions according to a foreordained plan and according to universal justice, so as to reward or punish each person—the righteous according to their merits and the sinners according to their misdeeds, without overt intervention by God.[54] At every stage we are acutely aware of God's hidden intention. Seemingly chance events are in truth part of a clear and preordained program. Jacob does not know where he is sending his son; Joseph, inquiring after his brothers, does not know where his feet are leading him; and the man does not know where he is sending Joseph. Nor do the brothers know the significance of their deeds.

There are also parallels between chapter 37, the sale of Joseph, and chapter 38, the episode of Judah and Tamar. Judah, whose idea it was to sell Joseph into slavery, receives his just deserts after he impregnates his daughter-in-law Tamar. When the brothers send the coat of many colors to their father, after dipping it in the blood of a kid, they tell him, "Please examine it; is it your son's tunic or not?" (37:32). Judah similarly dispatches a kid to Tamar. Thinking her to be a harlot, he instructs that she be taken out and burned. He too is told, "Examine these" (38:25).

Jacob "refused to be comforted" (37:35), whereas "when he was comforted, Judah went up to Timnah to his sheepshearers" (38:12). When Joseph tells his brothers, "It was to save life that God sent me ahead, ..." (Gen. 45:5–8, 50:20), he clearly acknowledges the role of divine Providence. That acknowledgment is emphasized with even greater compass regarding the future of the family and the future of the nation in God's words to Jacob: "Fear not to go down to Egypt, for I will make you there into a great nation. I Myself will go down with you to Egypt, and I Myself will also bring you back" (Gen. 46:3–4).

---

54. S.v. "Joseph," *EMiqr* 3:614.

SOLOMON'S DREAM (1 KINGS 3: 3-15)

A comparison of the story of Solomon's dream at Gibeon with biblical and extrabiblical material reveals a resemblance in its motifs and language to other ancient Near Eastern stories. The offering of sacrifices, the dream theophany, and divine gifts tendered to kings in dreams are a frequent motif. Herrmann long ago noted that the divine revelation to Thutmoses IV is similar to the Solomon's theophany at Gibeon. Thutmoses leaves his capital, Memphis, and goes to offer sacrifices in Giza, which was a holy place.[55] After the deity appears to the king in a dream, the monarch instructs his escort to return to the city and offer sacrifices.

Herrmann goes further and tries to show that the story of God's appearance to Solomon takes the Egyptian royal novella as its literary model. We are told that the gods proclaimed Sesostris I, Thutmoses III, and Thutmoses IV as their chosen representatives when they were still children and that they were consecrated as kings even before they were born. Similarly, "But I am a young lad" (1 Kings 3:7), "You have ... [given] him a son to occupy his throne, as is now the case" (v. 6), and the phrase "in faithfulness and righteousness and in integrity of heart" (ibid.) all describe a ceremonial coronation during which the biblical king is enthroned and given his royal epithets.[56]

Scholars have long warned, however, against finding too many parallels and disregarding differences. Fensham notes that the situations are not similar. Thutmoses IV had his theophany when he was still a prince, not after he had ascended the throne. Furthermore, the theme of gods appearing to kings was a commonplace of the ancient world and offering sacrifices was a routine event.[57] Zalevsky adds that Thutmoses' silence and concealment of the content of his dream stemmed from personal motives and was not part of the revelation ceremony.[58] In Solomon's case, we are told neither that he kept his dream to himself nor that he disseminated it in public. As for the content, we dispute Herrmann's contention that Solomon's dream is based on the Egyptian royal novella. Many of the elements of the dream, such as Solomon's request for discernment in dispensing justice, the blessings enumerated by the

---

55. John A. Wilson, "Egyptian Oracles and Prophecies," trans. John A. Wilson, *ANET*, p. 449.

56. S. Herrmann, "Die Königsnovelle in Ägypten und in Israel," *Wissenschaftliche Zeitschrift der Karl-Marx-Universität* (Leipzig, 1953–1954), 3: 51–52.

57. F. C. Fensham, "Legal Aspect of the Dream of Solomon," in *Fourth World Congress of Jewish Studies* (Jerusalem, 1967), vol. 1, p. 67.

58. S. Zalevsky, "The Revelation of God to Solomon in Gibeon," *Tarbiz* 42 (1973), p. 224.

Lord that Solomon did not ask for, and the motif of the gods granting gifts to kings can also be found in Mesopotamian sources.[59]

Kapelrud, following another path, sees an affinity between Solomon's dreams and those of Gudea of Lagash.[60] In both, the deity appears and gives instructions for the construction of a temple. According to Kapelrud, the injunction to build a temple was originally found in the story of Solomon's visit to Gibeon. The narrative author, however, focused on the theme of wisdom as the centerpiece of the story, along with the episode of the two prostitutes and the list of Solomon's officials and prefects. These changes, he argues, led to the change in the ancient narrative unit, which dealt chiefly with the construction of the Temple.

Weinfeld follows Hermann in noting the similarity of Solomon's dream to that of Thutmoses IV. In his opinion, however, the resemblance is limited to the external setting. On the other hand, Weinfeld expands on Kapelrud's analogies and enumerates biblical and extrabiblical sources in which the construction of a sanctuary must be confirmed by a deity.[61] In addition to the example of Gudea of Lagash, he offers the examples of Esarhaddon, Nabonidus, and Baal, who waited for a dream theophany before starting to build temples to the gods.[62] According to Weinfeld, the story of the dream at Gibeon originally contained the Lord's instructions to Solomon to build the Temple in Jerusalem. The Deuteronomistic editor of the Book of Kings excised the original content and left only the framework of vv. 4–5 and 15, which he filled in with the theme of judicial discernment.

I find Weinfeld's contention strange, because the construction of the Temple was a key event for the Deuteronomist. Why would he delete this theme

---

59. Ibid., pp. 226–227.

60. A. S. Kapelrud, 'Temple-Building: A Task for Gods and Kings," *Orientalia* 32 (1963), pp. 56–62.

61. Weinfeld brings a long series of examples from the Bible to show that divine revelation precedes the construction of temples and sanctification of places. Moses erected the sanctuary in the desert only after he had seen its pattern in the revelation at Sinai (Ex. 25:9, 26:30; cf. 1 Chron. 28:19). David required divine assent before he began building the Temple in Jerusalem, but the Lord expressed His opposition (2 Sam. 7:4ff.). The Patriarchs, too, erected cult sites after various revelations (Gen. 12:7, 26:24–25; 28:12–19). Gideon built an altar to the Lord after the Lord came to him in a dream (Judg. 6:25). We may rebut Weinfeld and note that all his examples assert a link between the new sanctuary, on the one hand, and appearance of the Lord and the place where He appeared to His elected one, on the other. Here the Lord appears to Solomon in Gibeon, but the Temple is to be in Jerusalem.

62. Moshe Weinfeld, *Deuteronomy and the Deuteronomic School* (Oxford: Clarendon Press, 1971), p. 250.

from Solomon's dream at Gibeon? Victor Hurowitz in his book points to a large number of extrabiblical building accounts that contain no dream and that do not assume that the building project was undertaken on divine initiative.[63] To the contrary, in some stories it was the king who initiated the project and requested divine permission for the construction. According to Hurowitz, the divine consent is found in a pre-deuteronomic passage telling of Solomon's correspondence with Hiram.[64]

The story of the dream as it appears in the Book of Kings indicates that there is a link between the dream and later events. Solomon receives certain promises, whose realization is described in the later stories about him. Motifs and language in subsequent chapters in the Book of Kings draw on the dream episode.[65] Given that both the framework of the dream and its content have many lines of resemblance to both early and late biblical and extrabiblical literature, it seems likely that the entire story is ancient.[66]

The divine promises made to Solomon in his dream bear a limited resemblance to God's promises to Abraham in the Covenant between the Pieces.[67] There Abraham responded to the Lord's overtures with the question "What can You give me?" (Gen. 15:2); here the Lord tells Solomon, "What shall I give you?" (1 Kings 3:5). The Lord promises Abraham "You shall go to your fathers in peace; you shall be buried at a ripe old age" (Gen. 15:15). In addition, his descendants will leave Egypt "with great wealth."

The motif of the request for and promise of wisdom also appears in the Joseph cycle, where we read, "Accordingly, let Pharaoh find a man of discernment and wisdom (נבון וחכם), and set him over the land of Egypt" (Gen. 41:33), and again, "Since God has made all this known to you, there is none so discerning and wise as you (נבון וחכם כמוֹך)" (v. 39). Scholars have compared these verses with the Lord's promise to Solomon: "I grant you a wise and discerning mind (לב חכם ונבון); there has never been anyone like you (כמוֹך) before, nor will anyone like you (כמוֹך) arise again" (1 Kings 3:12). In the tale of the pretended appeal by the clever woman from Tekoa, she compares David to an angel of God, "understanding everything, good and bad

---

63. Victor (Avigdor) Hurowitz, *I have Built You an Exalted House: Temple Building in Light of Mesopotamian and Northwest Semitic Writings*, Journal for the Study of the Old Testament, Supplement Series 115, (Sheffield: Sheffield Academic Press,1992), p.165.

64. Ibid, p. 166.

65. Zalevsky, "The Revelation of God to Solomon in Gibeon," pp. 247ff.

66. Moshe Garsiel, "King Solomon's Descent to Gibeon and His Dream," *The Dr. Ben Yehuda Book,* ed. Ben-Zion Luria (The Israel Bible Society, Tel Aviv, 1981), p. 205 (Hebrew).

67. Ibid., p. 198.

(לשמע הטוב והרע)" (2 Sam. 14:17). When David penetrates her meaning, she tells him, "My lord is as wise as an angel of God (חכם כחכמת מלאך האלוהים), and he knows all that goes on in the land" (v. 20). This should be compared to the language of Solomon's dream, "Grant, then, Your servant an understanding mind (לב שמע) to judge Your people, to distinguish between good and bad (בין טוב לרע)" (1 Kings 3:9). These qualities are echoed again at the end of the episode of the two prostitutes: "When all Israel heard the decision that the king had rendered, they stood in awe of the king; for they saw that he possessed divine wisdom (חכמת אלהים) to execute justice" (1 Kings 3:28).[68]

Parallels can also be found between Solomon's request for discernment and the proposal for a judicial reform in the time of Moses (Exodus 18 and Deuteronomy 1). Weinfeld believes that all of Solomon's dream, except for the frame (vv. 4–5 and 15), was produced by the Deuteronomist redactor. He notes especially the resemblance between 1 Kings 3:6–14 and Deuteronomy 1, in both of which the burden of judging the people is a heavy one and requires discernment and wisdom.[69] The resemblance is no coincidence–the authors obviously intended for readers to compare the two leaders. It is interesting to note that whereas Moses could not bear the burden and required assistance, Solomon wanted to succeed alone in his task: "I grant you a wise and discerning mind; there has never been anyone like you before, nor will anyone like you arise again"[70] (1 Kings 3:12).

The story of Solomon's dream can also be compared with the David cycle. We have already noted the episode of the woman of Tekoa (2 Sam. 14:17). The expression "I ... do not know how to go out and come in" (v. 7) is also applied to David: "So Saul removed him from his presence and appointed him chief of a thousand, and he went out and came in at the head of the troops" (1 Sam. 18:13; see also ibid. 16; 2 Sam. 5:2). Additional expressions are found in 1 Kings 1–2, the so-called succession story: "And further, this is what the king said, 'Praised be the Lord, ... who has this day provided a successor to my throne, while my own eyes can see it'" (1 Kings 1:48); and "You have continued this great kindness to him by giving him a son to occupy his throne, as is now the case" (1 Kings 3:6).

---

68. Ibid., p. 200.

69. Zalevsky, "The Revelation of God to Solomon in Gibeon," pp. 238–239. Zalevsky rejects Weinfeld's view and points out the differences between 1 Kings 3 and Deuteronomy 1. Among other things, he notes that in Deuteronomy 1 the judicial reform is instituted in order to ease the heavy burden on Moses of judging the entire nation. By contrast, in the Book of Kings, Solomon requests judicial discernment so that he will be able to fulfill his role faithfully and does not appoint a bench of judges to ease his burden.

70. Garsiel, "King Solomon's Descent to Gibeon and His Dream," p. 203.

One can conclude from these comparisons of Solomon's dream with other biblical literature that the content and phrasing of the story are ancient. Who, then, was the author of the story in 1 Kings 3? Zalevsky, noting the connection between this episode and other chapters of 1 Kings dealing with Solomon, believes that Solomon received certain promises in Gibeon and that the rest of the stories about him detail their fulfillment.[71] He adds that sometimes the Solomon stories give the impression of being meant to emphasize their connection with the dream.[72] A reading of the subsequent chapters reveals not only plot connections with the dream story but the same narrative voice. Whoever wrote the chapters about Solomon in the Book of Kings was also the author of the dream episode. The central theme of all these chapters is Solomon's wisdom, as is reflected in key words like *wise, wisdom, discerning, discernment.* This central topic and its characteristic idioms do not appear elsewhere in the Books of Kings; consequently some believe that the wisdom motif was not original with the author of the book but goes back to an ancient source from which he derived his material about Solomon. Perhaps that source was the "Annals of Solomon" mentioned in 1 Kings 11:41, where, evidently, the topic of Solomon's extraordinary wisdom was a central theme.[73]

As for the purpose of the story of Solomon's dream, we have already mentioned Herrmann's view, based on comparisons with Egyptian royal novellas, that the ceremony at Gibeon was Solomon's coronation as king of Israel. Hermann also notes similar motifs in the coronation ceremonies in the "royal psalms," such as Psalms 2, 21, and 89. Gray, taking his cue from Herrmann, sees the use of the royal novella model as a means of buttressing Solomon's legitimacy–agreeing that the pericope deals not only with Solomon's legitimacy but also with that of the entire Davidic dynasty, as expressed in Isaiah 9:6–11.[74]

Zalevsky accepts the idea of a coronation ceremony, but believes that Herrmann goes too far in accentuating the story's dependence on the Egyptian royal novella. He examines other motifs in the dream and holds that the phrase "in faithfulness and righteousness and in integrity of heart" (1 Kings 3:6), as well as Isaiah 11:1ff and Psalm 45, reflect an ancient Israelite coronation tradition that expresses the hope that the new king will lead his people

---

71. Zalevsky, "The Revelation," pp. 247–258.

72. Ibid., p. 247.

73. Jacob Liver, *Studies in Bible and Judean Desert Scrolls,* pp. 83–105; Garsiel, "King Solomon's Descent to Gibeon," p. 204.

74. John Gray, *1 and 2 Kings,* pp. 121–122.

with justice and equity.[75] Similarly, the expression "You have ... [given] him a son to occupy his throne, as is now the case" refers to the problem of succession and was part of the coronation ceremony. Finally, Zalevsky points out that in Gibeon, Solomon received two forms of wisdom that a king needed to succeed—judicial wisdom, essential for domestic policy, and general wisdom, necessary for the conduct of foreign policy.

According to 1 Kings 1:33–48, Solomon was proclaimed king during David's lifetime. Why, then, does the coronation have to be repeated? An answer can be found in the events surrounding Solomon's ascent to power, which was accompanied by bitter struggles. His brother Adonijah asserted his right to the throne and had the support of broad circles, including Joab the son of Zeruiah, Abiathar the priest, his brother princes, and leading figures of the tribe of Judah. Accordingly after the executions of Adonijah and Joab, Solomon required the ceremony at Gibeon to unite the people and to emphasize his unchallenged rule over all Israel. The offering of sacrifices at the great shrine was part of Solomon's coronation. So too Saul, when he renewed his kingdom, marked the event by offering sacrifices at the sanctuary in Gilgal (1 Sam. 11:12–15). Absalom accompanied his own coronation with festive sacrifices in Hebron (2 Sam. 15:10–12). Adonijah's abortive coronation, too, was the occasion for many sacrifices offered at the Zoheleth stone near En-rogel (1 Kings 1:9–19, 25).

The festivities in Gibeon were evidently paralleled by a ceremony in Jerusalem, where Solomon offered sacrifices before the tent of the Ark of the Lord. Perhaps he conducted these two ceremonies in order to broaden his popular support—one to bind the northern tribes to the monarchy, and the other in the capital. During the ceremony in Gibeon Solomon recounted his dream to the assembled throng. That is how its contents came to be included in the "Annals of Solomon."[76] Later the story was inserted into the Book of Kings. Solomon may also have recounted his dream as a declaration of intents; that is, to tell the people that he would judge them fairly and continue in the path of his father, who had walked with the Lord ""in faithfulness and righteousness and in integrity of heart" (1 Kings 3:6).[77]

In summary, then, the story of the dream at Gibeon, in its present form, is an ancient tale whose sole function was to legitimize Solomon's rule. There was no pact between him and the people, as had been concluded between David and the Israelites in Hebron. Solomon was selected by David as his

---

75. Zalevsky, "The Revelation of God," p. 230.
76. Garsiel, "King Solomon's Descent to Gibeon," pp. 197.
77. Ibid., pp. 197–198.

heir, and it was the first time that succession had applied to the monarchy in Israel. Nevertheless, a king of Israel required divine confirmation and recognition by the people to justify his election and provide legitimacy to his reign. Accordingly, the story of the dream was written by the counselors and scribes of the royal court during Solomon's lifetime.

NEBUCHADNEZZAR'S DREAMS (DANIEL 2 AND 4)

The scholarly and critical literature on the Book of Daniel abounds with questions regarding its author and period of composition. As early as 1674, Spinoza noted that chapters 7–12, written in the first person, were by Daniel, whereas chapters 1–6 were derived from "Chaldean chronicles."[78] Sir Isaac Newton thought that the last six chapters were written by Daniel, but the first six by other hands.[79] These views notwithstanding, early biblical scholars originally believed that Daniel was all of a piece.[80]

By the end of the nineteenth century and into the first half of the twentieth,

---

78. Benedict Spinoza, *Theologico-Political Treatise,* trans. R. H. M. Elwes (New York: Dover, 1955), Ch. 10, vol. 1, p. 150; H. H. Rowley, "The Unity of the Book of Daniel," in *The Servant of the Lord and other Essays on the OT,* second edition, revised (Oxford: Blackwell, 1965), p. 250, n. 3; John J. Collins, *Daniel,* p. 26.

79. Isaac Newton, *Observations upon the Prophecies of Daniel and the Apocalypse of St. John* (1733), in *Sir Isaac Newton's Daniel and the Apocalypse,* edited by William Whitlam (London: Murray, 1922), p. 145; Collins, *Daniel,* p. 26.

80. The argument for the unitary character of the book is based on the fact that Daniel appears in both parts, that identical historical errors are found in both halves, and that the resemblance between the kings of Babylonia and Persia and their decrees in the first part of the book and the description of Antiochus and his decrees in the second part. Rowley maintained that "a point can be found for every story in the first half of the book in the setting of the Maccabean age." Nevertheless, a scrutiny of chapters 1–6 proves just the opposite; these chapters cannot be associated with the period of Antiochus Epiphanes, because nothing in them alludes to the mass persecution characteristic of his reign. Instead, we find that religious persecution and extreme tests of faith applied only to individuals–Jews who had attained high positions in the royal court. In the second half of the book, by contrast, an entire nation is put to the test, as indeed was the situation produced by the decrees of Antiochus. In the first half of the book, no one can harm the loyal adherents of the Jewish religion and pagan kings praise and exalt the God of Israel. Nebuchadnezzar, who recognizes the God of Israel, is not a stand-in for Epiphanes. The scholars who believe that the Book of Daniel is all of a piece include von Gall, Bevan, Driver, Charles, Porteous, Polger, Rowley, and others. A detailed survey of scholarly opinion regarding the composition of Daniel can be found in Rowley, "The Unity of the Book of Daniel," pp. 249–260; O. Eissfeldt, *Einleitung in das AT,* third edition (Tübingen: Mohr, 1964), pp. 700–704; K. Koch, *Das Buch Daniel* (Darmstadt: Wissenschaftliche Buchgesellschaft, 1980), pp. 55–57; Collins, *Daniel,* pp. 26–28.

however, that view was abandoned in favor or the recognition that the book of Daniel has two parts, almost like two books. Part one (chapters 1–6) contains six legends about Daniel and his colleagues, written in the third person, that reflect the life of the Jewish Diaspora in Persia, where some Jews held posts in the royal court and Daniel was an intrepid sage and magus. In part two (chapters 7–12), a passive Daniel recounts the visions and secrets revealed to him.

The dual structure of the book is made more conspicuous by the fact that the chronology starts over in the second part.[81] Belshazzar is the son of Nebuchadnezzar and Darius is a Median king. The order of the kingdoms after the collapse of Babylon is Media, Persia, Greece. The earliest date and royal name in the stories refer to the third year of Jehoiakim of Judah (1:1), meaning the beginning of the reign of Nebuchadnezzar, followed by the second year of Nebuchadnezzar (2:1). Later we have Belshazzar in chapter 5 and Darius the Mede in chapter 6, which ends with a reference to Cyrus the Persian. The kingdoms are not referred to chronologically from then on, but go back to Belshazzar (chapters 7 and 8), then to Darius the Mede (9:1), and conclude in the reign of Cyrus the Persian. Another indication of their independence of each other is that there are several idioms that appear in only one or the other half of the book.[82] For example, the expression אֱלָהּ שְׁמַיָּא to designate the Lord occurs seven times, all of them in chapters 1–6.[83] The term "Chaldeans," in the sense of astrologers, is found only in the narrative section of Daniel (2:2, 5, 10; 3:8, 4:4; et passim); elsewhere in the Bible it is an ethnic designation.[84] Particularly prominent is the use of about twenty Persian terms and designations in the narrative chapters. (There are only two in the apocalyptic sections—a strong indicator of the difference between the tales and the visions.[85])

---

81. Haran, *The Biblical Collection* (Jerusalem: Magnes Press, 1966), pp. 104–105.

82. Ibid., pp. 105–107.

83. The designation אלוה שמייא or אלוהי השמים is characteristic of the Second Temple period and is also found in 2 Chron. 31:23, Ezra 1:2, 5:11 and 12, 6:9 and 10, 7:12, 21, and 23; Neh. 1:4 and 5, 2:4 and 20. It is also found in the apocryphal books of Judith (5:8, 6:19, and 11:17) and Tobias (10:11 and 13), as well as in the Elephantine papyri. The Persians used this term to describe the God of the Jews. See Louis F. Hartman and Alexander A. Di Lella, *The Book of Daniel,* AB (New York: Doubleday, 1978), p. 139; Collins, *Daniel,* p. 159. For the use of the phrase in the Elephantine papyri, see A. E. Cowley, *Aramaic Papyri of the 5th Century B.C.* (Oxford: Clarendon, 1923), Nos. 30:2 and 28; 31:27; 32:4; 38:3 and 5; and 40:1.

84. As an ethnic designation it also appears in Daniel: 3:8 and 5:30.

85. For a detailed discussion of the Persian words in Daniel, see H. H. Rowley, *The Aramaic of the Old Testament* (Oxford: Oxford University Press, 1929), p. 138; Rosenthal, *A*

Among the twenty are the titles of Persian functionaries, some of them derived from Akkadian, chiefly late Akkadian. They are mentioned in the stories of the three lads in the furnace (3:1–30) and of Daniel in the lions' den (chapter 6). Some of the Persian titles are mentioned elsewhere in the Bible, but always in texts that date from pre-Hellenistic Second Temple period: סגניא גדבריא אחשדרפניא, and פחותא.[86] On the other hand, some posts in the Persian civil service are mentioned only in Daniel: סרכיא סרכין דתבריא אדרגזריא and תפתיא. The clothing of the three lads—פטישיהון סרבליהון, and כרבלתהון (3:21; and cf. v. 27) also seem to be borrowed from the Persian.[87]

The stories first appeared individually[88] and were not part of a series, as the differences among them make clear. Thus chapter 2 begins, "In the second year of the reign of Nebuchadnezzar." This is a difficult verse, because it is also the second year of the three-year education of Daniel and his friends (Daniel 1:5). But it was only "when the time the king had set for their presen-

---

Grammar of Biblical Aramaic, pp. 58–59; K. A. Kitchen, "The Aramaic of Daniel," in D. J. Weisman, T. C. Mitchell, R. Joyce, W. J. Martin, and K. A. Kitchen, *Notes on Some Problems in the Book of Daniel.* (London: Tyndale 1965), p. 35–44; Collins, *Daniel,* pp. 18–19; Haran, *The Biblical Collection,* p. 107, n. 33; Montgomery, *The Book of Daniel,* p. 21.

86. אחשדרפן comes from Persian, but also appears on cuneiform tablets in the form *aḫšad(a)rapannu.* Just as the administrative mechanisms of the Assyrian Empire were adopted by the Babylonian Empire, so too the Babylonian royal bureaucracy was taken over by the kingdom of Media and Persia. The term appears in Esth. 8:9, and 9:3 as well as Ezra 8:36. גדבריא designates the officials in charge of the exchequer; it is also found in Aramaic with *zayin* instead of *dalet.* Hartman and Di Lella believe the word is borrowed from the Old Persian *handarza-kara.* סגן is borrowed from the Akkadian *saknu,* which means the deputy to a functionary. Pseudo-Jonathan used the term to render "Zephaniah, the deputy priest" (2 Kings 25:18 = Jer. 52:24). Finally, פחות / פחה occurs in the prophetic books (2 Kings 18:24; Jer. 51:23, 28, 57, et passim), in Ezra (5:3, 5, 14, et passim), and Esther (3:12 and 8:9), and always designates the provincial governors of Assyrian, Babylonian, or Persian Empire. See Hartman and Di Lella, *The Book of Daniel,* pp. 156–157; Robert H. Charles, *A Critical and Exegetical Commentary on the Book of Daniel* (Oxford: Clarendon, 1929), p. 61; Collins, *Daniel,* pp. 182–183.

87. James A. Montgomery, *Critical and Exegetical Commentary on the Book of Daniel,* ICC (Edinburgh: T. & T. Clark, 1927), pp. 211–213; Collins, *Daniel,* pp. 188–189. As for כרבלתהון, R. Samuel ben Nissim Masnut explained that it was like a diadem or hat; this gloss seems likely, since the word resembles the Hebrew כרבולת, which is s cockscomb, as in Talmudic Aramaic כרבלתיה דההוא תרנגולא (BT Erubin 100b). Some, however, trace it to the root כרבל 'wrap', and cite the statement about David, "wrapped [מכרבל] in robes of fine linen" (1 Chron. 15:27). Rosenthal believes that the word is neither Persian nor Akkadian but an item of Persian dress. See Franz Rosenthal, *A Grammar of Biblical Aramaic* (Wiesbaden: Harrassowitz, 1968), p. 59.

88. Montgomery, *The Book of Daniel,* pp. 92–94; Collins, *Daniel,* pp. 29 and 35; Haran, *Biblical Collection,* pp. 110–113.

tation had come [that] the chief officer presented them to Nebuchadnezzar" (1:18) and he became aware of their wisdom. In chapter 2, however, it seems that Daniel and his friends are already recognized as being among the wise men of the kingdom (2:13).[89] Chapter 3, which recounts the tale of the idol erected by Nebuchadnezzar, does not mention Daniel at all. And in chapter 5, Belshazzar is ostensibly Nebuchadnezzar's son but is not aware of Daniel's existence or that he had interpreted his father's dreams. These discrepancies reinforce the hypothesis that the stories in the first six chapters originally existed separately, whether orally or in writing. That hypothesis was further strengthened by the discovery in Cave 4 at Qumran of an Aramaic scroll whose contents are associated with the Daniel cycle.

The scroll tells the story of the prayer of Nabonidus, which is an older version of the episode recounted in Daniel 4. The Qumran version may well be closer to the Babylonian original, whereas the biblical variant is a reworking produced in the Land of Israel, where Nebuchadnezzar and the city of Babylon were more familiar than Nabonidus and his oasis of Tema. Still other works associated with Daniel survived in separate scrolls after the consolidation of the book and were incorporated in the Greek version: the Prayer of Azariah, the Song of the Three Holy Lads, Susannah, and Bel and the Dragon. These stories indicate that fragments of the Daniel cycle survived after others were canonized and provides further evidence that the stories composing the book were originally separate and only later merged.

Still, we must emphasize that there are also similarities between the two parts of the book, which may explain why they were joined into one. The author of chapters 7–12 seems to have made use of ancient materials and written and oral traditions that preceded the Hellenizing period. The narratives of chapters 1–6 were relevant to this period, inasmuch as they too were meant to encourage those who remained faithful to the Torah. The hero who is willing to give his life and who interprets Nebuchadnezzar's dreams as referring to the four kingdoms—to be followed by the kingdom of the Lord

---

89. The Talmudic sages understood "in the second year" to mean two years after the destruction of the Temple, indirectly stating that his "reign" dated only from his conquest of Jerusalem, since Jerusalem is the place of the Lord's abode—as David put it, "for the Lord has chosen Zion; He has desired it for His seat" (Ps. 132:13)—and the location of His throne, on which the kings of Judah sat (1 Chron. 29:23). According to Sa'adia, too, "when Nebuchadnezzar destroyed Jerusalem the Bible considered that he became king then." For the views of modern scholars and the various solutions they have offered, see: Hartman and Di Lella, *The Book of Daniel,* pp. 137–138; Norman W. Porteous, *Daniel: A Commentary,* OTL (Philadelphia: Westminster, 1965), p. 39; E. W. Heaton, *The Book of Daniel,* Torch Bible Commentary (London: SCM Press, 1956), p. 123; Montgomery, *The Book of Daniel,* pp. 140–141; Collins, *Daniel,* pp. 154–155.

(chapter 2)–could reinforce the Jews who remained steadfast in their faith during the dark days of the Antiochian persecution.[90] Thus the author of chapter 7 assigned to that hero the detailed vision of the fourth kingdom, Greece, down to the persecution by Antiochus and the redemption that would follow (chapters 7–12).

Evidence that it was the author of the apocalyptic dreams who collected the narratives to serve as introduction to his visions is provided by the "fingerprints" he left on both parts–e.g., common idioms.[91] For example: the expression "a dream and a vision of [the] mind in bed," followed by verbs of fright and alarm (2:28 and 4:2; 7:1 and 7:15). So too, "peoples and nations of every language," in reference to the entire population of the kingdom (3:4, 5:19, and 6:26; 7:14); and "His kingdom is an everlasting kingdom, and His dominion endures throughout the generations" (3:33 and 4:31; 7:14 and 27).

Particularly noteworthy is the link between Nebuchadnezzar's dream of the colossus (2:31–45) and the vision of the beasts who emerge from the sea (chapter 7).[92] In the latter, four beasts appear–a lion, a bear, a leopard, and the beast with ten horns. In the dream, however, the sections of the statue are made of four different materials: the head of fine gold; the breast and arms of silver; the belly and thighs of bronze; and the legs of iron. The feet were part iron and part mud. Both scenes relate to the theme of the four kingdoms. Yet whereas in chapter 7 and the other vision chapters the allusion is to the decrees of Antiochus Epiphanes, nothing hints at them in chapter 2 and the rest

---

90. The fact that the Daniel stories were topical in the time of the Maccabees is one of the points alleged by Rowley as proof that Daniel is a single work. At the end of the article, however, he says that the author evidently used materials derived from various written and oral sources. See Rowley, "The Servant of the Lord," pp. 276–280.

91. Haran, *Biblical Collection*, p. 115.

92. Rowley, *The Servant of the Lord*, pp. 262–264; Hartman and Di Lella, *The Book of Daniel*, p. 142; Haran, *The Biblical Collection*, p. 116ff. On the other hand, some scholars who think that there is a certain resemblance between chapters 2 and 7. Collins says that chapter 2 certainly influenced chapter 7. But there are also differences between them that must not be overlooked. Kaufman, for example, points out that in chapter 7, the last kingdom revolts against God and persecutes Israel and its religion, but there is no mention of this in chapter 2. In chapter 7, the four kingdoms are symbolized by four animals who emerge from the sea, whereas in chapter 2 the four kingdoms are represented by four parts of the statue. For other differences, see Kaufman, *Toledot*, 4:423ff.; Collins, *Daniel*, p. 173. Rappaport says that the differences noted by Kaufman exist, "but they stem from the fact that what we are dealing with are two different apocalypses and do not prove that the object of the description is different. The differences involve additions and subtractions, but not self-contradictions" (A. Rappaport, "The Fourth Kingdom in the Book of Daniel," *Beit Mikra* 22 (1964), p. 15).

of the narrative half of the book.[93] What does appear in chapter 2 and is repeated in chapter 7 is the messianic and eschatological expectation that a new kingdom–the kingdom of Israel–will be established, will overthrow its predecessors, and endure forever (2:54; 7:18 and 27). In chapter 2, the fourth kingdom is destroyed by a stone that shatters the statue and then turns into a large mountain that fills up the earth. In chapter 7, however, it is divine agents that destroy the fourth beast (7:9–11, 21, 22). Haran believes that the feverish expectation of the destruction of the Greek kingdom and the deliverance of Israel, which are so prominent in both the dream and chapter 7, indicates the link between Nebuchadnezzar's dream and the vision of the four beasts.[94] He hypothesizes that there was a story about a king who had forgotten his dream and demanded that his wise men tell him what it was and what it meant. Daniel, to whom the Lord had appeared and interpreted the dream, came to the king, thereby saving the wise men from death and also compelling the pagan king to honor his God. The innovation of the author of the vision chapters was to incorporate the dream story into his work; in this way, "a sort of apocalyptic vision was woven into the context of the story without dispossessing it of its original meaning."[95]

Another reason for the linking of the narratives with the visions is that the former are the only source that can establish Daniel's preeminence as an apocalyptic prophet.[96] Ultimately, the visions were incorporated into the Bible because they were associated with the narratives and included with them

---

93. Ginsberg held that the core of chapter 2 was written between the years 292 and 261 BCE, with two or three verses added between 246 and 220. Later he thought that the bulk of the chapter was written in the year 304. Bickerman argued that the story of the dream was written during the reign of Nebuchadnezzar, was revised during the period of the Diadochoi at the end of the fourth century BCE, and was given its final form, including the addition of two or three verses, in the period 246–242 BCE. See: Harold L. Ginsberg, *Studies in Daniel* (New York: The Jewish Theological Seminary of America, 1948), pp. 5–9 and 29; idem, "Daniel," *EMiqr* 2:691; Elias J. Bickerman, *Four Strange Books of the Bible* (New York: Schocken, 1967), pp. 63–70; Haran, *The Biblical Connection,* p. 117, n. 47.

94. Haran, *The Biblical Collection,* p. 118.

95. Ibid., p. 119.

96. Dan'el, written without a *yod,* is mentioned three times in Ezekiel (14:14 and 20, 28:33). These references do not elucidate his character to a degree consonant with his prominence in apocalyptic literature. The wise king and righteous judge Dan'el, the father of Aqhat in the Ugaritic epic, is remote from the figure of the biblical Daniel, and an association between the Gentile king and apocalyptic prophet seems far-fetched. The mentions of Daniel in Ezra 8:2, Neh. 10:7, and 1 Chron 3:1 add nothing to the figure of the apocalyptic visionary. See Haran, *The Biblical Collection,* p. 122; on the name Daniel, see André Lacocque, *The Book of Daniel,* trans. David Pellauer (Atlanta: John Knox Press, 1979), pp. 2–4.

as a single work.[97] It was difficult to question the authenticity of the stories because of their solid background in the Babylonian exile. Without them, the visions would have fared no differently than other apocalyptic writings. Their linkage with the historical narratives gave them the stamp of reliability and made possible their inclusion in the biblical canon.[98]

Scholars agree that the final redaction of the Book of Daniel dates from the period of the Antiochian persecution (167–164 BCE), at its height or after. This is when chapters 7 through 12 were assembled as a single unit and grafted onto the trunk of chapters 1–6. There is no similar consensus about the narratives, although all agree that they were composed earlier. Most scholars believe the stories were written at the beginning of the Hellenistic Age—more precisely, in the third century BCE. Others, however, assign them to an earlier date, in the Persian period.[99] The inclusion of Greek words, however, indicates that the stories were edited a number of times, at least until the Hellenistic Age. In contrast, the apocalyptic visions contain explicit allusions to Antiochus and his decrees: that "he will think of changing times and laws" (Dan. 7:25), that the perpetual daily sacrifice was suspended because of him (8:11–14, 23–26), and that an "appalling abomination" was erected in the Temple in Jerusalem (9:27). In addition, it is apparent that the political and military history of the Seleucid and Ptolemaic kingdoms in the preceding decades was well known to the author of the visions. All this indicates that they were composed after the start of Antiochus' persecution (167 BCE) but before the victory of the Maccabees and purification of the Temple in 164, an event of which the author of the visions was not aware.[100]

Resonances of the Joseph cycle can be found in both Esther and Daniel.

---

97. Some have held that the Book of Daniel was included in the biblical canon because it provides a basis for the belief in the resurrection of the dead (Daniel 12:2–3). This notion can be found in Emil Schürer, *The History of the Jewish People in the Age of Jesus Christ* (175 B.C.–A.D. 135), rev. and ed. by Geza Vermes, Fergus Millar, and Martin Goodman, 3 volumes (Edinburgh: T. & T. Clark, 1973–1987), 3:247. It seems, however, that the Jewish belief in resurrection took firm root because Daniel became part of the canon, and not the other way around. It should be remembered that belief in the resurrection of the dead antedated the Book of Daniel; for instance, in Hannah's thanksgiving psalm—"The Lord deals death and gives life, casts down into Sheol and raises up" (1 Sam. 2:6)—and the Ha'azinu ode—"I deal death and give life; I wounded and I will heal" (Deut. 32:39); see also Isa. 26:19, Ps. 30:4, et passim.

98. Haran, *The Biblical Collection,* pp. 123–124.

99. Kaufman, *Toledot,* vol. 4, pp. 406–420, 432; Collins, *Daniel,* p. 35; Eissfeldt, *Einleitung,* p. 708. Eissfeldt says that the material of these stories, but not the literary treatment, is rooted in the Persian period.

100. Haran, *The Biblical Collection,* pp. 109–110.

Indeed, some have maintained that the story in Daniel is a retelling of the story of Joseph.[101] In both stories the king has a dream, which leaves him perplexed and disturbed. The wise men are summoned, but are unable to interpret his dream. Then in both cases a Hebrew lad interprets it, with God's help—impressing the foreign king so much that he appoints him to a high position. It must be noted that the stories in the first part of Daniel are court legends and that courtiers who interpret dreams can be found in a number of Near Eastern legends, of which that of Joseph in Genesis is one.[102]

The similarities between the Joseph and Daniel stories are also conspicuous in their use of language.[103] Thus, the youths in Daniel 1:4 are "handsome"(טוֹבֵי מַרְאֶה), just as Joseph is "well built and handsome" (יְפֵה תוֹאַר וִיפֵה מַרְאֶה) (Gen. 39:6). After their ten-day dietary test, Daniel and his friends are described as looking "better and healthier" [מַרְאֵיהֶם טוֹב וּבְרִיאֵי בָּשָׂר] (Dan. 1:15) than the other youths, precisely the terms used to describe the cows in Pharaoh's dream (Gen. 41:2). Not only are the professional oneirocritics in both Genesis and Daniel referred to as "magicians" (חַרְטֻמִּים), but the term applied to the interpretation of the dream is identical—פִּשֶׁר / פִּתְרוֹן. The two kings' reactions to their dreams are also identical: they are "agitated," as expressed by forms of the root פ.ע.מ (Gen. 41:8, Dan. 2:1 and 3). Joseph is "a man in whom is the spirit of God" (Gen. 41:8) and Daniel "has the spirit of the holy gods in him" (Dan. 5:11 and 14). Both declare that an interpretation of a dream must come from God (Gen. 40:8 and 41:15; Dan. 2:28), and both receive golden chains around their necks (Gen. 41:42; Dan. 5:29). The verse in Daniel continues that they "proclaimed that he should rule as one of three in the kingdom," which echoes the proclamation before Joseph, "Abrek" (Gen. 41:43).

There are also many similarities between the Books of Esther and Daniel (especially chapters 1–6), most probably because the two books describe relatively contemporaneous periods.[104] These similarities allow us to understand unintelligible phrases in Esther that become clear from a reading of Daniel.[105]

---

101. Heaton, *The Book of Daniel,* p. 122; Samuel R. Driver, *The Book of Daniel,* The Cambridge Bible for Schools and Colleges (Cambridge: Cambridge University Press, 1900), p. 17.

102. The two stories belong to the court tale genre. See: Susan Niditch and Robert Doren, "The Success Story of the Wise Courtier: A Formal Approach," *JBL* 96 (1977), pp. 179–193; Collins, *Daniel,* p. 173; W. Lee Humphreys, "A Lifestyle for the Diaspora: A Study of the Tales of Esther and Daniel," *JBL* 92 (1973), pp. 211–223; Redford, *A Study,* pp. 94–97.

103. Hartman and Di Lella, *The Book of Daniel,* p. 57; Collins, *Daniel,* p. 39.

104. Hartman and Di Lella, *The Book of Daniel,* pp. 57–59; Collins, *Daniel,* p. 47; Humphreys, "A Lifestyle," pp. 211–223.

105. In Esther we read that "Mordecai sat in the palace gate" (Esth. 2:19 and 21). From

The king's rank and court life are described in detail in both books. The king is omnipotent and all matters of state depend on him. A royal edict sealed with the king's signet is valid in perpetuity and cannot be revoked (Esth. 1:19 and 8:8; Dan. 6:9–16). The king is flanked by counselors and asks their advice (Dan. 2:27 and Esth. 1:3). And both books devote attention to the drunken revels that were part of court life (Dan. 5:1–4 and Esth. 1:1–12).

In both kingdoms, handsome young people are brought to the royal court. In Persia, all the "beautiful young virgins" are assembled (Esth. 2:3), whereas the Babylonian court prefers "handsome boys" (Dan. 4:4). In both stories the young beauties are pampered for a long time (Esth. 2:12 and Dan. 1:5). Those responsible for their care show them favor (Esth. 2:9 and Dan. 1:9). In the end they are selected for high office (Esth. 2:17 and 10:3; Dan. 2:5).

In both stories, a Jew is ordered to prostrate himself and refuses (Dan. 3:10 and Esth. 3:2). The Jews' enemies who sought to destroy them are themselves punished: those who had Daniel's friends cast into the fiery furnace are incinerated by that same fire (3:22). Daniel's enemies are thrown into the lions' den (6:25), and Haman is impaled on the stake he had set up for Mordecai (Esther 7:10).

Much of Daniel is written in Aramaic, which complicates linguistic comparison with Esther, but it is evident that many names and phrases are common to them both. The titles of the leading bureaucrats and officials are the same, and the terms פרתמים and אחשדרפנים are found only in these two books.[106] The noun דת 'law, decree' occurs frequently in both, as do idioms appropriate to it such as "there is only one law / verdict" (Dan. 2:9 and Esth. 4:11), "may not be abrogated" (Dan. 6:9 and Esth. 1:19), and תקף (Dan. 12:17 and Esth. 9:29). Thus it seems that the authors or editors of Daniel were familiar with and influenced by the Book of Esther, even though Esther and Mordecai are not mentioned in Ecclesiasticus and no copy of Esther has been found at

---

Daniel we learn that the expression designates the incumbent of a high-ranking position, as we also know from external sources (cf. also Dan. 2:49). In Esther we read that "Mordecai would not kneel or bow low" (Esther 3:2); and this too is explained by Daniel. It is hard to understand why Mordecai would refuse to bow low before Haman, given that the patriarchs bowed before human beings as a sign of respect (Gen. 23:7 and 42:6), and Esther herself fell on her face before the king (Esth. 8:3). Evidently prostration before Haman involved idolatry. This is alluded to by the expression "kneel and bow low," which occurs three times in 3:3–5. In the Bible, the two acts of reverence together appear only in the context of idolatry. In order to refrain from idol worship, Mordecai was willing to endanger his own life and that of his people. From Daniel we learn that in the Babylo-Persian milieu there was a real danger of idol worship. Daniel and his friends refused to bow down and are punished for this (3:8), although in the end they are saved.

106. Except for one mention of אחשדרפנים in Ezra 8:36.

Qumran. Evidently the Book of Esther was not well known and certainly had not been included in the canon before the Maccabean period.[107]

Another influence on Daniel is Deutero-Isaiah with its Babylonian background.[108] One of the motifs in chapters 2 and 4 is the contrast between the helplessness of the Babylonian wise men and the power and wisdom of the God of Israel, who knows and directs world history. In Isaiah, the professional astrologers, Chaldeans, and wise men are unable to predict the future because their gods are devoid of power and wisdom.[109] Daniel 2:24–30 emphasizes that the Chaldeans cannot interpret the king's dream; nor can Daniel, until the Lord has provided him with the key. The royal counselors fail again with Nebuchadnezzar's second dream (4:4). Here too Daniel is summoned to interpret the dream after the wise men are unable to do so.[110]

The stories in the first half of Daniel reflect the beginning of Judaism's war against paganism. In chapter 2, Daniel proclaims to the king his faith in the God of Heaven, the God of the Jews, who alone rules the world and who had made known to the king the transient nature of human dominion. In response, the king falls on his face and proclaims that the God of the Jews is the true God—a motive that runs throughout the first six chapters of Daniel. When (in chapter 3) we read that Nebuchadnezzar erects a giant statue, commands all the nations to fall down and worship it, and decrees that anyone who violates the king's ordinance will be thrown into a fiery furnace, Hananiah, Mishael, and Azariah do not obey the decree and tell the king that they trust in their God to save them from the flames. The story concludes with the king's praise for the God of the Jews.

In chapter 4, Daniel interprets Nebuchadnezzar's dream to mean that he will turn into a beast and advises him what he should do. This story, too, ends with Nebuchadnezzar acknowledging the wondrous deeds and greatness of the Creator. In chapter 5, Daniel rebukes Belshazzar, who has not humbled

---

107. Collins, *Daniel,* p. 40.

108. John J. Collins, *The Apocalyptic Vision of the Book of Daniel* (Missoula, MT: Scholars Press, 1977), pp. 44–45; John J. Gammie, "On the Intention and Sources of Daniel I-VI," *VT* 31 (1981), pp. 287–291; P. von der Osten-Sacken, *Die Apokalyptik in ihrem Verhältnis zu Prophetie und Weisheit,* Theologische Existenz Heute 157 (Munich: Kaiser, 1969), pp. 18–27.

109. Isa. 44:8–20 and 25; 47:13.

110. The obvious question is why, after Nebuchadnezzar's experience with his earlier dream, he did not summon Daniel at once. Meir Leibush Malbim answered that Nebuchadnezzar thought that Daniel's special talent involved general dreams that relate to all humanity and focus on the end of days. Since his second dream of the tree was personal in nature, which do not fall into the Lord's purview, he did not expect that Daniel would be able to interpret it. Only when his wise men proved unable to do so did he summon Daniel as a last resort .

himself before the God of Heaven, has profaned with his revels the sacred vessels of His Temple, and has given divine honors to idols of wood and stone. Belshazzar submissively accepts Daniel's rebuke. In chapter 6, Darius orders all inhabitants of his kingdom to worship him exclusively for 30 days. Daniel, who ignores this writ and continues to pray to his God, is thrown into the lions' den. At the end, however, Darius enjoins all his subjects to honor the God of Daniel. The theme of all these stories is the Jewish struggle against paganism. The victory over idolatry may have been an idea, a legend. But in Judaism it was a belief based on real emotional need.[111]

God reigned in Heaven; but on earth there were Gentile rulers who did not know God and enslaved His people Israel. Although the pagan nations ruled over the earth, their gods were powerless, so their reigns would be ephemeral. The author of Daniel proclaims that the Lord will destroy the empires created by men and erect His own kingdom to endure forever over the entire world. It is the Lord who plans the course of all human history, who "changes times and seasons, removes kings and installs kings" (Dan. 2:21). God reveals the future to His elect and sometimes to the kings of the nations. Just as the Lord, through Joseph, informed Pharaoh of what was going to befall his kingdom—"God has told Pharaoh what He is about to do" (Gen. 41:25)—so the Lord informs Nebuchadnezzar in his first dream of events that will befall the human race in the future (Dan. 2:28), and in his second dream, what will happen to the king himself (chapter 4). Why did the Lord grant these prophetic dreams to the wicked king who destroyed His Temple and exiled His people from their land? According to Don Isaac Abravanel, "It was part of the Lord's wisdom to reveal all this to Nebuchadnezzar, the destroyer of Jerusalem, to make known to him that neither by might nor by power does he accomplish this, but by the sentence of the Watchers and the verdict of the Holy Ones, and that he, too, will perish, as will all the kingdoms that come after him and persecute Israel—'all who devour [them] shall be held guilty; disaster shall befall them'" [Jer. 2:3].

Chapter 4 expands the idea first presented in 2:21, that the Lord "removes kings and installs kings." The core of the story is the downfall of Nebuchadnezzar, who until that moment had felt himself to be exalted above all. Brought low like a beast, here he expresses his awe of God and recognizes the greatness of the Lord. This miraculous transformation adds a legendary dimension to the narrative cycle of chapters 1 through 6. It rests on the biblical concept that "the Lord makes poor and makes rich; He casts down, He also lifts high" (1 Sam, 2:7); that "God it is who gives judgment; He brings

---

111. Kaufman, *Toledot,* vol. 4, p. 433.

down one man, He lifts up another" (Ps. 75:8). After all, the royal constitution in the Book of Deuteronomy is instituted so that the monarch "will not act haughtily toward his fellows" (Deut. 17:20). As Nebuchadnezzar writes at the end of his epistle, "The King of Heaven ... is able to humble those who behave arrogantly" (Daniel 4:34). The narrative also reflects the utterances of the prophets of Israel condemning the Gentiles for their pride in ephemeral glory. Isaiah proclaimed of the king of Babylonia, "How are you fallen from heaven, O Shining One, son of Dawn! ... Once you thought in your heart, 'I will climb to the sky; ... I will match the Most High.' Instead, you are brought down to Sheol, to the bottom of the Pit" (Isa. 14:12–15).[112] Ezekiel condemns Pharaoh "because you towered high in stature, and thrust [your] top up among the leafy trees, and [were] arrogant in [your] height" (Ezek. 31:10). Similarly, the Lord denounces the king of Tyre: "O mortal, say to the prince of Tyre: Thus said the Lord God: 'Because you have been so haughty and have said, "I am a god; I sit enthroned like a god in the heart of the seas," whereas you are not a god but a man, though you deemed your mind equal to a god's'" (Ezek. 28:2).

Living in exile, far from their homeland and enslaved by pagan peoples, Jews fantasized and embellished the notion of God's kingdom. Such longings no doubt spawned descriptions and visions of God of the sort found in Ezekiel and Zechariah. Similarly, in Daniel 2, the statue symbolizes the human kingdoms, whose dominion is ephemeral, while the stone represents the fifth monarchy, the kingdom of Heaven and Israel that will endure forever. The stone is quarried out of the mountainside without the intervention of human hands. Its antithesis is the statue erected by human beings. The Gentile kingdoms will vanish from the world; but the Kingdom of Heaven and Israel will endure eternally.

In sum, despite the power of the idolatrous kingdom and the Jews' subjection to it, the stories in Daniel constitute an absolute rejection of paganism. It is the God of Israel who guides world history and decrees who shall dominate the earth. Kaufman believes that the major theme in these stories is religion triumphant, not religion being persecuted The absolute superiority of the God of Israel is not eschatological but realistic, firmly anchored in the present.[113] Daniel and his friends express their scorn for idols. Paganism is

---

112. Rabbinic sources point to the association between Daniel 4 and Isaiah 14, in which the Babylonian king is scornfully referred to as the "shining one, son of dawn." See *Mekhilta d'Rabbi Yishmael,* Tractate Shirta, section 6; D. Satran, "Early Jewish and Christian Interpretations of the Fourth Chapter of the Book of Daniel," Ph.D. dissertation, Hebrew University of Jerusalem, 1985, pp. 102–103.

113. Kaufman, *Toledot,* 4:437.

routed. Its kings bow down before the Eternal God and recognize that their own kingdom is provisional and fleeting.

In all the biblical stories the Lord is the source of dreams and the pilot of human action. Jacob's dream at Bethel severs Canaanite associations with the place and establishes that its sanctity derives from the Lord's appearance there to Jacob. The stories of Joseph manifest that all human action is directed by God and that what has already been dreamed will indeed take place. In addition, the narrative echoes with determinism, recounting the Israelites' descent to Egypt, which was part of the plan foreordained by Heaven. Solomon's dream at Gibeon provides divine legitimacy for his reign. Finally, the stories in the Book of Daniel were written to show that the rule of human kings is temporary and evanescent, whereas the kingdom of God is everlasting.

7

Conclusions

We have seen that in much of biblical literature, dreams serve as a medium of communication between human beings and God. In referring to the future, they depict events of major significance for the dreamer, sometimes including divine promises and encouragement, other times warnings about actions to be avoided.

There are two types of those communicative dreams in the Bible—prophetic and symbolic. Prophetic dreams contain an annunciation, injunction, or warning, spoken to the dreamer in clear and intelligible terms by God Himself, who addresses a human being directly. Symbolic dreams, in contrast, rely on tokens with an esoteric or hidden meaning. God Himself is not present, and His message can be understood only with the assistance of a qualified dream interpreter.

Our survey of prophetic dreams in the Bible shows that they comply with the three-part model originally identified by Oppenheim in dreams of the ancient Near East. In part one of that model, the *setting*, descriptions such as "He came," "He appeared," "I make myself known," "And the Lord was standing beside him and He said," emphasize that God is the source of dreams. Sometimes God even addresses the dreamer by name. The dreamer, in contrast, is quite passive.

In the second part, the *message*, an annunciation, injunction, or warning tells the dreamer how he should act. In the Jacob cycle, God gives the patriarch instructions every time he sets out on a journey and promises to escort, defend, and guide him until he returns home. Similarly, the Lord appears to Solomon at the beginning of his reign and endows him with the charismatic qualities required of a king, such as "a wise and discerning mind." And God appears to both Abimelech and Laban to warn them not to harm His favorites.

The third part of Oppenheim's model presents the *response* of the dreamer or hearer. Abimelech restores Sarah to Abraham, compensates him in the form of livestock and slaves, and gives Sarah a thousand pieces of silver to make amends for his damage to her good name. Similarly, Laban heeds

God's warning not to harm Jacob. Other dreamers, however, are left in a state of psychological arousal. Jacob, for example, "awoke from his sleep and said, 'Surely the Lord is present in this place, and I did not know it!' Shaken, he said, 'How awesome is this place.'" The stone Jacob anoints bears witness to the fact of the dream and God's promises, and his vow is a reaction to its verbal content. In the same vein, Solomon's feast and rites, in the wake of his dream at Gibeon and God's promise to support his kingship, are an expression of gratitude for the promises made in the dream.

At first glance symbolic dreams seem to be autonomous creations of the dreamers, meant to satisfy needs and desires that are not met in waking life. This is how Joseph's brothers view their brother, "that dreamer" (Gen. 37:19): "Do you mean to reign over us? Do you mean to rule over us?" (Gen. 37:8). They consider his dreams to be juvenile fantasies. But the Bible sees matters differently, emphasizing that it is God who is the source of symbolic dreams and provider of their interpretation. Hence the dreams of Pharaoh and Nebuchadnezzar come from the Lord (Gen. 41:25, 28: Dan. 2:28, 45; 4:21); so do the symbolic dreams of Joseph, which ultimately come to pass (Gen. 37:1-11; cf. 42:9). When Joseph interprets the dreams of the imprisoned courtiers and later of Pharaoh he declares that it is God who makes their meaning known to him (Gen. 40:8; 41:16, 38-39). Daniel, too, interprets dreams thanks to his prophetic gift. God informs him of Nebuchadnezzar's first dream and its meaning in a vision (Dan. 2:17ff.); it is by means of the divine spirit that he is able to interpret Nebuchadnezzar's second dream (ibid. 4:5, 6, 15) as well.

We have also seen that the biblical milieu does not include professional oneirocritics or refer to a literature of dream interpretation. There are only two Hebrew oneirocritics in the Bible—Joseph and Daniel. Both, interestingly enough, are active in royal courts—one in Egypt, a land renowned for its sorcerers, and the other in Babylonia, the home of the Chaldean astrologers. The two Hebrews' appearance in royal courts and their success in interpreting the rulers' dreams constitute a polemic against those foreign oneirocritics, while their success attests to the superiority of the God of Israel. At the same time it must be emphasized that the Bible states explicitly that the interpretation of dreams is strictly the province of God, who vouchsafes interpretations to Joseph and Daniel.

In Mesopotamia and Egypt, in contrast, there were professional dream interpreters who, applying a special mantic sense or various signs and omens, attempted to lay bare the significance of dreams. These experts tried to correlate the overt action of a dream with its underlying meaning. Another method they employed was an appeal, through prayer and magical rites, to the deity who sent the dream to interpret it for them. Still another method relied on dream books, which anthologized dreams from the past alongside their interpretations.

Whereas there are no professional oneirocritics in the Bible, in the Talmudic era, as we have seen, there was a guild of them in Jerusalem with dozens of members who interpreted dreams on the basis of their associative links with biblical verses and popular sayings. The dream interpreter had to be an expert in sounds, connotations, and wordplay, and the Talmud even incorporates a short dream book for guidance. It should be emphasized, however, that there is no Talmudic consensus about the legitimacy of dreams as communication from God. A skeptical attitude coexists with one that takes such divine "messages" very seriously.

The prophetic literature, too, expresses ambivalence about the source of dreams. The prophets describe their visions, never their dreams, and when dreams are considered, one school totally rejects them as deceitful. The most prominent advocate of this position is Jeremiah, who comes out forcefully against the false prophets who lead the people astray. Here Jeremiah reflects the Deuteronomic evaluation of the dreamer as a prophet who incites the people to idolatry (Deut. 13:2-6). Zechariah, too, considers dreams to be the imaginary creations of false prophets and not messages from God. We must not, however, assert that they totally rejected the dream medium, given that the Lord explicitly tells Aaron and Miriam that He appears to his prophets in dreams: "I make Myself known to him in a vision, I speak with him in a dream" (Num. 12:6). But there does seem to be absolute rejection of dreams in a number of passages (Isa. 29:7-8, Ps. 73:20, Job 20:8; Eccles. 5:2), which maintain that dreams are vain and meaningless attempts to satisfy dreamers' desires not filled in waking.

More favorable attitudes can be found in Joel and Job. Joel, referring to the messianic era when the Lord will pour out His spirit on all flesh, describes how the old men will dream dreams (Joel 3:1). And though Job says that the Lord frightened and afflicted him in dreams, the crucial point is that the dreams do serve as an authentic medium of communication between man and God (Job 7:13-14 and 33:14-16).

As we have seen, most biblical dreams are found in Genesis and in Kings chapter 3; from there until Daniel, biblical authors describe only visions. Thus in addition to חֲלוֹם the Bible employs terms such as מַחֲזֶה and מַרְאָה, both usually rendered as "vision" and referring to the same phenomenon. Biblical authors do not seem to have made a meticulous distinction among these terms, because the experiences have much in common. God appears in all of them and delivers a message, and whether the epiphany takes place when the recipient is awake or asleep is not always clear.

Our study of the use of the מַחֲזֶה indicates that revelations using this term have two parts: in one the recipient is awake; in the other, asleep. When the Lord appears to Abram in a vision (Gen. 15:1), He confides to him both a personal and a national message. In the first part of this scene, during which Abram is awake, the Lord identifies Himself. This introductory formula is found in other dreams in Genesis (28:13 and 31:13). The dialogue between Abram and the Lord resembles that in Abimelech's dream: a divine statement (v. 1-b), Abram's reply to Him in a question that is a complaint (vv. 2-3), and God's response, which explains His position (vv. 4-5). This is followed by a description of the rites performed by Abram. In the second half of the scene Abram is asleep, as indicated by the word תַּרְדֵּמָה 'sleep', which parallels the dream in Job 33.

Another epiphany in a vision is the Lord's appearance to Balaam; this revelation also has two parts, sleeping and waking–"Prostrate, but with eyes unveiled" (Num. 24:4). The message conveyed to Balaam refers to the Israelites. It is interesting that Balaam's epiphany, like Abram's, is preceded by ritual actions.

As for the word מַרְאָה, the Lord's appearance to Jacob in a vision by night (Genesis 46) seems to be identical in form, structure, and language to the descriptions of dreams in the Bible. What is more, the description indicates that we are dealing with an incubation dream. This divine revelation continues the series of epiphanies experienced by Jacob each time he sets out on a journey, revelations in which God appears and encourages him. The word מַרְאָה is also used when God makes himself known to Samuel. Although we tend to accept the conjecture that he was awake, the element and language employed could very well refer to a dream. The description of Samuel lying in bed at the sanctuary at Shiloh when the Lord appears to him is identical to biblical and extrabiblical descriptions of epiphanies. The future-oriented message warns of the grim fate awaiting the House of Eli. The language that depicts Samuel's fearful reaction to the message is similar to what we find with respect to the members of Abimelech's court when they hear his dream (Gen. 20:8) and with respect to Jacob after the Lord appears to him in Bethel (Gen. 28:17).

In our final chapter we examined the literary functions of dreams in the Bible. What are these stories meant to teach and why are they included in the Scriptures? We found that Jacob's dream at Bethel serves to explain the sanctity of the place and detach it from its Canaanite context. The biblical author ignores all earlier consecration and attributes the holiness of the site exclusively to God's appearance there to Jacob. The dreams in the Joseph stories are an integral and inseparable part of the Joseph cycle and serve two different purposes. First, they lead to the descent to Egypt and eventual ascent to the Promised Land of the bones of Joseph and his brothers. Second, the dreams show how divine Providence steers human actions according to a foreordained plan. The actions of Joseph and his brothers and subsequent events in Egypt are determined not by human free will, but by concealed divine guidance.

We also conjectured that Solomon's dream at Gibeon is an ancient story intended to legitimize Solomon's rule. Solomon was not chosen by the people and there was no contract between him and them, as had been concluded by David and the northern tribes at Hebron. Solomon was selected by his father David, thereby inaugurating the idea of hereditary monarchy in Israel. Nevertheless, this king by right of birth still required divine confirmation and recognition by the people. Hence this story of the dream—in which the Lord endows Solomon's kingship with full legitimacy and gives it divine sanction—was written during Solomon's own lifetime by the court scholars and scribes in order to justify his assumption of power.

Nebuchadnezzar's dreams also reinforce the idea that the Lord guides universal history. It is the Lord who "changes times and seasons, removes kings and installs kings" (Dan. 2:21). In Nebuchadnezzar's first dream the Lord informs him of coming events that will affect all humanity (Dan. 2:28); in his second dream, details of his individual future (chapter 4). In the first dream, the idol symbolizes ephemeral human monarchies—Gentile kingdoms that will vanish from the earth—while the stone represents the fifth monarchy, which is the kingdom of heaven in Israel that will endure forever.

The second dream expands on the idea found in chapter 2 (v. 21), where we read that the Lord "removes kings and installs kings." Its core is the story of the abasement of Nebuchadnezzar, who, having considered himself above everyone and everything, is reduced to the level of a beast. The central theme of this story is the biblical view that "the Lord makes poor and makes rich; He casts down, He also lifts high" (1 Sam. 2:7). As Nebuchadnezzar says at the end of his letter, "The King of Heaven ... is able to humble those who behave arrogantly" (Dan. 4:34). Thus the dream sequences in Daniel also serve to express awe and wonder and praise the greatness of the Lord.

Appendix

The Incubation Dream

In chapter 1 we examined cases in which the deity causes the human being to have a dream or "brings" the dream to the dreamer. But there is also a type of dream that seems to be "invited" by the dreamer, who attempts to impose his will on God. In this variation, the dreamer goes to a particular spot considered to be sacred, offers sacrifices to God, and falls asleep in the holy place, hoping he will be visited by Him in a dream. The content of the dream is supposed to provide advice and guidance: for example, how to cure a serious illness or end a woman's barrenness. Sometimes a long period must pass before the dream comes. And while waiting the person prays, fasts, or engages in some complex ritual activity such as bathing and anointing with oil. A dream of this type is called an *incubation.*

Hebrew Bible

In the Bible, this category includes the dream of Solomon at Gibeon (1 Kings 3:4). According to the text, Solomon went to Gibeon because that was the site of the great high place.[1] He offered a thousand animals on the altar there, and the Lord appeared to him in a dream. The sacrificial offerings seem to reflect the emotional need of human beings to honor their God and placate Him as a condition for receiving His bounty. Similarly, sleeping in sacred precincts is a way of drawing closer to God. Indeed, such places have been consecrated because that is where gods have appeared to mortals. People accordingly went back there, believing that if the Lord appeared there once He would do so again. We should also remember that it is only reasonable to expect that the gods would appear in the temples built especially for them.

---

1 The parallel story in 2 Chronicles 1:3–5 adds that Gibeon was also the site of the Tent of Meeting that Moses had built in the wilderness and of the bronze altar made by Bezalel. The inclusion of these details is meant to emphasize the religious importance of Gibeon. It may also be intended to draw a connection between Moses and Solomon. In other words, it follows that the tradition that began in the days of Moses continued in the time of Solomon.

God's appearance to Solomon at Gibeon unquestionably fits our definition. Several other biblical passages, however, have been alleged to be incubation dreams but are less likely to be so.[2] One of these occurred at Bethel, where Jacob went to sleep in a sacred place and the Lord appeared to him in a prophetic dream.[3] Jacob, however, arrived in Bethel purely by chance. He did not know that the place was holy: "Surely the Lord is present in this place, and I did not know it!" (Gen. 28:16). In fact, the place became sacred only after Jacob's dream.[4]

Some also suggest that the story of the angel's appearance to Hagar (Gen. 21:16-19) fits this genre.[5] Hagar's weeping and the angel's initial question, "What troubles you, Hagar?" (v. 17), are paralleled in descriptions of incubation dreams. Similarly, the angel's statement to Hagar, "Fear not," is found in the description of other dreams in the Bible. Finally, "then God opened her eyes" (v. 19) may indicate that Hagar had been asleep. At the same time, it should be noted that this expression is not used to describe waking from a dream in any other biblical passage, and seems rather to indicate that God gave her the ability to comprehend what she had not seen previously. Evidently Hagar had not seen the well because of her exhaustion; or perhaps God made it break through the ground miraculously.[6]

Another incubation attempt might be found in 1 Sam. 28:6: "And Saul inquired of the Lord but the Lord did not answer him, either by dreams or by Urim or by prophets" (1 Sam. 28:6). In his distress, Saul seeks help from the Lord. Some scholars believe that he performed the ritual actions associated with incubation but to no avail.

In the Balaam pericope we are told that the servants of Balak attempted to persuade Balaam to come and curse the Israelites. In response, Balaam says, "So you, too, stay here overnight, and let me find out what else the Lord may

---

2 Anton Jirku, "Ein Fall von Inkubation im AT (Ex. 38:8)," *ZAW* 33 (1913), pp. 151–153.

3 According to Kutscher, Jacob made preparations to receive the word of the Lord in a dream. He points to the association with the Mesopotamian dream-god Zaqar, the meaning of whose name is unclear, though some trace it to 'tower' or 'pillar'. In order to summon a dream, Jacob sets a stone by his head—a stone that is chosen deliberately because it has the shape of a pillar. According to Kutscher, this biblical episode describes an incubation in a fashion not found in Mesopotamian sources, which do cast light on the background of Jacob's action. See Raphael Kutscher, "The Mesopotamian God Zaqar and Jacob Massebah." *BeerSheva* 3 (1988), pp. 125–130 (Hebrew).

4 For the rejection of the idea that Jacob's dream is an incubation dream, see: Oppenheim, *Interpretation*, p. 187; Gnuse, *Dream*, p. 68, n. 43.

5 Gnuse, *Dream*, p. 66.

6 J. Skinner, *A Critical and Exegetical Commentary on Genesis*, p.324.

say to me" (Num. 22:19). In the very next verse we read that the Lord did appear to Balaam that night. Thus the text may indeed be alluding to an incubation dream.

In Daniel 2:17-18, King Nebuchadnezzar has a dream but cannot remember its content. He summons all the magicians, sorcerers, astrologers, and Chaldeans, demanding that they tell him his dream and its meaning, but none can do so. In his rage, the king orders that all the wise men of Babylonia be killed. While the massacre is in progress, Daniel asks the king for a short extension so that he can interpret the dream. In Midrash Tanhuma (*Miqqeṣ* 2), the aggadist adds the dialogue between Nebuchadnezzar and Daniel: "He said to him, 'Are you Daniel?' 'Yes,' he replied." The midrash asks, "Didn't he know him?" before proceeding to explain the sense of the king's question:

"Do you have the power to tell me my dream and its meaning?"
"Yes," he said to him.
He said to him: "When?"
He said to him: "I do not ask you for time, neither 30 days nor 20 days.
Only wait for me tonight and in the morning I will tell you."

Afterwards Daniel goes to Hananiah, Mishael, and Azariah, his friends, and asks them to entreat the God of Heavens for mercy—although the Bible does not report the words of their prayer. In verse 19, we are told that the Lord appeared to Daniel in a nocturnal vision. Was it only the prayers that moved the Lord to appear to Daniel or were there other ritual actions that are not mentioned in the text?

Some scholars believe that sections of certain Psalms—notably 3:6, 4:9, and 17:15—allude to incubation in the Temple.[7] However, Johannes Lindblom doubts whether these descriptions are realistic, in view of their figurative language and paucity of detail. An exception, in his opinion, is Psalm 3, which he does consider to represent an incubation dream.[8]

None of the examples cited thus far, however, mention sacrifices or sleeping in the sacred precinct. In sum, there are very few biblical dreams that completely fit our definition of incubation. This is probably no happenstance—biblical authors were probably strongly motivated to minimize the phenomenon. As we have seen, the thrust of scriptural dream literature is that the Lord guides universal history according to His preordained

---

7 These views are summarized by Johannes Lindblom, "Theophanies in Holy Places in Hebrew Religion," *HUCA* 32 (1961), p. 105, n. 23.

8 Ibid., 104.

plan.[9] In that view, the Almighty does not need the prompting of humans to decide when to appear in a dream.

Mesopotamia

In extrabiblical sources, incubation is a widespread phenomenon. The dreamers are usually kings and priests and their dreams are preceded by prayer and sacrifices. In an Akkadian poem we find an address to the goddess Mamu: "Reveal thyself unto me and let me see a favorable dream. May the dream that I dream be favorable, may the dream that I dream be true, may Mamu, the goddess of dreams, stand at my head; let me enter E-Sagila, the temple of the gods, the house of life."[10]

The incubation phenomenon also makes an appearance in the saga of Gilgamesh. This applies especially to Tablet IV, where we find the following description:

82 (It was) a march of one month and fifteen days, (but) they arrived at the mountain of Lebanon on the third day.
83 They dug out a pit before Shamash. 84 They placed (...)]...[to? (.)
85 Gilgamesh went up to the top] of the mountain?. 86 [He presented his offering of cheapscented flour to (....)].
87 (He said):
"[O Mountain], bring me a dream! Let me see [a message (of good luck?)!]"
88 (Meanwhile) [Enkidu] made a house? of Zaqiqu' for him, for [Gilgamesh)].
89 [He fastened] a door (against) the storm in its doorway. 90 [He] made him (Gilgamesh) lie down (in it), and (he surrounded the site) [by a circle (....)] diagram. 91[He] himself?, like the corn of the mountain [(....)., and he laid] down at its doorway.
92 Gilgamesh leant his chin on his knees. 93 Sleep, (which) is poured out over mankind, fell upon him. 94 (However), [during] the middle watch (of the night) he woke up (*lit.*, he ended his sleep). 95 [He] arose, speaking to his friend (Enkidu):
96 "My friend, (if) you did not call to me, why am I awake? 97 (if) you did not touch me why am I bewildered? 98 (if) a god did not pass by,

---

9 Some believe that incubation underlies the Covenant between the Pieces in Genesis 15, God's appearance to Jacob in Genesis 46:1–4, and the Lord's appearance to the prophet Samuel (1 Sam. 3:1–18). These texts are considered in detail in chapter 5.

10 H. F. Lutz, "An Omen Text Referring to the Action of a Dreamer," *AJSL* 35 (1918–19), p. 146; Gnuse, *Dream*, p. 34; Ehrlich, *Traum*, p. 52.

why is my flesh numbed? 99 My friend, I have seen a third dream, 100 and the dream which I saw was totally bewildering.[11]

In this description, Enkidu is building a *bīt zaqīqi*. Evidently this refers to "the house of *zaqīqu*," a structure used for incubation purposes--in other words, "a temple of the Dream God Zaqiqu."[12]

We also encounter incubation in the story of Atrahasīs:

59 And he himself, the man Atrahasis, 60 complains in tears daily. 61 He carries *maššakku* (to) a river meadow. 62 When the *miṭirtu* canal was still, 63 he divided the night, and he performed a sacrifice. 64 (As) sleep came... 65 He addresses the *miṭirtu*-canal, 66 "May the *miṭirtu*-canal take (it)! May the river carry (it)! 67 May the gift be delivered before Ea, my lord! 68 May Ea see (it), and may he heed me 69 so that I myself may see a dream during the night!" 70 After he commissioned the *miṭirtu*-canal, 71 he sat down facing the river, (and) he cries? 72 Facing the river, the man. (.) .. 73 (Meanwhile,) his favour descends to the Apsu. 74 Ea heard his call."[13]

Ea's reply takes the form of two messengers dispatched to Atrahasis—Iahmus and his vizier, Ushmu. We must stress that the text does not state explicitly that the messengers appeared in a dream, although this seems to be the most plausible reading.[14] As for the rites mentioned in the text, scholars including F. N. H. Al-Rawi and A. R. George believe that Atrahasis poured the *maššakku*-powder on the water both as an offering and as a means of divination. It should be emphasized that we have a number of texts in which *muššakku* (*maššakku*) appear together with the *šā'ilu,* the dream interpreter mentioned in chapter 3.

Oppenheim believed that the dream of Nabonidus, too, belongs to the category of incubation dreams.[15] According to the text, Nabonidus, after seeing Nebuchadnezzar II in his dream, requested an additional message from the gods.

1-5 I placed a very large offering (before) Venus, Saturn, [....], Arcturus, the *ŠÀM*-star (and) Jupiter, (who) dwell in heavens. 6-10 I

---

11 Sally Butler, *Mesopotamian Conceptions of Dreams and Dream Rituals* (Munster: Ugarit-Verlag, 1998), pp. 224–225.

12 Ibid., pp. 225–227.

13 Ibid., pp. 228–229.

14 Ibid., p. 229.

15 Oppenheim, *Interpretation,* p. 205.

inquired of them in front of Marduk, my lord, regarding (my) long life (*lit.*, life of distant days), established rule, lasting reign, (and) my very favourable matters. 11 I lie down, and during the night 12-15 I saw Nintinugga (i.e., Gula), my lady, the one who heals the dying, the river of long life.

Butler, unlike Oppenheim, believes that the text is part of Nabonidus' consultation of various astral beings.[16] She also stresses the fact that we do not know the nature of the appearance by Gula. What is more, the text does not indicate whether this is a dream and whether any message was received. In her opinion, we are to understand Gula's appearance as a response to the king's request for long life and a secure reign.[17]

In 1986 a library was discovered at the temple of Sippar. It contained another exemple of the Weidner Chronicle,[18] a letter from the king of Isin to the ruler of Babylon, evidently from Damiq-ilishu (1816-1794 BCE) to Apil-Sin (1830-1813 BCE) or Rim Sin I (1822-1763 BCE) at Larsa.[19]

10 I performed a sacrifice to Ninkarrak (i.e., Gula), my lady, the mistress of Egalmah (the temple of Ninisina (again Gula) in Isin).
11 I prayed to her. I besought her with supplications, and I [told] her the matters <which?> my heart constantly strives after. Indeed, I myself (spoke) <thus>: (lines 12-13). Holy Gula, the exalted lady, stood by me during the night. [She heard] my words, and spoke with me truthfully (lines 15-32)
33 Apart from the oracular decision which was pronounced in my dream.[20]

This episode is considered to be an incubation because it includes a request to the goddess who subsequently appears in a dream. On the other hand, F. N. H. Al-Rawi saw it as a "nocturnal vision." In his opinion, the offering of sacrifices and prayers are a standard way of approaching the deity and do not necessarily indicate an incubation.[21]

---

16 Butler, *Mesopotamian Conceptions,* p. 233.

17 Ibid., pp. 233–234.

18 Ibid., pp. 234. 234–235.

19 A. K. Grayson, *Assyrian and Babylonian Chronicles* (Locust Valley, New York: J. J. Augustin, 1975), pp. 145–151.

20 Butler, *Mesopotamian Conceptions,* p. 234.

21 F. N. H. Al-Rawi, "Tablets from the Sippar Library: I. The 'Weidner Chronicle': A Supposititious Royal Letter Concerning a Vision." *Iraq* 52 (1990): 1.

Hittite

In times of distress, kings would have recourse to incubation to obtain advice or assistance from the deity. In the Hittite version of the legend of Naram-Sin, we read that "Naram-Sin purified himself, undertook incubation of his bed, cried to the gods, and began to complain to his gods."[22] Here weeping is an integral part of the process of incubation: a human being cries to the deity, entreating him to appear. We also find crying associated with incubation in the dream of Ashurbanipal, who feared an invasion by the Elamites.[23] The king went to the temple of the goddess Ishtar, where he cried and prayed while prostrating himself before her statue.

The Hittite ruler Mursilis I refers to incubation in his Plague Prayers, where he asks the Hittite storm god to inform him whether he should fast in order to stop the plague. The reference may be to a dream for himself, for the priests who slept on a purified bed, or for any person.[24] Incubation is recommended against impotence. Here we have ritual actions performed by the dreamer, in addition to the spells that were part of the rite to obtain a dream.[25] It seems that not only did the god send dreams, but also slept alongside the dreamer:

(5) During the three days on which he is entreating the deity he tells all the dreams which he has, whether the deity appears to him and whether the deity (10) sleeps with him.[26]

Ugarit

Possible incubation also appears in Ugaritic literature, in the saga of Keret. The saga recounts the adventures of King Keret, in one of which the king closes himself up in his room and cries bitterly to the deity for a son. After that, he falls asleep; in his dream the god appears and tells him how to proceed. The seclusion and weeping described here remind us of the incubation process.

In the epic of Aqhat, the allusion to incubation is much clearer. The tale begins with the introduction of Dan'el, who in distress appeals to the gods and entreats them for a son. After Dan'el lavishes food and drink on them for seven days, Baal appears and successfully urges El to grant Dan'el's request—which he does.

---

22 Gnuse, *Dream,* p. 35; H. G. Guterbock, "Die historische Tradition and literarische Gestaltung bei Babylonien und Hethitern bis 1200," *ZAW* 94 (1938), pp. 56–57.

23 Oppenheim, *Interpretation,* p. 201.

24 "Hittite Prayers," trans. Albrecht Goetze, *ANET*, pp.394–396.

25 "Hittite Rituals, Incantations, and Descriptions of Festivals," op. cit., pp. 349–350.

26 Ibid., p. 350.

The text, as stated, mentions a number of ritual actions, such as offerings and lustrations. In the former context, the text specifies *uzr*, which is evidently the food of the gods and includes both solid food and drink.[27] Dan'el enters the sleeping chamber where he leaves his garments. He sprinkles a certain liquid on the garments, evidently in order to purify them. He also sprinkles the liquid in the room where he spent the night. Evidently this fluid is part of the *uzr* sacrifice. He repeats these ritual actions for seven days. On the seventh day the author adds the notation that prayer, too, accompanied the rituals.

Egypt

Crying as part of incubation is also found in the dream of Sethos in the temple of Hephaistos.[28] The king cries to his god in his sleep. The deity appears to him in a dream and promises him victory:

> The monarch ... entered into the inner sanctuary, and before the image of the god bewailed the fate that impended over him. As he wept, he fell asleep, and dreamed that the god came and stood at his side, bidding him be of good cheer, and go boldly forth to meet the Arabian host, which would do him no hurt, as he himself would send those who should help him.

In Egypt, incubation was associated with the diagnosis of diseases and discovery of remedies for them. One of the famous centers of incubation was the well-known temple in the city of Memphis. In the story of Satni we read about Mahituaskhit, who goes to the temple of Imuthes in Memphis to pray to the god. Afterwards she falls asleep in the temple; the god appears to her in a dream and gives her a recipe to cure her barrenness:

> (1,1–[One night] she dreamed that one spoke to her, [saying: "Are you

27 Julian Oberman, "How Daniel was Blessed with a Son," *JAOS* 20 (1946), p. 9, believes that the word *uzr* is related to the Hebrew נזר; consequently he renders it as "consecration, votive offering." It may be that this term referred specifically to an incubation in which the dreamer temporarily isolated himself from his family. In Hebrew and Aramaic, the sense of the word נזר is "separation, isolation." Oberman believes that the word refers to separation or seclusion for ritual tasks that lead to consecration. G. R. Driver, *Canaanite Myths and Legends,* p. II; 10, translates *uzr* as "nectar." Ginsberg ("Oblation," *ANET* 149), renders it as "oblation." The true meaning may well be "holocaust" and "full libation," as found in the stories of Gideon and Manoah and the angel (Judg. 6:21 and 13:20), as well as with Elijah and the prophets of Baal (1Kings 18:38), when both the sacrificial animal and the libation are totally consumed by fire.

28 Herodotus 2:114; Gnuse, *Dream,* p. 29; George Foucart, "Dreams and Sleep; Egyptian," in *Encyclopedia of Religion and Ethics,* pp. 34–35.

Mehuusekhe] [the wife] of Setne, who is lying [[here in the temple]] so as to receive healing?–[When tomorrow has come] go to [the place where your husband] [bathed]. You will find melon vines grow there. [[Break off a branch]] with its grounds and grind it. [Make it into a remedy, put it [in water and drink it.]–You will receive the fluid of conception] from the [night.][29]

In addition to incubation, there were evidently Egyptian magicians who could summon dreams by drawing magic pictures and repeating thaumaturgic names:

> Take a clean linen bag and write upon it the names given below. Fold it up and make it into a lamp-wick, and set it alight, pouring oil over it. The words to be written are: "Armiuth, Lailamchouch, Arsenophrephren, Phtha, Archentechtha." Then in the evening, when you are going to bed, which you must do without touching food, do thus: Approach the lamp and repeat seven times the formula given below, then extinguish it and lie down to sleep. [The long formula is omitted here. The passage concludes;] I require, O lords of the gods, give me the information that I desire.[30]

Greece

Our knowledge of incubation sanctuaries in Greece goes back to the fifth century BCE. The institution spread gradually, until sources for the second century CE report that there were more than 400 incubation centers in temples in Greece and throughout the Roman Empire. These temples were dedicated to various gods, some of them Egyptian and others Greek. As in Egypt, the main use of incubation was to find cures for disease; consequently many of the temples were dedicated to Asklepios.[31] Homer recounts his bravery and skill in medicine, which he learned from the Centaur Cheiron. The temples dedicated to Asklepios became the best-known incubation sanctuaries. Especially prominent was the temple in the city of

---

29 Miriam Lichtheim, *Ancient Egyptian Literature* (Berkeley: University of California Press, 1980), vol. 3, p. 138; Serge Sauneron et al., "Dans l'Egypte ancienne," in *Les Songes et leur interprétation,* p. 41.

30 Wallis Budge, *Egyptian Magic* (Evanston and New York: University Books, 1899), pp. 216–217; Papyrus 122 in the British Museum, 1.359ff.

31 Carl Alfred Meier, "The Dream in Ancient Greece and its Use in Temple Cures," in *The Dream and Human Societies,* ed. G. E. von Grunebaum and Roger Caillois (Berkeley and Los Angeles: University of California Press, 1966), pp. 303–319.

Epidaurus, Asklepios's birthplace. Sufferers would sleep in the temple and then regain their health, thanks to the dreams they had in the temple.[32]

Inscriptions have been discovered on the walls of many incubation temples, with testimony of persons who were cured and wished to glorify the name of the god and increase the faith of believers. From these and other testimonies we may infer that the temple priests had devised ritual ceremonies in which the dreamers bathed in a pool to whose waters various chemical substances were added, and then anointed themselves with oil. Sometimes the priests also interpreted dreams that were excessively vague. If the patient was critically ill, a priest or some emissary would be sent to the temple to dream for the patient. The Greek sources also contain instructions given after the dream to promote convalescence. It was the custom that those who had been cured offered a cock to Asklepios as a thanksgiving offering.

---

32 Strabo, 8.6, 15; Pausanias 2.27.3; E. J. and L. Edelstein. *Asclepius: A Collection and Interpretation of the Testimonies* 2 (Baltimore, Johns Hopkins Press, 1945), pp. 145ff.

Bibliography

Abusch, T. *Babylonian Witchcraft Literature.* Atlanta: Scholars Press, 1987.
——. "An Early form of the Witchcraft Ritual Maqlû and the Origin of a Babylonian Magical Ceremony." In *Lingering over Words: Studies in Ancient Near Eastern Literature in Honor of William L. Moran.* edited by T. Abusch, J. Huehnegars, P. Steinkeller, 1–57. Atlanta: Scholars Press, 1990.

Albright, W. F. *Archaeology and The Religion of Israel.* Baltimore: Johns Hopkins Press, 1942.
——. "The North-Canaanite Poems of Al'êyân Ba'al and the 'Gracious Gods'." *JPOS* 14 (1934): 101–140.

Alexander, T. D. "Are the Wife/Sister Incidents of Genesis Literary Compositional Variants?" *VT* 42 (1992): 145–153.

Alter, R. *The Art of Biblical Narrative.* New York: Basic Books, 1981.

Amit, Y. "The Story of Samuel's Consecration to Prophecy in Light of Prophetic Thought." In *Moshe Goldstein Volume,* edited by B. Z. Luria, 29–36. Jerusalem: Society for Biblical Research, 1987 (Hebrew).

Anbar, M. "Abrahamic Covenant Gen 15." *Shnaton* 3 (1978): 34–52 (Hebrew).

Barr, J. "Theophany and Anthropomorphism in the *OT.*" *VTSup* 7 (1960): 31-38.

Batten, L. W. "The Sanctuary at Shiloh, and Samuel's Sleeping Therein." *JBL* 19 (1900): 29–33.

Barton, G. A. *A Critical and Exegetical Commentary on the Book of Ecclesiastes. ICC.* New York: Scribner's, 1908.

Baumgartner, W. "Zu den vier Reichen von Daniel 2." *THZ* 1 (1945):17–22.

Behnk, F. "Lexikalische Beiträge zur ägyptisch-semitischen Sprachvergleichung." *ZAS* 62 (1926): 80–83.

Bentzen, A. *Daniel.* 2d ed. *HAT* 19. Tübingen: Mohr, 1952.

Beyer, K. *Die aramäischen Texte vom Toten Meer.* Göttingen: Vandenhoeck & Ruprecht, 1984.

Bickerman, E. J. *Four Strange Books of the Bible.* New York: Schocken, 1967.

Blau, J. "Notes on the Vocabulary of the Bible." In *Sefer Yosef Braslavi,* 439–444. Jerusalem: Kiryat Sefer, 1970 (Hebrew).

Blommerde, A. C. M. *Northwest Semitic Grammar and Job. Biblica et Orientalia* 22. Rome: Pontifical Biblical Institute, 1969.

Breasted, J. H. *Ancient Records of Egypt.* 5 vols. New York : Russell and Russell, 1962.

Brenner, A. "מַרְאָה and מִרְאֶה." *Beit Mikra* 83 (1980): 373–374 (Hebrew).

Bright, J. *Jeremiah. AB* 21. Garden City, NY: Doubleday, 1965.

Briggs, C. A. and E. G. Briggs. *A Critical and Exegetical Commentary on the Book of Psalms. ICC.* Edinburgh: T. & T. Clark, 1907.

Brinkman , J. A. *A Political History of post-Kassite Babylonia, 1158–722 B.C. AnOr* 43. Rome: Pontifical Biblical Institute, 1968.

Brockington, L. H. "Audition in the *OT." JThs* 49 (1948): 1–8

Brueggemann, W. "David and his Theologian." *CBQ* 30 (1968): 156–181.

Budde, K. *Das Buch Hiob.* 2nd ed. Göttingen: Vandenhoeck & Ruprecht, 1913.

Budge, W. *Egyptian Magic.* Evanston: University Books, 1899.

Burrows, E. *The Oracles of Jacob and Balaam.* Edited by F. Sutcliffe, London: Burns Oates & Washbourne, 1938.

Butler, S. *Mesopotamian Conceptions of Dreams and Dream Rituals.* Munster-Verlag, 1998.

Caminos, R. A. *Late Egyptian Miscellanies.* London: Oxford University Press, 1954.

Caquot, A. "Selon Canaan et Israel." In *Les Songes et leur interprétation,* S. Sauneron et al., 101–124. Paris: le Seuil, 1959.

Cardascia, G. *Les Lois assyriennes.* Paris: Cerf, 1969.

Carlson, R. A. *David, the Chosen King.* Translated by E. J. Sharpe and S. Rudman. Stockholm: Almqvist & Wiksell, 1964.

Carmignac, J. "Un équivalent français de L'araméen 'Gazir'." *RevQ 4* (1963): 277–278.

Carroll, R. P. *The Book of Jeremiah.* OTL. Philadelphia: Westminster Press, 1986.

Cartledge, T. W. *Vows in the Hebrew Bible and the Ancient Near East. JSOT* Sup 147. Sheffield, England: *JSOT* Press, 1992.

Cassuto, U. *A Commentary on the Book of Genesis: From Noah to Abraham Genesis VI–XI.* Part II. Jerusalem: Magnes Press, 1964 (Hebrew).

——. *Commentary on the Book of Exodus.* Translated by I. Abrahams. Jerusalem: Magnes Press, 1967.

——. "Biblical Literature and Canaanite Literature." *Tarbiz* 14 (1942): 1–10.

Charles, R. H. *A Critical and Exegetical Commentary on the Book of Daniel.* Oxford: Clarendon, 1929.

Childs, B. S. *Memory and Tradition in Israel. SBT* 37. Naperville, IL: A. R. Allenson, 1962.

Clark, W. M. "A Legal Background to the Yahwist's use of 'Good and Evil' in Genesis 2–3." *JBL* 88 (1969): 266–278.

Clements, R. E. *Isaiah 1–39. New Century Bible Commentary.* Grand Rapids: Eerdmans, 1980.

Clines, D. J. A. *Job 1–20. WBC* 17. Dallas, TX: Word Books, 1989.

Coats, G. "A Threat to the Host." In *Saga, Legend, Tale, Novella, Fable,* edited by G. W. Coats, 71–81. *JSOT* Sup 35. Sheffield, England: JSOT Press, 1985.

Cohen, H. R. *Biblical Hapax Legomena in Light of Akkadian and Ugaritic. SBLDS* 37. Missoula, MT: Scholars Press, 1978.

Cohen, J. M. "An Unrecognized Connotation of *nšq peh* with Special Reference to Three Biblical Occurrences." *VT* 32 (1982): 416–424.

Collins, J. J. *The Apocalyptic Vision of the Book of Daniel. HSM* 16. Missoula, MT: Scholars Press, 1977.

_____. *A Commentary on The Book of Daniel.* Edited by F. M. Cross. Minneapolis: Fortress, 1993.

Conard, E. W. "The 'Fear Not' Oracles in Second Isaiah." *VT* 34 (1984): 129–152

Cooper, J. S . "Gilgamesh Dreams of Enkidu: The Evolution and Dilution of Narrative." In *Essays on the Ancient Near East in Memory of Jacob Joel Finklestein,* edited by Maria de Jong Ellis, 39–44. Hamden, CT: Archon Books, 1977.

Cooper, J. S. and W. Heimpel. "The Sumerian Sargon Legend." *JAOS* 103 (1983): 67- 82.

Couroyer, B. Review of *Joseph en Égypte,* by J. Vergote. *RB* 66(1959): 588–594.

Cowley, A. E. *Aramaic Papyri of the Fifth Century B.C.* Edited, with Translation and Notes. Oxford: Clarendon, 1923.

Craghan, J. F. "The *ARM* X 'Prophetic' Texts: Their Media, Style, and Structure." *JANES* 6 (1974): 39–57.

Crenshaw, J. L. *A Whirlpool of Torment.* Philadelphia: Fortress Press, 1984.

_____. *Joel: A New Translation with Introduction and Commentary. AB* 24. New York: Doubleday, 1995.

_____. "Method in Determining Wisdom Influence upon 'Historical' Literature." *JBL* 88 (1969): 129–142.

Cross, F. M. "A New Qumran Biblical Fragment Related to the Original Hebrew Underlying the Septuagint." *BASOR* 132 (1953): 15–26.

_____. "Fragments of the Prayer of Nabonidus." *IEJ* 34 (1984): 260–264.

Dahood, M. J. *Psalms III 101–150, Introduction, Translation and Notes. AB* 17A. Garden City, NY: Doubleday, 1970.

_____. "Northwest Semitic Notes on Genesis." *Bib* 55 (1974): 76–82.

_____. "Eblaite ha-ri and Genesis 40,16." *BN* 13 (1980): 14–16.

———. "Ebla, Ugarit, and the Bible." In *The Archives of Ebla*, edited by G. Pettinato, 271–321. Garden City, New York: Doubleday, 1981.

———. "Eblaite and Biblical Hebrew." *CBQ* 44 (1982): 1–24.

———. Review of H. R. Cohen, *Biblical Hapax Legomena in the Light of Akkadian and Ugaritic*. *Bib* 62 (1981): 272–274.

———. and T. Penar. "Ugaritic-Hebrew Parallel Pairs." In *Ras Shamra Parallels*, edited by L. R. Fisher, vol 1:71–382. *AnOr* 49–51. Rome: Pontifical Biblical Institute,1972.

Daiches, S. "Balaam: A Babylonian Bārû." In *Assyriologische und archaeologische Studien Herman von Hilprecht gewidmet*, 60–70. Leipzig: J. C. Hinrichs, 1909.

Davies, N. de G. *The Rock Tombs of El Amarna*. Vol 6. London: Egypt Exploration Fund, 1908.

Dhorme, E. *A Commentary on The Book of Job*. Translated by Harold Knight. London: Nelson, 1967.

Dijkstra, S. "Is Balaam Also Among the Prophets?" *JBL* 114 (1995): 43–64.

Dillman, A. *Genesis: Critically and Exegetically Expounded*. 2 Vols. Translated by W. B. Stevenson. Edinburgh: T. & T. Clark, 1897.

Dossin, G. "Sur le prophétisme à Mari." In *La Divination en Mésopotamie ancienne et dans les régions voisines*, 77–86. *RAI* 14. Paris: PUF, 1966.

———. "Le Songe d'Ayala." *RA* 69 (1975): 28–30.

Driver, G. R. *Canaanite Myths and Legends*. *OTS*, 3. Edinburgh: T & T. Clark, 1956.

——— and J. C. Miles. *The Assyrian Laws: Edited with Translation and Commentary*. Oxford: Clarendon Press, 1935.

Driver, S. R. *The Book of Daniel*. The Cambridge Bible for Schools and Colleges. Cambridge: Cambridge University Press, 1900.

———. *The Book of Genesis with Introduction and Notes*. London: Methuen, 1904.

———. *Notes on the Hebrew Text and the Topography of the Books of Samuel*. 2nd ed., revised and enlarged. Oxford: Clarendon, 1966.

———. and G. B. Gray. *A Critical and Exegetical Commentary on the Book of Job*. *ICC*. Edinburgh: T. & T. Clark, 1950.

Duhm, B. *Das Buch Hiob*. *KHC(AT)* 16. Leipzig und Tübingen: Mohr, 1897.

Dupont-Sommer, A. "Exorcismes et guérisons dans les écrits de Qoumrân." In *Congress Volume: Oxford 1959*, 246–261. *VTSup* 7. Leiden: Brill, 1960.

Durand, J.M. *Archives épistolaires de Mari I/1*. *ARMT* XXVI:1(Paris: Editions Recherche sur les Civilisations, 1988.

Eddy, S. K. *The King is Dead: Studies in the Near Eastern Resistance to Hellenism, 334-331 B.C.* Lincoln: University of Nebraska Press, 1961.

Edelstein, L. and E. J. eds. *Asclepius: A Collection and Interpretation of the Testimonies.* 2 vols. Baltimore: Johns Hopkins Press, 1945.

Ehrlich, A. B. *Randglossen zur Hebräischen Bibel.* 7 vols. Leipzig: Heinrichs, 1908.

———. *Miqra Ki-Pheshuto.* 3 vols. New York: Ktav, 1969 (Hebrew).

Ehrlich, E. L. *Der Traum im Alten Testament. BZAW* 73. Berlin: Topelmann, 1953.

Eichrodt, W. *Theology of the Old Testament.* 2 vols. Translated by J. A. Baker. Philadelphia: Westminster, 1961–67.

Eisenman, R. H. and M. Wise. *The Dead Sea Scrolls Uncovered.* Rockport, Massachusetts: Element, 1992.

Eissfeldt, O. "The Prophetic Literature." In *The Old Testament and Modern Study,* edited by H. H. Rowley, 115–161. Oxford: Clarendon Press, 1951.

———. *Einleitung in das AT.* 3rd ed. Tübingen: Mohr (Siedek), 1964.

Elat, M. *Samuel and the Foundation of Kingship in Ancient Israel.* Jerusalem: Magnes Press, 1998.

Emerton, J. A. "The Origin of the Promises to the Patriarchs in the Older Sources of the Book of Genesis." *VT* 32 (1982): 14–32.

Evans, G. "'Coming' and 'Going' at the City Gate: A Discussion of Professor Spieser's Paper." *BASOR* 150 (1958): 28–33.

Encyclopaedia of Religion and Ethics, 1922 ed. S.v. "Dreams and Sleep," by various authors.

Falk, Z. W. "Ruler and Judge." *Leshonenu* 30 (1965–66): 243–247 (Hebrew).

Fensham, F. C. "Legal Aspect of the Dream of Solomon." In *Fourth World Congress of Jewish Studies,* Vol 1:67–70. Jerusalem: World Union of Jewish Studies, 1967.

Finkel, J. "The Author of the Genesis Apocryphon Knew the Book of Esther." In *Essays on the Dead Sea Scrolls in memory of E.L. Sukenik,* edited by C. Rabin and Y. Yadin, 163–182. Jerusalem: Hekhal Ha-Sefer, 1961 (Hebrew).

Fishbane, M. *Biblical Interpretation in Ancient Israel.* Oxford: Clarendon Press, 1985.

Fisher, L. R. "Two Projects at Claremont." *UF* 3 (1971): 25–32.

Fitzmyer, J. A. *The Aramaic Inscriptions of Sefire. BibOr* 19. Rome: Pontifical Biblical Institute, 1967.

———. *The Genesis Apocryphon of Qumran Cave I.* 2nd ed. *BibOr* 18A. Rome: Pontifical Biblical Institute, 1971.

———. "Review of Aramaic Text from Deir 'Alla." *CBQ* 40 (1978): 93–95.

Flusser, D. "The Four Empires in the Fourth Sibyl and in the Book of Daniel." *IOS* 2 (1972): 148–175.

Fokkelman, J. P. *Narrative Art in Genesis.* Assen-Amsterdam: Van Gorcum, 1975.

Fox, Nili S. *In the Service of the King: Officialdom in Ancient Israel and Judah.* Cincinnati: Hebrew Union College Press, 2000.

Freedman, D. N. "The Prayer of Nabonidus." *BASOR* 145 (1957): 31–32.

Freud, S. *On Dreams.* New York: Norton, 1952.

——. *The Interpretation of Dreams.* In *The Standard Edition of the Complete Works of Sigmund Freud.* Vols. 4–5. Translated and edited by James Strachey, Anna Freud, Alix Strachey, and Alan Tyson. London: Hogarth, 1953.

——. "A Metapsychological Supplement of the Theory of Dreams." In *Standard edition.* Vol. 14. London: Hogarth Press, 1958.

Gadd, C. J. "The Harran Inscriptions of Nabonidus." *Anatolian Studies* 8 (1958): 35–92.

Gammie, J. G. "On the Intention and Sources of Daniel I-VI." *VT* 31 (1981): 282–292.

Gardiner, A. H. *Hieratic Papyri in British Museum.* Third Series.1:9–23. Papyrus Chester Beatty no. 3, 2, plates 5–8a,12–12a. London: British Museum, 1935.

——. *Late Egyptian Miscellanies.* Bibliotheca Aegyptica, 7. Brussels: Éditions de la Fondation Égyptologique Reine Élisabeth, 1937.

——. *Ancient Egyptian Onomastica.* Oxford: Oxford University Press, 1947.

Garsiel, M. "King Solomon's Descent to Gibeon and His Dream." In *The Dr. Ben Yehuda Book,* edited by B. Z. Luria, 191–217. Tel Aviv: The Israel Bible Society, 1981 (Hebrew).

Gaster, T. H. *Thespis: Ritual, Myth, and Drama in the Ancient Near East.* New York: Schuman, 1950.

——. *Myth, Legend, and Custom in the Old Testament.* New York: Harper and Row, 1969.

——. "Dreams in the Bible." *EncJud.* Vol 6: 208–209. Jerusalem: Keter, 1971.

Gerber, I. J. *Immortal Rebels.* New York: Jonathan David Publishers, 1963.

Gibson, J. C. L. *Canaanite Myths and Legends.* 2nd ed. Edinburgh: T. & T. Clark, 1978.

Ginsberg, H. L. *The Ugarit Texts.* Jerusalem: Vaad Halashon, 1936.

——. *Studies in Daniel.* Texts and Studies of the Jewish Theological Seminary of America, 14. New York: Jewish Theological Seminary of America, 1948.

Gnuse, R. K. *The Dream Theophany of Samuel.* Lanham, Md: University Press of America, 1984.

——. "A Reconstruction of the Form-critical Structure in I Sam. 3: An Ancient Eastern Theophany." *ZAW* 94 (1982): 379–390.

Goitein, S. D. *Bible Studies.* Tel Aviv: Yavneh, 1963 (Hebrew).

Goldziher, I. *Abhandlungen zur arabischen Philologie.* Erster Teil. Leiden: Brill, 1896.

Gordis, R. Koheleth: *The Man and His World.* New York: *JTS,* 1951.

——. *The Book of Job.* New York: *JTS,* 1978.

Gordon, C. H. *Ugaritic Handbook. AnOr* 25. Rome: Pontifical Biblical Institute, 1947.

——. *Ugaritic Literature.* Rome: Pontifical Biblical Institute, 1949.

——. *Before the Bible: The Common Background of Greek and Hebrew Civilisation.* London: Collins, 1962.

——. *Ugaritic Textbook. AnOr* 38. Rome: Pontifical Biblical Institute, 1965.

——. *Ugarit and Minoan Crete.* New York: Norton, 1966.

——. "The Patriarchal Age." *JBR* 21 (1953): 238–243.

——. "Sabbatical Cycle or Seasonal Patteren?" *Orientalia* 22 (1953): 79–81.

Graesser, C. F. "Standing Stones in Ancient Palestine." *BA* 35 (1972): 33 63.

Grapow, H. *Die bildlichen Ausdrücke des Ägyptischen.* Leipzig: Hinrichs, 1924.

Gray, G. B. *A Critical and Exegetical Commentary on Numbers. ICC.* Edinburgh: T. & T. Clark, 1903.

Gray, J. *I & II Kings: A Commentary.* 2nd ed. Philadelphia: Westminster Press, 1963.

Greenberg, M. *Ezekiel 1–20. AB* 22. Garden City, NY: Doubleday, 1983.

Greenfield, J. C. "The Zakir Inscription and the Danklied." In *Proceedings of the Fifth World Congress of Jewish Studies,* Vol 1: 174–191. Jerusalem: World Union of Jewish Studies, 1969.

Griffith, F. L. *Stories of the High Priests of Memphis, the Sethon of Herodotus and the Demotic Tales of Khamuas.* Oxford: Clarendon Press, 1900.

Griffiths, J. G. "The Celestial Ladder and the Gate of Heaven (Gen.28:12 and17)." *ExpTim* 76 (1964/65): 229–30; 78 (1966/67): 54–55.

——. *The Conflict of Horus and Seth.* Liverpool: University Press, 1960.

Grintz, Y. M. *The Book of Genesis.* Jerusalem: Magnes Press, 1983 (Hebrew).

Gressmann, H. "Die literarische Analyse Deuterojesajas." *ZAW* 34 (1914): 254–297.

Von Grunebaum, G. E. and Roger Caillois, eds. *The Dream and Human Societies.* Berkeley: University of California Press, 1966.

Guillaume, A. *Prophecy and Divination among the Hebrews and Other Semites.* London: Hodder and Stoughton, 1938.

Gunkel, H. *Einleitung in die Psalmen.* 2nd ed. *HKAT* II/2. Göttingen: Vaendenhoeck & Ruprecht, 1966.

——. *The Legends of Genesis.* Translated by W. H . Carruth. Chicago: Open Court, 1907.

Gunn, B. "Notes on Ammenemes I." *JEA* 27 (1941): 2–6.

Gurney, O. R. "The Myth of Nergal and Ereshkigal." *Anatolian Studies.* 10 (1960): 105–131.

———. and J. J. Finkelstein, eds. *The Sultantepe Tablets.* London: British Institute of Archaelogy at Ankara, 1957–1964.

Ha, J. *Genesis 15: A Theological Compendium of Pentateuchal History.* Berlin: Walter de Gruyter, 1989.

Hackett, Jo Ann. *The Balaam Text from Deir 'Alla.* Chico, CA: Scholars Press, 1984.

Hakham, A. "The מַרְאֶה of Moses versus מַרְאָה." In *Sefer Gevaryahu,* edited by B. Z. Luria, Vol 1: 60–67. Jerusalem: Kiryat Sefer,1989. (Hebrew).

Haldar, A. *Associations of Cult Prophets among the Ancient Semites.* Uppsala: Almqvist & Wilksells, 1945.

Hall, C. S. and G. Lindzey. *Theories of Personality.* London: Wylie, 1957.

Hallo, W. W. "Lugalbanda Excavated." *JAOS* 103 (1983): 165–180.

Hamilton, V. P. *The Book of Genesis: Chapters 18–50. NICOT.* Grand Rapids: Eerdmans, 1994.

Hammer, R. *Sifre on Deuteronomy.* New Haven: Yale University Press, 1986.

Haran, M. *The Biblical Collection.* Jerusalem: Magnes Press, 1996.

Hartley, J. *Book of Job. NICOT.* Grand Rapids: Eerdmans, 1988.

Hartman, L. F. and A. A. Di Lella. *The Book of Daniel. AB* 23. Garden City, NY: Doubleday, 1978.

———. "The Great Tree and Nebuchadnezzar's Madness." In *The Bible in Current Catholic Thought,* edited by J. L. Mckenzie, 75–82. New York: Herder, 1962.

Hayes, J. H. "The Tradition of Zion's Inviolability." *JBL* 82 (1963): 419–426.

Heaton, E. W. *The Book of Daniel.* Torch Bible Commentary. London: SCM Press, 1956.

Held, M. "Philological Notes on the Mari Covenant Rituals." *BASOR* 200 (1970): 32–40.

Henry, K. H. "Land Tenure in the Old Testament." *PEQ* (1954): 5–15.

Herrmann, S. "Die Königsnovelle in Ägypten und in Israel: Ein Beitrag zur Gattungsgeschichte in den Geschichtsbüchern des Alten Testament." In *Wissenschaftliche Zeitschrift der Karl-Marx-Universität,* Vol 3: 51–62. Leipzig: Karl-Marx Universität, 1953–1954.

Hertzberg, H. W. *I and II Samuel, A Commentary.* Translated by J. S. Bowden. Philadelphia: Westminster, 1964.

Hess, R. S. *Amarna Personal Names. ASOR* Dissertation Series 9. Winona Lake: Eisenbraun's, 1993.

Hoffmeier, J. K. *Israel in Egypt.* Oxford: Oxford University Press, 1996.

Hoffner, Jr. H. A. "Second Millennium Antecedents to the Hebrew *'ÔB.*" *JBL* 86 (1967): 385–401.

———. "Hittite Tarpis and Hebrew Teraphim." *JNES* 27 (1968): 61–68.

Hoftijzer, J., and G. van der Kooij, eds. *Aramaic texts from Deir 'Alla.* Leiden: Brill, 1976.

———. *Die Verheissungen an die drei Erzväter.* Leiden: Brill, 1956.

Holladay, W. L. *Jeremiah 1: A Commentary on the Book of the Prophet Jeremiah Chapters 1–25.* Hermeneia. Philadelphia: Fortress, 1986.

———. *Jeremiah 2: A Commentary on the Book of the Prophet Jeremiah Chapters 26–52.* Hermeneia. Minneapolis: Fortress, 1989.

Holscher, G. *Das Buch Hiob.* Tübingen: Mohr, 1952.

Honeyman, A. M. "Merismus in Biblical Hebrew." *JBL* 71 (1952): 11–18.

Houtman, C. "What Did Jacob See in His Dream at Bethel? Some Remarks on Genesis xxviii 10–22." *VT* 27 (1977): 337–351.

Humphreys, W. L. "A Life-Style for the Diaspora: A Study of the Tales of Esther and Daniel." *JBL* 92 (1973): 211–223.

Hurowitz, V. *I Have Built You an Exalted House: Temple Building in Light of Mesopotamian and Northwest Semitic Writings. JSOT,* Supplement Series 115. Sheffield: Sheffield Accademic Press,1992.

Hurvitz, A. "The Uses of שש and בוץ in the Bible and its Implications for the Date of P." *HTR* 60 (1967): 117–121.

Husser, Jean-Marie. *Le Songe et la parole: Étude sur le rêve et sa fonction dans l'ancien Israël. BZAW* 210. Berlin: Walter de Gruyter, 1994.

Hyatt, J. P. "A Neo-Babylonian Parallel to Bethel-Sar-Eser, Zech. 7:2." *JBL* 56 (1937): 387–394.

———. "The Deity Bethel and the *OT.*" *JAOS* 59 (1939): 81–98.

——— and S. Hopper "Introduction and Exegesis, Jeremiah." *IB* 5: 775–1142.

Jacob, B. *The First Book of The Bible: Genesis.* Abridged, edited, and translated by E. J. Jacob and W. Jacob. New York: Ktav, 1974.

Jacobsen, T. *The Harps that Once–: Sumerian Poetry in Translation.* New Haven: Yale University Press, 1987.

Janssen, J. M. A. "Egyptological Remarks on the Story of Joseph in Genesis." *JEOL* 14 (1955–56): 63–72.

Jastrow, Marcus. *A Dictionary of the Targumim, the Talmud Babli and Yerushalmi, and the Midrashic Literature.* New York: Putnam, 1903.

Jastrow, Morris. *Aspects of Religious Belief and Practice in Babylonia and Assyria.* 2nd ed. New York: B. Blom, 1971.

———. *A Gentle Cynic.* Philadelphia: Lippincott, 1919.

Jensen, P. "Die Joseph-Traume." *BZAW* 33 (1918): 233–245.

Jepsen, A. "Chazah." *TDOT* 4:280–290.

Jirku, A. "Ein Fall von Inkubation im AT (Ex 38:8)." *ZAW* 33 (1913): 151–153.

Johnson, A. R. *The Cultic Prophet in Ancient Israel.* 2nd ed. Cardiff: University of Wales Press, 1962.

Jones , G. H. *1 and 2 Kings.* NCBC. 2 vol. Grand Rapids: Eerdmans, 1984.

Josephus, F. *Jewish Antiquities.* Translated by H. St. J. Thackeray. Cambridge, MA: Harvard University Press, 1930.

Jung, C. G. *Memories. Dreams and Reflections.* New York: Random House, 1961.

——. *Psychology and Alchemy.* Princeton, NJ: Princeton University Press, 1968.

Kaiser, O. "Traditionsgeschichtliche Untersuchung von Genesis 15." ZAW 70 (1958): 107–126.

Kapelrud, A. S. *Joel Studies.* Uppsala: A. B. Lundequist, 1948.

——. "Temple Building: A Task for Gods and Kings." *Orientalia* 32 (1963): 56–62.

——. "The Number Seven in Ugaritic Texts." *VT* 18 (1968): 494–499.

Kaufman, Y. *Toldot Ha'Emunah Ha'Yisre'elit.* 8 vols. Jerusalem: Bialik Institute, 1956.

Kees, H. "Der sogenannte oberste Vorlesepriester." *ZÄS* 87 (1962): 119–139.

Kelso, J. L. et al. *The Excavation of Bethel* (1934–60). *AASOR* 39. Cambridge: American School of Oriental Research, 1968.

Kitchen, K. A. "The Term *Nśq* in Genesis xli. 40." *ExpTim* 69 (1957): 30.

——. "Asenath." *The New Bible Dictionary.* Edited by J.D. Douglas. Grand Rapids: Eerdmans, 1963.

——. "Joseph." *NBD*

——. "Potiphar." *NBD*

——. "Cupbearer." *NBD*

——. "The Aramaic of Daniel." in *Notes on Some Problems in the Book of Daniel.* edited by D. J. Weisman, T. C. Mitchell, R. Joyce, W. J. Martin and K. A. Kitchen, 31–79. London: Tyndale, 1965.

Klein, R. W. *1 Samuel. WBC* 10. Waco, Texas: Word, 1983.

Knudtzon, J. A. *Die El-Amarna-Tafeln. VAB* 2/22. 2 vols. Leipzig: J. C. Hinrichs, 1915. Reprinted, Aalen: Otto Zeller, 1964.

Koch, K. *Das Buch Daniel.* Ertrage der Forschung 144. Darmstadt: Wissenschaftliche Buchgesellschaft, 1980.

Von König, E. "Die sprachliche Gestalt des Pentateuch in ihrer Beziehung zur ägyptischen Sprache." *JBL* 48 (1929): 333–353.

Kraus, H. J. *Worship in Israel: A Cultic History of the Old Testament.* Translated by G. Buswell. Richmond: John Knox, 1965.

——. Psalms 60–150. Translated by H. C. Oswald. Minneapolis: Augsburg, 1989.

Kramer, S. N. *The Sumerians: Their History, Culture, and Character.* Chicago: The University of Chicago Press, 1963.

Kselman, J. S. "The Recovery of Poetic Fragments from the Pentateuchal Priestly Source." *JBL* 97 (1978): 161–173.

Kutscher, R. "The Mesopotamian God Zaqar and Jacob Massebah." *Beer Sheva* 3 (1988): 125–130 (Hebrew).

Labuschagne, C. J. "The našû-nadānu Formula and its Biblical Equivalent." In *Travels in the World of the Old Testament: Studies Presented to M. A. Beek.* Edited by M. S. H. G. Heerman van Voss, Ph. H. J. Houwink ten Cate, and N. A. van Uchelen, 176–180. Assen: Van Gorcum, 1974.

Lacocque, A. *The Book of Daniel.* Translated by D. Pellauer. Atlanta: John Knox, 1979.

Laessøe, J. *Studies on the Assyrian Ritual and Series bīt rimki.* Copenhagen: Munksgaard, 1955.

Lambdin, T. O. "Egyptian Loan Words in the Old Testament." *JAOS* 73 (1953): 145–155.

Lambert, W. G. *Babylonian Wisdom Literature.* Oxford: Clarendon Press, 1960.

Leibowitz, N. *Studies in Bereshit (Genesis).* Translated by A. Newman. 4th rev. ed. Jerusalem: World Zionist Organization, 1981.

Levine, B. A. *In the Presence of The Lord: A Study of Cult and Some Cultic Terms in Ancient Israel.* SJLA 5. Leiden: Brill, 1974.

———. *Numbers 1–20.* AB 4A. New York: Doubleday, 1993.

———. "The Righteousness of the Lord." *Eretz Yisrael* 20. *Yigal Yadin Volume.* Edited by A. Ben-Tor, J. C. Greenfield, A. Malamat, 202–214. Jerusalem: Israel Exploration Society, 1970 (Hebrew)

———. "The Deir 'Alla Plaster Inscriptions." *JAOS* 101–102 (1981): 195–205.

———. "The Balaam Inscription from Deir 'Alla: Historical Aspects." *In Biblical Archaeology Today. Proceedings of the International Congress on Biblical Archaeology, Jerusalem, April, 1984,* 326–39. Jerusalem: Israel Exploration Society, 1985.

Lewin, I. *The Psychology of Dreams.* Tel Aviv: Dekel, 1980 (Hebrew).

Licht, J. *Storytelling in the Bible.* Jerusalem: Magnes Press, 1978.

Lichtenstein, M. "Dream Theophany and the E Document." *JANESCU* 1–2 (1969): 45–54.

Lichtheim, M. *Ancient Egyptian Literature.* 3 vols. Berkeley: University of California Press, 1973–1980.

Lieberman, S. *Hellenism in Jewish Palestine.* 2nd ed. New York: Jewish Theological Seminary, 1962.

Lindblom, J. *Prophecy in Ancient Israel.* Philadelphia: Fortress, 1973.

——. "Theophanies in Holy Places in Hebrew Religion." *HUCA* 32 (1961): 91–106.

Liver, J. *Studies in Bible and Judean Desert Scrolls.* Jerusalem: Bialik, 1971 (Hebrew).

Loader, J. A. "Esther as a Novel with Different Levels of Meaning." *ZAW* 90 (1978): 417–421.

Loewenstamm, S. E. "אנכי אחטנה." *Leshonenu* 29 (1965): 69–70 (Hebrew).

——. "Ruler and Judge." *Leshonenu* 32 (1968): 272–274 (Hebrew).

——. "The Divine Grants of Land to the Patriarchs." *JAOS* 91 (1971): 509–510.

Lohfink, N. *Die Landverheissung als Eid. Eine Studie zu Gn 15.* Stuttgart: Verlag Katholisches Bibelwerk, 1967.

Long, B. O. "Prophetic Call Traditions and Reports of Visions." *ZAW* 84 (1972): 494–500.

Lutz, H. F. "An Omen Text Referring to the Action of a Dreamer." *AJSL* 35 (1918–19): 145–157.

Mabee, C. "Jacob and Laban: The Structure of Judicial Proceedings (Genesis xxxi 25–42)." *VT* 30 (1980): 192–207.

Macintosh, A. A. "A Consideration of Hebrew gʻr." *VT* (1969): 471–479.

Maimonides, M. *Mishneh Torah.* Translated by P. Birnbaum. New York: Hebrew Publishing Company, 1944.

Malamat, A. "Cushan Rishathaim and the Decline of the Near East about 1200 B.C." *JNES* 13 (1954): 231–242.

——. "History and Prophetic Vision in a Mari Letter." *Eretz Israel 5, B. Mazar Volume.* Edited by M. Avi-Yonah, H. Z. Hirschberg, Y. Yadin, H. Tadmor, 67–73. Jerusalem: Israel Exploration Society, 1958. (Hebrew).

——. "Aspects of the Foreign Politics of David and Solomon." *JNES* 22 (1963): 1–17.

——. *Mari and the Bible: A Collection of Studies.* 2nd enl. ed. Jerusalem: Hebrew University, 1984.

——. "A Forerunner of Biblical Prophecy: The Mari Documents." In *Ancient Israelite Religion: Essays in Honor of Frank Moore Cross.* Edited by P. Miller, Jr., et al, 33–52. Philadelphia: Fortress, 1987.

——. *Mari and the Early Israelite Experience.* Oxford: Oxford University Press, 1984.

Margaliot, A. "Numbers 12: The Nature of Moses's Prophecy." *Beit Miqra* 81 (1980): 132–149 (Hebrew).

Margalit, B. *The Ugaritic Poem of Aqhat.* BZAW 182. Berlin and New York: De Gruyter, 1989.

May, H. G. "Ephod and Ariel." *AJSL* 56 (1939): 44–69.

———. "Pattern and Myth in the Old Testament." *Journal of Religion* 21 (1941): 285–299.

Mazar, B. "The Historical Background of the Book of Genesis." In *Canaan and Israel.* Jerusalem: Bialik, 1974. 131–143 (Hebrew).

McAlpine, T. H. *Sleep, Divine and Human, in the OT. JSOT* Suppl. 38. Sheffield: JSOT Press, 1987.

McCarter, P. K, Jr. *I Samuel: A New Translation with Introduction, Notes, and Commentary. AB* 8. Garden City, NY: Doubleday, 1980.

———. "The Balaam Text from Deir 'Alla: The First Combinations." *BASOR* 239 (1980): 49–60.

McCarthy, D. J. *Treaty and Covenant. AnBib* 21. Rome: Pontifical Biblical Institute, 1963.

McNamara, M. "Nabonidus and the Book of Daniel." *ITQ* 37 (1970):131- 149.

Mendelsohn, I. "Samuel's Denunciation of Kingship in the Light of the Akkadian Documents from Ugarit." *BASOR* 143 (1956): 17–22.

———. *Religions of the Ancient Near East. Sumero-Akkadian Religious Texts and Ugaritic Epics.* New York: Liberal Arts Press, 1955.

Meyer, E. *Ursprung und Anfänge des Christentums* 1–2. Stuttgart and Berlin: J. G. Cotta, 1923–1925.

Meyer, R. *Das Gebet des Nabonid: Eine in den Qumran-Handschriften wiederentdeckte Weisheitserzählung.* Sitzungsberichte der Sächsischen Akademie der Wissenschaften zu Leipzig. Phil.-Hist. KL. Bd. 107, Heft 3. Berlin: Akademie-Verlag, 1962.

Meyers, C. L. and E. M. Meyers. *Zechariah 9–14. AB* 25C. Garden City, NY: Doubleday, 1993.

Michel, W. L. *Job in the Light of Northwest Semitic. BibOr* 42. Rome: Pontifical Biblical Institute, 1987.

Milgrom, J. *Cult and Conscience. The Asham and The Priestly Doctrine of Repentance. SJLA* 18. Leiden: Brill, 1976.

———. *Numbers: The JPS Torah Commentary.* Philadelphia: Jewish Publication Society, 1990.

Milik, J. T. "'Prière de Nabonide' et autres écrits d'un cycle de Daniel." *RB* 63 (1956): 407–415.

Millard, A. R. "The Celestial Ladder and the Gate of Heaven (Genesis xxviii.12,17)." *ExpTim* 78 (1966/67): 86–87.

Miller, P. D, Jr. "Sin and Judgment in Jeremiah 34:17–19." *JBL* 103 (1984): 611–613.

Miqra'oth Gedoloth [The Rabbinic Bible], commentaries of Rashi, Abraham ibn Ezra, David Kimḥi, & Meṣudoth. New York: Pardes, 1961.

Miscall, P. D. "Literary Unity in the Old Testament Narrative." *Semeia* 15 (1979): 27–44.

Mitchell, H. G., J. M. P. Smith, and J. A. Bewer. *Haggai, Zechariah, Malachi, and Jonah. ICC.* New York: Scribner's sons, 1912.

Montgomery, J. A. *A Critical and Exegetical Commentary on the Book of Daniel.* ICC. Edinburgh: T. & T. Clark, 1927.

_____. *A Critical and Exegetical Commentary on the Books of Kings.* ICC. Edited by H. S. Gehman. New York: Scribner's, 1951.

Moore, M. S. *The Balaam Traditions. SBLDS* 113. Atlanta: Scholars Press, 1990.

Morag, S. "Layers of Antiquity: Some Linguistic Observations on the Oracles of Balaam." *Tarbiz 50* (1980/1981): 1–24 (Hebrew).

Moran, W. L. "The Scandal of the 'Great Sin' at Ugarit." *JNES* 18 (1959): 280–281.

_____. "New Evidence from Mari on the History of Prophecy." *Biblica* 50 (1969): 15–56.

_____. ed. and trans. *The Amarna Letters.* Baltimore: John Hopkins University Press, 1992.

Mowinckel, S. *Psalmenstudien.* I-VI. Amsterdam: P. Schippers, 1966.

Müller, M. *Egyptological Researches: Results of a Journey in 1904.* Washington, DC: Carnegie Institution of Washington, June 1906.

Nagera, H. *Basic Psychoanalytic Concepts on the Theory of Dreams.* London: Allen and Unwin, 1969.

Newton, I. "Observations upon the Prophecies of Daniel and the Apocalypse of St. John(1733)." In *Sir Isaac Newton's Daniel and Apocalypse.* Edited by W. Whitla. London: Murray, 1922.

Nichols, H. H. "The composition of the Elihu speeches." *AJSL* 27 (1910–11): 97–186.

Niditch, S. and R. Doren. "The Success Story of the Wise Courtier: A Formal Approach." *JBL* 96 (1977): 179–193.

Niehoff, M. "A Dream Which is Not Interpreted is Like a Letter Which is Not Read." *JJS* 43 (1992): 58–84.

Noth, M. *A History of Pentateuchal Traditions.* Translated with introduction by B. W. Anderson, W. Bernhard. Englewood Cliffs, N. J. : Prentice-Hall, 1972.

Nowack, W. *Die kleinen Propheten, HAT.* Göttingen: Vandenhoeck und Ruprecht, 1903.

Obermann, J. *How Daniel was Blessed with a Son: An Incubation Scene in Ugaritic.* Supplement to the Journal of the American Oriental Society, Vol. 66.2. 1–30. New Haven: American Oriental Society, 1946.

Oppenheim, A. L. *The Interpretation of Dreams in the Ancient East: With a Translation of an Assyrian Dream Book.* Transactions of the American Philosophical Society, New Series, vol. 46. Philadelphia: American Philosophical Society, 1956.

———. *Ancient Mesopotamia: Portrait of a Dead Civilization.* Chicago: University of Chicago Press, 1964.

———. "Mantic Dreams in the Ancient Near East." In *The Dream and Human Societies,* edited by G. E. Von Grunebaum and Roger Caillois, 341–350. Berkeley: University of California Press, 1966.

———. "Dream." *EMiqr* 3:143–149 (Hebrew).

Osten-Sacken, Peter von der. *Die Apokalyptik in ihrem Verhältnis zu Prophetie und Weisheit,* Theologische Existenz Heute 157. Munich: Kaiser, 1969.

Bergman, J., M. Ottosson, and G. J. Botterweck. "Chalam." *TDOT* 4: 421–432

Parker, S. B. "The Vow in Ugaritic and Israelite Narrative Literature." *UF* 11 (1979): 693–700.

Pedersen, J. "The Role Played by Inspired Persons Among the Israelite and the Arabs." *In Studies in OT Prophecy,* edited by H. H. Rowley, 127–142. Edinburgh: T. & T. Clark, 1950.

Perowne, J. J. S. *The Book of Psalms.* 3rd ed. Andover: Warren F. Draper, 1882.

Pfeiffer, R. H. *Introduction to the Old Testament.* New York: Harper, 1948.

Polak, F. *Biblical Narrative.* Jerusalem: Bialik, 1994.

Polzin, R. "'The Ancestress of Israel in Danger' in Danger." *Semeia* 3 (1975): 81–98.

Pope, M. H. *El in the Ugaritic Texts.* VTSup 2. Leiden: Brill, 1955.

Porteous, N. W. *Daniel: A Commentary. OTL.* Philadelphia: Westminster, 1965.

Postgate, J. N. "Some Old Babylonian Shepherds and Their Flocks." *JSS* 20 (1975): 1–21.

Pritchard, J. B. *The Ancient Near Eastern Texts Relating to the Old Testament.* Princeton, NJ: Princeton University, 1954, 1969.

de Pury, A. *Promesse divine et légende cultuelle dans le cycle de Jacob Gen 28 et les traditions patriarcales.* Études bibliques. Paris: Gabalda, 1975.

Quaegebeur, J. "The Egyptian Equivalent of Ḥarṭummîm." In *Pharaonic Egypt,* edited by S. Israelit-Groll, 162–172. Jerusalem: Magnes Press, 1985.

Rabinowitz, J. J. "The 'Great Sin' in Ancient Egyptian Marriage Contracts." *JNES* 18 (1959): 73.

von Rad, G. *Genesis: A Commentary.* Translated by J. H. Marks. London: SCM Press, 1961.

———. "The Joseph Narrative and Ancient Wisdom." In *The Problem of the Hexateuch and other essays,* translated by E. W. Trueman Dicken, 292–300. New York: McGraw-Hill, 1966.

Rapport, A. "The Fourth Kingdom in the Book of Daniel." *Beit-Miqra* 22 (1964): 10–25.

Rattner, R. "Three Bulls or One? A Reappraisal of 1 Sam 1,24." *Bib* 68 (1987): 98–102.

Redford, D. B. *A Study of the Biblical Story of Joseph (Gen 37–50). VTSup* 20. Leiden: Brill, 1970.

Reiner, E. *ŠURPU: A Collection of Sumerian and Akkadian Incantations. AfO*Beiheft 11. Gratz: By the editor, 1951.

Rendsburg, G. A. *The Redaction of Genesis.* Winona Lake, IN: Eisenbrauns, 1986.

Rendtorff, R. "Genesis 15 im Rahmen der theologischen Bearbeitung der Vätergeschichten." In *Werden und Wirken des Alten Testaments: Fs. C. Westermann.* Edited by R. Albertz, H. P. Muller, H. W. Wollf, and W. Zimmerli, 74–81. Göttingen: Vandenhoeck and Ruprecht, 1980.

———. "Jacob in Bethel, Beobachtungen zum Aufbau und zur Quellenfrage in Gen 28:10–22." *ZAW* 94 (1982): 511–523.

Resch, A. *Der Traum im Heilsplan Gottes: Deutung und Bedeutung des Traums im Alten Testament.* Freiburg: Herder, 1964.

Richter, W. "Traum und Traumdeutung im Alten Testament." *BZ* 7 (1963): 202–220.

Ritter, E. K. "Magical Expert (=Āšipu) and Physician (=Asû): Notes on Two Complementary Professions in Babylonian Medicine." In *Studies in Honor of Benno Landsberger on his 75th Birthday.* Ed. Hans Gustav Guterbock, 299–321. *AS*16. Chicago: University of Chicago Press, 1965.

Roberts, J. J. M. "On Signs, Prophets, and Time Limits: A Note on Psalms 74:9." *CBQ* 39 (1977): 474–481.

Robertson, E. "Old Testament Stories: Their Purpose and Their Art."*Bulletin of John Rylands Library.* 28 (1944): 454–476.

Rooning, J. "The Naming of Isaac: The Role of the Wife / Sister Episodes in the Redaction of Genesis." *WTJ* 53 (1991): 1–27.

Rosenthal, F. *A Grammar of Biblical Aramaic.* Wiesbaden: Harrassowitz, 1968.

Rowley, H. H. *The Aramaic of the Old Testament.* Oxford: Oxford University Press, 1929.

———. *Darius the Mede and the Four World Empires in the Book of Daniel.* Cardiff: University of Wales Press, 1964.

———. "The Unity of the Book of Daniel." In *The Servant of the Lord and Other Essays on the Old Testament,* 249–280. 2nd ed. rev. Oxford: Blackwell, 1965.

Ruppert, L. *Die Josephserzählung der Genesis.* Munich: Kosel, 1965.

Sarna, N. M. *Understanding Genesis.* New York: Schocken Books, 1966.

_____. *Genesis: The JPS Torah Commentary*. Philadelphia: Jewish Publication Society, 1989.

Sasson, J. M. "Mari Dreams." *JAOS* 103 (1983): 283–293.

Satran, D. "Early Jewish and Christian Interpretation of the Fourth Chapter of the Book of Daniel." Ph.d. diss., Hebrew University of Jerusalem, 1985 (Hebrew).

Sauneron, S. et al., *Les Songes et leur interprétation*. Sources orientales 2. Paris: Le Seuil, 1959.

Schott, S., ed. & tr. *Altägyptische Liebeslieder: mit Märchen und Liebesgeschichten*. Zurich: Artemis-Verlag, 1950.

Schulman, A. R. "On the Egyptian Name of Joseph: A New Approach." *SAK* 2 (1974): 235–43.

Schürer, E. *The History of the Jewish People in the Age of Jesus Christ (175 B.C.-A.D. 135)*. 3 volumes.; revised and edited by G. Vermes, F. Millar, and M. Goodman. Edinburgh: T. & T. Clark, 1973–1987.

Scott, R. B. Y. "Meteorological Phenomena and Terminology in the Old Testament." *ZAW* 64 (1952): 11–25.

Segal, M. Z. "Problems of Words." *Leshonenu* 9–10 (1938–1940): 150–156 (Hebrew).

van Seters, J. *Abraham in History and Tradition*. New Haven: Yale University Press, 1975.

_____. *Prologue to History*. Louisville, KY: Westminster/John Knox, 1992.

_____. "Confessional Reformulation in the Exilic Period." *VT* 22 (1972): 448–459.

Skinner, J. *A Critical and Exegetical Commentary on Genesis*. ICC. New York: Scribner's, 1910.

Smith, H. P. *A Critical and Exegetical Commentary on the Books of Samuel*. ICC. New York: Scribners, 1899.

Smith, W. R. "On the Form of Divination and Magic enumerated in Deut. XVIII. 10,11." *Journal of Philology* 14 (1885):113–128.

Snijders, L. A. "Genesis XV: The Covenant with Abraham." *OTS* 12 (1958): 261–279.

von Soden, W. "Zum akkadischen Wörterbuch 89–96." *Orientalia* 26 (1957): 127–138.

Soggin. J. A. "Jeremiah 29: 8b," In *Old Testament and Oriental Studies*, 238–40. *BibOr* 29. Rome: Biblical Institute Press, 1975.

Spanel, D. *Through Ancient Eyes: Egyptian Portraiture*. Birmingham, AL: Brimingham Museum of Art, 1988.

Speiser, E. A. *Genesis*. AB 1. Garden City, NY: Doubleday, 1964.

_____. "Coming and Going at the 'City Gate'." *BASOR* 144 (1956): 20–23.

———. "The Royal Rule." In *The Patriarch and the Judges*, 297–300. Tel Aviv: Masada, 1967.

Sperling, D. "Studies in Late Hebrew Lexicography in Light of Akkadian." Ph.D. diss., Columbia University, 1973.

———. "Akkadian *egerrû* and Hebrew בת קול." *JANESCU* 4 (1972): 63–74.

———. "Genesis 41:40: A New Interpretation." *JANESCU* 10 (1978): 113-119.

Spinoza, B. *Theological-Political Treatise*. Translated R. H. M. Elwes. New York: Dover, 1955.

Stinespring, W. F. "The Participle of the Immediate Future and other Matters Pertaining to Correct Translation of the Old Testament." In *Translating and Understanding the Old Testament: Essays in honor of Herbert Gordon May*. Ed. H. T. Frank and W. L. Reed, 64–70. Nashville: Abingdon, 1970.

Stockton, E. "Sacred Pillars in The Bible." *ABR* 20 (1972):16–32.

Strugnell, J. "A Note on Ps. 126:1." *JTS* 7 (1956): 239–243.

Swain, J. W. "The Theory of the Four Monarchies: Opposition History under the Roman Empire." *CP* 35 (1940): 1–21.

Sweek, J. "Dreams of Power from Sumer to Judah." Ph.D. diss., University of Chicago, 1996.

Sweeney, M.A., Knierim, R.P. and Tucker, G.M., eds. *Isaiah 1–39. With An Introduction to Prophetic Literature*. Forms of Old Testament Literature Vol. 16. Grand Rapids: Eerdmans, 1966.

Thompson, J.A. *The Book of Jeremiah*. NICOT. Grand Rapids: Eerdmans, 1980.

Thompson, R.C. *The Reports of Magicians and Astrologers of Nineveh and Babylon*. London: Luzacs, 1900.

Thompson, S. *Motif-Index of Folk Literature*. Bloomington: Indiana University Press, 1955.

Tigay, J.H. *The Evolution of the Gilgamesh* Epic. Philadelphia: University of Pennsylvania Press, 1982.

———. *Deuteronomy: The JPS Torah Commentary*. Philadelphia: The Jewish Publication Society, 1996.

Tur-Sinai, N.H. *The Book of Job*. Jerusalem: Kiryat Sefer, 1957. (Hebrew).

———. "Ariel." *EMiqr* 1:558–560. (Hebrew).

Uffenheimer, B. *The Visions of Zechariah*. Jerusalem: Kiryat Sefer, 1961. (Hebrew)

———. "Gen. 15." *Studies in Bible. Dedicated to the Memory of Israel and Zvi Broide*. Ed. J. Licht and G. Brin, 15–21. Tel Aviv: Tel Aviv University, School for Jewish Studies, 1976.

———. *Ancient Prophecy in Israel*. 2nd edition. Jerusalem: Magnes Press, 1984. (Hebrew).

de Vaux, R. "Jérusalem et les prophétes." *RB* 73 (1966): 481–509.

——. *The Early History of Israel.* Translated by D. Smith. Philadelphia: Westminster Press, 1978.

Vergote, J. *Joseph en Égypte: Génèse ch. 37–50 à la lumière des études égyptologiques récentes.* Louvain: Publication Universitaires, 1959.

Volten, A. *Demotische Traumdeutung (Papyrus Carlsberg XIII und XIV Verso).* Anal. Aegypt. 3. Copenhagen: Einar Munksgaard, 1942.

Ward, W. A. "The Egyptian Office of Joseph." *JSS* 5 (1960): 144–150.

Watts, J. D. W. *Isaiah 1–33. WBC* 24. Waco, TX: Word, 1985.

Weidner, E. F. "Aus den Tagen eines assyrischen Schattenkonigs." *AFO* 10 (1935–36): 1–52.

Weinfeld, M. "The Covenant of Grant in the Old Testament and in the Ancient Near East." *JAOS* 90 (1970): 184–203.

——. *Deuteronomy and Deuteronomic School.* Oxford: Clarendon, 1971.

——. "The Loyalty Oath in the Ancient Near East." *UF* 8 (1976): 379–414.

——. "Ancient Near Eastern Patterns in Prophetic Literature." *VT* 27 (1977): 178–195.

——. "The Prophecy of Balaam in the Inscription from Deir 'Alla (Sukkoth)." *Shnaton* 5–6 (1982): 141–147.

——. "Sarah and Abimelech (Genesis 20) Against the Background of an Assyrian Law and the Genesis Apocryphon." In *Festschrift Delcore*, 431–435. AOAT 215. (1985)

Weisberg, D.B. "Polytheism and Politics: Some Comments on Nabonidus' Foreign Policy." In *Crossing Boundaries and Linking Horizons. Studies in Honor of Michael C. Astour,* edited by Gordon D. Young, Mark W. Chavalas and Richard E. Averbeck, 547–556. Bethesda, Maryland: CDL Press, 1977.

——. "Loyalty and Death: Some Ancient Near Eastern Metaphors," *Maarav* 7 (1991): 253–267.

Weisman, Z. "Paradigms and Structures in the Visions of Amos." *Beit Miqra* 39.4 (1969): 40–57.

——. "The Charismatic Personality in the Bible." Ph.D. diss., Hebrew University of Jerusalem, 1972.

——. *From Jacob to Israel.* Jerusalem: Magnes Press, 1986.

Wellhausen, J. *Der Text der Bucher Samuelis.* Göttingen: Vandenhoeck und Ruprecht, 1871.

——. *Die Composition des Hexateuchs und der historischen Bücher des Alten Testaments.* Berlin: Reimer, 1899. Reprint Walter De Gruyter, 1963.

Wenham, G. J. "The Symbolism of the Animal Rite in Genesis 15: A Response to G. F. Hasel." *JSOT* 19 (1981): 61–78; *JSOT* 22 (1982): 134–137.

——. *Genesis 16–50*, vol.2. Dallas, Texas: Word Books, 1994.

Westermann, C. "The Way of the Promise through the Old Testament." In *The Old Testament and Christian Faith.* Edited by B. W. Anderson, 200–224. New York: Harper, 1963.

——. *The Promises to the Fathers.* Translated by D. E. Green. Philadelphia: Fortress, 1980.

——. *Genesis 12–36. A Commentary.* Translated by J. J. Scullion. Minneapolis: Augsburg, 1985.

——. *Genesis 37–50. A Commentary.* Translated by J. J. Scullion. Minneapolis: Augsburg, 1986.

Wiseman, D. J. "Abban and Alalah." *JCS* 12 (1958): 124–129.

——. "The Vassal-Treaties of Esarhaddon." *Iraq* 20 (1958): 59–72.

Wolff, H. W. *Joel and Amos.* Translated by W. Janzen, S. D. McBride, Jr., and C. A. Muenchow. Philadelphia: Fortress, 1977.

Wreszinski, W. "Bäckerei." *ZÄS* 61 (1926): 1–15.33

Wright, C. H. H. *Zechariah and his Prophecies.* 2nd ed. London: Hodder and Stoughton, 1879.

——. *The Book of Koheleth.* London: Hodder and Stoughton, 1953.

Yahuda, A. S. "Hapax Legomena im Alten Testament." *JQR* 15 (1903): 698–714.

——. *The Language of the Pentateuch in its Relation to Egyptian.* London: Oxford University Press, 1933.

Young, D. W. "The Ugaritic Myth of the God Hōrān and the Mare." *UF* 11 (1979): 839–848.

Zalevsky, S. "The Revelation of God to Solomon in Gibeon." *Tarbiz* 42 (1973): 215–258 (Hebrew).

Zimmern, H. *Beiträge zur Kenntnis der Babylonischen Religion.* Assyriologische Bibliothek 12. Leipzig: Hinrichs, 1896–1901.

Index